LITERATURE, CASTE AND SOCIETY
The Masks and Veils

LITERATURE, CASTE AND SOCIETY
The Masks and Veils

Edited by
S. JEYASEELA STEPHEN

Publications

KALPAZ PUBLICATIONS
DELHI-110052

Literature, Caste and Society
The Masks and Veils

Rs. 750

ISBN: 81-7835-448-9

Published in 2006 in India by
Kalpaz Publications
C-30, Satyawati Nagar, Delhi-110052
E-mail : Kalpaz@hotmail.com

Laser Typesetting at : Master Computers, Delhi
Printed at : Salasar Imaging System, Delhi

Contents

Acknowledgements

In this volume are included papers mainly presented to a National Seminar on "Society and Culture in Pre-Modern and Modern India" held at the Visva-Bharati University, Santiniketan, 24-25 November 2002. A large number of scholars had participated in the intensively deliberated discussion of the seminar and I would like to express at first my deep appreciation to all of them. The seminar aimed at drawing together three groups of participants doing multi-disciplinary research in history, sociology and anthropology who do not often meet. The aim of the seminar was also to bring together the scholars of Indian literature and socio-linguists studying society, so that focus could be laid on to look at the Indian society in a holistic perspective, to know and understand the past afresh to be able to address the issues more effectively. The discussions that took place provided a backdrop for a number of more concrete ideas about history and society and it was an opportunity for scholars to present and review research in social history. Scholars using largely European documents and Indian literary sources enhanced our understanding of the society at this seminar through their research findings and I express my deep sense of gratefulness to all whose sincere efforts have included, enriched, embroidered and adorned this volume. It is regretted that, for various reasons, out of the seventeen papers presented, only six could not be included in this volume.

Though this book has developed from the national seminar conducted, a few more papers that have been invited from individuals both for the seminar and the present volume present a welcome enlargement of the scope of the social, literary and historical discourse. I wish to express my sincere thanks to them for agreeing to contribute their revised or earlier published papers. It was realized by both the editor and publisher that between scholars who published in the same field and currently working on the same theme may be invited for meaningful interaction and to make the book a comprehensive one. Thus there was an enormous amount of material for the readers for this book. The result is a set of articles which are just attempts and experiments and the scope was not restricted.

The writings of Ramesh Chandra Sharma and Ajit Neogy in this volume are from *"India Past and Present*" Vol. II, Nos. 2 1985, pp. 197-228 and 241-248. Further, the papers of M. Krishna kumari and P. Swarnalatha are from "Castes, *Communities and Culture in Andhradesa; 17th and 18th Centuries*", Hyderabad, 1996, edited by R. Soma Reddy, M. Radhakrishna Sharma and A. Satyanarayana, vide pp. 45-63, and 84-103. The article of K.S. Mathew is from Jacques Weber, (ed.,) *"Les Relations Entre la France et L'Inde de 1673 a Nos Jours*", Paris, 2002, vide pp. 349-371. Therefore, I am thankful for the permission, co-operation and assistance granted by concerned authors, editors/institutions, original publishers, copy right holders and publishing houses to reproduce articles either wholly or in part.

A major purpose of the volume is to bring together smaller studies already conducted by scholars rich, critical and varied. Each had been amplified in scope and theme, based upon original research using primary sources. There is much continuity although themes in this book vary from region to region such as Tamil Nadu, Pondicherry, Andhra Pradesh, Orissa, Bengal and North India. Thus, the present anthology brings together an invaluable collection of papers on literature, caste and society. I hope this book gives some unexpected insights into historian's craft and other readers a new way of looking at social history. The matrix around which the book is organized is, however, my own and responsibility for whatever limitations this has imposed on the themes covered rests with me alone. It is a small effort with a definitive purpose throwing light on the social history of several centuries of a crucial phase in India's history and so it involves an unusually large measure of selection and compression. The thematic selection of articles is made clear and transparent, and the whole text offers a coherent vision, filtered through the insights of disparate groups of researchers in this volume. Hence the collections have been in every sense instructive and meaningful.

The importance of the publication of this book lies in the fact that it would not only help the academic world but also all those who are interested in the undertaking of the vexed problems of society. I have taken a little more than the usual time in giving shape to the volume due to various reasons beyond my control. I could not put it better manner and my good fortune is even greater that I was soaked in the academic and administrative work amidst the usual and frequent electricity failure at Santiniketan and the poor infrastructural facilities in the Department of History which none writes often find it elsewhere.

The Seminar was sponsored by the Anthropological Survey of India, Calcutta, and so I thank them for the award of a generous grant in support of it. Many thanks to its Director for the humane way he responded to help organizing the seminar. Further, I thank also the authorities of the Visva-Bharati University for the grant of funds towards conducting the seminar. It is indeed a matter of great pleasure for me to express my gratitude, Last but not least, to Mr. Amit Garg, Gyan Books Pvt Ltd, New Delhi for undertaking the book production with expert efficiency Kalpaz Publication.

I hope the papers in this volume will make a contribution worthy of India's society in the past as a rich source of historical, anthropological and sociological studies. Towards a fuller understanding of society, the present book contributes in an enormous way and I am sure that this will stimulate further research, analysis and progress in this important field of social history.

S. Jeyaseela Stephen
University of Connecticut
Storrs, USA
March 2004

Contributors

Ajit Neogy is Emiritus Professor of History at Visva-Bharati University, Santiniketan. His publications include *"The Paramount Power and Princely States of India, 1858-1891*, (K.P. Bagchi and Co., Calcutta, 1979), *"Partitions of Bengal*", (A. Mukherjee and Co. Pvt. Ltd., Calcutta, 1987), and "Decolonization of French India" (IFP, Pondicherry, 1997).

Amiya Ghosh, is Reader in History at Vidyasagar College, Suri, West Bengal. He is the author of *"Bangaleer Bastumukhi Atmasadhana O Prabartak Samgha*" (Prabartak Samgha, Chandernagore, 2000) and *"Jatio Andolan O Zilla Birbhum, 1915-1947*", (Granthaneer, Bolpur, 2001).

Bipasha Raha is Reader in History at Visva-Bharati University, Santiniketan. Her doctoral dissertation is on "The Agrarian Question and the Bengali Intelligentia".

Chinna Rao is Research Officer at the Educational Research and Records Unit, School of Social Sciences, Jawaharlal Nehru University, New Delhi. His publications include *"Dalit's Struggle for Identity: Andhra and Hyderabad, 1900-1950*" (New Delhi, 2003), Dalit Studies: A Handbook of Bibliography (New Delhi, 2003) and co-edited (with Sabayasachi Bhattacharya), *"Development of Women's Education in India, 1850-1920*, (New Delhi, 2001) and *"Educating the Nation: Documents on the Discourse of National Education in India, 1880-1920*" (New Delhi, 2003).

Chhanda Chatterjee, is Reader in History at Visva-Bharati University, Santiniketan. She is the author of *"Ecology, the Sikh Legacy and the Raj: Punjab, 1858-1887*, (Minerva Associates, Calcutta, 1997) and *"Ideology, the Rural Power Structure and Imperial Rule: Awadh and Punjab, 1858-1887* (The Asiatic Society, Calcutta, 1999).

S. Jeyaseela Stephen is Professor and Head of the Department of History at Visva-Bharati University, Santiniketan. He is the author of *"The*

Coromandel Coast and its Hinterland: Economy, Society and Political System, 1500-1600", (Manohar, New Delhi, 1997), "*Portuguese in the Tamil Coast. Historical Explorations in Commerce and Culture, 1507-1749*" (Navajyothi, Pondicherry, 1998), "*The Diary of Muthu Vijaya Thiruvengadam Pillai, 1794-796*" (in Tamil, Institute for Indo-European Studies, Pondicherry 1999), "*The Diary of Rangappa Thiruvengadam Pillai, 1760-1766*, (2 vols in Tamil, Pondicherry Institute of Linguistics and Culture, 2000); "*The Diary of Rangappa Thriuvengadam Pillai, 1760-1768: Translated from original Tamil with Notes*" (IIES, Pondicherry, 2001), "*Portuguese-Tamil Grammar: Modernisation and Democratisation of Tamil*" (IIES, Pondicherry, 2001), "*Letters of the Portuguese Jesuits from Tamil Countryside, 1666-1668*", (IIES, Pondicherry, 2001), co-edited with K.S. Mathew *Indo-French Relations*, (ICHR Monograph Series No. 2, Pragati Publications, Delhi, 1999) and edited *Trade and Globalisation: Europeans, Americans and Indians in the Bay of Bengal, 1511-1819* (Rawat, Jaipur/New Delhi, 2003).

M. Krishna Kumari is Professor at the Department of History and Archaeology in Andhra University, Visakhapatnam. She has authored (in Telugu and English) eight books and edited two volumes dealing with Andhra history and culture. She has been honoured with 'The Best Teacher Award' by the Andhra Pradesh State Government in 2001.

K.S. Mathew is the Director of the Institute for Research in Social Sciences and Humanities, Tellicherry, India. He was Professor and Founder-Head of the Department of History at the Pondicherry University. He is the author of "*Society in Medieval Malabar*" (Jaffe Jo books, Kottayam, 1979). "*Portuguese Trade with India in the Sixteenth Century*" (Manohar, New Delhi, 1983), "*Portuguese and the Sultanate of Gujarat*", (Mittal, New Delhi, 1985), and "*Indo-Portuguese Trade and the Fuggers of Germany*" (Manohar, New Delhi, 1997).

JBP More was a Research Fellow of the Ecole des Hautes Etudes en Sciences Sociales, Paris, France. His significant publications include "*The Political Evolution of the Muslims of Tamil Nadu and Madras, 1930-1947*" (Orient Longman, Hyderabad, 1997) "*Freedom Movement in French India : The Mahe Revolt of 1948*," (Irish, Tellicherry, 2001) and L' Inde Face a Bharati, Le Poete Rebelle (Pondicherry, 2003).

Pratyusa Kumar Mandal is Reader in History at the National Council of Educational Research and Training New Delhi. He had taught at the Arunachal University (1992-2002). He was the Associate Editor of the Arunachal University Research Journal.

L. Ramamoorthy is Lecturer in Linguistics at the Pondicherry Institute of Linguistics and Culture, Pondicherry. He is the author of *"Modernisation of Tamil"* (PILC, Pondicherry, 2000) *"Language Loyalty and Displacement"*, (PILC, Pondicherry, 2000) and edited *"Atchi Tamil"*, (Pondicherry, 2001) He was the former chief-editor of PILC Journal of Dravidic Studies and currently editor of Yanar.

Ramesh Chandra Sharma was Former Head of the Department of History, St. John's College, Agra. His publications include *"A Mughal Hunting Carpet : The Boston Shikargah"* (1988) and *"Historiography and Historians in India Since Independence"* (1991). He is the president of Sardar Bhagat Singh Shahid Smarak Samiti.

B. Ravi Kumar is Lecturer in Tamil at S.R.M. College of Arts and Science, Chennai. He is the author of *"Naan Yethu Seyvenanda"*, (Chennai, 2002). His area of specialization includes modern plays in Tamil.

Shouvik Mukhopadhyay is Lecturer in History at Visva-Bharati University, Santiniketan. His doctoral dissertation is on the *"Military Organization and Society in Early Medieval South India"*.

Sovon Sanyal is Assistant Professor at the Centre of Spanish Studies, Jawaharlal Nehru University, New Delhi. He has edited (with Indrani Mukherjee) *"Reading Culture in Spanish and Luso-Brazilian Studies"*, New Delhi, 2004. He has specialized in Portuguese literary and cultural studies. He is also the editor of Hispanic Horizon.

G. Subbiah is Professor and Head of the Department of the Ancient Indian History, Culture and Archaeology at Visva-Bharati University, Santiniketan. He is the author of *"Roots of Tamil Religious Thought"* (PILC, Pondicherry, 1991). He is also the editor of Visva-Bharati Quarterly.

Suchibrata Sen is Professor of History at Visva-Bharati University, Santiniketan. He is the author of *"The Santals of Jungle-Mahals: An Agrarian History, 1793-1861"*, (Calcutta, 1983); *"The Santals: Crises of Identity and Integration"*, (Calcutta, 1999) and *"Purba Bharater Adibasi Astitter Sankat"* (Kolkata, 2003).

P. Swarnalatha. was Lecturer in History at the Department of History, University of Hyderabad. She is now an independent researcher.

Syed Ejaz Hussain is Reader in History at Visva-Bharati University, Santiniketan. He is the author of "*The Bengal Sultanate: Politics, Economy and Coins, (A.D 1205-1576)*", (Manohar, New Delhi, 2003). He has edited (in Hindi, with Surendra Gopal) "*Mauj-i-Sultani: A Memoir of the Mughal Prince Zubair-ud-din Bahadur, Gurgaon*" (Darbhanga, 2003).

Introduction

S. Jeyaseela Stephen

Historia vero testis
Temporum, lux veritatis,
Vita memoriae, magistra vitae
(History is the witness of the times, the light of truth, the life of memory, the mistress of life.)

—Cicero, De Oratore

In the quest for historical knowledge, especially to the study of Indian society given the time scale and the geographical diffusion historians who have written the social history of India in the past found it always convenient to quote the religious and puranic literature to describe the caste system. They failed to observe the collective mentalities and social problems to develop an 'underlying conceptual framework' by drawing information from a variety of corroborative sources such as court literature, travel literature, poetry and prose literature. Primarily we find four inter-related reasons for such a development in research. At first it may be said that the social history has not well developed in India owing to heavy concentration made on the study of economic history. The reason for this precisely rests with the priorities of historical research assigned by the Marxist scholars. Secondly the study of sociology came to be oriented more closely to the issues and developments on village studies, castes, tribes and process of their social change and continuity. On exploring India, scholars slowly began to study the people in society (instead of the rulers) who could not be banished from history. While writing such a social history of India narrative gave way to description, topic dominated continuity in time. Thirdly the unique characteristics of the various groups found in different regions of India are not available for writing a comprehensive social history during the long historical span of time. Fourthly the stereo-type tradition of *varna* theory attempting to explain the historical experience of the Indian society had prevented scholars attempting to formulate social theories.[1] Hence the historians could not go into deeper analysis and did not feel the nuances and complexity of the Indian society, the oldest living on earth. The significant strands of Indian society and culture had been over-layered by newer ones from time to time without being smothered or eradicated in the process of the evolution of society. Over a period of time the writing of social history of India has undergone review and reform in keeping with the populist temper. In order to provide fresh insights into the discussions here, it is thought fit in this introduction to discuss the divergent approaches that have been appearing now while interpreting the various aspects of society.

Existing historical scholarship is almost silent about the variations in the formation of regional societies in India under different periods. The major writings of the social history of ancient India are chiefly a product of sacred literature. These religious texts tell of a period when society was divided into four castes only. In the medieval period, we find that many writers have put forth a critique of their own society as found in the travel literature, court literature, and other forms of secular literature which carried different pronouncements on caste and society which have been largely overlooked. Therefore it is imperative on the part of social historians to review and reassess the established notions and recorded wisdom pertaining to the evolution of the Indian society. A systematic study of the past society should begin recognizing the importance of different literatures. This new approach to social history which was chiefly missing so far is the additive history, that is, history written after a re-examination of the sources to discover the society.

Society in Ancient India

In the opinion of many scholars, the society of ancient India is considered to be a traditional one and they chiefly base themselves on the classical Hindu religious philosophy. The *Dharma*, *Karma* and *Samsara* had dominated and the *varna* (pollution and purity) determined the moral and material parameters of human existence. The organization of Hindu society in ancient India is therefore characterized by a number of endogamous social units called *jatis* (sub-castes) which are located in the specific regions. These *jatis* in a particular region are linked to each other through an ideal scheme of social organization called the *caturvarna* system such as the *Brahmin* (priest and scholar) *Kshatriya* (king and warrior) *Vaisya* (herder, trader, cultivator) and *Sudra* (menial servant). This age old doctrine of the divisions of society into four *varnas* is the key aspect of the whole system of ancient Indian social life as mentioned in the *Smritis* (Smiriti law). What after all gives its specific character to Hindu society in ancient India is the fact that the life style of an individual within a *jati* is determined by rigorous usage, just as the hierarchical relationship between different *jatis* in a region which is determined with reference to the *varna* order of a society.[2] Thus the *caturvarna* system had provided only ground for intellectual development or expression of the early Indian society. D.D. Kosambi had rejected the concept that the period following the end of primitive communism in India was one that of the slave society. He argued that there were slaves, but no slave society.[3]

Megasthenes in his travel literature had described society in ancient India as being divided into seven classes (a) philosophers who offered sacrifices and performed other sacred rites (b) husbandmen who formed the bulk of the population (c) shepherds and hunters (d) those who worked at trades and vend-wares and employed in bodily labour (e) fighting men (f) inspectors and (g) counsellors and assessors of the king.[4] It is important to note that he makes no reference to the *varna* theory. Therefore it is opined that he compared the society of Greece with India. It is also possible that he perhaps refers to the urban society of ancient India. As Kautilya in his court literature *Arthasastra* mentions the different quarters of a city to the *Brahmins*, *Kshatriyas*, *Vaishyas* and *Sudras*, so also Varahamihira in his *Brihat-Samhita* does it.[5] It may be said that the urban areas and rural areas had completely a different background and setting with its own distinctive features.

In the social setup of ancient India emphasis was laid on religion, in behaviour norms and values. It widely accepted rituals, sacrifices and feasts. The individual status was determined by his birth and one did not strive for social mobility. Kinship relations predominated in interaction. People were conservative. The tool economy prevailed and it was simple (and not machine economy). Mythical thought predominated in society (and not logical reasoning). It is also made crystal clear that the Brahmins had introduced caste distinctions and they were successful in maintaining it among the people since no one understood its impact and effect. The Indian society in the process of evolution had slowly developed distinct roles to be played by different groups. The intellectual, military, commercial and menial activities were not assigned only to the four major castes. We find that two distinct groups viz., the aristocracy and traders emerged outside the four major castes. Some were elevated to dizzy heights while others were pressed down to the earth.

The *caturvarna* caste system became a social problem in the ancient period itself since the situation confronted one group or a section of the Indian society which inflicted injurious consequences. This social problem became a crucial issue which described human conduct as right and wrong in group relations (social ethics) and which concerned with the promotion of the common good or the welfare of its members and the preservation of public order (society) considered as unfavourable. With the passage of time the caste system affected a significant number of people in ways considered undesirable. The Brahmins remained indifferent since it did not affect them and they took no interest because they stood to gain so long as the problem existed. As the changes in caste have to be initiated by a change in outlook they remained unconcerned about finding alternative possibilities. It was at this hour Buddhism and Jainism had emerged and criticized the so-called hierarchy (belief in *varna* and caste system). These two new religions rejected the rituals of sacrifice in Hindu temples. Jainism obtained the patronage of urban mercantile community while Buddhism had princely patronage and they had played a key role in igniting the minds of the people through their new ideas in transforming the Hindu society.

Over a period of time, we find that the ruling class often used religion for managing the social order. In the Gupta age (established by Chandra Gupta I in A.D 319) we find social changes where the *varna* system of ancient India had been considerably modified owing to the proliferation of castes. The services of crafts were transformed into castes. We find aesthetic examples of inter-marriages between *varnas*, not only in the *anuloma* (hypergamy) but also in the *pratiloma* (hypogamy) order during the Gupta period. These *anuloma* and *pratiloma* marriages between Aryans and non-Aryans groups resulted in the rise of mixed castes. In the *Dharma Sastras* of Vasistha and Bauddhayana we find that an attempt has been made in this direction and we find that the Brahmins had tried their best to fix these mixed castes and tribes in the Aryan social order.[6] Suvira Jaiswal opines with a strong view that there was no *Kshatriya* community in South India.[7]

Although the society was in transition, the major four castes however were kept as a framework. Hiuen-Tsang in his travel literature records the existence of the four hereditary castes of Indian society together with their respective occupations. But he adds that the members of a caste group generally marry only within the caste. While escaping from a group of robbers in the Jakla country Hieun-tsang and his companions in the Seventh Century had encountered a Brahmin who was ploughing the land. Thus we find that the Brahmins had already begun to change their occupations. The *caturvarna* system remained only as a theoretical concept derived from the Vedic Aryans but the ancient Indian society had departed away from the *caturvarnadharma* and underwent several changes. According to A.L. Basham, *Jati* (sub-caste) appears to be comparatively a late phenomenon and it is largely ignored in ancient social theory.[8] Cyndia Talbot opines that the sub-caste membership was not an outstanding or memorable feature of an individual's identity in his/her transactions with the larger society.[9]

Scholars like R.S. Sharma have opined that from the Seventh Century onwards in Indian history it was as a period of feudalism and they mention it as a major breakthrough in the understanding of the evolving society. It has been now accepted widely by many that there were not many institutions of European feudalism such as vassalage, serfdom and the manorial system found in India in the same form. They record a process of acculturation as Aryans expanded eastwards and southwards in the Indian sub-continent.[10] At this time we find social mobility which is of two types, the horizontal and the vertical. The reasons for this may be due to pressure of population, political disturbances and religious conflicts. Horizontal mobility is geographical i.e., movement from one place to another. Vertical mobility is either upwards or downwards in the social stratification of a family or a group of families.[11] In this process the number of people excluded from the four *varnas* had increased. Many aspects of social dimension reserved for the *Sudras* were transferred into the principles of untouchability.

Society in Medieval South India under the Cholas

Sub-castes possessed many properties of caste in South India. Diverse groups had to become crystallized in various castes. As a result many occupational groups faced increasing functional differentiation in society. Even in the Rig Vedic period priesthood was not hereditary. The occupation of individuals in various groups had passed on from father to son (endogamic). Hindu religion in ancient India was well protected by liberal grants to the learned Brahmins.[12] We find Brahminic supremacy in the early empires in South India like the Satavahanas, Ikshvakus, Vakatakas and the Pallavas. However, Hindu rulers of later period also depended upon the Brahmins to advise the king about his duty as well as sacrifices to be offered to the gods. The position of the Brahmins had become somewhat different as they were appointed as *dewan* (prime-minister), bureaucrats and officials in the South Indian kingdoms. Hence they continued to attempt and possess much religious control in society. The others in the society functioned completely with a different social control but for the sake of religious practices they depended on the Brahmins. During the reign of Kulotunga I (1070-1120) several land grants were given to members of *Sudra* community who were generals and royal officials. We find a lot of proliferation within the castes, sub-castes and communties.[13] South Indian society under the age of the Cholas was more or less stratified. We find the existence of castes with certain hierarchy found mention in the inscriptions. These castes started rather as occupational groups than kin groups, though inferred hierarchy applied as broad outline to the entire period of the Cholas. Many tribal communities which had been on the fringes of the plain society until the Tenth century began to be incorporated into the latter as new castes such as *Pallis*, *Curtiman*, *Nattaman* and *Srigopala* in the Eleventh century and later period too.[14] However *caturvarna* system was replaced through the introduction of two social divisions such as *Valangai* (Right hand) and *Idangai* (Left hand) and it had been an important feature of South Indian society and the origin of the nomenclature is traced to Raja Raja Chola (A.D 985-1014). At this time we find the two divisions in a rudimentary form of social feature only. Later clear manifestation of these *Valangai* and *Idangai* appears in the inscriptions of the Twelfth and Thirteenth Centuries. The nature of right and left hand classification did not remain the same all through the centuries and it underwent tremendous and gradual changes in the entire medieval period. Pamela Price described this process as a long term mystery of South Indian history. Burton Stein opined that the *Valangai* caste people were not to be identified with the low based cultivating castes. He said that the *Idangai* included the traders and artisan castes at least during the early phase of history.[15] This view of Burton Stein has been called into question by Y. Subbarayalu who mentions that the emergence of the dual social divisions called right and left hand castes should be applicable to the wars of this period.[16] The caste of *kaikolars* (weavers) had started functioning as a military group in the Chola period being mentioned in the inscriptions are quoted by Subbarayalu.[17] Even this argument is not maintainable because if it is for the purpose of war, it was possible for the *kaikolars* to participate in the Chola army only for a very short period. Further, the *kaikolars* did not have any formal military training and skill required for the Chola army. There is no mention as to why it was not possible for the *Kshatriyas* and *Sudras* (agricultural labourers) to participate in war or ready to join in the Chola army. Details of how and why the *kaikolars*, a military group turned later into a weaving caste are not also available in the literary and inscriptional sources. It is also significant therefore to note here that why the entire society was divided by the Chola ruler into two groups and this is shrouded in mystery. Again how could some groups like the traders and *vaishyas* be fixed and treated in this left and right hand classification is posing a problem. It may be true that the artisans helped in producing the necessary weapons and required war equipments. Even then what was the role of the Brahmins who are outside the system of right and left hand divisions had to be known. Further, we find evidences that even in *Brahmadeyas* (Brahmin settlements) non-Brahmana *kani* (land) holders are seen along with the Brahmins.[18] By this time the idea of *varna* came to be mixed up with *jati* which was known as sub-caste.[19] In the inscriptions of the period we find mention such as *nammudidya jati* (our sub-castes).[20]

The social organization under the Cholas was complex in nature since we find the society in South India divided into innumerable number of social groups or sub-castes. Each caste remained hereditary and constituted an occupational group. The Brahmins received land grant privileges and combined with the religious authority they rose to heights with economic power. Their main duties did not confine to learning and reciting of the Vedas, performing rituals and ceremonies, serving as priests in temples. They enjoyed land grants with royal support and were exempted from payment of taxes also. They were even given lighter punishments in case of offences committed. Some Brahmins engaged in trade as *vaishyas*. These priestly group of Brahmins (the so-called scholars and teachers) were also recruited into military services by the kings and subordinate chiefs being *Dhandanayaka* and *Senanai* in the army besides appointed as *pradhani* and *mahapradhani* in civil service. Those Brahmins who followed the *Smirits* in their daily rituals and religious practices were (worshippers of both Siva and Vishnu) called the *Smartas*. Most of them followed the Sankara school of *Advaita* and offered daily worship to *pancayatana*.[21] The other group of Brahmins who were not satisfied with the *Smarta* system but were attracted to the devotional cults of Saivism and Vaishnavism were known as the *Aradhayas*. According to K.A. Nilakanta Sastri, they are semi-*Lingayats* half converted *smarta* who wore the sacred thread and the *linga* and they worshipped Ganapathi. They did not take *prasadam* from temples.[22] There was also another section of Brahmins called *Srivaishnavas* who propagated Vaishnavism and established *mathas*. Thus there were multiple groups within Brahmins in South India.

There was "resurgence of the Hindus" in the form of Puranic theism which supported the caste system when Buddhism and Jainism declined. As the castes based upon occupations had increased we find in the medieval inscriptions that the society was characterized by the *Astadasa Mahaparaja* (eighteen major communities) in the Telugu country.[23] Each occupational group came to be called a *jati*. Thus ancient theory of *caturvarnadharma* was replaced by the medieval concept of *Astadasa Mahapraja*. Ethnic factor is also an important one and we find the process of assimilation of *varnas*. These ethic groups in the society multiplied the number of castes and economic factors such as taxation already led to the rise of sub-castes based upon the specialised skills. The dyer, (*vastrabadhaka*) the spinner, (*devanaga*) the weaver, (*tantuvaya*) and sewer (*vastrarakshka*) are mentioned in the Telugu inscriptions.[24]

Slavery existed under the rule of the Cholas. Slaves were sold to the temples. Untouchable settlement (*Tindacheri*) is found mention in AD 1014 in the inscription of Raja Raja Chola (985-1016).[25] The Bahur inscription of Raja Raja Chola II in AD 1028 mentions *tindaar* (untouchables) living separately in villages.[26] Epigraphs do record untouchable slaves separately.[27] Thus untouchability a social problem was very commonly prevalent in the medieval period.

Religion and Society

A continuous struggle between the forces of social rejects, belief in pre-destiny determinism and the forces of social dynamism took place in medieval India. This struggle has been the most distinctive feature of India's social, cultural and ideological transformation. This age was dominant by Bhaktism, casteism, and Sufism. The Bhakti movement brought about a new awareness among the Hindus and it instilled a sense of commitment to their religion and culture. Hindu beliefs and values were further affected by the preachings of Shankaracharya (Ninth century) Ramanujacharya (1017-1137) Madhvacharya (Fourteenth century) who propagated monotheism. Hatred within religious groups, (Saivites and Vaishnavites) intolerances and communal divisions were common phenomena largely known to Indian society at that time. From the Thirteenth century onwards the devotionally oriented Bhakti movement provided a series of outstanding saints who were drawn by their sincere love and they bridged the gap between their respective communities by stressing that common aim which all sacred traditions have described. They lived in an age when the Hindu society had to face the expanding Buddhism. Therefore Sankaracharya attempted to re-emphasise the supremacy of the Vedas to counter the spread of Buddhism. Inter-caste marriages *anuloma* and *pratiloma* had been present at that time. *Virasaiva* or *Lingayat* movement challenged the authority of the Vedas and rebirth. This movement encouraged late post-puberty marriages and the remarriage of widows which were some of the social practices discouraged by the Brahmins. Indian culture and society did not remain stagnant and monolithic, but on the other hand it had every vibrant and receptive of various social groups from outside. The propagators of *Virasaivism* namely Basaveswara and Mallikarjuna Pandita preached that women should have equal rights with men. The women could disobey their husbands in certain matters and certain times, e.g a wife should teach her husband to become a devotee of Siva if he was not so and more he does not obey her, she should divorce him. *Sivatatvasara Virasaivism* propagated at this time the abrogation of caste distinctions. *Virasaivism* appears to be revolutionary but the propagators were unable to put forth their ideas into practice. We find that Mallikarjuna Pandita continued to wear his sacred thread. The study of R.N. Nandi shows that the *Virasaiva* movement was basically anti-Brahminical.[28]

Caste distinctions were opposed by the writers of the medieval period. In this context it is useful to analyse the text of *Lakshmi Purana*, a poem from Orissa composed in the Sixteenth century by poet Balaram Das. It is mentioned that one year Lakshmi the goddess decided to go into the city of Puri disguised as an old woman, in order to observe the level of devotion during the month of November on the day of Lakshmi Puja. Going from place to place here and there, she was increasingly discouraged and thoroughly dismayed, after noticing the prevailed religious superficiality and even apathy among the women. Finally she came to the house of an untouchable and she found that the woman in the house had prostrated on the ground praying fervently to Mahalakshmi. The goddess was overjoyed and she entered the house and shared a meal with the family. This event was reported to Lord Jagannath who is the presiding deity in the temple of Puri. Denouncing the ritual impurity, Jagannath had ordered the goddess to remain out of the temple. However, Lakshmi fully rose to the occasion and with the help of the divine architects she had built a new palace for her near the seashore. At the same time she had the temple in Puri cleared of all contents, including morsel of food. Faced with this desolation and deprived of sustenance Lord Jagannath and his brother were eventually forced to go into begging for food. Having been ignored at every house, the starved gods finally came to the palace of Lakshmi whom they entreated to return to the temple in Puri but she proved obstinate. In the end Lakshmi agreed to come to the temple in Puri but with a condition that in the temple there would be no distinction of caste and that everyone would be allowed to enter freely. We do not know whether this poem had any impact on society. But this proves that social inequality continued to exist and temple entry was denied to the *Sudras*.

South Indian Society in the Vijayangara Period

In the times of the rulers of Vijayanagar, Allasani Peddana in his *Manucharitam* mentions that four castes had existed such as the Brahmins (*Vipurulu*) the *Rachavaru* (the *Rajgular* or generally the ruling class) the

Matikaratalu (merchants) and the *Nalavajativaru* (the *Sudras* who were mainly agriculturists.). Thus it is evident that *Kshatriya varna* was absent in the Vijayanagar period. It may be mentioned here that King Deva Raya II (1419-1449) gave orders to enlist Muslims as soldiers in his service and he even allotted them estates and erected a mosque in the city of Vijayanagar. He also caused that no one should molest them in the exercises of their religion. He ordered the Quran to be placed before his throne on a rich desk. Allasani Peddana mentions the artisans, herders, *kaikolars* and the *thottiyans* in the society. The Hindu theory of the origin of man thus clearly postulates a hierarchy–twice born *varna* consisted the core with the Brahmins at the apex, the vast humanity of peasantry and artisans (the *sudras*) in the middle and those of the fifth order (the *panchamas*) were not even accounted for in the four fold division and were posted to the lowest position in medieval period.

The concept of the absence of a civil society or absence of linkages between the mass of the people and the ruling elites (as if these were the features not of a phase as in the West but characterized oriental society at all times) has made some scholars to put forward the idea of segmentary state or a disaggregated society.[29] Burton Stein therefore mentions the castes for enhanced status within a narrow, localized ranking system. He says that in medieval South India the social mobility involved spatial mobility and the units of mobility were individual families. The need as well as the facilities for corporate mobility therefore did not exist. Noboru Karshima and S. Jeyaseela Stephen had argued chiefly based on the inscriptional evidences of the Vijayanagara period in opposition to the views of Burton Stein and they point out the existence of caste solidarity becoming an important feeling.[30] This caste solidarity can also be mentioned on the basis of the imprecatory verses found in the epigraphs. We find clearly social ostracism and denial of certain caste privileges for those who violated the stipulations made in the grants. Occupations of different caste people became interchangeable in the society is also known through epigraphs. Several sub-castes tried to exalt their social status by *prasasthis* tracing mythical origin of its own. This can be viewed as the legitimizing mechanisms by certain dominant castes to win special recognition. Social conflicts for certain privileges and rights between the artisan and agricultural groups had emerged in the Tamil and Kannada speaking regions only. The two important features like the migration from the north to the south and process of commercialization constituted towards the dynamics of society at this time first around the royal courts and temples and later around the port settlements in South India.

With the advent of Islam, The status of a Hindu had continued to be restricted upon his birth in the caste system. But for Muslims it was on their religious faith. Ibn Battuata speaks of the exclusiveness and social insularity of the Hindus of medieval Malabar. He mentions that no Muslim could enter the house of a Hindu or use their vessels for eating purposes. If a Muslim had been fed by their vessels, they should either break the vessel or give them away to the same Muslim.[31] Thus there has been not much social contacts and interaction among the Hindus and Muslims in medieval South India.

Medieval Society in North India

Arab invasion of Sind under Muhammad bin Kasim in A.D 712 gave rise to Islamic power. In the Eleventh century Muhammad Ghazni conquered North India. On the death of Muhammad Suri in 1206 his general Qutbudin-Aibak, a Turk took possession of the acquisition of his master. Muhammad Ibn Ahmad Al-beruni (973-1048) who visited India refers also to seven classes (similar to the one mentioned by Megasthenes) of the division of the Indian society. He conducted research for fourteen years between A.D 1017 and 1031 and he is very familiar with the Sanskrit sources. There is no mention of the four *varna* theory of the Indian caste system in his *Kitab-al-Hind* (The Book of India). He is the man who deserves the title of the first anthropologist.[32] Changes as part of transition or evolution from untouchability were in progress in Hindu society had been noted by Alberuni in his account of the 'Reality of Hindustan'. He mentions that "great difference do not exist between the *Vaisyas* and *Sudras*". This picture painted and presented on the Hindu society shows that there was a vast difference in actual theory and practice. Alberuni had noted the insular attitude of the *Brahmins*, the then so-called learned people of India and he was inspired by the intellectual subtlety and metaphysical speculation of the Brahmin philosophers and also was shocked by their closed mindedness.

Muhammad Ghori laid the foundations for the Muslim empire in India in A.D 1175. Different dynasties such as the Slave (1206-1290) Khilji (1290-1320) Tughlak (1320-1412) Sayyid (1412-1451) and Lodhi (1451-1525) had ruled India from time to time. It is to be noted here that Islam does not believe in idol worship. It is monotheistic, non-hierarchical and it believes in equality. However, among the Muslims the Shia-Sunni divide had existed in the then society. Though Both Islam and Hinduism are oriented to the principles of holism (collectivism) yet holism is linked with hierarchy. During the Islamic rule Amir Khusro interpreted the Hindu traditions to the Muslim world. The state, the Muslim rulers had set up in India was a theocracy, which envisaged direct intervention and authorship of God through revelations in government of society. Abul Fazal in his *Ain-i-Akbari* says "They one and all believed in the unity of God and as to the reverence they pay to the images of stone and wood and the like, which simpletons regard as idolatry, it is not so". In order to understand the changing concept of the state in medieval India, it is necessary first to examine the concepts of some of the leading thinkers especially Jalaluddin Dawwani and Abul Fazal of the period. In other words to study the state not in isolation but as an essential component of medieval society, its culture, ethos and economic and social developmental trajectory need to be taken into account.

Abul Fazal presents the view that the four *varnas* were produced from the body of *Brahma* at the creation of the world. He recognizes that thereafter internal divisions came within the four *varnas*.[33] In his writings we see strong support for a hierarchical state and society, side by side with egalitarian notions and precepts. Abul Fazal's concept of state and sovereignty has to be seen in the context of his understanding of society, as also his religious and spiritual notions. Following the ancient Hindu traditions, as also influenced by thinkers such as Jalaluddin Dawwani, Abul Fazal classified the human beings into four categories: the first being the warriors, second the craftsmen and merchants, third the learned, and fourth the peasants and labourers. By relegating the learned that is religious classes (*Brahmins* and *Ulema*) to the third not to the first category as in the *Dharma Sastras*, Abul Fazal tried to downgrade the high pretensions and self-opinionated ideas of these sections. He also based himself on the existing social reality. Interestingly, Dawwani had put the learned above the craftsmen and merchants, but below the warriors.[34]

Jean Baptiste Tavernier a French merchant who travelled in India (between 1631-1667) mentions in his account that he had conversations with the Brahmins and says that there were seventy-two sub-castes. According to him that these seventy-two sub-castes are reduced to four principal castes from which all others derive their origin.[35] It is therefore clear that the society was divided and grouped on the basis of their resident status, caste and position as office holders. We find that cultivators or peasants were of three types such as the *Riyayatis*, or *Khudkasht*, the *Pahi-kasht* and the *Muzzarian*. Generally those belonging to the higher castes formed the *Khudkasht*, the *Muzzarian* generally belonged to the middle castes such as *Jat*, *Gujar*, *Ahir* and *Mali*. The bulk of the service designated as *Kamin* or low included a sizeable sect of untouchables. However, the traditional Hindu society remained "decentred". The Sultanate and Mughal states interfered with the social order and so their rule significantly altered the social structure.

W.H. Moreland had inaugurated a new chapter in medieval Indian historiography and the focus of historical research was shifted from institutional to society.[36] Nurul Hasan put forward the thesis that the *zamindars* constituted the dominant class in rural society in India except in tribal areas.[37] Satish Chandra was the first to question the medieval Indian society being largely stagnant and of the marginal ruling class being allergic or hostile to trade and commerce.[38] The social structure was changing in the early modern era and we find consolidation and expansion of the holders of superior rights in land (*zamindars*, *talluqedars*) emergence of trading cum banking community, several men of means trying to use political connections for maximum profits depicted by some scholars as portfolio capitalism.[39] The political and administrative institutions of Mughal India did not inhibit the growth of a market oriented economy and that in fact despite limitations there was fairly a rapid growth of merchant capital. Indian traders were not peddlers though operated on family networks. Therefore we need to analyse the world economic relations in the early modern era and there is a need to study the commonalities of Eurasian form rather than outdated oriental and occidental stereotypes.[40]

Akbar, the Mughal Emperor (1556-1605) removed the disabilities imposed on the majority of the people of India i.e., the Hindus. The first revolutionary step he took was to abolish the hated discriminatory pool tax called *Jizyah* to be paid by each adult Hindu *Zimmis*. He felt that the Hindus had become second class citizens because of this tax. With its abolition in 1564 Akbar brought Hindus on par with Muslims as common citizens of the Mughal state. Akbar also removed restrictions in the public religious worship by non-Muslims and abolished the pilgrim tax on Hindus in 1563. He issued orders permitting those Hindus who had been forcibly earlier converted to Islam to reconvert to Hinduism. He also prohibited making slaves of prisoners of war. According to Badaoni, Emperor Akbar challenged the doctrine of Islam itself being a. Sunni Muslim. He had respect for Hindu religion and culture as well as for other religions. In 1575 therefore hc established a house of worship (*Ibadat-Khana*) at Fatepur-Sikri where people of all sects such as the Hindu poets, the Muslims, the Jesuits from Goa and the Zoroastrians gathered together to discuss religion wth Akbar and among themselves. The outcome of the debates was a modified version of monotheism, known as *Din-i-Illahi* composed of strands from Hinduism, Sufism and Zoroastrianism which Akbar himself professed.

Emperor Jahangir (1605-1627) is well known for his liberal attitude who participated in all major Hindu festivals. He even performed the *shraddha* of Akbar. Some of the Hindu festivals such as *Deepavali* and *Holi* became popular among the Muslims during his rule. All these evidences clearly show the process of assimilation of the twin cultures. The process of reciprocity and fusion was continuously going on between the Hindus and the Muslims. The Mughal emperor Aurangzeb (1658-1707) was a different man who had expressed his reservation when his son Azim Uh-Shan took part in the *Holi* festival celebration.[41] Thus we find Akbar had experimented with the secularism. Jahangir instituted a liberal oriented state, while Aurangzeb had the orthodox outlook. Thus three different Mughal rulers emerged in India and the Mughal state under their leadership could be said to be secularist, liberal and orthodox.

It is believed that a wholesome study of the society in Mughal India would be incomplete without a study of religion and customs in the right perspective. Many changes occurred wherein the Muslims had adopted a number of social customs of the Hindus in due course of time and they practiced it faithfully. It is mentioned that the Muslims began to remove the body of the dying man out of his bed like the Hindus. The custom of *jauhar* was one such and we find that Mirza Nathaon who wrote the *Baharistan-i-Ghaibi* had instructed Sadat Khan. Further, the Hindu custom of shaving the head, beard and moustache of men after the death of some one closely related to them had come into vogue at the time of Emperor Akbar.[42] Further, the ceremonial lighting of lamps in the house of the deceased was practiced among the Muslims as well.[43] These changes were going on in the sixteenth and seventeenth centuries owing to social encounters of the time. An important feature we find is that the culture and religion had come into close contact between Hinduism and Islam and it had an impact on every day life.[44]

Medieval Social Institutions

> *"The Past is a permanent dimension of human consciousness, an inevitable component of institutions, values and other patterns of human society".*[45]
>
> **-E.J. Eric Habsbawm**

Of late scholars have been highlighting the role of women in history and other social sciences since it is reported that history has chiefly been concerned with exploits and activities of men serving as 'his story'. Many writers in the past have felt that women's roles have been considered unimportant or have been underplayed or ignored for, in the patriarchal society down the ages. It has been generally said that men have always enjoyed a dominant position over women in society. Studies of women are now done in cross-disciplinary approach since the subject spills over different vistas of life. Some researchers have concentrated their attention to see the position held by women in society in the course of history through the centuries and they underline the important contributions while others endeavoured on the problems faced by women in various fields of their activities. Some scholars in their studies have divided women into elite and folk and then they look at the different sections that depend within each group. [46]

Sexual divisions have been one of the basic distinctions within the society encouraging one group to view its interests different from another. Hindu theorists made distinction between the types of women in the Indian society and they classified women into three broad categories such as *Kula-Stri* (family woman), *Bhoga-Stri*, (public woman) *Ganikal* (cultured courtesan) *Nartaki* (mere dancers) and *Veshya* (prostitute or loose women without moral).[47] For a Hindu woman the husband was God and she had no other right but to accept him whether he was morally good or not. Woman married once, had no other chance to withdraw from it. This unequal treatment was possible because woman was uneducated and ignorant of her status and privileges. Woman was told that she was unclean and the concept of woman's impurity was related to menstruation and child birth. Thus pollution was referred to woman and not to man and she was set aside as inferior to man. A Hindu woman was also not permitted to read or learn the Vedas.

We find some restrictions extended only towards woman in ancient India. Manu says that the name of a woman should be easy to pronounce, not imply anything dreadful, possess a plain meaning, be pleasing and auspicious, end in long vowels and contain a word of benediction.[48] Further, it is said that do not marry a woman named after a constellation, a tree or a river nor one bearing the name of low caste or of a mountain nor one named after a bird, a snake, or a slave nor one whose name inspires terror.[49] Again it is said that a slave like wife was considered ideal. We learn that the *Aitrateya Brahmana* had declared a daughter as a source of misery while the son was the saviour of the family. *Atharva Veda* mentions the birth of a daughter is a calamity may perhaps imply infanticide was committed with the difficulty of getting daughters suitably married.[50] According to Manu, a girl should be given in marriage before she attains puberty.[51] The Brahmins favoured the early marriage of the girls. Widow re-marriage was considered a disrespectable practice.[52] This shows that through the religious literature Brahmins were propagating wrong ideas.

Devadasis (female slaves of God) were found common in the Hindu temples. These women surrendered themselves in the service of god in the temples, dancing, singing and playing music where the idol was kept. In this institution of dancing girls, they were connected to the spiritual world and sensual world. As they were in the service of the temples and dedicated their lives to the service of god they obtained training from the fifth year till the age of fourteen. In case if they are married they lost their profession of serving in temples. The girls took an examination in the temple compound if successful, they were appointed as *Sanis* or *devadasis*. In the medieval period the *manusmriti* had become impractical for application to marriage, divorce, succession, hereditary, adoption, guardianship and maintenance. Hence commentaries of classical law books were composed by re-interpreting and re-adjusting to suit the reality of medieval society. The most influential work of this period was *Mitaksara*, a commentary on Yajnavalkya-Smirit which was composed under the Western Chalukyas in the Twelfth century.[53] Temple women separately came to be constituted as a social category that was distinct[54] and we find that once the temples lost their institutional power the *devadasis* also lost their position. The system of *devadasis* fostered the growth of temple prostitution which led to the growth of loosening of moral codes among the men and women. Contemporary writers and travellers describe the social conditions of Hindu women.[55] Allasani Peddanna in his *Manucharitira* mentions that "it is love which blinds a man permanently to a single woman and vice versa; and it is a lie that one person can love several woman".[56] Domingo Paes in his travel literature mentions that women who were courtesans attached to the temples were of loose character.[57]

The Muslims followed a different policy with regard to marriage of women in society since the Holy Quran permitted the Muslims to have four wives at a time. Scholars like Misra Rekha point out that Muslims although generally followed polygamy, many poor Muslims perhaps thought of domestic happenings and they practiced monogamy. Widow re-marriage was also prevalent amongst the Muslims.[58] Strict seclusion became the order of the day as a result Muslim women remained confined to the four walls of their house. *Purdah*, the custom of covering the face with a veil was adopted as protective measure to have the honour of their women in Islamic society. Thus women were subjected to several discriminatory practices, customs and traditions.

There also emerged another trend in society in the early medieval period to institutionalize woman as a sensual object. Most important among them was harems of the kings. Women were kept as sensual objects and for the sexual needs of the rulers. Women living with kings and nobles were not married but remained in contact with one man just like married ladies and remained single on his desire. Such women are called *lanja pendlamu* in inscriptions. They had a respectable status in society in India. The commodity concept of women is reflected in the practice of polygamy. Their worth as human being often got scant respect. Sultan Alauddin Khilji married a Hindu Princess. Feroz Shah Thuglaq married the daughter of Deva Rai.[59] Emperor Akbar married Rajput princess such as the daughter of Uday Singh who was the son of Raja Maldeo in 944 A.H. and the daughter of Bihari Mal in 968 A.H.[60] Emperor Jahangir also married a number of Hindu and Rajput ladies.[61] Thus Hindu–Muslim inter-religious marriages were limited to the upper strata of the society.

Social Problems

Alberuni mentions that "the child belongs to the caste of the mother and not that of father".[62] Bernier says that no one marries outside his own trade and profession.[63] Dowry was a social malady and it encompassed both *stridhan* which was usually jewellery and clothing belonging to bride alone and a wide array of household goods and valuables that were gifts to the groom's family with whom they lived. We learn from Amir Khusrau that the fate of a girl was doomed if any aspersions were cast on her chastity, even though they were false allegations because if such a thing happened the poor girl could not get any respectable partner to marry her.[64] Barani records that men were particular about the chastity of women and the lack of chastity among men was completely ignored.

The education for women was stopped and they became victims of evil practices like the early child marriage. Tavernier observed that the people of India marry their children between seven and eight years.[65] Albert Mandelso also says that the Hindus marry their children very young.[66] Thevenot affirms and confirms the same view.[67] Manucci says that Indians offered their daughters in marriage even before they have learnt to talk.[68] Thus it is confirmed that child marriages had continued. Akbar formulated several regulations in order to save the women from the effects of child marriage. Abdul Fazal observed "he (Akbar) abhors marriage which takes place between man and woman before the age of puberty. They bring-forth no fruit and his majesty thinks them even harmful, for afterwards when such a couple ripens into manhood or womanhood by dislike having dispute and their home is desolate".[69] Al Badaoni also refers to the regulation enforced by Akbar forbidding girls before fourteen and boys before sixteen years of age to be married.[70] Thus a serious and whole-hearted effects for creating necessary public awareness was made to show the direct relationship between age of marriage and attitude towards size of a family in the medieval period.

Sati was found common among the Kshatriyas. Alberuni says that if a Hindu wife lost her husband by death she could not marry another man. She has only to choose between two things either to remain a widow as long as she lived or to burn herself.[71] But we find there has been some change over a period of time and widow re-marriages were prevalent among the lower section of Hindu society as noted by Careri.[72]

Sex is basically an individual biological phenomenon, but every society has to create some norms for regulating sex such as marital sex, pre-marital sex and extra-marital sex so that it may not become an unregulated act of pleasure. The necessity of the individuals and the social need should also correspond with each other in this regard. Vatsayana had judged the question of sex in India only as a part of an intelligent give of values preserved by Hindu religion, *dharma*, (religion) *artha*, (material prosperity) *kama*, (sexual pleasures) and *moksha* (heaven). Therefore *kama* or sex is to be viewed in an isolated manner. There were *vesyas* who indulged in immoral traffic by attracting rich men by evil devices and made these men paupers. They lived in *vesyavatikas* or *sanivadas*. Prostitution was recognised as an institution in the Mughal period. The number of female-sex-workers (public women) in Delhi had increased more than before as Al Badaoni records.[73] According to Manucci there were 6000 houses of public women.[74] Emperor Akbar took steps to control selling sex. He ordered for a particular red-light area to be set up for the public women. A *kotwal* was appointed in the area for the purpose of maintaining law and order. He also collected tax every week and it was an important source of the state revenue. Any individual who wanted to visit any of these prostitutes or to take the prostitutes to their own home he had to give the *kotwal* his name and address.[75] Manucci informs us that Emperor Aurangzeb ordered these public women and girls must either marry or move out of the empire.[76] He laid down rules to suppress prostitution since prostitute-houses had increased in number. He stipulated that even *kanchans* should either marry or else leave the empire.[77] The overall status and taste of women in Mughal India is depicted in Aini-i-Akbari "buy a Khursani woman for her wok, a Hindu women for her capacity for nursing children, a Persian woman for the pleasures of her company".[78]

Advent of the Europeans in India and the Hindu Society

Duarte Barbosa, the Portuguese traveller mentions that the high positions were occupied by the Brahmins in South India in the Sixteenth century.[79] He records the significance of the pollution in relation to untouchability, [80] the bars to commensality among endogamous groups, [81] the relationship of occupation to caste, [82] the application for sanctions within castes to maintain caste customs, [83] and the relationship between caste and political organization.[84] However there is no reference to the Hindu theory of the *varnas* and no moralizing about the benefits or evils of the system.

There was a common idea that woman had no independent existence and stature except being the wife of some man. It was also believed that her duty was to make her husband happy both while he was alive and there after his death and so the practice of *sati* was in full swing which was a curse on the society. The self immolation of the widow gained an upper hand even in Southern India among the members of the royal family. In Madurai we find that Muthammal, the queen of Ranga Krishna Muthu Virappa was pregnant when her husband died. She at that time decided to commit *sati* but was persuaded to postpone the performance of *sati* till her delivery and she committed *sati* after the birth of the child. In another case we find that Mangammal, the mother-in-law of Muthammal did not commit *sati* after the death of her husband Chokkanatha by that time social conditions had improved much. Rani Mangammal had acted as the regent of her grand son Vijaya Raghava Chokkanatha (the son of Muthammal). According to Duarte Barbosa, the Portuguese traveller those who did not commit *sati* were held in great dishonour.[85]

The word caste ('Casta' in Portuguese and 'Castus' from Latin) was referred to community, bloodline or birth group by the Europeans and it came to be equivalent with the Sanskrit term *jati* meaning birth. It is confused by the scholars often with the term *varna* (literally colour). In Brahamanical sociological thinking *varna* is an abstract best translated as category or class. Whether or not caste and the modern caste system is a by product of colours or of Brahminical collaboration is an issue that is not addressed by many scholars.[86] The word caste is referred to groups and categories but two types of distinctions are made (a) between *varna* and *jati* (b) between caste and sub-caste. Thus studies have pointed out that division was deep rooted in Indian society.[87]

In the European trading settlements of Madras, Pondicherry, Tranquebar, etc., there were many caste conflicts between the right hand and left hand castes. As early as November 1652 and 1655 we find caste disputes between the Hindus in Madras.[88] E.R. Leach states that wherever caste groups acted as corporations in competition against like groups of different caste, then they acted in defiance of caste principles.[89] The Hindu society was an unequal one. Based on caste and class the measure of social acceptance as it stood was very high. The situation was not critical or explosive. This is reflected in the statement of Ananda Ranga Pillai, The chief *dubash* and courtier of the French East India Company in Pondicherry who was not a member of high caste. He says "No good can come of treating low born with *varna* in a customaries respect or of employing any one in the occupation for which he is by descent unqualified. The foundation of property, prosperity and good go that is due to the subordination of the castes".[90] It is difficult to determine various castes belonging to each of the two divisions in a water-tight compartment and there had been change from one to the other. In the end of the Eighteenth century Francis White, a police officer in Pondicherry has mentioned that each caste had adopted what it pleases and preserved even complete neutrality. There had been plenty of variations in the castes.[91]

It is necessary to give greater emphasis to the role of weaving, dyeing and commercial technology in stimulating change in the age of the European commercial expansion in coastal India. The main paradigm shifts (from agriculture) to industries and commerce was chiefly made visible with the expanding European trade and commercial networks at this time. The weavers, artisans and merchants in the European port settlements claimed for social privileges because their action and employment had dramatically altered the social situation of the ports. Urban centres in the hinterland provided the political basis for change and they also provided linkages which forged with rural communities. Migration of the weavers, artisans and merchants from the hinterland to the coast had transformed the society and it represented the common strategy employed by them in their self interest pursuit of security and wellbeing. The traders and businessmen in the society had their own paradox mix of institutions and culture all serving to maintain and maximize social strategies. European sources have glorified chaos and disorder in the ports. The natives required peaceful conditions in the society to maintain business confidence. Thus the Indian society in the pre-British period (1500-1750) on the whole experienced a fundamental change in the nature of their interconnections.

Christians in Indian Society

Vasco da Gama sailed the ocean blue. Afterwards we find that the Portuguese missionaries began to convert Hindus in large numbers in India. At first it is to be borne in mind that conversion is not always a corollary of conquest nor is necessarilly restricted to the dissemination of religious beliefs. There is a need to examine the relations between the Christian converts and the Hindus. In the age of the Portuguese expansion, missionaries insisted and wanted the converts to follow the Christian habits. Therefore a ban was imposed on the use of areca nuts and betel leaves by the Christians in Goa. The giving of food cakes (*fugues*) at weddings or at other occasions, the singing of vovios which was followed at marriages were not allowed. Hindu functions and festivals were also prohibited. The anointing of the bride and the bridegroom with a mixture of coconut oil, rice and saffron powder crushed from leaves of abolim on the day of betrothal or any other day preceding or following the marriage was ordered to be stopped. Even the wearing of *purdem* (dhoti) by men and *chotis* (blouses) by women came to be forbidden in Goa.[92] In the other Portuguese trading centres on the East Coast of India native Christians continued to retain their own distinct culture and identities following Hindu manners and customs. This is chiefly because of the absence of inquisition.[93] The Catholic missionaries were more tolerant of the social distinctions of caste and of encouraging mass conversions in which entire group changed their faith. This led to the perpetuation of caste differences even after conversion. The Portuguese *Estado da India* had also played a key role in the conversions and helped the missionaries. The French missionaries in Pondicherry respected existing caste and culture norms.[94]

The arrival of the Danish missionaries at Tranquebar on the Coromandel Coast led to many conversions of the Hindus to Christianity. There were many social changes which took place at this time. Vedanayagam Pillai in his dialogue '*Jatiyacara Campavinai*' (on the difference of caste) composed in 1824 had described how within a single building of worship (the church) the European Christians sat on benches, *Vellalar* Christians on grass mats, *Pariaya* Christians or lower castes on the bare floor and women sat separately from the men.[95] Since Christianity preached egalitarian principle, it is found that the Danish missionaries had tried to force all caste to be of one caste and to make them eat and drink together and to have these of higher and lower castes connected to each other through marriage. Vedanagyam therefore published pamphlets publicly accusing the Danish missionaries of committing four cruelties, (a) tampering with Tamil scripture replacing old versions with their own translations (b) trying to combine the *pallar* and *paraiyar* (both from the lowest level castes) and every other people into one caste by excommunicating them from the Lord's Supper through reforming to abandon caste codes (c) restoring the festivals celebrated by the natives and protecting the same with the use of fines at weddings, funerals and important occasion (d) removing Tamil lyrics and music from worship, services, other festivals and events.[96] Thus we find Tamils like Vedanaygam Pillai made reinterpretations of their newly embraced Christian religion. The Protestant evangelists, found it more different to come to terms with group conversions because of their much greater emphasis laid on individualism. The degree of conversions and castes varied from place to place.

The Indian converts to Christianity had always continued to form a caste feeling even after the conversion. They perhaps feared the loss of caste or respect of their orthodox countrymen, if they did not conform to caste protocols. European Missionaries highlighted the evils of the indigenous society and they took the task of reforming it. During the British rule missionaries had no access to state forces to bring about conversion. The Protestants seem to be have regarded the caste system as an obstacle to evangelization and attempted to foster individual councils but the mass movements of the Nineteenth century caused them to re-assess their attempt.[97] Thus all the Christian missionaries did not have a single attitude towards caste.[98] K.N. Pannikar opines that the Christian missionaries worked within the framework of a colonial society and that their institutions created an illusion for western ideas and institutions.[99] This view calls for reconsideration since this could not be said to be true of all missionaries as explained above.

The British and the Indian Society: 1757-1857

Pre-colonial South India had a good population that cultivated the land. Irrigated cultivation was only possible in the fertile riverine tracts that run through the plains. Paddy was the main crop harvested twice a year. However, it has become increasingly difficult to depict the pre-colonial South Indian society in a larger measure as a peasant society since we find very strong commercial networks, developing independently of the European presence within the Indian society. In such a context several castes particularly belonging to artisans and traders came to be reformulated during the Eighteenth century and so the conventional understanding of caste could not continue to be maintained. India's economy had expanded under the Mughals. It became more urbanized and commercialized because trade networks extended deep into the countryside. The production of goods and commodities in the hinterland reached the coasts of Gujarat, Malabar, Coromandel and Bengal.[100] Fifteen per cent of the British exports and imports came from Bengal in 1670 and sixty-six per cent in 1740 and it continued to increase more till 1770s.[101] Indian trade in silk and cotton textiles which had been estimated annually to the tune of £ 800, 000 in silver during the Seventeenth century had increased phenomenally during the Eighteenth century and the British trade annually was around £ twenty-six million worth of goods.[102] This made the British to desire to turn the balance of trade in their favour when the Mughal empire declined in the Eighteenth century. The British were successful to obtain 123 million worth in reparations together with territorial and political rights, by the collecting land revenue that went to the state. The English East India Company was thus able to finance its trade deficit, after 1760 it steadily drained India and we find that over next fifty years a sum of £ five billion made its way to Britain.[103]

The Battle of Plassey (23 June 1757) made the English king-makers in Bengal and Bihar and it paved way for the foundation of the future British empire in India. The Battle of Buxar (22 October 1764) and the consequent '*Diwanee*' gave the British a legal status with revenue of three provinces which provided them with the sinews of trade, war and administration. The British impact on India particularly the social effects considerably took the form of the displacement of classes. The first upset followed the famine of 1770 when the cultivators were too few for the revenue demand to be met. The farming of revenue took time in the place of revenue settlement and in the mean while Warren Hastings was appointed the first Governor-General of India in 1774. Later we find that there was disturbance in Bengal, where by the smaller landholders were reduced to the condition of tenants at will caused by the permanent settlement of 1793. The second upset had come with this permanent settlement, when the revenue figure was fixed in many cases too high for the existing cultivation and there were also problems among the *zamindars* at this time.

Three major approaches to the study of the Indian society during the Eighteenth century had developed that include the orientalists, the administrators and the missionary and each of them had a characteristic view. The orientalists such as Alexander Dow (1768-1771) in his work "*The History of Hindustan*" dealt with the four *varnas*. Further, N.B. Halhead in his work "*A View of the India Society*" (1777) also mentioned that Brahmins at the top of the social order were dominant in the society. People of the other *varnas* were prohibited from learning the Vedas and certain other Hindu religious texts. The acceptance of a textual view of 2the society by the orientalists led to a picture of Indian society as being static and timeless. In this view, there was no regional variation and questioning the relationship between prescriptive statements derived from the texts and the actual behaviour of individuals and groups.

British administrators like H.T. Colebrooke summarized the four *varna* theory in practice. He says "little attention is paid to the limitations to which we have alluded daily observation shows, even Brahmins exercising the menial profession of a *Sudra*. We are aware that every caste forms itself into clubs or lodges consisting of the several individuals of that caste residing within a small distance. And these govern themselves by particular rules and customs or by laws." Thus we find description for rural society.[104]

The early Eighteenth century also witnessed development of considerable literature by the missionaries on Indian society such as Claudius Buchanan, Sir John Shore, William Carey and William Ward.[105] Here we find that there was an attempt to condemn Hindu society and ridicule it with translations from the Sanskrit texts. William Ward described that "caste system under the fatal influence of the abominable system the Brahmins have sunk into ignorance, without abating an atom of their claims to superiority, the *Kshatriyas* became almost extinct before their country fell into the hands of Muslims, the *Vaishyas* are no where to be found in Bengal almost all have fallen into the class of *Sudras* and the *Sudras* have sunk to the level of their own cattle".[106] Charles Grant was another missionary who served in Bengal from 1774 to 1790 and he wrote a tract on the Indian society in 1792. We find that the major thrust of these missionaries in their writings was to condemn Hindus and Hindu society and they often made contributions to the empirical study of the Indian society. This partially came from their need for preparation of the Christian religious tracts into the Indian vernaculars. William Carey wrote a work called '*Dialogues Intended to Facilitate the Acquiring of the Bengali Language*' and it was published at the press in Serampore in 1801. The different social and occupational groups in Bengal are recorded speaking the language as they would in the normal conversation. The venom that heaped on the caste system appears here not to have been accidental, as the missionaries considered it necessary to destroy what they thought was the social basis of Hinduism. For James Mill, who wrote the "History of India" in 1817 the principal value of culture was the degree to which it contributed to the furtherance of rationalism and individualism. Since these two values he did not see in Hindu civilization therefore he condemned it severely. The reification of caste as a category in Hindu sociology seems to owe much to the proposition that Hindus lacked a sense of history, for history records change. James Mill therefore wrote from the time of Alexander's invasion to British rule, the Indian society was static.[107] It may be said here that there is some truth in it because Hindus were continued to be governed by institutions moulded by laws that were codified 2000 years ago which were completely outdated.[108]

The orientalists and the missionaries were polar opposites in their assessment of Indian culture and society but they agreed in common to what the central principles and institutions of their society were. They accepted the Brahminical theory of *catur varna* and saw the origin of castes in the intermixture through marriage of the members of the four *varnas*. The orientalists admired in theory the civilization and religion embodied in the texts and they saw the difficulties of Indian society departing from a golden age. The missionaries saw the society as pernicious and filled with absurdities. Those Baptist missionaries who came from the lower orders in the British society were committed to reform the Indian society and they were concerned with changing India rather than with maintaining the status quo.

Many of the works that appeared had till now had taken for granted the centrality of caste in Hindu society. Anthropologists have been only fascinated by the ritual aspects of caste. This tendency has been intensified by the influence of Louis Dumont on recent theorisation of caste. He studied caste in India by placing it at the centre of the sociological endeavour with a critique of individualism claiming Karl Marx and Durkheim as his sociological ancestors. Some scholars opine that caste was chiefly religious and it was a religious doctrine. Grand Duff also held that caste was civil. Some others have argued that the attention paid to caste has tended to orientalism emphasizing those features of Indian society that make it 'exotic' from a western point of view. These approaches have been fundamentally questioned. While it is hard to write about caste without referring to Dumont, his theoretical assumption that hierarchy is indeed central to an understanding of the nature of Hindu society needs to be questioned.[109] Dumont confuses two separate ideas distinctiveness (which is a logical concept) and typicality (which is a statistical or empirical concept). Scholars have therefore criticised Dumont for he serves to perpetuate important elements of the colonial construction of India.[110] Most the works of scholars who followed him also depicted castes as arranged in a ladder-like vertical order. The sociologists have also tended to emphasis this stratification regarding the ideological and ritual manifestation of caste, such as the pervasive concern with purity and impurity as epiphenomenal. Anthropologists view caste as a recent colonial artefact, others as an indigenous category. Many have been heavily influenced by the ideological reductionism of Louis Dumont's theory of Hindu society. Anthropologists have often contrasted caste (based on hierarchy) and tribe (tribal society is undifferentiated and egalitarian) as forms of social organization based on opposite principles. Thus the caste system in India has been examined by scholars with three different perspectives. The indologists have viewed caste from the scriptural point of view and according to them the origin of caste was the division of labour. Social anthropologists viewed the caste from the cultural point of view in four directions such as organizational, structural, (Houton) institutional (Risley) and relational. Marxist scholars like S.G Sardesai, noted that the peculiar combination of village community and caste system has considerably inhibited the development of the forces of productivity in India and prevented the growth of social conditions which are necessary for the combination of manual labour and mental work.[111] Another consequence of the caste system was that it permitted "Great Walls of China" not only between the exploiting, ruling castes and the suppressed lower castes, but likewise also between the lower castes themselves, each of which considered itself higher or lower in rank than the others.[112] Social state is a broad term that included such entities as social classes, occupational specializations, caste organizations, tribes and perhaps even gender. Class for Marxists is the dominant social structure and they believe the utility of class analysis to be universal despite cultural differences. The argument that social structures might affect the capacity of a society for economic growth has been made by a number of authors beginning from Max Weber. India is different-because of the system of castes and sub-castes that structure social life. The factors that affect the operation of caste had been grouped by Burton Stein under three headings such as (a) legal and institutional changes (British judicial system and establishment of principle of equality) (b) technological changes (industrialization and introduction of new technology besides (c) occupational changes (old pattern of occupant replaced by new ones).

Movements, Social Reforms and Legislations

When the British conquered India, Hindus (particularly the Brahmins) were quick to change to the new circumstances while the Muslims in general remained with orthodox views. Therefore *Tariqa-i-Muhammadia* known as Wahabi movement was established in 1820 and it stressed for reforming and restoring Islam to its pristine glory discarding all pernicious practices that had crept into the Muslim society and religion in India.[113] Sir Syed Ahmad Khan (1786-1831) urged the Muslims to accept moderate western education. The *ulema* of Deobard issued a *fatwa* declaring Sir Syed Ahmad was a *kafir*. It may be said that the *ulema* felt anything modern was irreligious.

Conversion in India and missionary activities for bringing social changes had stimulated the Hindus for reforming the caste system. The caste Hindus felt at that time that they had to change their attitudes towards those expelled from caste due to conversion and also to reform the rules of their re-entry. Hindus also felt that the evils in Indian society were the most crucial factors to have handicapped the progress of humanity. The coming of the British brought another phase in the social and cultural development of India where we find the western political influence of education gave rise to new type of social thinking which had never occurred during the Islamic rule. People began to reshape their social and intellectual life in a large measure in accordance with strands adoptive from western thought and culture. The British listened to the wise counsel of such social reformers like Raja Ram Mohun Roy (1772-1833) and Swami Dayanand Saraswati (1824-1883). Socio-religious reform movements such as *Brahmo Samaj* counteracted the activities of the Christian missionaries by reviving the essentials of Hinduism and emphasized on one absolute God and revolted against idolators, polytheism, rituals, rites and caste system. It is to be noted that social reform refers to a change in the attitudes of the people and in their belief, value systems and it precedes social change.

It may be mentioned that Ram Mohun Roy was married three times at the age of nine, ten and twenty-one years. His first wife died soon after marriage. The second wife died in 1826 and the third wife outlived him. Ram Mohun advocated reforms in Hindu society and accepted some features of western thought. He denounced *sati* and championed the cause of the Indian widow and wife. *Brahmo Samaj* (Divine Society) was established in 1820 by him and it emphasised upon the humanistic contents of religion. He advocated the English education as a means of bringing western knowledge to India. He denounced idol worship and proclaimed monotheism. Lord William Bentick abolished *sati-pratha*, the evil social custom by The Act of Prohibition of the Practice of Sati in 1829, with the help of Ram Mohun. This Policy of the British introduced in social sphere encouraging the prohibition of *sati* was the first event of considerable impact in raising Hindu consensus. It also created increasing fears that the British Government (in league of with the Christian missionaries) had embarked on a course of interference with the Hindu practices.[114]

The *Arya Samaj* was founded by Swami Dayanand Saraswati and it attempted to remodel Hindu society on traditional lines and tried to appreciate the Vedic ideas.[115] Dayanand had made it clear that he would not defend the falsehood of the Hindu religion but would unveil them just as he had exposed the errors of the other religions. He condemned marriages between partners of unequal ages, dowry and polygamy.

Pundit Ishwar Chandra Vidyasagar (1820-1891) desired to create a more humane society. He conducted a study of 133 *Kulin Brahmins* of the Hooghly district. Using this data he argued that the practice of *Kulinism* was inhuman. He pointed out that Bolonath Bandopadhyay a man aged fifty-six years had eighty wives. Similarly Bhagaban Chattopadhyay another man aged sixty-four years had seventy-two wives. He was completely against polygamy and was responsible for enacting The Hindu Widow Remarriage Act which was passed in 1856. Vidyasagar and Dayanand Saraswati were trained in Hindu classics and saw India as recovering from a dark age. They argued that there has been a golden age when women were hailed and they held high status in society. These concepts seem to be useful only in the development of an ideology legitimating social reform. However, both the golden and dark ages are problematic for historians.

Virasalingam Pantulu (1848-1919) had worked for marriage reforms in Andhra. He published his journal *"Viveka Vardhani"* to encourage social reforms. He believed in the necessity of purifying the Hindu religion by opposing wrong customs and so he attempted to stop wrong conduct in society. In 1891 he founded a Widow Remarriage Association. In Western India Mahadev Govind Rande (1842-1901) founded The National Social Conference to focus attention on social reforms. R. Venkata Ratnam Naidu opposed the *devadasi* system in Madras presidency. From time to time thus there have been reformers in India who introduced a certain reorientation in the character of social structure, religious concepts and usage.

In the study of social change, two concepts such as westernization and modernization have been often counter posed in the debate which runs through the entire gamut of the various movements of cultural renaissance of India since the beginning of the British rule. This is possibly to describe in cultural and not structural levels. The structure of society in India relates to the network of groups, classes, castes besides religious sects and ideologies. Sociologists called sanskritization where the people of the lower castes in their attempts to improve their status adopted the customs and manners of a higher caste. Westernization involves acceptance of western dress, diet, manners, education and values. M.N. Srinivas's formulation of the concepts sanskritization and westernization had been utilized by a number of anthropologists in varied settings.[116] Marriott's use of universalization and parochialization has also contributed in a large measure to the discussion.[117] Yogendra Singh mentions that there are four categories of sociologists from the stand point view of their approach to the problem of caste such as cultural universalistic, cultural particularistic, structural universalistic and structural particularistic.[118] The view that social is the product of internal forces has a certain basis in historical fact. The obvious difficulty is to separate facts from reflections upon them. New emphasis has been made to the old view that social change is internal to the society changing and social changes originate in the division of labour and consequently the states are products of the social structures.

Social changes in British terms as 'social reforms' are often embedded with discussions on *sati*, child-marriage widowhood and polygamy. Various legislations came to be introduced by the British. The abolition of slavery culminated in the Act of 1843 was a bold step targeted into India's social progress. The Caste Disabilities Removal Act XXI of 1850 was another indication though it did not work against the castes behaviour. The Missionary efforts were very much involved in bringing into operation this act. Some important other enactments include The Christian Marriage Act of 1872, The Special Marriage Act III of 1872 and The Married Women's Property Act of 1874. All these acts were very good but, since there was no matching enforcement, they largely remained on paper only and were not reflected in actual society at large. During the British Rule reforms were called for changes in the cultural practices and values of Hindus on the pattern of primordial tradition of the Vedas. The British government did not desire and want to abolish the caste system. But all this attempts also did not remove the rigidity of the caste system. In British India 'reform' represented a specific reading of the need for change. Social malpractices within the Hindu society were deeply rooted in religious belief.[119]

Some scholars opine that social reform movements took place in India as part of an intricate political agenda to resist British domination and simultaneously to effect positive change in the various princely states. Others attribute the rise of social movements to the traditional reactions of alienated individuals to social changes or disruptions. Contemporary approaches appreciate social movements as conscious and rational activities. In fact social movements are conscious, organized and collective actions to bring about or resist social change. The Nineteenth century India can boast of a wide range of social and religious reform movements and their aim was initially to create an atmosphere to lessen social tension produced by caste on the one hand and to remove political and religious animosity on the other. These reform movements stood for some change and caused a stir in the minds of ordinary people. Scholars who have studied the socio-cultural transformation of the traditionalist society of

India under the impact of colonial modernization emphasize the role of movements and ideas. The colonial state was keen to acquire a more minute knowledge about the Indian society in order to face the sensitive question of social reforms without hurting the sentiments of the masses at large.[120] Remarkable transformation in the social ideas took place primarily because of the introduction of western education. Faith and belief began to slowly replace by reason and judgment among the educated Hindus and so they came to get rid of the social abuses like meaningless rites and infanticide which was a new experience. Reform movements such as the Prarthana Samaj, Ramakrishna Mission and the Theosophical Society also created social awakening among the Hindus through efforts of Rama Krishna (1836-1886), Vivekananda (1861-1902) and Annie Besant. Scholars like Dharampal opine that when the British started establishing themselves in India, the Indians were not technologically primitive. The archival records of British India prove the existence and functioning of the society extremely competent in the field of sciences and arts in the Eighteenth century.[121] By 1835-36 all caste distinctions were abolished in South India.[122] Right hand and left hand caste disputes disappeared in society in the late Nineteenth century since it had been transformed under the colonial rule.

In recent years we find the writings of the revisionists who employ Foucaultian analysis of the nexus between power and knowledge. They utilize social ideas connected with the study of invented traditions. Indian society was passive and plastic in the opinion of David Washbrook.[123] Ronald Inden who analysed the Nineteenth century western discussion about India says, end to present the construction of the other as an enterprise had been exclusively conducted by the Europeans.[124] The study of Nicholas Dirks over-emphasizes the capacity of the British to codify and restrict Indian society in accordance with their own interest.[125] To him it is primarily the British or colonialism that invented India as a rigid depolitised society. This was so even in the semi-independent or princely state of Pudukottai. The study of Eugene Irschik criticised Nicholas Dirks for viewing the South Indian temple (of the Nineteenth century) as an institution reinvented by the British administration.[126] His model of the colonial dialogue also implies that colonialism is seen not as a cultural damage but as a creative process. He argues that dialogue and inequality are not necessarily incompatible. Irschik also opposed the model of colonial discourse of Edward Said. The studies of C.J Baker and David Washbrook tried to explore the non-Brahmin identity and debated on the changes in the colonial situation.[127] We find River's studies on *Todas*, Grigson's work on the *Gonds*, Sarat Chandra Roy's studies on the tribals of Chotanagpur, Aiyappan's work on *Nayadis* and *Izhavas*, Ronald Inden's writings on Bengali *Kaasthas* and Brahmins, Karen Leonard's work on *Kayasthas* of Hyderabad, Robert Hardgrave's studies on South Indian *Nadars* and David Rudner's writings on *Nattukottai Chettiars* which throw light on different groups of caste which began to emerge in the Nineteenth and Twentieth centuries. These communities have responded differently to the new economic, legal, educational and other changes affecting the society under the colonial rule.[128] Some significant writings also include the works of F.G. Bailey, Stephen Alan Bernett, André Beteille, Brenda E. F. Beck, Janet Bensens, Geofrey Burhat, Kathleen E. Gough, Eric J. Miller and Moffatts.[129] In the discourse on caste, the major issues discussed by them were caste ranking, purity-impurity, elite emulation, *jajmani* system, dominant caste traditions, caste associations, caste as a system, caste structure and caste culture.

Following the Industrial Revolution in England, western culture soon came to be spread in India when the English East India Company established its rule in the beginning of the Nineteenth century. Dominance of that culture found place in Indian social and cultural fields and we find four types of changes as an impact. The first may be said to be eliminative change where we find the abolition of *sati* which took place. As examples of additive change we notice adoption of new cultural traits such as divorce in Hindu society and giving shares to daughters in father's property. As supportive change we find the *Hundi* system functioning effectively in India in loan transactions in a large measure. Further, synthetic change took place where we find new forms of existing elements plus those which came as adoptions, for which mention may be made of the dowry system but putting restrictions and associating children along with parents in mate selection.

Social Thinkers in Modern India

Social thinkers felt that the ritualistic disabilities of caste was chiefly based on misunderstanding of Hindu tradition and so they called for their rejection. Guru Nanak (1469-1539) denounced the very idea of impurity attached to god's creation. He refused to admit any one being low by birth. The treatment of the high caste people towards the *sudras* and the untouchables had been condemned by him as most inhuman. The two main subordinate groups of slaves and untouchables in Indian society were the main concern of the social thinkers. However, slavery came to be abolished by the British in India, but the untouchables continued to face problems in society. It may be worth quoting the words of Pandit Jawaharlal Nehru.[130]

"How can it be that Brahma
Would make a world and keep it miserable?
Since if all powerful He leaves it so,
He is not good, and if not powerful
He is not God!"

Social discrimination such as no entry to temple by the depressed castes (untouchables) prevailed in India. This made Sri Narayana Guru to consecrate a Siva temple separately at Arvuvippuram in 1808 in South Travancore. This was against the monopoly of the Brahmins and against tradition too. Similarly, for the first time in 1874 the *Shanars* asked for right to enter the Meenakshi temple in Madurai but were denied. These *Shanars* who were traditionally palm distillers had improved their social status by abandoning palm distilling and took to other professions like trading. On 14 May 1897 they forcibly entered the Meenakshi temple. Zamindar of Ramnad, the trustee of the temple, sued in the Madurai district court for a declaration that *Shanars* were not entitled to enter the temple. He also asked for a compensation of Rs. 2500 for conducting the purification ceremony needed by the temple. The subordinate judge of Madurai declared in favour of the plaintiff. Against this judgment, the *Shanars* appealed to the Privy Council, the First Tribunal for all the appeals from the High Courts in India.[131] In 1908 the legal committee of the Privy Council decided in the appeal case from the Madras High Court that the custom of excluding a depressed caste from entry into a Hindu temple was legal. This made the *Shanars* once again forcibly to enter into the Meenakshi temple at Madurai in a procession bearing troches and also accompanied by music. The temple entry question simmered throughout the following years until the Temple Entry Act was passed by many states in India in 1930s which provided the rights of entry to Hindu temples to the scheduled castes. In 1932 Temple Entry Enquiry Committee was also appointed to review the matter.

Role of Periyar

E.V. Ramasamy Nayakkar, (1879-1973) called Periyar (The Great) joined the Indian National Congress in 1919. He became disillusioned with its Brahminic leadership and left the congress in 1925. Therefore he joined the justice party, the first anti-Brahmin group (founded in 1916).[132] He claimed that three conditions were necessary for India to gain its freedom. They are namely destruction of Indian National Congress, the so-called Hindu religion and the Brahmin domination. Periyar in his journal "*Kudiarasu*" published articles and he declared all the religions to be abolished, the caste system and the dominance of Brahmins also to be destroyed. He founded "The Self Respect Movement League" in 1926. It was a new militant, mass-oriented movement chiefly consisting of the depressed classes. Periyar said the following words:

"There is no God
There is no God
There is no God at all.
He who invented God is a fool.
He who propagates God is a scoundrel.
He who worships God is a barbarian."

The radical nationalism of the Self Respect Movement inspired many intellectuals at that time and among them was the famous Tamil poet Bharatidasan who published his writings in 1938. The Self Respect Movement involved original Tamil values not as in the sense of seeking a revivalistic return to a golden age but as an inspiration of an autonomous identity. Singaravelu another follower wrote articles in *Kudiarasu*, dealing with socialism and also materialistic interpretation of history. The Self Respect Movement emerged into *Dravida Kazhagam* as a party under Periyar in 1944 and it had anti-Brahmin as its ideology. This Dravidian movement came as a protest against Vedic Hinduism and Brahmin dominance. The Dravidian Movement of the early Twentieth century first accepted the theory of the primacy of ethnicity but later asserted the primacy of language.[133]

Bhimrao Ramji Ambedkar

Ambedkar (1891-1956) another social thinker was prompted on the belief that so far as the people of India remained within the Hindu society they can not attain equality. He opined that orthodox traditions and narrow minds had given rise to untouchability. Casteism at that time had grippled the Indian social structure so firmly and it had sown the seeds of discord instead of brotherhood. On 25 December 1927 Ambedkar burnt the Manusmriti in the fire and gave a new speech to the suppressed and helpless. He wanted an alternative paradigm of a social order to an existing social order based upon the caste system. Hence he led mass conversion of Maharashtra Mahars to Buddhism.[134]. His alternative is on ideal society or a casteless society based upon the principle of justice. To him Budhha's *Dhamma* was the new paradigm of life which offered full liberation to all human beings in this world. He said that conversion was the only possible way which offered the *dalits* a real 'social equality'. According to him, the constitution of India was not just to provide rules and regulations to govern the country, but it was actually a process of creating a mechanism to help in establishing a democratic social order or a society based upon the principle of justice.[135] It is to be mentioned here that Ambedkar resolved to die as a Buddhist. He said that "there will be outcastes as long as there are castes and nothing can emanate the outcaste except the destruction of the caste system".[136]

The study of *dalit* movement by Mark Juergensmeyr was the first one which traced the lower caste struggles for social change. The impact of the missionaries, English education, modernization and changing economic conditions helped the rise of *dalits* and responsible for the *dalit* movements. The study of Geil Omvedt traced the rise and growth of such movements in the various parts of India and focused on ideological influence of Ambedkar. Rober Delige had discussed the formation of the distinct *dalit* consciousness since the middle of the Nineteenth century and comprehensively dealt with the variations in *dalit* assertion.[137]

Caste Associations, Peasant Revolts and Indian Society under the Crown

Indian society was one of the most diverse and complex societies in the world at that time with people of multiple and overlapping identity found on religion, caste, class and region.[138] Therefore it has given rise to a tremendous variety and density of groups, associations and movements during the Nineteenth century. The Cambridge school of scholars have argued that the caste categories were rather arbitrary, constructed by the colonial government and that the caste associations were deployed by the caste leaders and big-men to pursue their political ends.[139] It is to be noted that the caste associations formed at that time began to function as a political interest group. But some scholars opine that the society of India suffered from social disabilities and superstitions in the early Twentieth century and so as a part of reform activity, a number of castes were organized into caste associations by the educated members of the respective castes to implement social reforms. They published journals, evinced interest in caste welfare and collected funds for their caste students. They paid special attention to women's education, and the reform activity included in child-marriage and widow-remarriage.[140]

Scholars have so far highlighted revolts of the peasants under the British rule in their studies. The Sannyasi revolt is the first peasant revolt (1763-1800). Other revolts include the Chakma rebellion in the Hilly Chittagong (1776-1787), the indigo cultivators struggle (1830-1848) Baga's Wahabi Rebellion (1831) and the Santhal Rebellion (1855-57) in Bengal. British scholars like W.W. Hunter mentioned the cause of the Santal rebellion of 1855 and said that it was a misappropriation of sound administrative principles and the defeat of the rebels was necessary for the preservation of the British rule. However, the Marxist scholars in their studies had debated regarding the revolutionary role of the peasantry.[141] The English Governor-General of Madras also did not hesitate to interfere in the local social affairs and we find the breast cloth controversy of 1859 in South India.[142] André Beteille doubts the process of change taking place which represents a shift to social stratification in terms of social changes, especially if social classes are defined as interest groups in conflict with one another.[143]

The British began to have a fairly deep knowledge on Indian society through their direct experience such as Thomas Munro's land settlements in Baramahal (Salem district) in Madras, Malcolm's contacts with Mysore, Tod's assignments in Rajasthan and Elphinstone's administrative responsibilities in Maharashtra. Further, works relating to Bengal and Bihar such as Francis Buchanan had been very helpful for the publication of the Imperial Gazetteer of India. By this time we find that more than one third of the states in India had changed hands to the British through sale for arrears of land tax. The social link between the landholder and the cultivator had been broken. Cash nexus was replacing traditional rights. The literate class in Bengal that emerged came to be known as the *bhadralok*. In South India the ruling chiefs were dispossessed by Sir Thomas Munro. In western India particularly in Bombay we find the rise of enterprising Parsi community.

In 1870, W.W. Hunter published the statistical account of Bengal. With this for the first time we find the census of India undertaken in 1871. A whole new body of material on Indian society thus became available after every ten years when census was undertaken. William Crooke published the tribes and castes of the Northwestern Provinces and Oudh in four volumes in Calcutta in 1896. The castes came to alphabetically arranged and a good deal of space was given to marriage rules and sub-divisions of the caste usually termed exogamous sections. In 1901 effort was made officially to establish 'The Ethnographic Survey of India' which would develop as part of the ongoing census.[144] Sir Herbert Risley, the Director of Indian Census Operations completed the work and classified castes on the basis of social precedence as recognized by native public opinion.[145] Petitions were submitted by Indians for claiming different status than which had been granted earlier by Provincial Census Commissioners. These petitions were drafted in English by the people which shows that even the educated Indians were still within the caste system.[146] Various *jatis* particularly, the middle and low castes made efforts to get higher ranks for themselves referred to as members of twice born when Risley, the Director of Indian Census tried to rank all castes. Risley's justifications do give a fairly good idea of the motives and objectives underlying the official studies into the internal organization of the Indian society. According to him, "The native society is made up of a network of subdivisions governed by rules which affect every department of life. How that society will behave under novel conditions, what use will it make of any particular form of political representation are questions which can not be answered without fairly minute knowledge the internal organization of society".[147] By the 1901 census, we find that the definite and indefinite entries created have bear of the measures adopted by Risley to allow castes to petition if they had not been properly listed. It is true that Risley dubbed the classification of castes in the 1891 census as a patch work classification, in which occupation predominates, varied here and there by considerations of caste history, tradition, ethnic affinity and geographical position.[148] He was pessimistic about the general progress of India without reform. The concept of a multi-ethnic society and its central polarity had gradually acquired a definite shape in the minds of the imperial policy planners.[149] Detailed information about caste structure and its distribution at district, provincial and all-India levels had been collected with a view to reveal the essential attributes and vulnerability of each of the groups.[150] Now we find that the New Indian History remonstrates that caste was rigidified under colonisation as the British sought to categorize, systematize and privatize society for their rule.[151]

Indian society which has been analysed with three different perspectives such as religio-philosophical, historico-political and Marxism have on the one hand greatly strengthened the theoretical foundation of analysis and on the other hand it made the creative thinkers to present new approaches to western utilitarianism, welfare-egalitarianism and libertinism. The western historians attributed some features such as influence of caste, tribe and religion (Max Weber) selfishness and self indulgence of ruling class (W.H. Moreland) absence of private property in land (Bernier Wittfogel) village self sufficiency (Sir Henry Maine and Karl Marx) and they have concluded that there was absence of change in Indian society. The inelastic way of looking at the problem in our society by Indian philosophical and radical writers was different from western societies has shed new light on the current concerns.

Scholars have argued so far that India's appearance as a static and Hindu society should be seen more as a product of colonialism than as precondition for the subcontinent's subordinate to European dominance. It is a fact that the pre-colonial India itself had been dynamic and changing. Edward Said had presented orientalism as a hegemonic discourse created exclusively by the Europeans but Niels Brimnes demonstrated how the discourse embedded in the colonial encounter was produced mentally by European colonialists and indigenous leaders.[152] Sekhar Bandhyopadhyay points out that the prominent concern for the British was to put in place social controls that would ensure the maintenance of the expanded British empire after 1857 and that caused only by keeping Indian society neatly compartmentalized into caste.[153] India's society consisting of isolated village republics dominated by the peculiar institutions of caste and non-market *jajmani* exchange relations have become increasingly dubious.[154] This critique is against the discourse produced by the colonial activities of the Nineteenth century.

Caste remained a perennial topic of interest to indologists, social anthropologists, social historians and sociologists who argued the functioning of castes from different stand points. The first group is the one that used classical-scriptural texts by scholars like Wilson, Colebrook, Max Muller and Simmer. The second group is the cultural-anthropological one with emphasis on institutional and relational aspects by the British administrators, anthropologists and ethnographers like Dalton, Nesfield, Risley Horace, William Crooke, Edgar Thurston and Russel. Caste became a special target and site of knowledge for the ethnographers in British India during the three censuses held in 1911, 1921 and 1931. The third group is sociological, which explained a system of stratification functioning in a social matrix. Caste provided for a closed type of stratification where membership of each segment is fixed by birth and provided also for a compartmentalization of society (segmental division). Though hierarchy is an essential feature of caste the exact number of hierarchy among distinct castes had not been made clear (hierarchical division).[155] Dividing line between caste and occupation is so prominent that some writers like Nesfield define caste in terms of occupation. Ghurye does not accept such a position because the supposed linkage seems to be very tenuous.[156] The economic, political and religious dimensions of the system is very important in caste hierarchy, rights and disabilities of castes too.

Montague-Chelmsford Reforms or The Government of India Act of 1919 enabled a new category of social stratum called the depressed classes to be introduced and it included the marginal group of tribals as well. Pavlov opines that the Indian caste system has traits of tribal unity, servile submission as well as organization based on trade and social standing. These are all indication that its origins go for bad.[157] The British created tension in the society by passing government orders such as G.O. No. 1129 dated 15 December 1928 (Public service department) which mentioned that out of the twelve posts, five had to be given to non-Brahmin Hindus, two to the Brahmins, two for the Muslims, two to the Anglo-Indians or Christians and one to the depressed class.[158]

Some important social legislations were introduced and enacted from time to time by the British such as The Child Marriage Act of 1929, The Hindu Gains of Earning Act of 1930, The Parsee Marriage and Divorce Act of 1936, The Hindu Women's Right to Property Act of 1937 and The Dissolution of the Muslim Marriage Act of 1939. Further, The Government of India Act of 1935 permitted introduction of scheduled castes. The Scheduled castes were listed in a schedule with the Government of India order of 1936.

The study of Indian society undertaken by the scholars had different approaches. At the first place we find a broad scale humanistically oriented situation which emphasized the relationship between textual studies and a static model of contemporary Indian society. Next we find an administrative tradition centered on the census for the study of caste which sought to see the Indian society as a collection of discrete entities whose traditions and customs could be classified and studied. Then we see a tradition of economic study which sought to describe the working of village economies with some attention to the social structure of villages. Fourthly we have an anthropological tradition centered on the study of the tribals and also an historical-administrative strain which centered on the general category of village organization in a broad comparative framework but without an intensive ethnographic base. Thus changing views of Indian society are described and we find among the four, distinct components of social system of which two of them deal with structural and the other two on cultural (*jati*).

Various castes had undergone complex and profound changes in the colonial period also owing to secular education, opening of new jobs, rule of law, scientific and rational outlook. This new situation created not only to claborate their traditional caste status but also to increase their bargaining capacity in politics and centres of power. Some scholars like Conrad Wood, Stephen Frederick Dale and Millar in their studies give either the views of Cambridge school of thinking on the impact of conversions or new education and economic and political changes that indirectly initiating and emphasizing on the changes for assertion of castes in the new situation.

Nationalism, Secularism, Communalism and Society

The Indian National Movement was launched by Indians against the British Government to free India. It can be broadly classified into four distinct phases. The first phase (1885-1905) is that of the moderates. The second phase (1906-1919) is known as the middle class movement. The third phase (1920-1928) is referred to be the mass movement under the leadership of Gandhi and the fourth phase (1929-1947) is described as the period of complete revolution under the guidance of Jawaharlal Nehru. The study of Geil Omvedt points out that the Indian National Congress and the Left parties had ignored historical realities about secularism. He calls them as pseudo-secularists and says that religious pluralism in India had been a struggle and an achievement. He adds that secularism was not something that had sprung up automatically from the basic values of dominant religions and caste-class establishments.[159]

The social reformers of the Nineteenth century and leaders of the Indian National Congress were striving to arouse a sense of common nationality in India-the land of great diversities. The concept of the nation was itself a fluid category in princely states. Each kingdom had the notion in many ways yet these tendencies existed within British India where national qualities and points were discussed in their speeches about their own states with references to an Indian nation. In fact this is a true reputation of the historic experience of the Indian society.

Mahatma Gandhi and his colleagues in the anti-British campaign in India preferred *swadeshi* to nationalism. Gandhi avoided the language of nationalism primarily because he was fully aware that filtration with nationalist ideas in the first quarter of the Twentieth century by the Indian National Congress had frightened away not only the Muslims but also some of the Hindu lower castes. The Lucknow Pact of 1916 is the first political arrangement at all India level to divide two principal category Hindus and Muslims.[160] The All Parties Conference held in 1928 laid down the principles for the redistribution of provinces on a linguistic basis.[161] The Poona Pact of 1932 for the first time placed the backward classes, later classified as the *sudra* castes in the Government of India Act of 1935. This Poona Pact articulated arrangement in which scheduled castes were identified as a separate group within Hinduism.

Jawaharlal Nehru in his 'Discovery of India' comes closest to stating what the concept nationalism means to him. He says "nationalism is essentially a group of memory of past achievements, traditions and experiences, and nationalism is stronger today that it has ever been".[162] He does not answer the questions such as what is this nation round which the sentiment of nationalism crystallizes? Is it the territory a people occupy? Is it their ethnic identity? Is it a common religion? Is it a common language? Nehru emphasized the importance of the process of a fragmentation in arousing among the people a sense of their national identity.[163] The most important component of the Indian state's partition at the time of Independence was the task of constructing a unified national society out of a heterogeneous diversity of ethnic, religious and linguistic groups (secular state).

The formation of the Indian state, (The Mountbatten plan) the state building under Nehru Era (1947-1964) and the Indian state under transformation had been studied by scholars.[164] Ravindra Kumar opines that the political identity of the Republic of India should be defined in terms of a civilization state rather than a nation-state. The nature of a civilizational state calls for no formal change in the vocabulary of politics and it merely requires a new stance towards the overarching political identity of the country.[165]

It may be said here that the British were not foolish enough to divide the already divided communities in India that disagreed on all fronts. Nationalism had different meanings for Hindus and Muslims. The Muslim policy of the Indian National Congress had been very defective from the beginning. Cultural and religious nationalism could neither be neutralized nor eliminated by the British rule and in due course of time it changed into political nationalism.[166]

Ernest Gellener argues that it is not nationalism that imposes homogeneity, but on the contrary it is the imperative of homogeneity under modern-industrial conditions that takes the form of nationalism. Nationalism seeks to forge a new political community that will become the basis for common citizenship and it erases all markers of cultural difference and establishes one uniform culture.[167] Benedict Anderson gave the idea that nations are imagined communities.[168] Elie Kedourien believes that non-European cultures had traditions of accommodating cultural difference and so nationalism is specifically a European doctrine.[169] Partha Chatterjee has argued against Geller and Anderson that their viewing of nation converges, despite important differences, on a kind of sociological determinism whereby third world nationalism are reduced to mere types of original European ones. He says that nationalist ideology is 'inherently polemical and shot through with tension'.[170] The formulation of unity in diversity evolved by Indian nationalism really does not make serious attempts to deal with cultural difference. Therefore we need to ask questions such as which kinds of cultural differences does it actually recognize and to what extent? It seems the only kind of difference in the Indian nationalism had been linguistic difference.

The Indian social landscape as we have seen in the foregoing pages was chiefly marked by two elements called diversity and hierarchy. The pattern definition for both the *varna* and *jati* had also been repeatedly revised. There was no term in any Indian language in the ancient and medieval periods that could convey the meaning of categories such as nation, nationality and nationalism. Thus there was no nationale or conscious nationality in pre-colonial India. There appeared only two streams of national consciousness–pan-Indian (All India tradition and history) and regional (based on regional distinctive homogenities). The question arose as to what new challenges the social thinkers of India could encounter to analyze the emerging new forces of historical change with the spirit of Indian National Movement. The noticeable innovation that can be seen in this respect is the creation and rise in the feeling of nationalism, the emergence of a nationalist ideology with both communal and secular directions which had accompanied India's passage of the later period.

When the British established their dominance in India through the English East India Company they initially adopted a policy of patronizing Hindus. But after the First War of Independence in 1857 in which Hindus and Muslims fought shoulder to shoulder, the British adopted a policy of 'Divide and Rule' which resulted in fostering communal clashes deliberately for keeping intact their hegemony. The British at this time took full advantage of the inherent division of the Hindu society and contempt towards Muslims to divide the society. Bipin Chandra mentions that the Indian National Congress from its very inception adopted a policy "unity from the top" in which the effort was to win over the middle class and upper class. Those Muslims who were accepted as leaders of the Muslim community were left with the task of drawing the Muslim masses into the movement instead of making a different appeal to the anti-imperialist sentiments of both the Hindus and the Muslim masses. This "unity from the top" approach could not promote Hindu-Muslim cooperation in fighting imperialism.[171] There was an implicit acceptance within the early nationalist leadership that Hindus, Muslims and Sikhs were distinct communities which shared only the political and the economic concerns but not the religious, social and cultural practices. Thus the seeds of communalism were sown in the first and second quarters of the Twentieth century. However, the Muslim League and the Hindu *Maha Sabha* remained fairly weak organizationally till 1936. It was only after 1942, the Muslim League emerged as a strong political party. M.A. Jinnah described the Indian National Congress as 'Hindu' organization, a claim that the British supported. The slogan of Pakistan was first articulated in 1940 by the Muslim League in Lahore. Later the partition of India took place in 1947 and about two lakhs of people were estimated to have been killed in the riots and about six million Muslims and four and a half million Hindus and Sikhs also became refugees.

Communalism was one of the major social problems of Modern India. Various communal riots, communal bitterness and communal rivalry occurred mainly under the British Rule while Hindus and Muslims in India had lived in peace and amity is untenable and it is also uncorroborated by history. The study of T.K.Oommen has mentioned six dimensions of communalism and they are assimilationist, welfarist, retrealist, retaliatory, separatist, and secessionist. Of these six, the last three create problems engendering agitations, communal riots, terrorism and insurgency.[172] Further, it may be mentioned that different scholars have approached communal violence with different perspectives such as the Marxist, the political scientists, the religious experts and the sociologists.[173]

Rabindranth Tagore, Mohandas Karamchand Gandhi and Jawaharlal Nehru

Rabindranath Tagore (1861-1941) viewed the people of India not in terms of class struggle but of class harmony. He found that the account of the life and activities of the people of India had been concealed, and that unimportant and unnecessarily frightful legends and the arbitrary actions of the foreign rulers had been presented as the social history of India. He expressed his disappointment at this very sharply and exposed the real face of traditional Indian history. For Tagore, the gulf between the communities was largely due to the cultural forces. He said that the British colonialism had fractured the possibility of every sensitive exposed Indian and it had set up the west a crucial sector within the Indian nation itself.[174] As India's social system got disturbed, life departed argued Tagore, from her social system and in its place she is worshipping, with all the ceremony the magnificent cage of countless compartments that she has manufactured.[175] Tagore was alarmed by the drive to gloss over India's diversity for the sake of creating a nation-state as in Europe since it would strike at the very foundation of civilizational society that flourished in India over the centuries.[176]

Mahatma Gandhi (1869-1948) was against child marriage and *purdah* practice. He emphasised on the Hindu-Muslim unity and on the equality of man and woman. His ideal society was "*Ram-Rajya*". Gandhi directed a powerful spotlight on the injustices that ran through the Indian society such as the practice of untouchability, the pernicious caste system and the exploitation of low caste and tribal groups by high castes. He fought against these abuses with great energy. He was also disgusted by Christian missionaries who railed against Hindu superstition and idolatory.

Gandhi laid stress on decentralization and *swarajya* (self rule). Some scholars believe that Gandhian principles had brought about a more equitable society with less dependence on foreign countries, less pollution and also society built on our own past tradition and experience.

Jawaharlal Nehru had been impressed by the western democratic cultures as well as socialistic pattern of society by freely taking the large scale manufacture in public sector enterprises and simultaneously allowing private sector but with rigid controlling of licences, permits and price control. Nehru's effort had combined the science and technology with the concept of planned development with a view to achieving socialist pattern of society in India.[177] It was his unique contribution. Nehru rejected the suggestion of Gandhi on village industries and old tradition. Nehru was sensitive to protecting and preserving traditions and inadaptively integrating them in our institutions and values as we proceed towards cultural and social modernization. Gandhi and Nehru, the two chief architects of modern Indian society represented two different ideologies of modernization. They both felt the need for India to develop and balance between materialism and humanism. They also recognized how one sided development will merely contribute to brutalization of society.

Dimensions of Development in Contemporary Society in Independent India

The planning commission was set up in 1950 for India's development and the first five year plan (1951-1956) was mainly designed in a way to rectify the imbalances created by the Second World War and the partition of India in 1947 and the maladies continued in the economy as a legacy of the British rule. Agriculture and irrigation sector had been given priority by investing 44.6 per cent of the total plan budget. The second five year plan (1956-1961) aimed at rapid industrialization of the economy. It was also designed to bring about greater equality of income and wealth for the establishment of a socialist pattern of society in India. It stressed that the benefits of development should accrue more to the relatively under-privileged section of the society.

The third five year plan (1961-1966) once again emphasized on agriculture as the priority sector and about thirty-five per cent of the outlay was allocated. During this plan period some important happenings such as The Indo-Pakistan war, The Sino-Indian conflict and the successive failures of the monsoon had affected India very much and so the fourth five year plan to be launched in March 1966 was abandoned. The three year period (1966-69) was devoted to rectifying the problems and it aimed to complete the unfinished tasks of the third five year plan too.

The fourth five year plan (1969-1974) aimed at reducing inequality in income distribution and achieving social justice with equality. The fifth five year plan (1974-1979) aimed at the removal of poverty and attainment of self-reliance. Its main aim was to bring the larger sections of the poor masses above the poverty line by assessing a minimum income of Rs. 40 per individual per month calculated at the priced prevailed during the year1972-73. The sixth five year plan (1980-85) had the sole objective of removal of poverty and raising the life styles of the weaker sections of the society, by improving the public distribution system and control of the increasing population. The seventh five year plan (1985-90) aimed at a significant reduction in the incidence of poverty and an improvement in the quality of life. The eighth five year plan to be started in 1990 had actually been enforced from April 1992 and ended in 1997 and it chiefly aimed towards employment generation and large investment was made in small industries. The ninth five year plan (1997-2002) made its emphasis in certain areas which included agriculture, employment, poverty and infrastructure. This plan is therefore described as "delivery oriented'. Thus in India five decades of planning had been completed yet poverty and unemployment had always continued to increase. We do not know whether it has actually improved the quality of the life of the poor. So long as the implementation of the plans had remained in the hands of the political leaders who are prone to vested interests and to populism it is not certain to find whether actual progress has been made or not besides how and why? According to statistics now, India's thirty-six per cent people live below poverty line.[178]

After the independence of India various legislations were introduced to improve the condition of the people in the society. The Industrial Disputes Act of 1947, The Factories Act of 1948, The Employees State Insurance Act, The Maternity Benefits Act of 1961, The Payment of Bonus Act of 1965, The Employees Provident Fund Act of 1972, The Contract Labour (regulation and abolition) Act of 1970 and The Child Labour (protection and regulation) Act of 1986. These laws are meant to protect the labour but there are many loopholes. The public distribution system (of subsidies and food grains up to fifty-nine other essential commodities) is broad based, broadly distributive and very hard to fine tune. Tax evasion and communal violence the obstacles to development had already been questioned in their studies of India's industry by scholars like Milton Singer and Morris D. Morris. While Singer's ethnography showed Hindus beings used as a force for change, Gunnar Myrdal showed it 'inhibitions and obstacles' forces of inertia and irrationality all needing reform.[179]

II

Chapter Descriptions

The collection of articles in this book is not simply a string of haphazardly linked vignettes. The sequence of the chapters is held together by a line of argument which moves forwards in a very cautious and subdued manner. Thus the book is organized to deal with the manner in which society as a system of thought has altered with the changing tempo and character of Indian history. Chapters are arranged conforming to a chronological and sequential framework but sharing their affinities by linguistic region moving from South to North. Each chapter is a substantive and important contribution illustrating India's social and cultural landscape. There are five sections excluding the introduction which is the opening survey on Indian society.

Literature and Society

In medieval India, prior to the coming of the Muslim rulers Sanskrit was recognised as the language of high culture and so a number of kings and scholars wrote in it. Rajasekhar, the greatest Sanskrit poet lived at the court of Mahipala composed *Karpuramanjari*, *Bala Ramayana* and *Kavya Mimamsa* during the rule of Pratiharas. Vajra Datta, the Buddhist poet, author of *Lokesvara Sataka* lived in the court of Devapala, the Pala ruler. Bhoja wrote *Samaranganasutradhara* (art and architecture) under the Paramaras rule. Vgraharaja composed *Karikalinataka* in the period of Chahamanas. Lakshmidhara wrote *Kritya Kalpatrau* (on law and Procedure) during Govindachandra's regin under the Gahadvalas. Later many works in Jaina literature appeared such as Akalanka's *Ashtasati*, Vidynanda's *Astasahasri*, Manikyanandin's *Pakikshamukhasashta*, and Jinasena's *Parsvabhudhaya*. The Chalukyas of Kalyani had patronized Sanskrit and we find classics such as Bilhana's *Vikramacharita*, Vignanesvar's *Mitaksara*, Somesvara II's *Manasollasa*. Further, in Sanskrit we also find Trivikrama's *Nalachampu* and Halayudha's *Kavirahsya*. Tamil literature developed well during the medieval period and it was marked by the greatness of Tamil classics which include Kamban's *Ramayana*, Jayangondars' *Kalingattuparanai,* Pugalendi's *Nalavenba* and Sekkilar's *Periyapuranam* in the age of the Cholas. Similarly under the Rashtrakuta rulers, Kannada literature developed and we find Amoghavarsha composed *Kavirajamarga* (poetics). Pampa the greatest Kannada poet wrote *Adipurana* and *Vikramarjunavijaya*. Panna had also composed *Santipurana*. The first group of essays provides a close look at the society of India and the literature in various languages such as Telugu, Hindi, Bengali and Tamil.

Chinna Rao traces how Telugu literature reflected the experiences of the society in Andhra and explains the thoughts and emotions generated by the great poet Vemana, a social revolutionary of the medieval period characterized by *satakas* of didactic value. The untouchables as reflected in Vemana's writings are described where the poet scoffs at the Vedas, *Puranas* and *Dharama Sastras* which taught discrimination in the then existed society. According to him, Vemana opposed untouchability but wanted social equality and justice to be established in Andhra. However, the Brahmins had very consciously ignored his thought provoking ideas so that they continue to survive and dominate the other Hindus in society.

R.C Sharma uses Hindi literature as a source of information for the study of the social life in North India during the medieval period. He enumerates thirty-six social groups in the urban society which was composed of numerous castes and sub-castes. We find many subdivisions among the Brahmins. The hereditary occupation and endogamy of the occupational castes are broadly classified by him as the business groups, the occupational castes, tribal castes, untouchables, miscellaneous and those groups who did not fall within the purview of the urban society. According to him castes were found very common among the Muslims in North India during the medieval period.

Chhanda Chatterjee in her paper uses many famous Bengali novels which include *Bishabriksha* and *Krishnakanter* by Bankim Chandra Chattopadhyay (1838-1894), three other novels called *Shrikanta, Devdas* and *Charuraheen* besides another novel namely *Chokher Bali* by Rabindranath Tagore to paint the picture and condition of widows and fallen women in Bengal during the Nineteenth century. The ban of 1829 introduced by the British had forced *sati* out of existence in Bengal. She mentions that Ram Mohun Roy and Vidyasagar delved into the Hindu religious texts in order to authenticate norms which had arisen out of the needs of the times.

Ajit Neogy points out that Pondicherry became a distribution centre of seditious literature in the beginning of the Twentieth century. Printed pamphlets from London, Paris and New York came to this French colony where the anti-British groups passed them on to the various Indian political parties that functioned in the British Indian territories in order to inspire the people and revolt against the British rule. The role of M.M. Srinivasa Aiyengar, the journal editor of the "*India*" published from Pondicherry since 10 October 1908 is highlighted. There were also five other journals such as the *"Vijaya"*, the *"Bala Bharathi"*, the *"Karma Yogi"*, the *"Suryodhayam"* and the *"Dharmam"* published at that time which played a key role in the Tamil society. Some books written by Har Dayal and Savarkar were made available to the public for circulation in Pondicherry. Until then the Indian literature broadly classified broadly into two categories such as sacred and secular suddenly came to be known as seditious. It may be pointed out that what was seditious before the eyes of the Europeans was not so in the opinion of the Indians. This is completely a new development in the field of literature with the establishment of the British rule in India

Language and Society

The spread of European civilization and culture in India was accelerated by the twin wheels of trade and commerce between 1500 and 1800. In the wake of commerce came numerous trading settlements and the settlers brought with them their modes, manners and ways of European life. The Iberian civilization had encompassed three continents by the end of the Sixteenth Century through the efforts of the Portuguese and the Spaniards. In India, the two maritime regions in the Eastern coast namely the Coromandel and Bengal were close to each other culturally and linguistically even within administrative units where the Danish, Dutch, English and the French penetrated in the Seventeenth century. Cultural anthropologists like Nirmal Kumar Bose pointed out these culture zones of Tamil, Telugu, Oriya and Bengali also as products of history but these are sadly neglected by scholars. The language and culture in India with the arrival of the Portuguese, Danes,. Dutch, English and the French has undergone sea-change and the European presence and influence has brought also radical changes. It is, therefore, time for the historians who could give voice to the silence of the archives to examine the nature and development of Indian languages and the contributions made by the Europeans.

Language was a barrier for the Europeans to understand the Indians better. The European missionaries therefore recognized the significance of learning of language as an integral part of their work especially in the field of intercultural exchange. They felt that language was not independent of society since it reflected the social reality. The literary languages of India once a preserve of the Brahmins, *pundits* and court poets emerged in the course of these European contacts as modern languages and new forms such as novel, drama, satire and criticism were introduced and above all became the language of the common people. In these Indian languages Europeans have also faithfully mirrored every stage of social progress. The quality of literature and language also considerably changed. Talking with the Europeans generally being intermixed, Indian languages with words derived from European languages attained a new character. Thus native languages of India became an index of society and social change when compared to the previous centuries.

To facilitate popularization and promotion of Christianity the European missionaries in India studied regional languages with great interest. Their impact on the vernaculars of India was remarkable. Missionaries reformed the spoken Tamil to written Tamil since prose had been not considered significant at that time. Prose literature in Tamil did not develop independently and there had been various forms/types of Tamil prose existed prior to the advent of the Europeans. According to scholars there was commentator's prose style for ancient literature and grammar. Next we have the *manipravala* style of Sanskrit and Tamil mixed, written and spoken Tamil prose style found in the inscriptions.[180] Abbe Dubois, the missionary mentions that there was not a single old book in prose or in spoken language used by the ordinary people. *Tambiran Vanakkam* (1557) *Kristiyanni Vanakkam* (1579) *Flos Sanctorum* (1586) were prose works in Tamil translated from Portuguese. Roberto Nobili (1577-1656) wrote a high style Tamil for learned and spoken Tamil for the ordinary people. Constantius Beschi (1680-1747) wrote in prose without mixing foreign words and he was the pioneer of this pure Tamil prose style.

New Tamil prose writers rose among the Hindus such as Ananda Ranga Pillai, Rangappa Thiruvengadam Pillai and Muthu Vijaya Thiruvengadam Pillai who wrote their private diaries in Tamil. Some Tamil converts like Mariadass Pillai undertook the translation of *Bhagavada Purana* into French. Printing Tamil texts in Pondicherry appeared in 1840. Thus we find that two types of prose in Tamil such as liturgical prose with Jesuit experiments and public prose as found in the diary of Ranga Pillai and his family members.[181] A third type of literary prose in Tamil fiction writing also developed and Mayuram Vedanagayam Pillai is attributed for the development of it. He has outlined the features of this typical prose in the preface of his novel *"Pratapa Mudaliar Charitram"*.[182] However, critics point out that novel is essentially of the next representing a very difficult tradition from that of the Indian art of story telling, even going so far as to argue that the Indian concepts of life and literature are incompatible with the novel form. K.S. Ramamurthi does acknowledge that "the novel is an essentially alien form and form itself is related to three western concept of society and the place of the individual in that society".[183] T.W. Clark traces the new roots of Indian prose writing to the early decades of the Nineteenth century and related the first experiments in the genre directly to the British colonial presence.[184] R.S. Singh categorically states that the novel is in the modern sense came to be written in India only as a consequence of the British contact.[185] Literature in this period is seen as a social-functional and not an aesthetic object. Literary history is also noticed as a history of individual departures and initiatives, leading to change. Continuity is observed as 'no-progress'.

The period from 1550 to 1800 witnessed many perceptible changes in the languages of India. Therefore it is a distinctive period in the history of linguistics. This is also less explored by scholars when compared to the succeeding period in spite of a variety of numerous sources existing in the form of European accounts and records. Palm leaf and birch bark were replaced by paper as writing materials. Urdu became the language of North India and Portuguese had been the language of coastal India like Arabic was before. As language being a social fact it represented social identity and cultural value. In multicultural disposition nation at that time was not only comfortable with the existence of many languages but also served two purposes by maintaining group identity and articulation of the national identity. The central elements of Indian culture are language and religion throughout history. The distinction of languages in India has reflected the distribution of power in the subcontinent. In social psychology distinctiveness theory holds that people defined themselves by what made them different from others in particular context. People also defined their identity in India by what they are not.

Language stimulated the growth of regional literatures by setting up printing press, cutting types for various Indian scripts, printing books and founding journals, writing dictionaries, translating classics in the regional tongues. Devotional literature which was popular in medieval India began to decline. In the British enterprise of acquiring a mastery and command over Indian languages for the purpose of facilitating the governance of India, the intimate connections between knowledge and power underlined by Foucault are obvious. Bernard Cohan argues that the concept of India was a conquest of knowledge. From 1800, under the Governor-General of India of Lord Wellesly, the learning of Indian languages became an important part of training of new recruits to the English East India

Company's service. Cohan makes the point that "language as command was not only a domestic or personal matter, but matter of state".

Tani Tamizh Iyakkam (separate Tamil movement) started with Tamil quest for identity and self expression vis-a-vis the English colonial masters as well as the shastric. The Hindu domination that was implicit in the Congress ideology was met not by the Theosophical movement but by the *Tani Tamizh Iyakkam*. On 14 November 1938 women raised slogans down with English, Down with Hindi, interspaced with "*Tamizh Vazhga*" (May Tamil Flourish) in Madras and many were arrested in 1939. They condemned also all evidences of westernization whether in speech or culture.[186]

In North India, the Sufis practised the motto "*Sulk-i-Kul*" (peace with all). They had intense selfless devotion to God, with their rejection of the world and love for humanity. This made them universally attractive figures with their preaching and we find the rich and the poor, Muslims and the non-Muslims flocked to them. In this period we find the development of Sufi literature. Later we find also Urdu prose developed by Abd-ul Vali Uzlat (1692-1775) through his work *Divan* (1758-1759) *Karba Katha* (tale of Karbala) a religious narrative by Fazli composed in 1732.

Missionaries like D. Carey of the Serampore Mission with the help of the natives produced translation of the Bible in Bengali. These European missionaries compiled dictionaries and composed grammars in various Indian languages, prepared text books for the Europeans to learn. Their skill enabled them to translate some works and we find the Ramayana of Valmiki into English, although these translations were not devoid of their inherent defects. Prose literature developed in Indian languages and the Europeans immensely helped in building up the provincial literatures. In due course of time Indian languages had developed with enriched forms coining new words, ideas and expressions.

Portuguese introduced printing press in India and the Danish missionaries followed the same foot steps and both of them contributed much in the field of publication. Besides books, vernacular periodicals emerged. The Serampore mission was the first agency to print and issue periodicals and newspapers such as *Dig Darsan,* a monthly periodical and *Samachar Darpan*, a weekly newspaper in Bengali in 1818. Language communication and knowledge spread between Europe and India. Some Europeans became interested in Indian culture as evident from the foundation of the Asiatic Society of Bengal in 1784 by Sir William Jones.

We find the translation of works from Sanskrit into English and works like the *Bhagavad Gita* and *Abhinana Shakuntalam* in addition to Persian works like the *Ain-i-Akbari* at this time. Halhed wrote Bengali grammar in English and it was published in Hooghly in 1778. He was well known for his proficiency in colloquial Bengalee.[187] Alexander Dow wrote three volumes of the "History of Hindoustan" (1770-1772) and dedicated it to the King with the following words: "The success of Your Majesty's arms has laid open the East to the researches of the curious". The arrival of print and the emergence of new literary practices had brought print-culture or print-revolution in India. Natives began to entertain new ideas about language use whether translation or prose or dictionaries since it looked different from the speech and poetry. Texts and forms of information spread more quickly and widely. Scholars like Stuart Balckburn argue that print did not stimulate new ideas about language and literature.[188]

There were Indians who rejected all things western. There were those who were clients named employees of the British without any intention of giving up their traditional culture. There were also those who remained good Hindus/Muslims began to study western ways and thought. The English language became popular and it opened paths to employment and influence replacing Portuguese which was *lingua franca* for three centuries in India. Orthodox Hindus patronized the English schools and promoted the Hindu College (now Presidency College) in Calcutta (1816) became a centre of western influence and saw the rise of the Young Bengal Movement.

Language became the marker of cultural identity in India. Culture entered into the process of social change in many forms and at various levels. It defined the quality of social change as its indicator. In each main stream of culture one may find existence of sub-cultures and counter-cultures in India. Cultural studies of modern period begin with the debate how the Indian tradition in its essential form could be made to adapt with western culture without a loss of its core values or cultural identity. A sharp distinction was drawn between westernization and modernization, locating this process in the cultural-historical individuality of each society in India based on language, religion and region. Indian languages came to be broadly classified into five language families namely Indo-European, (Assamese, Bengali, Gujarati, Hindi, Kashmiri, Konkani, Marathi, Nepali, Oriya, Punjabi, Sanskrit, Sindhi and Urdu) the Dravidian, (Tamil, Telugu, Malayalam and Kannada) Austro-Asiatic, Tibeto-Burmese (Manipuri) and Semito-Hamstic. Most of the first two families trace their origin to Sanskrit.

The 1821 census reported about 237 languages (188 languages and 49 dialects). This figure has been reduced to 114 languages in 1991 census with 18 scheduled languages and 96 non-scheduled languages.

New historicism has brought the two disciplines of literature and history close to each other. New historicism is interested in the parallel reading of literary and non-literary texts, usually of the same historical period. Textuality of history and the historicity of texts are combined. New historicism situates a work of art in its historical context and also breaks down the boundaries between aesthetic production and other social kinds of social production, (i.e. between art and other historical traces). The old approach was interested in making use of historical data (poems). New historicism accepts Jacques Derrida's opinion that there is nothing outside the text and everything about the past is available to us only in the form of texts.

It may be said that Post-modernism seeks to explore culture by breaking the idea of system inside-out and by the process of deconstruction of culture's linguistic spoken or written text. The post-modernist response to the study of culture rests in its method. Language is a cultural phenomena and so we find now the study of language in relation to society (socio-linguistics) and the study of language in relation to culture (ethno-linguistics). Nations and states are indissoluably tied together. Contemporary writings on the nation-state have stressed how the two teams have become uncoupled to a larger extent both from below by the migration of people which diversifies the nation in counter point to the elite dominated state, and from above by the flow of culture and finance in the global market. There is problematic hypen in the nation-state. There exists a symbiotic relationship between language and nation. The nationalist school emphasizes one language one nation. Selection of a language as language of the nation is an arbitrary crafting of the notion of dominant language. In the framework of nation building the performance approach should be of integration through assimilation. The second set contains articles that deal with the spread of knowledge by Europeans in Indian languages, literature and linguistics with the advent of the missionaries in Coromandel and Bengal.

Sovon Sanyal highlights the interaction that took place in the field of linguistics and literature between the two cultures of Portugal and Bengal. The role of the Portuguese missionaries such as Francisco Fernando, Domingo de Souza, Manuel de Ascençã and Dom Antonio is dealt in detail. According to him these missionaries composed prayer books, booklets on Christian doctrine and catechism in Bengali in order to continue their dialogue with the native converts. Some works such as *Brahmo Roman Kayatholic Smabad* and *Crepar Xaxtrer Orth Bhed* were mere translations from Portuguese and these were (not original works) written in Roman script (but not in Bengali script). The Portuguese-Bengali-Hindusthani Vocabulary is the most famous work and we find enrichment of the Bengali vocabulary with Portuguese words here. Language being the most powerful instrument for creation and modification of the society, the socio-linguistic role of the Portuguese in Bengal had been discussed by him.

L. Ramamoorthy analyses the contribution of the Europeans to Tamil during the Eighteenth and Nineteenth centuries and tries to explain the shift in paradigm of Tamil development due to western impact. The use of Tamil language is determined by the demands made by the society on language and the development of Tamil is shaped by the social forces and social philosophy. Implementation of European ideology in Tamil society resulted in the social process called modernization and changes that took place in the society had reflected on Tamil language. Further, the language being a social and cultural institution, it flourished as an instrument of modernization. Paradigm shift in the society was chiefly caused by the social forces whereas in language development the shift was caused by its use. When we compare the use of Tamil in the present context with earlier use we certainly notice a paradigm shift. The author traces the influence of the then prevailing Sanskrit paradigm on Tamil language in the Sixteenth and Seventeenth centuries and mentions three elements that had constituted for the shifts in the developmental paradigm of Tamil such as the form, (which includes phonology, scripts, grammar and arrangement of words), the content of Tamil and the attitude of the people.

B. Ravi Kumar examines the private diaries, novels, short stories and new-verses in Tamil literature and argues that the advent of the Europeans had directly influenced the Tamils towards the development of such new literary genres. The natives contributed their might for the growth of Tamil prose which already existed in some kind of form. He opines that European literature had great impact on the Tamil writers and it paved way for new criticism, Marxism, modernism, post-modernism, and decentralization theory to be introduced in Tamil literature.

The Military, the Civil and the Tribal Society in India

India was internally fragmented by caste and sub-caste. It is difficult to mention that the caste system in which period was very rigid or not so.

Social divisions other than caste exist in India–those of linguistic, regional and religious origin. Theoretically speaking the followers of Islam and Christianity constitute a community held together in close bonds of allegiance to the doctrine set out in the Holy Quran and by the Holy See. In some recent writings, it has been argued that the Hindus and Muslims had no concept of a territorial state and they believed in a universal state.[189] These writings attempt to show that when co-relations at the world level change, western ideas about the orient, oriental society also change, as if the orient was always a subset of the west.[190] This view needs revision because the medieval Christian state belief was different. We find the Papal Bull dividing the world between Spain and Portugal. Further, the medieval states in India, (the Cholas and Vijayanagar in South India besides the Sultanates and the Mughals) were remarkably successful in centralizing many levers of power in their hands, without abolishing the para-local political entities. Moving to Mughal India we find Turkish speaking military elite governed a fragmented Indian society but was dependent on that society for military resources in ways that led to low levels of separation between the society and the Mughal military. Role of the military (both offensive and defensive had certainly contributed much to the medieval Indian society and history. The offensive military is the surplus of military power beyond what is needed to maintain the domestic order by the ruler which is projected also beyond the burdens of the state/kingdom. Defensive military power is actually the ability to resist foreign military invasion. Was there usable military power available to the Indian rulers in medieval India? is raised in this connection. It cannot be answered owing the paucity of information and studies dealing with social and military history of medieval Indian kingdoms and states. The study of society from the civil and the military view points shows the structural and functional analysis of the society.

Individuals are the primary units of civil society. Political theorists have traditionally assumed that civil societies are forged and shaped through (a) social and political transactions between the inhabitants of the sphere (b) the relationship between the inhabitants and the state. There are theorists and political leaders who work from the assumption that civil society is defined by its historical sociology. They identify the bases of western civil society in specific features of European history (articulated by liberals during the transformation of Eighteenth century Europe and the rise of solidarity movement in Poland). Suggesting that histories differing elsewhere make the development of civil society unlikely or impossible, this assumption has fed both western based predictions of a 'clash of civilizations' between western civil status and Islamic cultures and Asian elites' rejection of liberal civil society as culturally alien.[191] It is worth mentioning here the context of Adam Smith's work which was that of the transition from mercantile to commercial society or manufacturing capitalism. By the time he essayed his analysis of modern society, production has moved out of the household and out of the spatially delineated areas into increasingly expanding sphere which was marked by an intricate highly specialized and interdependent division of labour.[192] Georg Wilhelm Fredrik Hegel, (1770-1831) the German Idealist Philosopher is the first theorist who systematically distinguished the state from civil society. Hegel was socially influenced by the state. Writing a few decades after Hegel published his 'Philosophy of Right' (in 1821) Karl Marx (1818-1883) the greatest socialist thinker brought out the working classes on to the stage of history (22 years later) and 46 years after he published his work '*Das Capital*'.

Civil society is considered as a panacca to many ills of the country. Civil society covers all forms of voluntary associations and social interaction not constructed by the state. The existence of civil society in India remains a continuing question. It has been argued by Kaviraj that civil society in the sense of opposition to the state is developed while civil society in the sense of associated groups is not.[193] Further, Partha Chatterjee opines that civil society was the most important site of transformation in the colonial period while political society is the corresponding site in the post-colonial period.[194] The concept of civil society has captured the attention of a wide global community, its proponents find in the idea benefits such as empowering citizens for problem solving, counter-balancing the state, preserving individual privacy and deepening people's participation in government to increase effectiveness and improve governance.

Some scholars used the concept of oriental despotism to characterize the pre-British Indian states with the idea that in the societies all power and all property vested with the ruler. They felt that there was no civil society and believed that it was a stationery one. British administrative historians paid no attention studying the development of institutions such as the state and the civil society in India and it is well known through the writings that appeared in the last quarter of the Nineteenth century. Elliot described that there was nothing like the government institutions in India.[195] The shape of history writing in India has undergone a sea change. No one will today accept that the Indian society had remained largely static after the break down of the primitive communism, till the coming of the British.

Humans experienced changes and continuities in society. As social animals, humans have always pursued a range of collective strategies to endure their survival and well being. The cultural unification of India was an Aryan achievement but the administrative unification of India was a Turkish achievement and both were driven to it by circumstances rather than by conscious planning.[196] Humans have migrated, conquered, traded and technologically innovated. As societies grew larger and more inter connected, the range of strategies adopted tended to broaden. Conquest remained the dominant strategy. Conquering societies always ran out of lust to plunder or societies worth subjugating. Trading societies desired to monopolize trade and satisfy the lust for instant fortune frequently destroyed the potential for future market growth. Pluralism has been the core of Indian cultural life. Over the centuries, language, society and culture in India has been evolving its own progress and development. Undoubtedly she has been combating several challenges in tradition versus modernity.

Change faced new challenges in the form of adoption. Sociologists and anthropologists make distinctions between society and culture. Taylor, the Nineteenth century anthropologist had described culture as a "complex whole which included knowledge, belief, art, morals, law, custom and any other capabilities and habits acquired by man as a mention of society". So when defining culture it is always the society which gains predominance over the institutional or the group. Culture serves as an overall integrative function in the society. Culture has its own effect on society. Every culture had been characterized by a single central concern, a dominant tendency around which its efforts are built. Gurudev Rabindranath Tagore in his essay on Eastern and Western Civilization had cited Guizort in describing modern Europe culture as unique in one respect. The poet accepted entirely this ascription of uniqueness but his world-view was for more universalistic. Tagore also said, "The dominant objectives of any civilization was determined by history, but when pursuit of that goal destroyed some higher purpose the destruction of civilization itself could not be far off." The poet identified another basic difference between the Indian and European culture, and in developing his argument revealed his culture determined preferences. Indian civilization with society as its central focus was, in his opinion, concentrated more with the general well being of all concerned than with the pursuit of self interest-the quest for wealth, status, power through ruthless competition. The social boundaries of Indian culture by locality and region has been recognized in the study of caste, family and rural communities, the three basic institutions of India. Indian culture is characterized by enormous diversity. In the third group we find studies that dwell upon the construction, dimension and manifestation of the military society under the Cholas, civil society of the Sultanate and Mughal period, the social world of the weavers and artisans in Andhra and the tribal society of the Santals in Bengal.

Shouvik Mukhopadhyay in his paper records that the imperial expeditions of the Chola kings in the eleventh century had brought enormous wealth into the Tamil Country. The decline of *nadu* assemblies and the subsequent rise of *periyanadu* assemblies during the Thirteenth and Fourteenth centuries had not simply resulted in a shift in the political geography but led to major socio-political changes. According to him the waning of the Brahmin-*Vellalar* alliance and the rise of the martial communities like the *Maravars* and *Kallars* created a niche for their mechanism like *padaikaval* (protection fees) and donation to the temples. It is also said that re-emergence of the Murugan cult is noticed in Tamil country at that time.

Syed Ejaz Hussain mentions that during the rule of Qutbuddin Aibak, Iltutmish and Akbar the great, India forged a realm of harmony between the two principal socio-economic groups, namely the traders and the Muslims on the one hand and the ruled on the other hand. He argues that this harmony had largely qualified for a civil society in India and the social force of Sufism had played an important role for the creation of civil society. Using Abul Fazal's *Ain-i-Akbari*, and Ziauddin Barani's *Tarikh-i-Firuz Shahi* he mentions that Sufism eschewed violence and replaced pluralism in society. He adds that Sufism also pronounced civil rights by its role as mediator between the ruler and the ruled. He analyses the relationship of civil society to pluralism and liberalism and he traces the reality between the civil society and the Sultanate-Mughal states.

M. Krishna Kumari opines that the changing occupations of the people in Andhra in medieval times made the *Sudras* to become rulers of the land and it led the Brahmins to take the profession of arms. She has documented the various sub-castes within each caste as found in the inscriptions and literature besides explaining the dynamics of society in Andhra. According to her, harmony and coordination among the sub-castes in *Sudra* community prevailed in Andhra and the society was free from caste conflicts unlike the neighbouring Tamil and Kannada regions where the people of the same caste continued to strive for obtaining certain privileges and rights.

P. Swarnalatha describes the role of the weavers and their various castes such as the *Padma Sales*, *Pattu Sales*, *Devangars*, *Togatas*, *Jandra* weavers, *Paraiah* weavers and the *Malas* in the Northern Coromandel society. She examines how the intervention of the new political power, i.e., the British had transformed the weaving society and its character especially through their trade policies. According to her the ideology of the caste system manifested in the left hand and right hand caste divisions helped in a large measure to maintain order in the society which was frequently riven by caste conflicts that arose due to social customs and owing to religious practices because some castes followed *Saivism* while others *Vaishnavism*. These caste conflicts had seriously affected the economic life in Andhra. The weavers protested against the measures of control exercised by the British in this period over the production process of the weaver's economy.

Suchibrata Sen in his paper deals with *Santals*, the most important tribal community of Eastern India says that they regarded themselves as a superior race, although *Santals* are placed by others in the subaltern group. He analyzes in detail the background factors, various forces and the multiple facets of the *Santal* Rebellion of 1855. According to him these *Santals* called themselves *Har Hopan* (true sons of mankind) and this is due to the occupation of the land since nature has reserved it for them. They never settled down in the uncultivated areas in the region and when they found a suitable place for settling they went there in a body under the leadership of *Mondal* or *Majhi*. The clearer of the jungle in the *Santal* community became the owner of the land in the region.

Indian Society and the European Encounter

A fourth area that forms is the scholarship on the Portuguese, French and the British encounter and social interactions in India. S. Jeyaseela Stephen examines the various important crimes committed by the Portuguese in Coromandel with special reference to slavery, adultery, murder, dowry and marriage. He throws flood of light on the Indo-Portuguese mixed culture outlining the distinct characteristics. A life of licentiousness amidst luxury and plenty had been followed by the Portuguese in Coromandel during the Sixteenth Century. They were extravagant and vain-glorious rather than following high spirituality in their daily life as the medieval Christianity and the *padroado* missionaries expected. Portuguese settlers had fallen prey to many evil practices and the reason is the absence of a strong leadership in their social organization of the enclaves in Coromandel which led them to behave as they liked.

This Indo-Portuguese community was not a homogenous social group and it was considerably stratified in terms of race and status. The *castizos* or the Portuguese of purer blood living at that time in the Coromandel Coast were less and the descendants of mixed parentage or the *mestiços* were more. The wayward life style and lawlessness found common at that time created unusual social pressures. According to the author the crimes committed by the Portuguese and the Indo-Portuguese could be classified generally into three groups on the basis of their motives, i.e., economic, sexual and miscellaneous. These crimes could also be further sub-classified into four types based on the various purposes and nature such as (a) against women (assault and murder) (b) against property (theft and robbery) (c) against public decency or morality (disorderly conduct) and (d) against public justice (embezzlement and breach of trust). The above said crimes committed by men and women were very destructive to the smooth functioning of the society then.

K.S. Mathew highlights the role of the French Capuchins, the French Jesuits and the members of the Foreign Missionaries Society of Paris who played a key role in bringing about social changes in Pondicherry. He says that various indigenous customs of the native converts to Christianity were allowed to be practiced in respect of festivals, marriage ceremonies, funerals and other rituals. These converts tried to follow the customs of the upper castes irrespective of their previous affiliation to *varna* or *jati*. Several Hindu practices were retained by the converts under the specific instructions given by the Jesuits. The egalitarian message of Christianity was the logical anti-thesis of the inequality that prevailed in the Hindu world. The French missionaries tried several methods to win over the Christian converts of Pondicherry for an egalitarian behaviour but they failed. It is said that the Eighteenth century Pondicherry society was an extremely conservative one.

J.B.P. More traces the expansion of Christianity in Pondicherry and the problems met by the missionaries in converting Hindus to Christianity. He identifies the principal factors that impeded or retarded the progress of Christianity, besides the methods adopted by the missionaries and the administrators to attract the Hindus to Christianity. He explains why some Hindus converted at certain times and why some others resisted conversions. He opines that the high caste conversions to Christianity in Pondicherry during the early eighteenth century were numerous and the reason was trade which had been dominated by these castes members. Famines and epidemics were the major causes of conversions in the later period and many Hindus especially *paraiahs* embraced Christianity. The conversions diminished considerably after the famines and epidemics were over. He says that frontiers between the caste and religion were strictly maintained. The conventions governing sexual relationships were particularly severe and lapses were hardly tolerated. The conduct of the French administrators made the conversions extremely difficult given the conservative nature of the Tamil society. He questions the claims of Susan Bayly who asserts that Christianity spread because of its identification with Hinduism especially low Hinduism. Further the author questions the views of Louis Dumont that Muslims and other non-Hindus who functioned within the Hindu system had basic psychological dispositions. JBP More cites examples from Pondicherry and says that it is totally wrong and irrational to assume that the psychological disposition of Hindus all over the Indian subcontinent were homogenous. The principle of human hierarchy and inequality besides the notions of purity and impurity among the Hindus was always known and it was not the invention of Dumont though they were central to Dumont's thought.

Pratyusa Kumar Mandal records the agrarian and ritual bases of social stratification and change in Orissa under the colonial (1803-1865) and post-colonial period (1865-1947). He particularly deals with the horizontal division of society into groups/categories in Orissa before the famine of 1866 and the post-famine period. Ninety-nine castes were identified in the Balasore region according to the first census report of 1872. He says that the caste distinctions came up owing to the fundamental economic changes introduced by the British. Caste continued to exert considerable influence on the prospect of upward mobility. People began to make every possible effort to maintain hierarchical status quo in Orissa at that time.

Society, Nation-State and Culture

Growth of society and the evolution of state in India is important. Conflict with settled agricultural communities forced the tribals to develop their own state forms, generally after they had reached a certain stage of pastoral nomardism.[197] Building a larger and stronger units than the loosely knit systems of the state in India are found and the Vedic and socio-cultural state, Rashtra as state, republican states in the Buddhist era and empire state may be cited as some examples. Burton Stein brought out the shift of *nadu* (locality or region) in the governance of polity under the Cholas in South India.[198] David Ludden also affirms the role of local communities and their autonomy in the operation of the agrarian economy.[199] This marks an integrated convergence of different paradigms of analysis of social reality. Under the Vijayanagara empire, the Kannda, Telugu and Tamil speaking regions were brought together. With the establishment of the Delhi Sultanate, a strong centralized Islamic state gradually developed in North India. It played a larger role in agricultural expansion and improvement in other sectors. Muhammad Tughlaq's policy of the state giving loans (*taqavi*) for resuming agricultural production interrupted by natural calamities and human agencies, introducing superior crops such as sugarcane, cotton and indigo in the place of inferior crops besides improving irrigation is significant. Introducing a new *rehat* carried out by the Surs and the Mughals is noteworthy. The integration of North India under the Surs, followed by the Mughal integration under Akbar, showed that the era of small states was over. This also proves that the concept of a regional balance of power was unworkable. The Lodhis defeated the Sharqis and unified the Ganga valley. The groundwork of integration was laid out at that time. Without closing the space for other social groups and elements the Mughal integration also reaffirmed and re-established the power of hierarchical elites.

There has been a lot of discussion in recent years about the nature of state in medieval India. Was it feudal, patrimonial, bureaucratic, segmented, or basically mercantilistic. State in medieval India largely depended on the rural surplus extracted by the class of zamindars from the cultivators. Nurul Hasan designated the medieval state in India as feudal. The major controversies (with reference to the Seventeenth and Eighteenth centuries) are (a) the nature of Mughal state and whether it was an aid to or inhibiting factor in economic growth, (b) the distribution of power in medieval India and whether it permitted the establishment of a truly centralized state, (c) whether the establishment of British rule was essentially a foreign extrusion or a logical outcome of developments to which banking cum monied Indian sections contributed. British historians of the Nineteenth century have depicted the nature of states and state system after the decline of the Mughal empire as paragons of cruelty, oppression and licentiousness which is incorrect. India was moving towards a system of balance of power. The Marathas bid for supremacy in 1740 but failed by 1761. The British supremacy was not at all established till the beginning of the Nineteenth century. Burton Stein calls this state formation as patrimonial regimes which had access to core authoritative roles and offices depended upon personal relations to the rulers. Some scholars have also opined the state formation of this eighteenth century to military fiscalism.

Robert Clive founded a territorial state of a new type in India under the British by defeating the Nawab of Bengal. It was only with the start of the trading state that native societies became centered on the British state since these societies were not uniform or unitary but had diverse pluralities. Bonds of nationality and language strengthened by national boundaries grouped the fragments into more permanent contributions and the nation-state came up. The nation-state started speaking in the name of the entire society. We find the society is plural, whereas the nation-state is uniform and unitary.

A common language and contiguous common territory are the two essential elements absolutely necessary in the formation of a nation. Further we should remember that modern nation and nation-state are categories pertaining to the era of capitalism. The Marxists were greatly influenced by Stalin's formulations.[200] The imperialists argued that India can be a nation-state like the west European nations and all the more it had a conglomeration of disparate people. There was a plea for an aggressive and militaristic nation-state in India during the Nineteenth century which would wipe away the share of centre of subjugation of the Hindus by outsiders.[201] The Dravidian nationalists of Tamil Nadu depicted the Aryan invaders as the oppressors of the indigenous Dravidians replacing an egalitarian social system with a rigid and oppressive caste hierarchy.[202] These various nationalisms have all been rooted in a model of reasoning which treats history as a narrative of uni-linear progress towards an ideal.

One cannot understand the relationship between culture and nation-building only by analyzing the impact of logic, science and reason which are the three principles since they interact. These are the ones which depend upon the structure and function of entities that contribute the nation and central to the concept of modernization reflected in the nation building process. In addition as historians we confront challenges which are related to problem of polities. The strength of history as a discipline lies in its ability to unravel the mysteries of the surface social phenomena. It may be easy to define a nation and there is always a danger of reification. Nation is a process we call this process-nation building, to conclude nation building is essentially a structural-cultural process.[203] There existed, however the idea of a larger country in the minds of people in India living prior to the Nineteenth century. It formed the basis of a broader self-identity but came to be narrowed down in later period with language in a region. In this final section, role of state, society and culture is addressed and the image and perception of nation-state and nation building is dwelt.

G. Subbiah examines the inner dynamism of a nation-state and the applicability of the concept of nation-state to India. What makes unique in the case of India when compared to western countries/European nation-states is discussed at length. He argues that to think of the existence of the Indian nation in the pre-modern period is not an anachronism. In this context, he examines the (features) mechanism of integration, the process of expansion of the state and society in Indian History that involved the horizontal spread of monarchical polity. This has been replaced by the democratic polity or the horizontal spread of participation and cites the example of the Dravidian movement, a socio-political movement in South India.

Bipasha Raha traces the social and national consciousness dimensions of Poet Rabindranth Tagore. She mentions that Tagore openly expressed his patriotism in 1877. She says that Tagore was sad to note the arrangement of the Delhi durbar to celebrate Queen Victoria's accession as empress when a severc famine prevailed in India. In 1897 he condemned the Sedition Act and also the arrest of Bala Gangadhar Tilak. Further, he protested the partition of Bengal in 1905. He withdrew from active politics in 1907 and got himself involved in education, rural reconstruction and encouraged people to undertake the work in rural health, sanitation, agriculture, cottage industries, and water supply. He started a welfare society at Patisar. He also introduced the cooperative movement in rural Bengal. He won the Noble Prize for literature in 1913. He also condemned the Jallian Wala Bagh tradegy which took place on 13 April 1919 and surrendered his 'Sir' title. Tagore disagreed with Mahatma Gandhi on the issue of *charkha* and *khadi* and also he did not participate in the Civil Disobedience Movement in 1930.

Amiya Ghosh traces the emergence of the nation-making process through socio-cultural reforms introduced by *Prabartak Samgha* in Bengal. He mentions that Motilal Roy a revolutionary founded this *samgha* in 1905 at Chandernagore. A Bengali fortnightly "*Prabartak*" was first published from September 1915 to preach the message of creative nationalism and it emphasized also on nation-making. The *Samgha* started its first school in 1921 and later established several schools at various places. Numerous socio-economic programmes were launched by the *Samgha* in Bengal. The French Government in January 1925 suspended the publication of the fortnightly by an ordinance for three months as a measure to stop the voice of nation-making activities.

III

Society in Contemporary India

"As long as the society seeks knowledge of the past the historian must accept his responsibility to society without violating his responsibility to the varieties of history".[204]

—Fritz Stern

Today Indian society is no longer presented as a traditional society rather it is now viewed as a modern society. But changes have been brought about by various phases. The first volume of subaltern studies which appeared in 1982 heralded a new school of history focussing on the non-elite colonial subjects. Borrowing the term "subaltern" from Antonio Gramsci, these historians have explicated the interplay of coercion and context during the rule of the British in India. In their attempt to explain hegemonic processes subaltern historians have uncovered and articulated the studies of suppressed people. Antonio Gramsci has made the useful analytical distinction between civil and political society in which the former is made up of voluntary (or at least rational or non-coercive) affiliations like schools, families and unions, the latter of state institutions, the army, the police, the central bureaucracy whose role in the polity is direct domination. Marc Bloch said in his "Historian's Craft" that "a society that could be completely moulded by its immediately preceding period would have to have a structure so malleable as to be virtually invertebrate. It would also have to have a society in which connection between two generations was conducted so to speak children having contact with their ancestors only through the medium of their parents". Caste mobility is seen through first Sanskritisation, then Westernization and now through Politicisation. The Post-modern society is now concerned with critical awareness and about the damaging effect of applied science on nature, environment and humanity. Therefore the main question now is where has India reached after contact with the west? Has India progressed? Has it contributed to the welfare of the people? Is it possible to answer the questions objectively? Can subjectivism and philosophical partiality be avoided in such analysis? These are yet to be answered by scholars.

Some believe that India should not lose its strong in-built value system in the society for a western paradigm. In the name of modernising they are destroying Indian society. Caste remains a distributive feature of Indian society. The present day Indian society is a cross-breed between the western and Indian culture. There is only one society and it is made up of both women and men. In contemporary India, caste and class are inseparable aspects of India's social formation. However the dynamics of the nexus havc varied from region to region. Caste is also appropriated by a select group of people to their own economic and political advantage. Societies and social systems cannot be understood simply as collectivities of people. They have to be examined in terms of relationships, boundaries and missions. The analysis of social systems is important to understand how a society is ordered and how it changes.

Clearly caste was an important institution but the basis of caste as a social phenomenon will not be sufficient since it also has an economic basis. Occupation had largely determined the caste of an individual and it was always a constant factor. A society may be called in many ways such as, traditional, modern, post-modern, rural and urban. In the Twenty-first century, India is gearing up modernization. The progress is impressive in industrial and agricultural sector but socially we have not been able to keep up with the pace. What do we find in this society of ours today? Utter misery, wars and conflicts. The energy that should go to build up better order of society is spent on competition and destruction.

In India forty types of embezzlement and corrupt practices were adopted by the government servants out of the state revenue in the ancient period.[205] During the British rule bribes were accepted not only by the Indian officers but also by the highly-placed British officials. The fact that Robert Clive and Warren Hastings were found corrupt to an extent that they were tried by a parliamentary committee after returning to England may cited as examples. Corruption continues in India and it is one of the main social problems in the contemporary society. We have innumerable number of examples such as The Bofors payoff scandal of 1986, The cement scandal of 1982 and the involvement of the chief minister of Maharashtra, The securities scandal in Maharashtra, The treasury fraud scandal of Assam in 1995, The payoff scandal of 1993 involving the prime minister of India, The hawla scandal of 1991, The animal husbandry scam involving the chief minister of Bihar between 1990-1995 may be cited. India is viewed as the seventh most corrupt country in the world according to a non-government German organization called 'Trasperancy Interior'.[206] There is obviously something radically wrong in politics and governance. In building a better society we have to consider a method for changing the existing order.

Today communalism is a social reality which is generated and reflected in a distorted way. The nine-judge bench constituted had dwelt upon the term 'secularism'. It mentioned that, though the term was embedded in the constitution it was wisely left undefined because it was not capable of any precise definition.[207] Ethnic and communal violence continues in India. Communal riots are more politically motivated than fuelled by religion. The total number of communal riots in India which took place between 1954-55 and 1988-89 had been listed in a study.[208] After the demolition of the disputed structure of Babri Masjid on 6 December 1992 at Ayodhya, plenty of communal riots had flared up. Inter-religious and inter-caste conflicts in our society have grown. The religion has been politicized, the politicians had been regionalized. The unity in diversity of the society is threatened.

After fifty-seven years of independence, we cannot expect Indian society to remain static and completely traditional. The word '*kal*' in Hindi for yesterday and tomorrow–shows no sense of passage of time in India.[209] We have not succeeded in building a welfare state in India may be its foundation laid out and left. Many books have been published on Indian society. Most of them resemble in some way yet differ in many ways. Instead of state existing for the people, it was the people who are seemingly permitted to exist for the convenience of the state. Today our mother tongues are considered inferior to import the knowledge. We require Schumachar to understand small industry and appreciate technology and Fukuoka to understand sustainable agriculture. The Green Revolution gave spurt to changes in the contemporary stock of villages which till then was largely a presence of the residents in cities and metropolises. The White Revolution brought the largest gross producers of milk in the world. The per capita consumption of milk however, remains still inadequate.

Whatever its origin, the Brahminical system of caste based on birth had torn the Indian society into shreds and revealed it incapable of ever becoming a united community, much as a homogenous people or nation. Social problems of medieval and modern India are repeated and continued in contemporary society. In September 1987, Roop Kamar a twenty-one year girl at Deorala in Sikar district in Rajasthan state had committed *sati* on the funeral pyre of her husband and so the Government of Rajasthan passed an act in February 1988 prohibiting the practice of *sati*. Further, we find that the *Harijans* were prevented from entering the Nathdwara temple in Rajasthan in September 1988 and this provoked the then President of India, Shri. R. Venkataraman to declare that he was willing to lead a procession of the *Harijans* to enter the temple. In sum, the contemporary society should take lessons from the past.

In the capitalistic system it is the individual who gets priority over society. We have known that socialism and communism had failed in Europe and also in Asia. Today capitalism alone has become the only system throughout the world. In most of the literature on India, class, gender, religion and caste are typically understood not as social structures of accumulation, (SSA, especially labour, capital, the state, gender, religious plurality, caste) but as components of civil society. Caste ideology affects society. Schedule castes and tribal people are constitutionally entitled to positive discrimination (reveals) in the public sector to redress their social and economic backwardness and deprivation. Research had helped to enrich the importance of caste as a social institution for access to higher education and to jobs in the administration and public sectors enterprise. Social movements and the political mobilisation of untouchables in India in recent years have gained momentum in their search for respect and social status. They tend to the state for protection of their rights and for preferential access to public employment and education.[210]

Indian society has always been complex, and recent changes have made this truth more evident. Individuals and small groups have become more aware, well organized, skilled and assertive. This has undermined the old hierarchical, substantially self regulating character of the Indian society. The tendency has led people of India to shift their preoccupations with great fluidity. Changes in the caste system at first largely resulted from the reason of its material base (i.e. the old hierarchical *jajmani* system in which people tended mainly to perform tasks traditionally associated with their caste group (caste has increasingly come to denote difference more than hierarchy). Secondly impact on social attitudes from gradual political awakening among all the sections of society that democratic politics inspired. Thirdly rise of an increasingly vibrant civil society (a domain between the state and family) associations emerged. Individuals have a multiplicity of identities (social and political) religious, regional and linguistic in India.[211]

Globalisation gives a new dimension to the debate on modernisation in contemporary societies. The attention of the analysts is engaged in the debates of globalization relating to its economic, technological, communicational, cultural or socio-political implications for the developing societies. To what extent globalisation signifies features which conform with 'post-modernity' remains to be established. Globalisation offers a menace towards the native culture. Both caste and tribe have local existence in the sense that they are settled in the territorial boundary of a village.

The constitution that free India chose to adopt as a secular democratic nation reflects this in a large measure, the cultural policy of the state has and always been oriented towards preserving the best part of the Indian culture through institutional support. Vast changes cannot be brought about by the sudden passing of a few laws. A clash of interest seems inevitable. The past holds us together so why should the present or the future divide us in spirit. Political changes produce certain changes but essential changes are in the spirit and outlook of a nation.

Notes and References

1. As the process of human dynamism started in the West, each philosopher made his/her insights into the nature and functioning of society. Auguste Comte, the Father of Sociology stimulated academic activities in this discipline. Darwin's significant contribution on the theory of evolution in the middle of the Nineteenth century had brought an intellectual revolution in the world. His work *"On the Origin of Species"* marked a highly systematic organization of field data for deriving fundamental results regarding the evolution of man. This theory provided considerable influence on the philosophers of the succeeding period. In due course of time we find many sociological theories such as (1) functional theory of Auguste Comte, Herbert Spencer (1820-1903) and Emile Durkheim (1858-1917) (2) conflict theory of Karl Marx (1818-1883) and Max Weber (1864-1920) (3) exchange theory (utilitarianism) of Sir James Frazer (1854-1941) and Marx's theory of exchange and conflict (4) Interactionist theory of William James (1842-1910) (5) Structural theory of Karl Marx, Herbert Spencer and Emile Durkhiem. Thus new theories explained diverse phenomena through which mankind has surrendered to its present form.
2. M.N Srinivas, *Caste in Modern India and Other Essays*, London, 1962; See also, *Social Change in Modern India*, Berkeley, 1968; See, (ed.,) *India's Villages*, Bombay, 1960; See also Louis Dumont, *Homo Hierarchius : The Caste System and its Implications*, Chicago, 1970.
3. D.D. Kosambi, *Introduction to the Study of Indian History*, Bombay, 1956. See also his *Myth and Reality in Indian History*, Bombay, 1959. See also, S.C. Sarkar, *Some Aspects of Early Social History of India*, Calcutta,1948.

4. J.W. Mcrindle, *Ancient India: As Described in Classical Literature,* Westminster, 1901. pp. 47-53. Romila Thapar, *Mauryas Revisited*, Delhi, 1987.
5. Kautilya, *Arthasastra*, (ed.,) Sama Sastry, Benares, 1967.
6. G. Bulher, (trs.,) *Sacred Laws of the Aryans*, Delhi, 1984, Part B, Vasistha Dharama Sastra, Chapter XVII & XVIII; See also Bauddhayana Dharama Sasatra Prasna I, Adhyaya 9, Khardika 17.
7. Suvira Jaiswal, "Studies in Early Indian Social History: Trends and Possibilities", *The Indian Historical Review*, Vol. VI, Nos.1-2, pp. 1-63.
8. A.L. Basham, *The Wonder that was India*, New York, 1959, p. 148.
9. Cyndia Talbot, *Pre-colonial India in Practice: Society, Religion and Identity in Modern Andhra*, New Delhi, 2001, p. 52.
10. R.S. Sharma, *Material Culture and Social Formation in Ancient India*, Delhi, 1983, p. 146.
11. Romila Thapar, *Ancient Indian Social History-Some Interpretations*, Hyderabad, 1984, pp. 122-151.
12. A.L Basham, *The Wonder ... op. cit.*, p. 89.
13. M. Krishna Kumari, *The Rule of the Chalukaya Cholas in Andradesa*, Delhi, 1985. p. 206 & 246.
14. Y. Subbarayalu, *Studies in Cola History*, Chennai, 2001, pp 89-90. See also his article 'The Cola State', *Studies in History*, Vol. IV, No.2, 1982, pp. 265-306.
15. Burton Stein, *Peasant State and Society in Medieval South India*, Delhi, 1980, pp. 24, 55 and 173-215. See also, M. Arokia Swami, "Social Developments under the Imperial Cholas", *Transactions of the Archaeological Society of South India*, 1956-57, pp. 1-7.
16. Y. Subbarayalu, *Studies in ...op. cit.*, p. 85.
17. Y. Subbarayalu, "Social Change and the Valangai Idangai Divisions", in *Studies in Cola History, op. cit.*, pp. 23-24.
18. *South Indian Inscriptions*, (hereafter *SII*), Vol. XXIII, 381& 383.
19. Y. Subbarayalu, *Studies in ..op. cit.*, p. 30, see note.30.
20. *Annual Report on Epigraphy*, (hereafter *ARE*) 163 of 1938-39.

21. B.S.L, Hanumantha Rao, *Religion in Andhra*, Guntur, 1973, p. 314.
22. K.A. Nilakanta Sastri, *Development of Religion in South India*, Madras,1962, p. 64.
23. *Telangana Inscriptions*, 2 Vols, Hyderabad, 1935. Vol. I, pp 83-84. See also, *A Corpus Inscriptions in the Telugu Districts*, (hereafter ITD, Vol. III, pp. 16-17.
24. See, M. Krishna Kumari, *"Caste and Dynamics of Society in Andhra, 1600-1750"* in this book.
25. Noboru Karashima, *South Indian History and Society: Studies from Inscriptions, AD 850-1800*, Delhi,1984, pp. 40-55. N. Karshima, *History and Society in South India, from the Cholas to Vijayanagar*, OUP, Delhi, 2002.
26. K.V. Ramesh, and S.P Tewari, (eds.,) *Indian History and Epigraphy* (Dr. S. Gai Felicitation Volume) Delhi, 1990, pp. 87-91.
27. Noboru Karashima, "The Untouchables in Tamil Inscriptions and Other Historical Sources in Tamil Nadu", in Hiroyuki Kotani, *Caste System: Untouchability and the Depressed*, Delhi, 1999.
28. R.N. Nandi, *Social Roots of Religion in Ancient India*, Delhi, 1986.
29. Burton Stein, *Peasant State and Society...op. cit.*, p. 24 & 55.
30. Noboru Karashima, *Towards A New Formation, South Indian Society Under Vijayanagar*, Delhi, 1992; S. Jeyaseela Stephen, *The Coromandel Coast and its Hinterland : Economy, Society and Political System, 1500-1600,* Manohar, Delhi, 1997.
31. Ibn Battuta, *Rehla, The Travels of Ibn Battuta,* Delhi, 1980, p. 182. See also, Ibn Battuta, (trs.,) by B. Fuller, London, 1809, pp. 9-10; See also, K.S Mathew, *Society in Medieval Malabar : A Study Based on Vadakair Pattukal, Kottayam*, 1979. On social evils see, See, Pelaseart, *Jahangir's India* (trs.,) Qasimjan Sheik, Delhi, 1972, p. 78; Foster, *Early Travels in India*, London, 1921, p. 119.
32. Al-Biruni, *Alberuni's India*, Lahore, Government of West Pakistan,1962, pp. 132-140; Akbar Ahmed, *Discovering Islam: Making Sense of Muslim History and Society,* London, 1999, pp. 9-10; E.C. Sachan, (ed.,) *Alberuni's India*, Delhi, 1983, Indian edition, p. 100. The original title of the book is *Tahqiq ma al Hind* (Interpretation of India).
33. See, *Abul Fazal Allami*, Calcutta, 1786, Vol. III, pp. 82-84.

34. See, Jalaluddin Dawwani, *Akhlaq-i-Jalaini*, Nawal Kishore Press, Lucknow, n.d, pp. 259-60.
35. Valentine Ball, (ed.,) *Travels in India*, 2 Vols, London, 1889, p. 182.
36. W.H.Moreland, *The Agrarian System of Moslem India*, Cambridge, 1929.
37. K. Srivatsva, *The Position of Hindus under the Delhi Sultanates,1206-1526*, New Delhi, 1980; M.I. Khan, "The Attitude of the Delhi Sultanates towards Non-Muslims: Some Observations", *Islamic Culture*, 69, 1995, pp. 41-56. Savitri Chandra, *Social Life and Concepts in Medieval India, Bhakti Poetry*, Delhi, 1983, pp. 86-100; Irfan Habib, "Technological Changes and Society: Thirteenth and Fourteenth Centuries", Presidential Address, Section II, *Proceedings of the Indian History Congress*, 1969.
38. Satish Chandra, "Commercial Activities of the Mughal Emperors during the 17th Century", *Bengal Past and Present*, Vol. LXXXVII, July–December 1959, pp. 92-97; See also, "Some Aspects of the Growth of Money Economy in India during the 17th Century", *Indian Economic and Social History Review*, (henceforth *IESHR*) Vol. III, No.4, 1966, pp. 321-331; Satish Chandra, *Medieval India: Society, the Jagirdari Crisis and the Village Society,* Delhi, 1982.
39. Sanjay Subrahamanyam & C.A Bayly, "Portfolio Capitalism and Political Economy of Early Modern India" *IESHR*, Vol. XXV, No.4, 1988, pp. 401-24.
40. Stephen Dale, *Indian Merchants and Eurasian Trade, 1600-1750*, Delhi, 1994, p. 134.
41. J.N. Sarkar, *Alikam-i-Alamgiri*, Calcutta, 1932, p. 34.
42. Beveridge (trs.,) *Akbar Nama*, 1920, Vol. III, p. 1153.
43. Bernier, *Travels in India*, Delhi, 1983, p. 259.
44. Eugenia Vanina, *Ideas and Society in India, (from the 16th to 18th Centuries)* Delhi, 1996, p. 171.
45. E.J. Eric Habsbawm, *On History*, Abacus, 1999, p. 13.
46. Feminist historians have pointed out the invisibility of women in history. We find the entire focus was laid on the high caste Hindu women in the Altekarian model. Others focussed on *devadasis* and devoted some space to women. Thus we find misconception, perception and distortion in the existing knowledge of women. Description and analysis is given due place in history. The status of a daughter, a wife or a mother is

important and it is difficult to de-link one category in the family. Chakaravarty and Roy regard women as silent voices of history. See, Supriya Altekar, "Theory and Practice of Women's Movement in India", *Economic and Political Weekly* (henceforth *EPW*, 29 April 1995, p. 2; See also Uma Chakravarti, "Beyond the Atlekarian Paradigm: Towards a New Understanding of Gender Relations in Early Indian History", *Social Scientist*, Vol. 16, No.8, 1988, pp. 51-52. Kumkum Sangavi and Sudesh Vaid (eds.,) *Recasting Women: Essays in Colonial History*; Delhi, 1992; Aloka Parasher, "Women in Nationalist Historiography: The Case of Altekar" in Leela Kasthuri & Veena Mazumdar (eds.,) *Women and Indian Nationalism*, Delhi, 1989. See also, A.S. Altekar, *The Post-Utopian of Women in Hindu Civilization*, Delhi, 1962; Rekha Misra, *Women in Mughal India, 1526-1748*, Delhi, 1967; Saroj Gulati, *Women and Society in Northern India in 11th and 12th Centuries*, Delhi, 1985; Kamala Gupta, *Social Status of Women in North India, 1206-1705*, New Delhi, 1987; Mushid Ghulam, *Reluctant Debutante: Responses of Bengali Women to Modernization, 1849-1905*, Rajshahi, 1983; Borthwick, *The Changing Role of Women in Bengal, 1849-1905*, Princeton, 1984; Usha Chakarborty, *Condition of Bengali Women Around the Second Half of the 19th century*, Calcutta, 1963; Tanika Sarkar, *The Image of Women in 19th century Bengali literature: Some Poems, Plays, Novels and Short Stories*, Delhi, see chapter 8, pp 250-267.

47. A Padma, *The Socio-Cultural World of Women in Medieval Andhra, 11th-13th Centuries*, Delhi, 2001.
48. Manu, *op. cit.,* Vol. II, p. 33.
49. Manu, *op. cit.,* Vol. III, p. 9.
50. A. Macdonell, *A History of Sanskrit Literature*, London, 1900, p. 163. The text runs *"Sakhah Jayakirpan Hi Duhita, Jyotehirya Putrah Parame Vyavnin"*.
51. Max Muller, *The Sacred Books of the East*, 1879, Vol. II, Pt. I, Chapter XVIII, p. 269.
52. Manusamhita refers to remarriage but there is no proof for remarriage of the widows. See, Max Muller, *op. cit.,* Vol. XXV, 1886, p. 339.
53. H. Kotani, *op. cit.,* pp. 79-80.
54. Leslie C. Ort, Donors, *Devotees and Daughters of God: Temple Women in Medieval Tamil Country,* New York, 2000; See also,

K Sadasivam, The *Devadasi System in Medieval Tamilnadu*, Trivandrum, 1993.

55. Abdul Razzaq, in Elliot, *op. cit.,* Vol. IV, p. 111f.
56. *Manuschartira*, 6: pp. 73-75.
57. Robert Sewell, *A Forgotten Empire*, London, 1900, p. 234.
58. Rekha Misra, *Women in Mughal India*, Delhi, 1967.
59. J. Talboys Wheeler, *India Under the Muslim Rule*, Delhi, 1975, pt. I, p. 65.
60. Bloch, *Ain-i-Akbari, op. cit.,* IInd edition, 1927, p. 322.
61. Bloch, *Ibid.,* pp. 323.
62. Sachau, *Alberuni's India*, Vol. II, (reprint), Delhi, 1964, pp. 155-156.
63. Archibald, Bernier, *Travels in the Moghul Empire*, Westminster, MDCCXCI, pp. 309-310 & 314.
64. K.M. Asraf, *Life and Condition of the People of Hindustan, 1200-1350*, Delhi, 1970, p. 136n.
65. Ball, (trs.,) Tavernier, *Travels in India*, London, 1898, p. 437; See also Calcutta edition, 1905, Chapter XI, pp. 408-09, & 411.
66. Davies, (trs.,) *Travels of John Albert Mandleslo*, London, 1669, p. 58.
67. Surendranath Sen, *Travels of Thevenot and Careri*, New Delhi, 1949, p. 323.
68. Nicolao Manucci, *Storia do Mogor*, London, 1907, Vol. I, pp. 54-59.
69. Abul Fazal, *Ain-i-Akabari* (trs.,) Bloch, *A Statistical Survey of Bengal*, 2nd edition, Calcutta, 1927, p. 287.
70. Al Badaoni, *Muntakhabhu-i-Tawarikh,* (trs.,) by Sir W.H. Lowes, Asiatic Society of Bengal, 2nd edition, Calcutta,1924, Vol. II, pp 315-349.
71. *Alberuni's India, op. cit.,* Vol. II, p. 155.
72. Surendranath Sen, *Travels of Thevenot and Careri, op. cit.,* Chapter I, pp. 256-257, fn 35-37. See also, *Travels of Delle Valle in India*, London, MDCCCCII, p. 83.
73. Al Badoni, *op. cit.,* p. 311.
74. Niccolao Manucci, *op. cit.,* Pt. II, p. 186.
75. Al Badoni, *op. cit.,* pp. 311-312.
76. Nicolao Manucci, *op. cit.,* Vol. II, p. 9.
77. Biswanath Joardar, *Prostitution in Historical and Modern Perspective*, Inter-India Publishers, New Delhi, 1984, p. 49.

78. *Ain-i-Akbari, op. cit.,* Vol. I, p. 327.
79. Duarte Barbosa, *A Description of the Coast of East Africa and Malabar in the Beginning of the Sixteenth Century*, London, 1866, p. 121.
80. Durate Barbosa, *op. cit.,* p. 129.
81. *Ibid.,* p. 136.
82. *Ibid.,* pp. 135 & 137.
83. *Ibid.,* p. 133.
84. *Ibid.,* pp. 103-106.
85. *Ibid.,* p. 216.
86. See, Nicholas Dirks, "The Invention of Caste", *Social Analysis*, Vol. 25.1, 1989, pp. 42-52. See also his another article, The Conversion of Caste, *The Globalization of Christianity*, (ed.,) Peter Van der Meer, New York, 1995, pp. 115-137.
87. Robert L. Hardgrave Jr., *The Dravidian Movement*, Bombay, 1965; Rajini Kothari (ed.,) *Caste in Indian Politics*, New Delhi, 1970; M.N. Srinivas, "Varna and Caste" in M.N.Srinivas (ed.,) *Caste in Modern India and Other Essays,* Bombay, 1962.
88. Niels Brimnes, *Constructing the Colonial Encounter: Right and Left Hand Caste in Early Colonial India*, London, 1999.
89. E.R. Leach, (ed.,) *Aspects of Caste in South India, Ceylon and Northwest Pakistan,* Cambridge, 1960.
90. H. Dodwell & K. Rangachari, *The Private Diary of Ananda Ranga Pillai*, 12 Vols, Delhi, reprint, 1985, vol. XII, p. xxiii.
91. British Library, London, Oriental and India Office Collection (henceforth *OIOC*), *Mss. Eur; Mackenzie collection*, Misc. Vol.131 fls.1-26. OIOC P/253/34; *Madras Military and Political Proceedings* (henceforth *MMP*) 28 Oct 1794 fls.4310-4346 quoted from OIOC P/253/34; MMP 20 Oct 1794 fls. 4329.
92. A.K. Priolkar, *The Goa Inquisition*, New Delhi, Voice of India, 1991, p. 97.
93. S. Jeyaseela Stephen, "Societal Changes: Portuguese and the Native Christians in Tamil Country, 1537-1759" in (eds.,) K.S. Mathew, T.R. Desousa, & Pius Malekandathil, *The Portuguese and Socio-Cultural Changes in India, 1500-1800,* Tellicherry, 2001, pp. 479-513.
94. Kenneth Ballhatchet, *Class, Caste and Catholicism in India, 1789-1914*, Richmond, 1998.
95. British Library, London, *Oriental Books and Manuscripts*, Catalogue, No. UR11, 742, *'Jati Tirutalin Payittiyam'* (In

Foolishness of Annulling Caste) and '*Sathi Teratoo*' Tanjore, 1829; See also *Jati-arasan-bhavanai.*

96. Dennis Hudson, *Protestant Writings in India: Tamil Evangelical Christians, 1707-1835*, Richmond, 2000, pp. 148-51.
97. Duncan B. Forrester, *Caste and Christianity,* London, 1980.
98. G.A. Oddie, "Protestant Missions, Caste and Social Change in India, 1850-1914", *IESHR*, Vol. 6(3) 1969.
99. K.N. Pannikar, Presidential Address, Section III, *Proceedings of the Indian History Congress*, 36th Session, Aligarh Muslim University, Aligarh, 1975, p. 7.
100. Andre Gunder Frank, *Re-Orient, Global Economy in the Asian Age*, London, 1999, p. 91.
101. *Ibid.*
102. Andre Gunder Frank, *Re-Orient op. cit.,* p. 175; See also, Anupama Sen, *The State, Industrialization and Class Formations in India : A Neo-Marxist Perspective on Colonialism, Underdevelopment and Development*, London, 1982, pp. 38-39.
103. Anuapama Sen, *op. cit.,* pp. 52-53.
104. H.T Cole Brooke, *Remarks on the Husbandry and Internal Commerce of Bengal*, 1806, p. 174.
105. *Account of the Writings, Religion and Manners of the Hindoos*, 4 Vols, Serampore, 1811.
106. *Account of the Writings, op. cit.*, Vol.2. pp 64-65.
107. James Mill, *History of British India*, 1817, p. 35.
108. K.M. Pannikar, *The Foundations of New India*, London, 1963. p. 67.
109. Ahuja Ram, *Society in India*, Jaipur, 1999.
110. Louis Dumont, *Homo-Hierarchius*, London, 1972. See also Dumont, *Essays on Individualism: Modern Ideology in Anthropological Perspectives*, Chicago, 1986.
111. S.G Sardesai, "Science Versus Superstition in Indian Philosophy" in *Main Stream*, Vol. XV, No.9, 30 October 1976, p. 21f.
112. *Ibid.*
113. Q. Ahmad, *The Wahabi Movement in India*, Calcutta, 1966, pp 6-9 & 15-16.
114. A.F.Salahuddin Ahmad, *Social Ideas and Social Changes in Bengal, 1818-1835,* Leiden, 1965, pp. 30-32, 125-126; Kenneth W Jones, *Socio-Religious Reform Movements in*

British India, Cambridge, 1989; K.S. Singh, "Colonial Transformation of Tribal Society", *EPW*, Vol. 29, 1978, pp. 1221-1231. M. Carrin Bouez, *La Fleur et l'os Symbolism et Ritualchez les Santal*, Paris, 1986.

115. Andre Beteille, *Caste: Old and New*, 1969, pp. 73-78.
116. M.N. Srinivas, *Religion and Society Among the Coorgs*, London, 1952; See also "A Note on Sanskritization and Westernization", *Far Eastern Quarterly*, 1955, Vol.15 (4) pp. 481-96.
117. Marriott, *Village India*, Chicago, 1955.
118. Yogendra Sharma, *Social Stratification and Change in India*, 1997, p. 7.
119. Amiya Sen, *Social and Religious Reforms: The Hindus of British India*, Delhi, 2003, pp. 188-189.
120. Dharampal, *Indian Science and Technology in the Eighteenth* Century, Delhi, 1989, See also his book on *Civil Disobedience.*
121. Sekhar Badhyopadhyay, "Caste in the Perception of the Raj: A Note on the Evolution of Colonial Sociology in Bengal", *Bengal Past and Present*, 1985, Vol. CIV, Pt. I & II, p. 67-68.
122. See, Niels Brimnes, *Constructing the Colonial Encounter: Right and Left Hand Castes in Early Colonial South India*, London, 1999.
123. D.A. Washbrook, "Land, State and Agrarian Society in Colonial India", *Modern Asian Studies*, Vol.15, No.3, 1981, p. 720.
124. Ronald Inden, *Imagining India*, Delhi, 1990.
125. Nicholas Dirks, *The Hollow Crown,* Delhi, 1987.
126. E.R Irschick, *Dialogue and History: Constructing South India, 1795-1895,* Berkeley, 1994, pp. 93-94.
127. D.A Washbrook *The Emergence of Provincial Politics: The Madras Presidency, 1870-1929*, Cambridge, 1976; See also, *The Congress in Tamil Nadu: Nationalist Politics in South India, 1919-1937*, Cambridge, 1977.
128. Robert Hardgrave, Nadras of Tamil Nadu: *The Political Culture of a Community in Change*; Robin Jaffrey, *The Decline of Nayar Dominance: Society and Politics in Travancore*; Karen Leonard, *Social History of an Indian Caste: The Kayasthas of Hyderabad*; James Manor, *Vokkaligas of Mysore;* Irschick, *Political and Social Conflict of Non-Brahamins in Madras Presidency;* Robert Delige, *The Untouchables of India;* Gail Omvedt, *Dalits and the Democratic Institutions in India.*

129. F.G. Bailey, *Politics and Social Change in Orissa*, Berkeley, 1959; Stephen Alen Barnett, *The Structural Position of South Indian Caste: Kontakkatti Vellalars* (Ph.D. Thesis, Chicago, 1970; Andre Beteille, *Caste, Class and Power*, Berkeley, 1965; Brenda E.F. Beck, Kongus; Janet Bensens on *Jajmani System*, E.A.H. Blunt, *Caste System in North India*; Geofirrey Burhat, *Vellalars of Salem District*, Kathleen E. Gough, *Thanjavur, Village India*: Eric J. Millar, *Caste and Territory in Malabar,* Moffatts, *Untouchable Castes of Chingleput*,1979.
130. Nehru Memorial Museum and Library, New Delhi, *Jawaharlal Nehru Collection*, Excerpts dated 12 December 1928.
131. *Indian Law Reports Madras Series*, reprinted in Vol.31, pp 236ff. Case No. 31 M.236.
132. Eugene Irschick, *Politics and Social Change in South India: The Non-Brahmin Movement and Tamil Separatism, 1916-1929*, Berkeley, 1969.
133. Dagmar Hellman–Rajanayagam, (ed.,) *Is there a Tamil race?* Peter Robb, The Concept of Race in South Asia, New Delhi, 1995, pp. 136-137; See also Robert L. Hardgrave, *The Dravidian Movement*, Bombay, 1955.
134. K.R. Hanumanthan, *Untouchability: A Hindu Society up to 1500 AD With Special Reference to Tamilnadu*, Madurai, 1977.
135. James Massey, *B.R. Ambedkar: A Study in Just Society,* Delhi, 2003.
136. Hirendranath Mukherjee, *Gandhi, Ambedkar & the Interpretation of Untouchability*, New Delhi.1990. Gandhi insisted that the scheduled castes were a part of Hindu society and separating the two would be detrimental to the interest of the nation. See, T.K. OOmen, *State and Society in India : State in Nation–Building*, Sage, New Delhi, 1990. Colonialism separated the Hindus and Muslims by its strategy of divide and rule. The partition (the great divide) of India took place in 1947.
137. Mark Juergensmeyr, *Adi Dharmma Movement*, Berkeley, 1908; Geil Omvedt, *Dalits and the Democratic Institutions in India*, Delhi, 1994; See also, Rober Delige, *The Untouchables of India*, Oxford, 1998. Sail Omvedt, *Dalit Vision*, New Delhi, 1995.
138. C.J Fuller, (ed.,) *Caste Today*, Delhi, 1996.
139. D.A Washbrook, "The Development of Caste Organisations in South India 1800-1915", in C. J Baker and D.A Washbrook,

South India: Past Institutions and Political Changes, 1800-1915, Delhi, 1975.

140. AR Deasi (ed.,) *Peasant Struggles in India*, Delhi, 1979.
141. Lucy Caroll, "Colonial Perceptions of Indian Society and the Emergence of Caste(s) Associations", *Journal of Asian Studies*, Vol. XXXVII, No.2, February 1978, pp. 233-250.
142. Robert R. Hardgrave, *The Nadars of Tamilnadu*, Berkeley, 1969, pp. 65-69.
143. Andre Beteille, *Studies in Agrarian Social Structure*, Delhi, 1974, p. 110.
144. *Census of India, 1901 Report*, p. 138.
145. *Census of India, 1915 Report*, p. 111.
146. *Census of India, 1915 Report*, pp. 112-114) Simon Charsley writes that one commissioner after another struggled to discern some order amongst the differently based groups which might properly be regarded as castes. See, Simon Charsley, "Untouchable: What is in a Name?" *The Journal of the Royal Anthropological Institute*, Vol.2, 1996, p. 3.
147. H.H Risley, *The Tribes and Castes of Bengal*, 4 Vols, Calcutta, 1891-1896, Vol. I, P. vii; See also, L.S.S. O'Malley, *Bengal Bihar and Orissa under British Rule*, London, 1913, W.W Hunter, *Annals of Rural Bengal*, Calcutta; H.H. Risley, *The People of India, London,* 1915.N.B. Halhead, *A Code of Gentoo Laws, or Ordinances of the Pundits from a Persian Translation made from the Original Written in the Shanscrit Language*, 1777, London; J.H. Hutton, *Caste in India: Its Nature, Function and Origins*, Cambridge, 1946; See also, *Bengal, Bihar, Orissa and Sikkim, Census of India*, 5 Vols, Calcutta, 1913. William Ward, *A View of the History, Literature and Mythology of the Hindoos*, 3 Vols. London, 1822.
148. *Census of India, 1901 Report*, p. 538.
149. Sekhar Badhyopadhyay, "Caste in the Perception of the Raj: A Note on the Evolution of Colonial Sociology in Bengal", *Bengal Past and Present*, 1985, Vol. CIV, Pt. I & II, p. 76.
150. Bernard S. Cohan, "The Command of Language and the Language of the Command" in Ranajit Guha (ed.,) *Subaltern Studies*, Vol. IV, New York, 1985, p. 289.
151. Susan Bayly, *Caste, Society and Politics in India from the 18th Century to the Modern Age*, New York, 2001.

152. Edward Said, *Orientalism*, New York, 1978; See also, Niel Brimnes, *Constructing the Colonial Encounter: Right and Left Hand Castes in Early Colonial South India*, London, 1999.
153. Sekhar Bandyopadhyay, *Caste, Politics and the Raj: Bengal, 1872-1937*, Calcutta, 1990, pp. 10-30.
154. C.J Fuller, "Misconceiving the Grain Heap: A Critique of the Concept of Indian Jajmani System" in J. Parry & M. Bloch (ed.,) *Money and the Morality of Exchange*, Cambridge, 1989, pp. 33-63.
155. G.S. Ghurye, *Caste and Race in India*, Bombay, 1976, p. 6.
156. E. Senart, *Caste in India*, London, 1930, p. 42.
157. V.I. Pavlov, *India's Socio-Economic Structure from the 18th to mid 20th Centuries*, Moscow, 1975. p. 14.
158. M.N. Srinivas, *Social Change in Modern India*, Berkeley, 1966, p. 109.
159. Geil Omvedt, "Pseudo-Secularism, I & II" *The Hindu*, 20 January 2003, and 21 January 2003.
160. Hugh Owen, "Negotiating the Lucknow Pact", *Journal of Asian Studies*, Vol. 31, (3) May, 1972, p. 561.
161. *The Report of All Parties Conference*, Allahabad, 1928, p. 62.
162. Jawaharlal Nehru, *Discovery of India*, Calcutta, 1946, Signet press, p. 627.
163. M.S. Gore, *Unity in Diversity: The Indian Experience in Nation Building*, Rawat Jaipur, 2002. p. 70; Questioning utility of the very concept of a nation-state as the socio-political model for our society, See D.L. Sheth, "State, Nation & Ethnicity Experience of Third World Countries", *EPW*, 25 March 1989, Vol. XXIV, No. 12, pp. 619-26.
164. Shaileja Upmanyu, *State in the Political System*, Jaipur, Rawat, 1997.
165. Ravindra Kumar, "India : A Nation State or Civilization State", Occasional Papers No.VIII, Centre for Contemporary Studies, Nehru Memorial Museum and Library, Teenmurti House, New Delhi,1989 in *South Asia New Series*, XXV, No,2, August 2002 pp. 13-32. Francis Fukuyama mentions that people define themselves in terms of ancestry, religion, language, history, values, customs and institutions. They identify with cultural groups, tribes, ethnic groups, religious communities, nation and at the broadest level civilizations. See, "The End of History" *The National Interest*, 16, Summer, 1989, pp. 4-18.

Fukuyama advanced a thesis end of history and he argues that the end point of mankind's ideological evolution and the universalization of western liberal democracy is the final form of human government. He says that with the end of soviet empire, western universalism seemed to triumph and to encompass the whole world. Since history is a process of conflicts, the end of all conflicts in a uniform world would also mean the end of history. Samuel Huntington's book was an answer to Francis Fukuyama's the end of history. Huntington argued against this that new conflicts are arising in terms of his clash of civilizations. According to him there were seven early civilizations such as the west, the Islamic, the Russia, China, Japan, Hindu India and black Africa. He realizes that civilizations cannot be actors on the world stage.

166. The nationalism of the Hindus and Muslims turned into divergent directions clashing with each other and paved way for the partition of India in 1947. See, Anshu Singh, *National Movement and Communal Strife in India from 1937 to 1947*, Delhi, 2004. Se also, Anil Seal, *The Emergence of Indian Nationalism*, Cambridge, 1994; Bipan Chandra. *Rise and Growth of Economic Nationalism*, New Delhi, 1982; A.R. Desai. *Social Background of Indian Nationalism*, Bombay, 4th edition, 1993. Dilip Menon, *Caste, Nationalism and Communism in South India, Malabar, 1900-1948*, Cambridge, 1994; Tanika Sarkar, *Hindu Wife, Hindu Nation : Community, Religion and Cultural Nationalism*, Delhi, 2001.

167. Ernest Gellener, *Nations and Nationalities*, Oxford, 1983, p. 39.

168. Benedict Anderson, *Imagined Communities*, London, 1991, p. 7. A nation is an imagined community. In fact all countries larger than primodial villages of face to face contact are imagined. Benedict Anderson warns that the word imagined seems not to be taken to mean fabricated or false. He argues that a nation is a "cultural artifact" that acquires legitimacy in course of time. Imagining two nations at a time The Bengali, or Tamil nation and India is it possible? Sekhar Bandhyopadyay points out to say that nations are imagined or invented does not mean that they are in some way unreal or artificial. We must note that the concept of state as defined by Hegel for instance requires a sense of agency and scope for dialectical

mediation. Both of these are denied by Hegel to Hindu thought and the social and political reality were inseparable. See, Ronald Inden, *Imaging India*, Bloomington, 2000, p. 20. The Indian Marxists think that the mechanical application of Stalin's definition of nationality prompts them to argue that India is not a nation in view of the absence of a common language. See, Irfan Habib, "Emergence of Nationalities", *Social Scientist*, August, 1975, p. 16. Habib asks and answer the question thus, Is India then a nation? India is not a nation because it meets the requirement of neither a common language nor a common culture. The dictum "one language-one nation" is not a workable proposition in the Indian context. Among the four requirements, three criteria such as territory, economic life and psychological make up manifested in community of culture to define nationality are there in the case of India except the common language.

169. E. Kedourien, (ed.,) *Nationalism in Asia and Africa*, New York, 1970, p. 28.
170. Partha Chatterjee, *Nationalist Thought and Colonial View–A Derivative Discourse*, Zed books, 1986. p. 40.
171. Bipan Chandra, *Communalism in Modern India*, Vikas, New Delhi, 1984.
172. T.K. Oommen, *The Hindustan Times*, Delhi, 8 August 1989.
173. Suranjan Das, *Communal Riots in Bengal, 1905-1947,* Calcutta, 1991.
174. Ashis Nandy, *The Illegitimacy of Nationalism*, New Delhi, 1994, p. 89.
175. Rabindranath Tagore, *Nationalism*, London, 1917, p. 90.
176. Ashis Nandy, *op. cit.*, p. 88.
177. Louis Dumont, *Homo Hierarhicus, The Caste System and its Implications,* Revised Version, Chicago, 1980; See the criticism of Dumont by Ronald Inden, *Imagining India, op. cit.,* pp. 151-154; See also, Nicholas Dirks, *The Hollow Crown: Ethno-History of an Indian Kingdom,* Cambridge, 1987, p. 26, 238 & 404.
178. *The Hindustan Times*, 20 January 1997.
179. G. Myrdal, *Asia Drama: An Inquiry into the Poverty of Nations*, Penguin Books, Clinton. 1968.
180. See, *Nuttrandu Tamil Urainadai*, Manivasagar Pathipagam, Madras, 1987.

181. S. Jeyaseela Stephen, *Rangappa Thiruvengadam Pillai Naatkurippu*, (in Tamil) II Vols, Pondicherry Institute of Linguistics and Culture, Government of Pondicherry, 2000, See also the English translation, *The Diary of Rangappa Thiruvengadam Pillai, 1761-1768, Translated from Original Tamil with Notes*, Institute for Indo-European Studies, Pondicherry 2001. See also, *Muthu Vijaya Thiruvengadam Pillai Naatkurippu, 1794-1796*, Institute for Indo-European Studies, Pondicherry, 1999.
182. Mayilai Seeni Venkatasamy, *Kritavvamum Tamilum*, Kalaga Veliyidu, (reprint) Chennai 1980.
183. Ramamurthi, *The Rise of the Novel in India*, New Delhi, 1987.
184. T.W Clark, *The Novel in India*, London, 1970.
185. R.S. Singh, *Indian Novel in English: A Critical Study*, New Delhi, 1977.
186. C.S Lakshmi, *The Face Below the Mask: Women in Tamil Literature*, Delhi, 1984.
187. W.H.Carey, *The Good Old Days of John Company*, Calcutta, 1882, abridged edition, 1964.
188. Stuart Blackburn, *Print, Folklore and Nationalism in Colonial South India*, New Delhi, 2003, p. 10.
189. See, M.N Pearson, *Merchants and Rulers in Gujarat*, 1976; C.A Bayly, *Society and the Making of the British Empire*, 1987; Edward Said, *Orientalism*, New York, 1978; Burton Stein, *Peasant State and Society in Medieval South India*, Delhi, 1980; Frank Perlin, "State Formation Reconsidered", *Modern Asian Studies*, Vol. XIX, 2, 1985, Andre Wink, *Land and Sovereignty: Agrarian Society and Politics under the Eighteenth Century Maratha Swarajaya*, Cambridge, 1986.
190. Satish Chandra, *Essays on Medieval Indian History*, Delhi, 2003, p. 37; Amiya Sen, *Social Reforms: Some Legislations in Indian States, 1901-1939*, See Appendix B, pp. 219-221.
191. Samuel Huntington, *The Clash of Civilizations and the Remaking of the World Order*, New York, 1996. Robert Hefner shows that Islamic countries founded through trade differed greatly from those founded by conquest, providing a basis for pluralism. See, Robert Hefner, (ed.,) *A Muslim Civil Society*, pp. 285-321.
192. Adam Smith, *An Inquiry into the Nature and Causes of the Wealth of Nations*, Chicago, 1952. See also his another work, *The Theory of Moral Sentiments*, (1759) Oxford, 1976.

193. Kaviraj, *"Civil Society in India?"* A Paper Presented at the Seminar on Civil Society, Public Sphere and Organizational Behaviour : Approaches to the Study of State-Society Relations in the Non-Western World, University of Oslo, April, 1996. Theorists adopted Brahaminic version of caste in India. See, John Hall, "The Nature of Civil Society", *Society*, May-June 1998, pp. 32-41.
194. Partha Chatterjee, "Beyond the Nation State or Within?" *Economic and Political Weekly*, Vol. XXXII, Nos 1-2, January 4-11.
195. Elliot and Dawson, *History of India as Told by its Own Historians*, 8 Vols, London, 1867, see introduction.
196. K.A. Nizami, *Some Aspects of Religion and Politics in Sind during the Thirteenth Century*, Bombay, 1961, see, Mohammed Habib, Introduction, pp xviii-xix.
197. We have examples in the case of Ujjainayas of Bihar and the Dimanas of Assam. See, K.S.Singh, "A Study in State Formation Among the Tribal Communities" in R.S. Sharma and V. Jha (eds.,) *Indian Society: Historical Probings*, Delhi, 1974, pp. 317-36. See also J.B. Bhattacharya, The Economic Content of the Medieval State Formation Process Among the Masses of North East India, *Proceedings of the Indian History Congress*, 1987, pp. 222-23.
198. Burton Stein, *Peasant State and Society in Medieval South India*, Delhi, 1980.
199. David Ludden, *Peasant History in South India*, Princeton, 1985.
200. Joseph Stalin, *Marxism and the National and Colonial Question*, London, 1942, p. 8. Stalin defined a nation as a historically evolved stable community of language, territory, economic life and psychological make up (manifested in community of culture). Don Luigi Sturzo's analysis of the concept shows the nexus of a national community consists of tradition, customs, language, territory, social rights and economic interest. See, Don Luigi Sturzo, *Nationalism and Internationalism*, New York, 1946, pp. 16-17. E.H. Carr's exposition that although the nation is not a definable and clearly recognizable entity it has such national and universal elements as attachments to one's native land and speech and a sense of wider kinship. E.H Carr, *Nationalism and After*, New York, 1945, p. 40.

201. Ranajit Guha, *Dominance Without Hegemony: History and Power in Colonial India,* Cambridge, 1997, p. 206.
202. M.S.S Pandian, "De-nationalizing the Past: Nation in EV Ramasamy 's Political discourse, *EPW*, 16 Oct 1993, pp. 2284-85.
203. F. Fukuyama, *The End of History and the Last Man*, London, 1992.
204. Fritz Stern, *From Voltaire to the Present*, New York, 1972, p. 12.
205. Sama Sastry, (ed.,) *Artha Sastra*, 1967, pp. 15-17. During Asoka's time corruption prevailed on a lower scale. See, Majumdar, *Ancient India*, 1960, p. 113.
206. *The Hindustan Times*, 5 May, 1996.
207. S.R Bommai Case after the demolition of the Babri-Masjid deals with this affair.
208. Shankar Surolia, *The Indian Police: Issues and Perspectives,* Gaurav Publishers, Jaipur, 1987, p. 60. The Kelkar Commission Report in 1955 identified 2399 castes OBCs in India. The Mandal Commission Report in 1980 identified 3743 OBCs. Even before the destruction of Babri Masjid in December 1992 the secular state in India stood on shaky ground.
209. Kaushik Basu et al., (eds) *Unravelling the Nation: Sectarian Conflicts and India's Secular Identity*, Delhi, 1996.
210. Barbara Harris White, *India Working: Essays on Society and Economy*, Cambridge, 2003.
211. On state, see, *Society ande Discourse in India: Rethinking Society*. S. Guhan & S. Paul (eds.,) *Corruption in India: Agenda for Action & Vision*, New Delhi, 1997; J.B.Hansen, *The Saffron Wave: Democracy and Hindu Nationalism in Modern India*, Princeton, 1999; Barbara Harris-White & S. Subramanian (eds.,) *Illfare in India: Essays on India's Social Sector* (in Honour of S. Guhan), Oxford, New Delhi, 1999; A. Kohli, *India's Democracy: Analysis of Changing State-Society Relations*, Princeton, 1990.

PART I
OPENING A NEW ROAD : INDIAN LITERATURE AND SOCIETY

1

Medieval Telugu Literature and the Untouchables in Society

Chinna Rao Yagti

Literature is one of the oldest forms of human activity. It expresses through the medium of words, human emotions and thoughts generated during the course of human struggle with nature.[1] The literature of the people often serves both as mirror of reality[2] and of the structures of thinking that constitute the consciousness of the age they live in. Analytical studies of literature can therefore serve to illuminate an understanding of social relationships in any given period of history.[3] There is no doubt that 'literature of the transitory periods always has a valuable historical importance. It provides a panorama, showing the transition of the society from one phase to another.[4] The Seventeenth and Eighteenth centuries in South Indian history constitute the transitory phase between the disintegration of Indian polity and the advent of the British. The greatness and grandeur of Telugu literature in this period is characterized by *satakas* of didactic value. This paper is concerned with the relevance of and symbolism in *satakas* with a view to examine the socio-cultural conditions under which the "untouchables" were living as reflected in Telugu literature in general and Vemana's writings in particular.

Untouchables : The Background

The origin of untouchability is obscure and its development is also difficult to trace. It has become one of the truisms of historical process that the peasants of traditional societies are the 'silent actors' of history.[5]

The same is applicable in an even greater degree to "untouchable" communities in India. Untouchability with its manifold manifestations is rooted in the notions of "purity" and "pollution", which is believed to have developed in the later Vedic period, when Brahmanic literature emerged in the form of *smritis*, *samhitas* and *upanishads*. The *Rig Veda* shows no acquaintance with people with whom contact was even remotely tabooed. In the later Vedic period terms like *Chandala* [6] and *Paulaksa* [7] come into existence and they suggest such people as objects of spite and abhorrence existing at the lowest ritual and social level. But they are not treated as "untouchables".

According to the *Boudayana Dharma Sutra*, a *Chandala* is an offspring of a *Sudra* father and a Brahmin mother.[8] Although not all the Brahminical texts are unanimous on the origin of *Chandala*, he is represented as an instrument of derivative pollution as well as a transmitter of contagion through contact. Further references to infection from the *Chandala* through sight, speech or proximity occur.[9] *Chandalas* were forbears of several castes, *Nishads*, *Kaivarta*, *Dasa*, *Bidalakari* etc., who were subsequently treated as "untouchables". His shadow, however, not regarded polluting then, was a later development. The commensual and connubial taboos in relation to the *Chandala* became severe and absolute. The notion of pollution became a potent reality and it was seen in full play with respect to the *Chandala*.

Harsh restrictions upon "untouchables" imposed by the Brahminical "legal" texts, as a result of elaborate development of the concepts of "purity" and "pollution" are manifest in the *Manusmriti*. The idea of groups having "lower" status than the *Sudra* in the *Chaturvarna* scheme of social stratification repeatedly appears in the later Brahminical writings. These references are often characterized by immense contempt, hatred and castigation. By the fifth century A.D. many of the stern injunctions of the "theoretical legal texts" seem to have become a reality. Fa-He-In, the Chinese traveller, [10] (Fifth Century) and the Chinese pilgrim Yuan Chaung[11] (Seventh Century) observed that the *Chandala*s, dwell apart from others i.e., outside the village, in a separate quarters. The eleventh century Muslim scholar Al-beruni notes that the *Chandala*s and three other groups are not members of any caste or guild, perform dirty work and are considered illegitimate.[12] Indian legal texts, secular works and most foreign accounts prove that untouchability was a practice and segregation of these sections of society had assumed rigidity.

Telugu Literature and Society

When we look at the situation of Telugu speaking regions in South India, even a cursory glance at the history of Telugu literature, particularly the medieval texts, would reveal how literature was mainly confined to *zamindar darbars* and scholarly gatherings with an emphasis on literary gimmicks such as *satavadhana* and *asthavadhna*[13] which indulged in depicting *sringaraviraha* (erotica). Until mid-Seventeenth Century, all the writers, (primarily Brahmins) tried only to make it difficult the language to display their command over language (Sanskrit or sanskritised Telugu), and to score over their rivals.

There are no literary sources available other than the translations of Hindu epics till Fourteenth Century A.D. The preceding period was characterized by the waning of Buddhism and Jainism. It is a historical fact that Jainism and literature based upon it had been prevalent in Telugu and Kannada regions prior to Nannaya the first known Telugu poet (*Aadi Kavi?)*. And it is said that the scholars of the Jaina faith also wrote some books in Telugu. But these works must have been destroyed when Jainism was suppressed. Nannaya, must have been acquainted with some of them, because otherwise he could not have become an "eminent" poet all of a sudden to compose a Telugu version of the Mahabharata. Starting from Rajaraja Narendra (Eleventh Century) all the then rulers generously donated tax free lands to the poets, who in turn devoted all their intellect to praise their patron and depict some of their affairs with women and also to preserve the Vedic ritual and *Varnasramadharma* intact.

Some scant literary sources reveal that the *Chandala*s were employed as *Talayaries* or watchmen of the villages.[14] Edarupalli record mentions them as *Charmakaras*, [15] but not more than that. Fourteenth and Fifteenth Century literature like *Kridabhiramam* of Vallabhacharya refers to this *Chandala* caste but does not categorize it as separate i.e. outside the pale of Hinduism.[16] Proudhakavi Mallana in his *Rukmangada Charitra* mentions that *Chandala*s are prohibited from witnessing religious ceremonies performed by the "high caste". These sources evidently show that *Chandalas* were appendage to the *Chaturvarna* of Hindu society, but their main occupation was as agrarian labour, who played a major role in the society, [17] being a productive communities and worshipped deities such as *Ekavira* and *Mahuramma.*[18]

The late medieval period is better known as *Rayalu-yugam* in Telugu literature[19] and the poets of *Prabhanda* style included were Allasani

Peddana (author of *Manucharistramu*), Nandi Timmana (*Parijatapaharanam*), Ramabhadrakavi, (*Ramabhyudayamu*), Dhurjati (*Kalahasti Mahastyam* or *Kalashastisva Satakam*) and Pingali Surana (*Kalapornodayam*). But none of them took 'society' realistic as a subject. Under the local administration of Vijayanagara rulers we find an inscription of the Seventeenth Century which refers to eighteen professional association bodies. *Kurantakas* (shoe-maker) was one of them and seemed to have formed a recognized part of local assemblies.[20] The references to "untouchables" do not go beyond this.

After the Battle of Talikota, the city of Vijayanagar lost its importance and the *Nayaka* courts such as Gandikota, Siddhavatam, Nellore, Gingee, Tanjore and Madurai emerged. Literature began to flourish through Matli Ananta (1590-1210) of Siddnavatam (Cuddapah district), Pushpagiri Timmana at Nellore, Raghunatha Nayak, in Tanjore.[21] In Northern Andhra, in the royal courts at Pithapuram and Paddapuram, literature also enjoyed patronage.[22] There was a set of poets outside the patronage who made a considerable contribution to Telugu literature in this period and worth mentioning among them are Tyagayya, Potuloori Vira Brahmam, Paparaju and Vemana.

Since there was no dearth of patronage, there was also no dearth of poets and works.[23] Surprisingly no work deals with a social theme, and the society is reflected neither as a subject nor as an object. Whatever references about the untouchables are made was in the context of taboos, punishment and perpetuation of their servile status. These *Prabhanda* texts departed from the epic and *puranic* texts in several respects, a theme might have taken from the *puranas*, but restricted to one or two episodes. Importance is given to the *Sringararasa* (the erotic sentiment), but they were confined to the classical standard in usage and the narration is subordinate to the description and the two are not integrated.[24] The only qualitative shift is that the target of audience, for the *Puranas* were meant for the common people, but the *Prabandhas* were only for the pleasure-seeking upper class, i.e. the kings and the nobles. The prime aim of these texts was only to please the patrons and they lost relevance for society at large.[25]

Vemana : Time and Place

Vemana's poetry occupies a distinct place in Telugu literature both in literary style and content. He was a social revolutionary in literary circles and the remaining part of the paper, will discuss his contribution. Scholars, both Indian and Western have achieved very little success with regard to fixing the time of Vemana's birth and death. But based on the evidence of the manuscripts and from the various oral traditions, some critics have placed Vemana as early as the Twelfth Century.[26] William Howard Campbell places Vemana roughly in the middle of the Sixteenth Century.[27] However, most of the critics believe that he lived in the Seventeenth Century. C.P. Brown, for example, fixes the year of his birth as 1652,[28] while Abbe Dubois states that "we were told" that Vemana died towards the end of the Seventeenth Century.[29] If Vanguri Subba Rao makes a persistent effort to put back the age of Vemana, there is a pronounced tendency in Rallapalli Ananta Krishna Sharma to push it forward.[30] Bandaru Thammayya[31] places Vemana between AD.1650-1750, which is the time period agreed upon by most scholars. A lack of adequate sources has become an impediment to accurate accounts of his date of birth, the place he lived and what caused his death. However, since the manuscripts of Vemana literature have been found in different parts of Andhra and Tamilnadu states, it is probable that Vemana wandered through most of the southern parts of the sub-continent.[32] But his activities were concentrated in Andhra Desa. One of the oft-quoted verses, repeated in several manuscripts in different versions, places him in Kondaveedu in Guntur district. "Home town-Kondaveedu, district-Muga Chintapalle; first house; west street; caste-Edde Reddi; what shall I say it is?".

However, in 1874, J.D.G. Gribble wrote in a pamphlet that Vemana had lived in Cuddapah district. Both oral tradition and some critics maintained that Vemana died in Katarlapalle in Cuddapah district, but the Telugu scholar Rallapalli Anantha Krishna Sharma, to cut short that debate, concluded that Vemana spent the best part of his life in Cuddapah and Kurnool districts of Rayalaseema region in Andhra. It is doubtful whether the internal evidence of the manuscripts and oral traditions will ever conclusively establish a definite date and place for Vemana.

Another point, much debated, is the caste of Vemana. Rallapalli says that Vemana belonged to the *Kapu* caste. Vanguri Subba Rao, on the other hand affirms that he was a Reddi. Both of them call in Vemana as a witness. This is no equivocation on the part of Vemana, for he is at once a Kapu and Reddy. Till the beginning of the Twentieth Century these two terms "Kapu" and "Reddi" were used interchangeably.[33] Edgar Thurston[34] says that the same people were known under different nomenclature in different regions.

Vemana : The Resurgence

Vemana was dismissed as beneath notice by the Telugu literary world until the first quarter of the Twentieth Century. Until then, no Telugu poet, scholar, critic or even a conscious social reformer made any reference to Vemana either in their works or the debate on reform. It is speculative as to what were the reasons for the conscious negligence of a Vemana and his philosophy. Was it his non-Brahmin status or his philosophy of questioning society as a consequence of which he ridiculed the caste system, idol worship etc.? Probably the first available source of information about Telugu poets and writers in print is the *Biographical Sketches of the Deccan Poets* (1829) by Cavally Ventaka Rama Swami. It consists of 'memories of the lives of several eminent bards, both ancient and contemporary, who have flourished in different provinces of the Indian peninsula, compiled from authentic documents. It deals, in all with 108 poets, of whom forty seven are Telugu poets, but Vemana does not figure in it. Later on Kandukuri Viresalingam's *Andhra Kavula Charitramu* (1899), which includes many minor poets, even obscure ones, surprisingly, omits Vemana. With some more additions in his revised edition (1917) the total number of poets swells to 220 but still Vemana was excluded.[35] But this "scholastic" Brahmin negligence in including Vemana was compensated far by western scholars, who recognized and by enormous popularity among the masses.

The first recorded contact of the west with Vemana's literature (poems) was made by Etienne Le Gac, a French Jesuit, who in 1729 sent a manuscript from Pondicherry to Louis XIV, King of France. This manuscript is preserved in *Bibliotheque Nationale*, Paris.[36] In 1806, a French missionary called Abbe Dubois, writing about Hindu society and culture characterized Vemana as one of the Indian poets who wrote in "philosophic vein".[37] This description caught the attention of Charles Philip Brown, a British Civil Servant in Madras, who was interested in preparing a Telugu text, a possible aid to Englishmen in learning Telugu. In 1824, with the assistance of Telugu scholars, Brown started reading Vemana in the vernacular and began collecting from different areas of Andhra, palm leaf and paper manuscripts of Vemana's poems.

In 1829, the first edition of this collections was published by Brown, entitled *The Verses of Vemana: Moral, Religious and Satirical*. Here is an important point that needs to be mentioned. Out of 500 copies of this edition, fifty copies were presented to him as editor's copies and the remaining 450 copies disappeared mysteriously. It took Brown ten years to discover that, with an active connivance of the high caste-Hindu *pundits*(?) of the College Board, the missing copies were rolled up as waste paper and tucked away in the lumber room of the college library.[38] A host of western rendering of Vemana's work poured in following the translation by Brown. Worth mentioning among them are R.M. MacDonald (1866)[39], Charles E. Gover (1874), J.D. B. Gribble (1875) W.H. Campbell (1898),[40] and Leonel David Barnett (1908).[41]

Since C.P. Brown's editions there have been many editions of Vemana's poems, a few of them have been translated into English and other Indian languages such as Kannada, Sanskrit, Tamil and Hindi. Some of these editions are merely reprints of Brown's first and second editions, whereas other editions are based wholly or partly on new poems from the palm-leaf manuscripts. Three editions are chiefly worth mentioning here. R. Purnacharyulu collected and edited *Vemana Sukti Ratnakaramu* (Masulipatnam, 1913) which was later edited by Nadendla Purushottam Sastrulu with 4, 035 new poems of which about sixty five per cent occur in Brown's editions. The second important work P.T. Parthasarathi Ayya's [42] which contains nearly 1800 poems and the third one is by Mutyala Narsimha Yogi's[43] which includes a life of Vemana and some of entirely new poems, not found in Brown's editions. The most voluminous yet of the collections of Vemana's verses is by N.Gangadharam.[44] It contains over 5000 poems, of which many are slight variations of other poems.

Vemana :The Reformer

Vemana scoffs at the *Vedas*, *Puranas* and *Dharmsastras* which teach discrimination and uneven scales of social justice. Hence, Vemana as a social rebel was constantly at war with the upholders of the caste system, opposed the practice of untouchability and represents a non-Brahmin social category. His anti-systemic pronunciations in forceful and sarcastic tones with the potential of fuelling conflict in society might have led to the conscious silence and subtle boycott of Vemana's work. So strong and persistent was this contempt for Vemana that, when Vemana was made a text book in Government schools in the Nineteenth Century, both teachers and pupils did all they could to evade the order. In some instances the introduction of it into the classes, for which it was prescribed, was postponed under various excuses. In others, the teachers took on themselves the omission of certain verses on the ground that they contained profane attacks on their religion or caste. The Telugu literary authority was also represented this attitude and countered the use at Vemana's poetry.

Appakavi, an authority on Telugu poetics has laid down the rule that the work of a *Sudra* poet to be rejected without examination.

The poems that bear Vemana's name give us a portrayal of him. They make clear that Vemana was a *yogi*, a social critic and a poet whose knowledge ranged from the esoteric to the common place and who made use of that knowledge to enhance the teachings of his poetry. The poems exhibit knowledge of the various sects of the Hindu religion and of the multitudes of observances and practices associated with these religious sects. The poems also reveal his awareness of the different activities and events involving the peoples of many castes around him. As a social critique he attacked and scorned human's preoccupation with externals, i.e., rituals, image worship, caste prejudices. Moreover expressive language is a great factor in making Vemana's poetry so popular. It is rarely that he resorts to Sanskrit words and expressions. He found the local (*Desi*) dialect sufficient, powerful and expressive enough to convey his message. Vemana's philosophical thought is a matter of claims and counter claims. He criticizes the "auspicious times" (*Muhoortham)* fixed by the Brahmin and he says:

If Brahmins bring a husband and wife together
By mad utterances on a 'holy' timing of weather
With a sanction so vouch safed and careful
How can the wife be widowed to face the way other?.

Vemana is never more vigorous than when exposing the evils of the caste system and denouncing caste prejudice. "Why revile a *pariah*?" he says. "Are not his flesh and blood one with ours; and of what caste is he who dwells with-in him", "There is in the wide world no viler *pariah* than he who scorns others, calling them *Sudras*, after he has perished, hell is his portion." The trouble men take about caste seems to him utterly vain and ridiculous. Since all castes have had the same origin, it is absurd to consider one greater and one less. So far as birth is concerned all men are equal, for all are brothers. If we will draw distinctions, it is the liar and the hypocrite, the cruel and the sensual, who are real *pariahs*, not those who happen to have been born in a particular family. Had Vemana the power he would make a speedy end of caste pretensions. "Come", he cries, "set one dish before all men in the world, and make them eat together. Make them all equal, and then placing your hand on their heads, bid them believe this to be the true way". And it is not only caste distinctions, but all arbitrary social distinctions, which arouse Vemana's indignation. His attitude is that which was taken by the great English satirist when he uttered his famous protest: "The table of ranks and degrees is a lie and should be flung into the fire". Vemana recognizes the popular attitude and describes it in the most contemptuous terms. "When a man has wealth, people look on him as the fairest of the gods, when brought low, by want and unable to raise himself, though he be a very Cupic, they look on him as an outcaste". Vemana questions the meaningless caste distinction and Brahminical customs, he says:

You make morsels of food invoke ancestors
And feed the crows as part of memorial rite
Turd-eating crows, how can they be ancestors?
You donkeys!

He was very critical about high-caste traditions and against the idea of calling a *Sadhu*/Priest, who pretends to be the torch-bearer to *"Mukti"* (freedom) to do ritual and said:

If one wears saffron clothes for a bliss elect
Knowing well the ways of all guises and dialects
No bliss would ever follow there on to be proven
As nothing could shake by heads being shaven

Vemana rejected all distinctions based on caste. He distinguishes between the caste one is born into, which is the result of one's past *Karma*, and one's true caste, the caste determined by one's character. Thus a man is a true Brahmin because of his truth seeking and honest conduct, and not because of his birth. For Vemana, an honest untouchable is nobler than a dishonest Brahmin. He questions beef eating as the cause of untouchablity. He asks:

By slaying grass eating cattle and eating them,
Men became untouchables
What will be the caste of those who eat pigs and chicken
Which eat every one's faces!

Vemana, perhaps the first Telugu social revolutionary who questioned the inhuman practice of untouchability, he has no patience with the pretensions of the higher-castes, denounces the caste system and says that:

Why revile a Mala, [45] again and again
Aren't his flesh and blood same as yours
What is the caste of him who moves in him?

Vemana's thinking goes much further, far ahead of his times. Vemana was very critical about caste distinctions, and declared that "all humans are equal", and said:

You plunge into the water; after you touch a Mala
When you depart to the cremation ground
The Mala burns your body
The filth that touched you then; where did it go now?

Despite of being a social critic, he had his limitations. Vemana's perception of women is regressive. According to him women ought to be obedient and virtuous. For instance

"Wives who disobey their lords are as death as poison snakes
Wives who live to please their lords, wives indeed the best on earth".
Disobedient wives are not wives at all, but only gyres?

A good deal of Vemana's satire is directed against women. He speaks so bitterly of the whole sex that it seems as if he doubted the possibility of any woman being capable of truth and fidelity. "In time of wealth a wife looks to her husband. In time of want she will not even rise at his approach, she looks on him as dead though he is still alive". For Vemana, woman was inferior and had to be under male control, for "as the track of a ship on the sea, as the path of a bird in the sky, so is the way of a woman". Thus his ideas sanction a patriarchal social order and his conservative ideas on women denied freedom of movement and expression in accordance with the norms of the period in which he lived. It is in his references to women that Vemana fails most conspicuously to rise above the false conventionalism of Hindu society. Thus his advocacy of equality as a social philosopher was limited in scope.

Vemana's poetry has been popular with the Telugu speaking people of all sections including the semi literate, the ascetic, the common folk and non-scholar. He is regarded as popular wit, who spoke the truth. His poetry has thoroughly permeated Andhra social consequences and had an important influence in shaping the language. Perhaps more importantly his literature laid the foundation stone for the future non-Brahmin and social reform movements in Andhra. It is difficult to determine exactly to what persuasion Vemana belonged, for his ideas do not fit completely into any particular mould of thought. Since the time of Buddha, who rebelled against the Brahminic, priest dominated Hindu religion with its exclusive hierarchical caste system, its elaborate rituals, expensive sacrifices and exploitation of untouchables under the guise of their lower status. Buddhism, Jainism and Virasaivism are all part of the non-Brahminic tradition which refused to observe caste distinctions and did away with rituals such as image worship, wearing the sacred thread etc. Vemana's thought strongly resembles the teachings of Virasaivism, but does not share the metaphysical interest in *Sakti* which is central to Virasaivism; indeed he only mentions *Shakti* to criticize its worship.

His belief and thought was free from all religious influence and does not fall into any particular sect. Not only is Vemana's philosophy unique, so too is his poetry.[46] The language is simple, straight forward, local in dialect. The poems do not contain the emotionality, the religious devotion or the interest in nature which are characteristic of most of the Sanskrit and even vernacular poetry in India; nor are they merely didactic like the verses in Sanskrit technical or "legal" texts. Criticism, argument, sarcasm, outright scolding and moral and religious teaching characterize Vemana's verses. Many poems are filled with fresh, often striking imagery, contrasts, caricatures and phrasing. Finally there is no doubt that Vemana's literature served the ends of criticism and teaching. Through his literature, he laid-down the foundations for the social reform to purify the society and fought against the social evils in Andhra.

Vemana had no respect for kings and courts or of court poets. Writing poetry to please a patron and to earn a pittance he said, is to demean the calling of poet. Only a sturdy spirit, free and untrammeled, can, he believed, be a poet with an enduring message. Enraged by Vemana's philosophical thought and his ideology, the traditionalists of his time turned his bitterest enemies. They called him a village lout, an irrelevant wretch, a mad man.46 They tried to kill him by ignoring him totally. But Vemana was too powerful and could not be ignored. His potency lies in his master of the common speech of the common man. The source of his strength is to be traced to his stout championship of such human values, as social equality and justice. It was Vemana who launched a virulent attack against the evil practice of untouchability in the Telugu literary scene. His thought provoking ideas were so striking that, he was consciously ignored by the Brahminical social order of the time.

Notes and References

1. For details, See, *Literature and Ideology: A Study of Telugu Literature* (1920-42), unpublished M. Phil Dissertation, Jawaharlal Nehru University, New Delhi, 1992, Chapter 1.
2. P.C. Gupta., Literature and Society: Selected Essays, PPH, 1985, p. 181.
3. See, *Literature and Ideology*, op. cit., p. 128.

4. S.C. Roy Choudhary, *Socio-Cultural and Economic History of India*, New Delhi, 1982, p. 206.
5. Cited in Vasanth W. Moon, "From Dependence to Protest: The Early Growth of Education and Consciousness among Untouchables of Western India", in Barbara R. Joshi, (ed.) *Untouchablels: Voices of the Dalit Liberation Movement*, New Delhi, 1986, Indian Edition, p. 15.
6. *Ajasaneyi Samhita, XXX. 21; Bruhadaranyaka Upanishad, IV.3.22; Chandogya-Upanishad*, V.10.7, cited in Vivekananda Jha, "Stages in the History of Untouchables", in *The Indian Historical Review*, Vol. II, No.1, July, 1975, pp. 18-31; also see his *"Chandalas* and the Origin of Untouchability", *The Indian Historical Review*, Vol. III, Nos.1-2, July 1986-January 1987.
7. *Taitreya Brahmana, III.4.1.14; Vajasaneyi Samhita, XXX.17, Ibid.*, also see Genichi Yamazaki, "Social Discrimination in Ancient India and its Transition to the Medieval Period", in H. Kotani, (ed.), *Caste System, Untouchability and Depressed*, New Delhi 1997, pp. 1-19.
8. For an 'Inter-Varna marriages and their progenies' see Chinna Rao Yagati, *Dalits' Struggle for Identity: Andhra, 1900-1950*, New Delhi, 2003, pp. 230-233.
9. Hiroyuki Kotani, "Ati Sudra Castes in the Medieval Deccan" in H. Kotani (ed.) op. cit., pp. 55-57; also see Cynthia Talbot, "A Revised View of 'Traditional' India: Caste, Status and Social Mobility in Medieval Andhra", in *South Asia*, Vol. 15, no.1, 1992, pp. 17-52.
10. James Legge, *The Travels of Fa-Hein*, Delhi, 1971, (First published in 1886), p. 43.
11. For details see T. Waters (tr.) *On Yuan-Chaung's Travels in India,* 2 Vols, London, 1904-05; also see J. Tarakusu, (tr.) *A Record of the Buddhist Religion as Practiced in India and Malay Archipelago by I-Tsing,* Delhi, 1966, Indian Edition.
12. E.C. Sachau, (Tr.), *Alberuni's India*, London, 1914, pp. 101-102; Qeyamuddin Ahmed, (ed.), *India by Alberuni*, New Delhi, 1993, Second Edition, pp. 44-47.

13. Avadhana means, very learned person and a Versatile man and expert in Vedas and other texts. Astavadhana means who can attend to eight matters simultaneously, and Satavadhana means, who can attend to a hundred issues.
14. See G.V. Sitapati, *History of Telugu Literature*, New Delhi, 1968.
15. Inscriptions of Andhra Pradesh, Warangal District no.87; Sri Vasavi Kanyakapuranam, Chapter 46, verse 3, cited in K. Suryanarayana, *History of Minor Chalukya Families in Medieval Andhradesa*, Delhi, 1956, p. 265. See *Bharati*, Janaury, 1968, p. 3., Ibid.
16. *Kridabhiramam*, verse 73, Ibid.
17. David Washbrook, "Land and Labour in Late Eighteenth Century South India: The Golden Age of Pariah" in Peter Robb, (ed.) *Dalit Movements and the Meanings of Labour in India*, Delhi, 1996, (First Published in 1993) pp. 68-86.
18. *Praudhakavi Mallana, Rukmaugada Charitra*, I.V.95, also see M. Somasekhara Sharma, *History of the Reddi Kingdoms, (Circa 1325 A.D. to Circa 1448 A.D.)* Waltair, 1948, p. 279.
19. Nidadavila Venkata Rao, *Dakshina Desiyandhra Vangmayamu*, Madras, 1954, Introduction.
20. *Epigraphia Indica*, XX p. 90; *Madras Epigraphical Report*, 1918, Paras 84-85; K.R.R. Sastry, *South Indian Guilds*, pp. 6-32, Cited in T.V. Mahalingam, *Administration and Social Life Under Vijayanagara*, Madras, 1969, p. 229.
21. K.A. Nilakanta Sastri, *A History of South India: From Prehistoric Times to the Fall of Vijayanagara*, Madras, Fourth edition, 1976, (First published in 1955), pp. 405-417.
22. P.V. Chalapati Rao, "Satabdala Sahityam: Samajika Rajakiya Bhumika" in D. ChandraSekhra Reddy, (ed.) *Telugu Sahityam: Charitraka Nepadhyam*, Hyderabad, 1994, pp. 128-138.
23. For details see Velchuri Narayana Rao, "Kings, Gods and Poets: Ideologies of Patronage in Medieval Andhra" in Barbara Stroller Miller, (ed.), *The Powers of Art: Patronage in Indian Culture*, Delhi, 1992.

24. Bh. Krishnamurthi, "Shifts of Authority in Written and Oral Texts: The Case of Telugu", in David Shulman, (ed.), *Syllables of Sky: Studies in South Indian Civilization*, Delhi, 1995, pp. 77-102.
25. Velcheru Narayana Rao, *Telugulo Kavita Viplavala Swarooppam*, Hyderabad, 1978, pp. 50-60.
26. Charles E. Grover, *The Folk Songs of Southern India*, Madras, 1871. He says that "from the absence of reference to Mohammedanism and the Muslim rule, and the close resemblance in style and matter to the Tamil Poets of the tenth century are there about, it is suggested that the proper date of Vemana's life is not later than the end of twelfth century'. If this is to be considered to place him in a particular period, he is wrong. In fact there are at least three references to Muslims in Vemana's verses. For details see V.R. Narla, *Vemana*, New Delhi, 1969.
27. W.H. Campbell, "Vemana-A South Indian Poet" in *Madras Christian College Magazine* 1898. He says "it is generally believed that Vemana lived about 250 years ago". Western Scholar, Grierson also states that Vemana lived in Sixteenth Century.
28. C.P. Brown, (tr.) *The Verses of Vemana, (693 verses)* Madras, 1911, (reprint); *Verses of Vemana* (1215 verses) (in Telugu original with English rendering), Hyderabad, 1967, Introduction.
29. Abbe J. A. Dubois, *Hindu Manners, Customs and Ceremonies*, Oxford, 1916, (first published in 1817); Vanguri Subba Rao says that Vemana was born in early fifteenth century. See his *Vemana*, Narasapuram, 1951, also see his *Sataka Kavula Charitramu*, Narasapuram, 1957; Vemuri Viswanatha Sharma, "Vemana Kulam-Kutumbam", in *Andhra Patrika*, (Dundhubi Kartika) "Vemana Kala Nirnayanu-Vemana Kalam" *Andhra Patrika* (Raktashri, Akshaya Sanchikalu). For a more complete account of this controversy see, N. Gopi, *Praja Kavi Vemana*, Hyderabad, 1980, pp. 94-133.

30. Rallapalli Ananta Krishna Sharma, *Vemana*, (Sir R. Venkataratnam Endowment Lectures) Waltair, 1971. He says that Vemana lived in early part of the eighteenth century.
31. Bandaru Thammayya, *Vemana Charitramu*, p. 130; V.R. Narla, "Vemana", in Mohanlal, (ed.), *Encyclopaedia of Indian Literature*, Vol. 5, New Delhi, 1992, pp. 4535-4537.
32. J.S.R.L. Narayana Moorthy and Elliot Roberts, (trs.), *Selected Verses of Vemana*, New Delhi, 1995, p. 2.
33. Gurram Venkata Reddi and Pochana Rami Reddi, *Viplava Yogi-Viswakavi: Vemana Vedasastram*, Kurnool, 1988, p. 108.
34. For details see Edgar Thurston, *Castes and Tribes of Southern India*, Madras, 1909, Vol. III, pp. 222-249.
35. This conscious neglect was noticed by the Dalit Poet of the Twentieth Century, Gurram Jashuva (1895-1971) who said: Vemana's Poetry is immortal but Viresalingam has surely erred by ignoring this great poet in his treatise on Andhra poets. See his Gabbilam (tr) K.Madhava Rao, Hyderabad, 1996, p. 63.For details of Jashuva's Life and Works, see Yendhuri Sudhakar, *Jasuva Kadha*, Rajahmundry, 1992, Hemalatha lavanam, *Maa Naanna Garu*, Vijayawada, 1986.
36. J.S.R.L. Narayana Moorthy and Elliot Roberts, (tr.) *Selected Verses of Vemana*, New Delhi, 1995, Introduction.
37. Abbe J.A. Dubois, Hindu Manners, Customs and Ceremonies, op. cit. p. 48.
38. These instances can be found in *Some Account of the Literary Life of Charles Philip Brown*, London, 1866. Also see his, "Essay on the Language and Literature of the Telugus", *Madras Journal of Literature and Science*, 1840, (Reprinted in 1991); V.R. Narla, *Vemana*, op. cit., p. 15.
39. M. Macdonald, "Vemana", in *Madras Journal of Literature and Science, 1866.*
40. W. Howard Campbell, "Vemana–A South Indian Poet", *The Madras Christian College Magazine*, Vol. XV, July 1897-June 1898, pp. 522-537.
41. For details of these Western Writings on Vemana see V.R. Narla, *Vemana Through Western Eyes*, translated into Telugu by

Maravuru Kodanda Rama Reddi, *Vemana-Paschatyulu*, Nellore, 1971.

42. P.T. Partha Sarathi Ayya, (ed.), *Vemana Padyamulu*, Madras, 1908.
43. Mutyala Narsimha Yogi, *Vemana Jnanamarga : 3002 Padyamulu*, Madras, 1958.
44. Nedunuri Gangadharam, *Vemana Padyamulu*, Rajahmundry, 1960.
45. *Mala* is one of the two major untouchable communities in Andhra. It consists of nearly thirty five per cent of the scheduled caste population in Andhra.
46. See Katti Padma Rao, *Sanghika Viplava Rachayithalu*; See V.R. Narla, *Vemana*, op. cit. p. 15.

2

Caste System in North Indian Medieval Society : A Study Chiefly Based on Hindi Literature

Ramesh Chandra Sharma

Man is the pivot round which revolve society, literature and history, and his life is the *sine qua non* of their being. Society represents agglomeration of men in mutual cooperation and harmony. These depend on "the total network of relations between human beings,"[1] and these relations, in fact, form the components of society.[2] Literature is the vehicle which reflects and conveys something of the experience of the society[3] in such a way as to produce out of the apparent chaos of human life a pattern[4] through the efflorescence of the integrated human personality[5] so as to help a better organisation and understanding of the factors of existence[6] by its "essence of beauty, spirit of creativity and the light of the realities of life."[7] And history epitomizes society and literature by studying "the human phenomena as we see them move through time and space."[8] It, thereby, aims at understanding men both as individuals and in their social relationships, which embrace everything that affects life of mankind.[9] This is not a static study, [10] for history is 'life going on, changing and developing.[11] Thus this trinity manifests different facets of the one reality, namely, human life.

In view of the above, there can be no gainsaying about the necessity of the study of literature for a proper understanding of history. Since the historian is expected not merely to describe men, but make them "intimately known to us," he has to exhibit in his work "the character and spirit of his age in miniature."[12] This he does by representing the 'progress of life in its different phases and nothing can elucidate life better than literature.'[13] The writer does not write in a vacuum. He cannot avoid the influence of the circumstances through which he lives and carries on his work, for he himself is the part and parcel of the world he delineates in his writings. These influences work on him constantly. Therefore, it is natural for him to react to them. Besides, being a creative artist, a free thinker and an independent reviewer of life, he also shapes it and thereby influences the society.[14] He, thus, represents the ethos of his milieu, which finds reflection in literature. Hence literature becomes a veritable social document and as such yields such intimate glimpses of life as more conventional and direct sources of history, by their very nature, cannot be expected to reveal.[15] Literature thus becomes a unique source of information for the reconstruction of social life of an age.

I

Contemporary Hindi Literary Sources

An attempt is here made to examine the contemporary Hindi literature as a source of information for the study of social life in northern India during the medieval period, with particular reference to the caste, which with its elaborate and well-defined system formed the real basis of social organisation. It went not only to the roots of the Indian society but even embraced those who came from outside. Those who attacked and criticised it accepted it as a matter of course. Kabir, for example, could never forget that he was a *julaha* of Kasi.[16] Tulsidas, who upbraided those who troubled him about his caste because he became an orphan soon after his birth and was brought up by a *sadhu*, was conscious of not defiling the caste of others,[17] and at the same time regretted the falling off of the people from the *varanasramadharma.*[18] The Muslim society came to be influenced by the caste system[19] so much that Sir Muhammad Iqbal had to say, "there are castes and sub-castes like the Hindus! Surely we have out-Hindued the Hindu himself. We are suffering from the double caste system, the religious caste system, sectarianism, and the social caste system, which we have either learned or inherited from the Hindus."[20]

Despite being predominantly "devotional and erotic"[21] and bound by "formal conventions that not only laid down elaborate and rigid rules of composition but also determined the choice of subjects that merited literary treatment,"[22] Hindi literature of the medieval period forms a rich but not yet properly tapped source of information for social life. For it creators-the poets, were impelled by "the desire to feel the reality of life" and accepted the challenges of the "complicated and ever shifting fabric of custom and law, society and politics",[23] whether *bhaktas* or court poets. Kabir, Sur and Tulsi, for example, attempted to uplift the contemporary social life and sublimation of its thought through the progress respectively of the individual, the family and the society.[24] The court poets in spite of their close relations with their patrons never gave up their self-respect and boldness and tried to raise up the morale of the people through their historical-heroic poetry.[25] Thus their social-consciousness enabled them to transcend the crippling dead-weight of convention and to reveal some of the realities of the contemporary social life.

Rich information of varied type is available on social organisation in general and the institution of caste in particular in the Hindi literature of the medieval period. It is to be noted in this connection that while the Muslim writers-Sufis and others, treat the subject in a specific way, the Hindu writers take it for granted and in their works only incidental stray references to castes and sub-castes are to be found. However, certain delineations of castes appear to be conventional to the Hindi writers of the medieval period. Thus descriptions of towns and cities generally carry specific references to castes of the people inhabiting them.[26] A marked convention in such descriptions is a detailed account of the chief markets of the towns where shops kept by people of different trades, which had consolidated in most cases as separate castes are generally mentioned.[27] Again, references to castes occur in connection with the account of social ceremonies and domestic rites and rituals.[28] References to different occupations provide yet another occasion for the enumeration of castes.[29] In these frequent mentions of caste, it is interesting to note, the females figure quite prominently not only in connection with the different domestic rites and ceremonies but also as practitioners of varied sundry trades and avocations in society.[30] Their intimate connection with the performance of the family rites and ceremonies is quite natural, as women usually play the leading role on such occasions. The references to the women professionals make it clear that women of the lower orders of society activity participated in bread-earning for the family and as such might have enjoyed greater freedom and regard than their counterparts belonging to the higher orders of the society. Not only this, the analogy of the castes, *varnas* to be more precise, has been used in many other contexts, as for example, as a standard for indicating the classical correctness of the metre in poetry,[31] and indicating the gradation of horses,[32] white of which being regarded as *Brahmans*, red as *Kshatriyas*, yellow as *Vaisyas* and black as *Sudras*.[33]

II

Varna System and Social Organisation

Any inquiry into the caste system should invariably begin with the consideration of the *varna* system, traditional of the Indian social organisation since the later Vedic period. By the medieval period, however, the system had undergone complete change which came to be regretted in the late Sixteenth Century.[34] Yet references to the four *varnas* are very frequent in the Hindi works of the period under review.[35] But the general treatment of the *varnas* in these works is neither distinct nor specific except in the case of the *Brahmans*, who figure very prominently in the contemporary Hindi poetry as a caste. They appear to enjoy their traditional pre-eminence in the society.[36] It is interesting to note that some new bases for their special position in the society had been discovered in accordance with the changed times, as is indicated by their mention as inspiring the Hindus to resist the political domination of the Muslims.[37] Their subdivisions and traditional-cum-specific functions are frequently mentioned, as would be clear from Appendix-A. But by the period under review *Brahmans* had adopted numerous other avocations besides those assigned to them by the *Dharmasastras*.[38] Some of these avocations were despicable.[39] Partly because of this and largely owing to their fall from the age-old ideals of their excellence in spiritual knowledge and matchless equanimity,[40] their revered position in the society came to be challenged.[41] A few vigorous efforts to emphasise the significance of the Brahmans in society[42] appear to be the natural action to counter this challenge.

Despite the *Mahabharata* tradition of their extermination at the hands of Parasurama,[43] supported by the medieval commentators,[44] the *Kshatriyas* figure quite prominently in the Hindi literature of the period.[45] They are usually referred to as *Khattris*[46] and Rajputs,[47] and sometimes as *Thakurs*[48] as well. However, there is no clarity. The confusion increases all the more when one tries to investigate into the ramifications of the *Vaisya* and the *Sudra varnas* during the period under review. As a matter of fact, these two appear to have no clear distinction between them,[49] having transformed themselves into multiple occupational groups which had consolidated into so many different castes.[50] Thus the *varna*-model does not hold good for the medieval period, for in it the ancient system had been substituted by a different organization resembling the old one in externals only,[51] as a result of a process that had started long back.[52]

III

Hereditary Occupation and Endogamy

Social organization as reflected in the contemporary Hindi literature during the medieval period clearly distinguishes between the urbane society, composed of the numerous castes and sub-castes, beyond the pale of civilisation.[53] The latter were generally looked down upon. Yet whenever they came into contact with the urbane elite, they rendered them invaluable sevices.[54] The hierarchical order of castes with its manifold divisions and subdivisions formed the basis of the organized society during the medieval period. The exact number of castes is impossible to give, for varying numbers are given for them in different works.[55] It would be quite appropriate to declare the castes as innumerable, [56] as is clear from the medieval commentators on the *Dharmasastras*.[57] Yet the number thirty-six appears to have been recognized as the traditional standard number of castes. But here, again, nothing is clear, for this number has not only been used for the enumeration of the castes in general[58] but in varied other contexts as well. For example, the expression *chhattis kuri* (thirty-six families/branches) has been generally used for pointing out the sub-division of the Rajputs.[59] The same number, however, appears in relation to the S*udras*,[60] the P*aunias*,[61] and the business people.[62] Here it may be pointed out that in the enumeration of the thirty-six branches of the social groups, mentioned above, there is neither uniformity in the different sources of information with regard to the sub-divisions of each, nor does the actual number where given tally with the constant.

IV

The equation between occupation and caste has been well established by the medieval period, as is proved by the works like the *Brihaddharma Purana*, composed during the period under study.[63] In fact, occupation, besides birth, has been a major determinant of caste.[64] Even the original *varna* system had the rudiments of occupational divisions in society. The only thing was that except for the priestly profession and that of the warrior, all other occupations, were put within the broad general categories of the *Vaisya* and *Sudra* varnas.[65] But with the development of the *jati* system,[66] the *varna* system withered away in actual practice among other things through intermingling of the *varnas*. Attempts at arresting it led to the proliferation of castes.[67] At the same time, the exigencies of corporate life made people engaged in different occupations to organize themselves into well-defined guilds.[68] These guilds, in course of time, consolidated into closer groups of people whose occupations became hereditary. This closeness, in due course, embraced their social tradition, which separated them from other sections of society. Each one of such groups, in order to maintain its unity and speciality unbroken and continuous, increasingly withdrew from inter-caste marriages and inter-dining and ultimately there grew up on the basis of common regulation and prohibition of occupation, faith, marriage and dining and so on a special, definite and separate unit of society. Thus came into being the different occupational castes,[69] which came to be well established by the period under review. This is amply borne out by references to the abundance of artisans and workers of all types in the contemporary historical works.[70]

Two characteristic features-hereditary occupation and endogamy, of the occupational castes are generally mentioned.[71] These two traits actually separated one group from the other. It should, however, be noted that these two traits, while preserving and transmitting skills from generation to generation, did not interpose any effective barrier to the mobility of labour in the long term at any rate.[72] In determining the social status among the different occupational castes, the usual medieval differentiation between occupations requiring manual labour and those not needing it or what we call the white-collar jobs, and the polluting and the non-polluting nature of the work concerned, appear to be the main criteria. Of these the latter in both cases were accorded a higher social status.[73] However, in so far as they contributed their respective services towards the common life of the society, the castes were welded together and became interdependent. Through their certain special functions on certain occasions, especially social ceremonies, certain occupational castes, ordinarily considered to be low, were afforded importance and even opportunities of enjoying temporary superiority.[74] At the same time, being economically the most productive section, they held the strings of social prosperity, as is clear from the frequent references to business activities and the special notices of the *Banias* in the contemporary records,[75] which, however, are not chary of mentioning about the sufferings of these professionals at the hands of the ruling classes.[76] This has been regarded as the cause of the proverbial poverty of the artisans, because it not only meant low wages but also implied working for no payment quite often.[77] The abundant supply of artisans has also been regarded as a cause for low payments.[78]

Although in the medieval society, in which kinship organization depended on the patron-protege relationship,[79] they may not be expected to enjoy a place commensurate with their share in production, the occupational castes, nevertheless, formed the basis of social organization in those days, as is clear from their multiplicity and the number of groups into which they may be categorised.[80] One such group was formed by those castes which rendered traditional services to the society and received annual and occasional payments (*pavana*), usually in kind, in return.[81] They were generally called *Paunia*[82] or *Tahalua*,[83] who may be regarded as traders in social services. They worked under the age-old traditional kinship organization of the castes, known as the *jajmani* system.[84] Among these the barber-nai, also called *Hajamana* or *Vrati*,[85] was very prominent. He performed his usual tonsorial duties, but on occasions of domestic rites and ceremonies, especially marriages, he used to figure prominently along with the priest.[86]

Businesmen, Occupational Castes and Miscellaneous

Another well marked group was of those who were engaged in business activities. Generally called *Baniks* and *Banjaras*, they included a wide range of people who earned their living through transactions in goods and money.[87] At the apex of the group were the *Vaisyas*, who as *Banias* figure prominently in the accounts of the foreign travellers[88] The sectarian caste of Jains was also engaged in the *banik-vritti* (profession of a *Banik*, i.e., business).[89] Some of the members of the community in view of their intellectual and professional attainments, cultivated tastes and outlook, may be regarded as forming the nucleus of the Hindu middle-class, as will be clear from the perusal of Banarasidas's autobiography-the *Ardha-Kathanak.*[90]

Those practicing various crafts formed the third group of the occupational castes.[91] They included both practitioners of the fine arts as well as those engaged in the utilitarian crafts. They, especially the former, generally prospered under the patronage of the royalty and the nobility. But at the same time, they had to bear with the whims and frowns of their patrons,[92] in spite of the excellence of their workmanship and products.[93] The usual professional activities of some of them are found mention in the contemporary literature.[94]

In the fourth group may be included professionals of a miscellaneous type.[95] Among these the primarily official class of the *kayasthas*[96] by virtue of the epistolary and computational skills of its members is said to "rule all the courts".[97] Though they did not receive high pay, "they are still cherished by the great for their good service".[98] The bards[99] were also included in this group, in which may also be placed some of the tribal castes, like the *ahir*, the *nat*, the *kevat* etc., which were devoted to specific occupations.[100] Thus the occupational castes formed a major segment of society in North India during the medieval period.

V

Some of the tribes had become consolidated as castes during the medieval period.[101] Of these the Rajputs, who had adopted "the sword as their calling", [102] were the most important. They were considered to be divided into thirty-six families, [103] of the three branches–the *Suryavansi*, the *Chandravansi* and the *Agnikula*.[104] But there was no certainty and agreement on the names of the different families, and actually more than thirty-six have been mentioned, which included some other independent tribes such as the *Jats*, the *Gujars* and *Badgujars* as well.[105] These tribal castes are to be distinguished from those tribes which lived in the forests beyond the pale of the organized society, as pointed out earlier. The Jains came to be regarded as a particular caste during the medieval period.[106] They also came to think of themselves as such, having developed the common requisites of castes–the *kula*, *gotra* etc.[107] Thus in those days there existed sectarian castes as well.[108] Here it may be interesting to note that even in the Muslim society in medieval India traces of castes and their sub-divisions existed, which were not only confined to those converted to it from Hinduism.[109] Then there were those who were placed at the lowest rung of the social ladder. They were generally despised in spite of the services rendered by them to the society.[110] They were treated as *Pariahs* and as such as untouchables. Thus it is clear that the medieval North Indian society consisted of innumerable castes and sub-castes. They formed an intricate hierarchical order.

Notes and References

1. A.J.Toynbee, *A Study of History*, London, 1964, Vol. 12, p. 271.
2. *Ibid.*
3. *Ibid.*p. 580.
4. D.Daiches, *Literature and Society*, London, 1938, p. 268.
5. M.P. Singh, *Ritikalin Hnidi Sahitya ki Aitihasik Vyakhya*, New Delhi, 1977, p. 53.
6. D.Daichas, *op. cit.*, p. 268.
7. Prem Chand, *Sahitya Ka Uddesya*, Allahabad, 1954, p. 19.
8. A.J.Toynbee, *op. cit* p. 225.
9. J.H.Plumb, *The Death of the Past*, Harmondsworth, 1973, p. 84.

10. *Ibid.*
11. A.Kettle, *An Introduction to the English Novel*, Vol. 1, London, 1962, p. 28.
12. T.B.Macaulay, *History: The Varieties of History*, (ed., F.Stern) London, 1970, p. 86.
13. Prem Chand, op. cit, p. 25.
14. R.Wellek and A. Warren, *Theory of Literature*, London, 1961, p. 97.
15. S.Chandra, "Literature and Social Consciousness", *The Indian Historical Review*, VI, 1-2, p. 209.
16. B.S.Misra (ed.), *Kabir-Granthavali*, Agra, 1969, pp. 391, 405-406 (Abbrv. Kabir)
17. Dhuta Kahau, Avadhuta kahau, rajaputa kahao, Jolaha kahau Koul
    Kahu ki beti Saun beta na byahal,
    Kahuki jati bigara na Sau
    Mere na jati pati, na Chahaun kahu ki jati pati. R.C.Shukla, et al (eds.) *Tulsi Granthavali*, Vol, II, (Kasi, 2031 V), p. 187. (Abbrv. T.G., ii)
18. Tulsidas, *Ramacharitamanasa*, (Mula Majhala size) (Gorakhpur 2025 V) pp. 580-582.
    (abbrv. RCM). Also Nabhadas, *Bhaktamala*, Bombay, 1978, V, pp. 313-314. (abbrv. BM).
19. Tara Chand, *Society and State in the Mughal Period*, New Delhi, 1961, p. 29; M. W. Mirza, Muslim Religion and Society, in R. C. Majumdar et al (eds), *History and Culture of the Indian People*, Vol. VI, Bombay, 1960, p. 608.
20. Tara Chand, *op. cit*, p. 31.
21. S. Chandra, *op. cit*, p. 209.
22. *Ibid.*
23. G.M.Trevelyan, *English Social History*, London, 1962, pp. viii and ix.
24. G.B.Raman, *Kavitraya Samaj Darsan*, Chittur, 1971, pp. 7-8, 185.
25. *Ritikalin Hindi Sahitya ki Aitihasik Vyakhya*, pp. 82, 221. Indeed, the whole book deserves careful perusal in this context.
26. So far as poetical works are concerned references are generally to verse no./page no.: Banarasidas, *Ardhakathanak*, (ed). N.R. Premi, Bombay, 1957, 29/4-5 (For an English translation of

the work by the present author vide Indica, vii. 1-2, March and September 1970, pp. 49-73 and 105-120) (abbrv. A.K.); Daud, *Chandayana*, (ed.) P.L. Gupta, Bombay, 1964. 26/90 (abbrv. Ch.); V.P. Misra (ed.), *Keshav-Granthavali*, ii. (Allahabad 1959) *Rama Chandrika* (abbrv. RC), 43/233; iii. *Vira Charitra* (abbrv. VC) 5/557 (abbrv. K-G); Usman, *Chitravali*, (ed) S. Verma, Allahabad, 1929, 14/6 (abbrv.CV); Kutuban, *Mrigavati*, ed. S.G. Misra, (Prayag, 1885, Saka) 171/121, 172/122 (abbrv. MG).

27. M.P. Gupta (ed.), *Prithviraj Rasau*, (Jhansi, 2020), V.25/10 (abbrv. PR); Vidyapati. *Kirtilata*, (ed).V.S. Agrawal, Jhansi, 1962, 100-114/71-78, 121-122//80 (abbrv.KL); M.M. Jaisi, *Padmavat*, (ed). R.C. Shukla (Kasi 2008 V) 2/14-15, 3/80-81 (abbrv. Pd); S.B. Singh, *Abdur Rahim Khan Khanan*, (Jhansi, 2018, V) pp. 352-367, (abbrv.Rahim).
28. Ch. 251/222; Tulsi, *Ramalala Nahchhu* (abbrv. Rin), TG ii. 5-18/3-5; Manjhan, *Madhu Malti*, ed. M.P.Gupta, Allahabad, 1961, 52/43, 54/45, 286/242, 287/243, 441/387, 462/407, 15/459 (abbrv. MM); Pd, 3/80-81.
29. MG, 25-26/75-76; *Rahim*, pp. 352-367.
30. *Ibid;* Senapati, *Kavitta Ratnakar*, ed. U.S. Shukla (Prayag 1936) 59/63 (abbrv. Senapati).
31. Keshav, *Chhandamala* (abbrv.CM), K-G, ii, 13/450, 21/451, 32/452.
32. VC, K-G, iii, 46-47/555.
33. *Ibid*
34. RCM, Uttar, 98/580, 102/583; *Kavitavali*, ed. I. Narayan (Gorakhpur 2025 V) Uttar, 84/155, 183/223. (abbrv. KV)
35. Nanddas, *Nanddas Granthavali*, ed. V. Das (Kasi 2006 v) 56 (abbrv. Nand); *Gitavali*, (ed.) V. Sharma, Allahabad, 1926, Uttar, 1/275 (abbrv. GV); CV 14/6; *Rasikpriya* (abbrv.R), K-G ii, 43/233, VC, K-G iii. 31/479; Bhushan *Sivaraj Bhushan abbrv. SB*), Bhushan Granthavali, (ed.) S.B.Misra, (Kasi, 2015, V) 22/116 (abbrv.BG); Narottamdas, *Sundama Charita*, (ed.) P.C. Jain, Agra, 1966, 12/29 (abbrv. SC); A.K. 28/41, Lal Kavi, *Chhatraprakasa*, (ed). M.P. Singh, New Delhi, 1973, p. 102 (abbrv. Cp).
36. Nand 59, 207; Tulsi, *Kundaliya Ramayana*, ed. S.N. Pandey, Allahabad, 1941, pp. 60-61, 196 (abbrv. KR); *Parvati Mangal*

(abbrv. Pm), T. G. ii, 93/31; G. V. Bal, 2/7, 4/9, 6/15, 12/24; RCM Bal, 155/98, 165/102 *Kavipriya* (abbrv. K), K-G i, 77/174; RC, K-G ii, 14-20/342-343, 36/364, 55-56/410;A.K.417-427/46-48;Senapati, 54/2.

37. *Ratan Babani* (abbrv. RB), K-G iii, 22-23/469. The entire work of Bhushan centers round Shivaji and Chhatrasal, two principal opponents of Aurangzeb. It would be appropriate, here, to consider Zia-i-Barani's fulminations regarding Hindus in general and Beahmans in particular-Cf. The Patawa-i-Jahandari, (trans) Afsar Begum, *Medieval India Quarterly*, iii, 1-2, pp. 21-22, 62-65.
38. This phenomenon was, in fact, an earlier one-Cf. Manu Smriti, (ed.and trans) R. Bhatt, Bombay, 1929, 8/102/198.
39. Ch 432/323; Pd 1/30; *Society and State in the Mughal Period*, p. 26. Abul Fazl mentions ten categories of Brahmans according to their occupations, including Miechchha and Chandal-*Ain-i-Akbari*, iii, (trans.) H.S. Jarrett, Calcutta, 1948, p. 129.
40. RCM Ayo., 172/283; Uttar, 99-100/581; Senapati, 54/22. Yet the Brahmans continued to take pride in poverty and equanimity, as is clear from the following line of Narottam das- "Aurat ko Dhan Chahiye, Babri bamman ko Dhan keval bhichha"-SC, 10/28.
41. Kabir, 93; *Gorakhbani*, ed. P.D. Barthwal, (Prayag 1999 V), 42/136 (abbrv. GB); RCM Uttar, 100/581; BM, 235.
42. For instance, those by Tulsidas and Keshavadas.
43. Senapati, 26/103 and 27/104; *Ain* iii, p. 130.
44. *Society and State in the Mughal Period*, p. 26.
45. Cf. Appendix A.
46. *Ain* iii, 126. Even here there appears to be some confusion, for sometimes the khatris are referred to as a separate caste altogether, as, for example, in Ch. 251/222.
47. *Ain* iii, p. 131. Cf. Appendix C.
48. Ch, 26/90.
49. *Jahangir-Jas-Chandrika* (abbrv. JC), K-G iii, 16/618.
50. Cf. Appendex B.
51. *Society and State in the Mughal Period*, p. 34.
52. B.P. Mazumdar, *Socio-Economic History of Northern India (1030-1194 A.D.)*, Calcutta, 1960, p. 79.
53. Cf. Appendix F.

54. RCM Ayo., 250/320. CV 45-59/76/77. Also Appendix F.
55. For example, 41 in Ch, 31 in MG and more than 60 in Rahim.
56. KL, 121/122/80; K.M. Sen, *Bharat men Jawtibheda*, Calcutta, 1940 pp. 19-24; *Socio-Economic History of Northern India*, p. 79. Iravati Karve has shown how 204 castes can be derived on the basis of mixing of varnas as per Manu–*Hindu Samaj aur Jati Vyavastha* (Hindi translation) Hindu Society : An Interpetation, Delhi, 1975, p. 57.
57. P.V. Kane, *Dharmasastra ka Itihasa*, Lucknow, 1980, p. 120.
58. Ch, 35/98; MM, 515/459; Pd, 4/39; VC, K-G iii, 18/6/557. For further references in Hindi poetry vide M.G. Gupta, *Hindi Kavyamen Bharatiya Sanskriti*, Delhi, 1968, pp. 322-323.
59. PR, 13/114; Pd, 3/80/81; M.P. Gupta (ed.), *Madhu Malti Varta/ Madhu Malti Ram Vilas* (Kasi 2021 V), p. 1 and note on p. 249 (abbrv. MMV/MMR). Abul Fazl, however, says that the Rajputs were divided into "thousands of sects"–*Ain* iii, p. 131.
60. A. K., 28/4.
61. Ibid., 29/5; MM, 52/43, 54/45.
62. MG 298-299/172-173.
63. *Socio-Economic History of Northern India*, 79ff.
64. No doubt, from the beginning there was no rigidity with regard to the profession assigned to each varna and caste, and "there were groups of occupations like trading, agriculture, labouring in the field, and doing military service which were looked upon as anybody's, and most castes were supposed to be eligible for them"-G.S. Ghurye, *Caste, Class and Occupation*, Bombay, 1961, p. 15.
65. These two varnas were supposed to do all the productive as well as aesthetic labour in the society. Thus most of the occupational castes of the later days developed from these two varnas, although a few like the kayasthas might have been derived from all the four varnas–R. Thapar, Social Mobility in Ancient India, in R.S. Sharma, (ed.) *Indian Society: Historical Probings*, New Delhi, 1974, pp. 87-88, 100, 111-112. Moreover, we come across progressive assimilation of the vaisya with the sudra, as revealed by the medieval commentators-*Caste, Class and Occupation*, p. 100. This process started in the Gupta period (circa 200 B.C. to 500 A.D.)-R.S. Sharma, *Sudron ka Prachin Itihas*, New Delhi, 1979, p. 280.

66. For the period of the sutra literature (circa B.C.600 to A.D.300) see, V.C. Pandey, *Bharatvarsha ka Samajik Itihas (600 B.C.–100 A.D.*), Allahabad, 1960, pp. 2, 54, 98.
67. The intermingling of the varnas was not liked by the lawgivers like Manu, who were purists trying to guard against this by creating different social groups in the form of castes, especially in the case of the pratiloma unions, in which the varna of the father was lower than that of the mother-*Bharatvarsha ka Samajik Itihas*, pp. 56-63; *Caste, Class and Occupation*, p. 99.
68. R.C. Majumdar, *Corporate Life in Ancient India*, (Hindi transl.) Sagar, 1966, pp. 14-16, 18ff, 21.
69. *Ibid.*, pp. 323, 333, 357, 366, *Bharatvarsha ka Samajik Itihas*, pp. 53-55; *Indian Society*, pp. 118, 122.
70. Babur, dwelling upon the "advantages of Hindustan", says, "another good thing in Hindustan is that it has unnumbered and endless workmen of every kind.... Mulla Sharaf, writing... about the building of Timur Beg's stone mosque, lays stress on the fact that on it 200 stone-cutters worked from Azarbaijan, Fars, Hindustan and other countries. But 680 men worked daily on my buildings in Agra, Sikri, Biana, Dulpur, Gualior and Kiul. In the same way there are numberless artisans and workmen of every sort in Hindustan"-A.S. Beveridge (tanslr), *Babur-Nama*, New Delhi, reprint, 1970, p. 520 (abbrv. BN). He also mentions that "all artisans, wage-earners, and officials are Hindus"-*Ibid.*, p. 518, Father Monserrate refers to the "great number of artizans"-J.S. Hoyland and S.N. Banerjee (trans). *The Commentary of Father Monserrate, S.J.*, London, 1922, p. 36.
71. BN pp. 518, 520; W. Foster, *Early Travels in India*, Delhi, 1968, p. 322; E. Grey (ed.), *The Travels of Pietro Della Valle in India*, London, 1892, i. p. 71; W.H. Moreland and P.Geyl (trans), *Jahangir's India : The Remonstrantie of Francisco Pelsaert*, Cambridge, 1925, p. 60; R.C. Temple (ed.), *The Travels of Peter Mundy*, ii. London, 1914, p. 94; F. Bernier, *Travels in the Mogul Empire*, (trans) A. Constable, London, 1916, p. 259; J.B. Tavernier, *Travels in India*, (trans) V. Ball, ii, London, 1889, pp. 184-185; S.N. Sen (ed.), *Indian Travels of Thevenot and* Careri, New Delhi, 1949, pp. 38, 254.

72. Irfan Habib, Technology and Barriers to Technological Change in Mughal India, *The Indian Historical Review*, v. 1-2, pp. 170-171.
73. Caste, Class and Occupation, p. 242. The *kayasthas*, for example, largely being in the state service enjoyed greater regard.
74. Caste, Class and Occupation, p. 25; Cf. Rln. TG ii, 5-18/3-5 *History and Culture of the Indian People*, vi. pp. 575-577, 579-580.
75. For the contemporary literary references see Appendix B (ii) A. Rashid, *Society and Culture in Medieval India*, Calcutta, 1969, p. 229; *Early Travels*, pp. 226, 322, 323, 324; *Travels in the Mogul Empire*, pp. 152, 164, 285; *The Travels of Pietro Della Valle*, i, p. 178; *Jahangir's India*, pp. 13, 17; *Travels of Peter Mundy*, ii, pp. 93, 95; *Travels in India*, i. pp. 6, 59, 60, 74, 75, 77, 91, 104, 156, ii, pp. 63, 129, 183, 184; *Indian Travels*, pp. 88, 89, 256.
76. Pelsaert, for example, writes, "the second (scourge) is (the oppression of) the Governor, the nobles, the *Diwan*, the *Kotwal*, the *Bakshi*, and other royal officers. If any of these wants a workman, the man is not asked if he is willing to come, but is seized in the house or in the street, well beaten if he should dare raise any objection and in the evening paid half his wages, or nothing at all"-p. 60; *Travels in the Mogul Empire*, pp. 254-256. Banarsidas's autobiography abounds in references to such vexations at the hands of the government officials suffered by him and his kinsmen at Jaunpur-A.K., 22/4, 10-114/13-14, 467/473/52.
77. *Jahangir's India*, pp. 60-61.
78. *The Indian Historical Review*, v. 1-2, p. 169.
79. R.C. Sharma, Occupational Castes in Uttar Pradesh During the Mughal Period, A.D. 1526-1707, *The Quarterly Review of Historical Studies*, xxii, 4, p. 69.
80. Cf. Appendix B.
81. Appendix B (i).
82. A.K., 29/5.
83. BM, p. 97; Hargulal, *Madhyakalin Krishnakavya men Samajik Jivan ki Abhivyakti*, Delhi, 1967, p. 139.
84. R. Lannoy, *The Speaking Tree*, London, 1974, pp. 157-162.

85. Appendix B(i). Peter Mundy makes a special mention of the barbers of Etawah for their "neatness in shaving and artificial shampooing"-*Travels*, ii, p. 86.
86. Appendix B(i).
87. Appendix B(ii).
88. Ftn. 75 Supra.
89. A.K., 14/3.
90. R.C. Sharma, Life of a Middle-Class Man in the Seventeenth Century, *Journal of Indian History*, lix, 2 and 3, pp. 389-403.
91. Appendix B (iii).
92. Ftn.76.Supra.The poet Vrinda says:

Ve to rojagari rojagara ke Umedavara.
Tuma rojagari deta main naik. Na darat ho
Khijmati Chahen Khijamati bicha avain tuma.
Khijamati Kari kari Ulta Parata ho
Rakhiya tamama Sirapavatiyau Chahai tuma.
Kariya tamama Sirapava hi dharata ho.
Vrnda Kahai Chakara ki Chakari banata kaisen
Sahiba Kaha aisi Sahibi Karata ho.

("They are wage-earners expecting daily work, but you do not hesitate in abusing them. You expect service, but you not only interfere in the work but also show ill-temper to them. They work hard for reward, but in spite of all their efforts you put them down (lit. put your foot on their heads). Says Vrinda how can a servant work in the face of such a shoe of mastery (lit. what sort of mastery do you have) ?"-J.R. Cheler (ed.), *Vrinda-Granthvali*, Agra, 1971, p. 351.

93. *Travels in Mogul Empire*, p. 254.
94. For example, for the Sundar's exact weighing of gold and the Lohar's hammer beating the iron-Senapati, 44/18 and 43/57 respectively; Rln, TG ii, 5-18/3-5.
95. Appendix B(iv).
96. VC, K-G iii, 3/594, *Indian Society*, pp. 111-112.
97. N.Manucci, *Storia do Mogor*, (trans) W. Irvine, 2 Vols, Calcutta, 1966, p. 422.
98. *Ibid.*
99. Appendix B (iv).
100. Appendix C.101.*Ibid.*
102. *Ain*, iii. p. 131.

103. Cf.Discussion of the thirty-six castes and sub-castes in the text supra.
104. *Ain*, iii. pp. 130-131.
105. Appendix C; Also *Ain*, iii. p. 131.
106. Ch, 26/90; *Kabir*, p. 93.
107. A.K., 10/2.
108. Appendix D.
109. Rahim, p. 358; Jan, *Kym Khan Raso*, (ed.) D. Sharma, Jaipur, 1953, pp. 3, 6, 17, 19, 27, 37 (abbrv.KKR).
110. Appendix.E.

Abbreviations Used

Akbari	Akbari Darbar ke Hindi Kavi, S.P.Agrawal (Lucknow, 2007, V) Pad and Page No.
BB	Bihari Bodhini, (ed) B. Din (Banaras 2013 V) Doha and Page No.
BM	Bhaktamala, Nabhadas (Bombay 197; V) Page No.
Din	Din Dayal Giri Granthavali, (ed.) : S.S.Das, Page No.
DV	Dohavali, Tulsi (Gita Press) Dona no./Page No.
Jm	Janaki Mangal, TG ii, verse and page no.
KRV	Krishna-Rukmini Ri Veli, Prithviraj Rathod, (ed.) N. Swami (Agra, 1953) verse and page No.
Sur	Sur Sagar, 2 vols (Kasi 2009 V) Skand and Page No.
SS	Sant Sudhasar, (ed.) Viyogi Hari and Page No.
Vp	Vinaya Patrika, (ed.) R.N. Sharma (Agra 1963) Pad and Page No.
VP	Vidyapati ki Padavali, (ed.) N.N.Gupta (Allahabad, 1910) Pad and Page No.

APPENDIX-A
The Four Varnas

Varnas	*Sub-Divisions*	*Remarks and References*
Brahman	Sanadhya	A prominent sub-division of the brahmans in Sanaudhiya northern India-K, K-G I 1/99, RC, K-G ii 4/229, 14-20/342-43, 36/364, 55-56/410; BM 314.
	Kanaujia	BG 26/8; BM 152.
	Mathur	BM 171.
	Gotras/Alls	Gotras indicate exogamous sub-groups of sub-castes. Originally known after rishis, later they

	came to have a varied nomenclature and came to be known as alls, which appear to have substituted the gotra in the medieval period.
Tiwari	Ch 26/90.
Dube	Pd 4/268.
Misra	K-G I K 18/95, 9/100, ii RC 7/2;9, Cm 13/450, Kabir 344; Cp 158.
Pande	Pd 2/53; Ch 37-38/100; Cv 39-41/117, 1/125; SC 34/42, 37/43, 77/59; Cp 58, 70, 71, 72.
Kasyap	BG 26/8.
Dikshit	Senapati 5/2-3.
Bhatta Professional	BM 174; 257-260.
Purohit, Uprohit, Pir	Pd 6/189; GB 96/33; Jm 156/50; RCM Bal 169/104, Kulguru 172/105, 214/127, 323/179; Nand 243, 204, 326, 371; Ch 431/322; KR 12, 17, 24, 64; GV Bal 12/24, 100/107, 101/118; KRV 36/19; MG 31/123; MMR 290/304; K-G i. K 13/178; MG 115/102; 116/103; MMV 27; VP 92/; Senapati 59/24; Cp 77.
Jyotishi, Ganak, Gunitkar	Ch. 25/98, 39/101, 261/229; GV Bal 14/27, Lanka
Agami	19/269; RCM Bal 312/173; CV 30/113; MG 9/70; MM 50/42; 437/383, 438/384; Sur 10-88, 703, 704; Nand 194, 199, 231-32; Pd 3/19; CV 12/14; Pd 1/198; DV 149/78; BB 649/238; BM 287.
Ojha	DV 68/27; KL 196/112, 141/198; Pd 2/49.
Sagunia	KR 140; Ch 289-90/242-43; MMV 4; RCM Ayo. 121/213, 192/292. Teacher GV Bal 50/64; CV 13/15; SC 10/28.
Panda	BM 276.
	1. Most frequently referred to in all the works. 2. Considered to be the most important in the caste hierarchy and generally respected in the society-Cf. A.K. 417-27/46-48; K-G I K 77/174; GV Bal 6/15; RCM Bal 165/102, Aran. 34/383; Nand 59, 207. For (i) Learning called Pandits-Cf. Pd 2/53, 1/102; RCM Ayo. 323/353; CV 33/114. (ii) Consulted in all important matters-Cf. RCM Ayo. 3-4/20405; KR 90, 123, 133, 200. (iii) Acting as messengers and mediators in all sorts of negotiations-Cf. RCM Bal 91-92/66; CV 39/41/117, 1/125; Nand 202. 3. Challenges to their super4iority because of (i) Their falling from the age-old ideals-Cf. RCM Ayo. 172/283, Uttar 99-100/581. (ii) Adopting other professions, e.g., trade-Cf. Ch 432/323; Pd 1/30 (iii) Moral degeneration

		and some of them taking to despicable professions-Cf. Ain iii 129; State and Society during the Mughal Period 26.
	Kshatriya Khattri	GV Bal 14/6; PR 13, 186, 190, 213, 275, 288; K-G iii VC 17/507; M M 258/219, 356/309; R C M Bal 160/100, Aran 19/371, Kis. 1/394, Lanka 236-37/460; Pd 1/279; CV 42/97, 22/109; K-G ii RC 24/231, 22/249, Cm 13/450; Kabir 496; KR 54, 55, 57, 61; MG 103/99, 113/102; MM 50/42; MMR 299, 303, Cp 3, 57, 89, 102, 180; BM 275
	Chhatra-vandhu	RCM Bal 174/106.
Vaisya		K-G ii Cm 13/450; BM 118; Cf. Appendix B(ii).
Sudra		Kabir 341; DV 553/194; RCM Uttar 97/580, 99/581, 100/582; K-G Cm 13/450, 21/451; KRV 60/31. The sudras came to be identified with some of the professional and service castes-Cf. Appendix B(i) and (iii).

APPENDIX–B
The Occupational Castes
(i) The Paunias

Caste	*Sub-Division Alternative name*	*Remarks and References*
Kumhar	Kulal	GB 42/136; Kabir 47, 63, 245, 280, 496, 542; Ch 80/123; RCM Uttar 100/581; VP 457/232; Sur 10-4399; BB 675/246; A.K. 29/5; Akbari 65/415; Rahim 27-28/355; BM 249, 277, 308.
Dhobi	Rajak	Kabir 74; Ch 260/228; Sur 10-3037, 3038, 3042, 3057, 3655; KV Uttar 66/142; BB 675/246; MG 387/202; A.K. 29/5; Akbari 89/328, 166/443; Rahim 37-38/366; BM 185.
Kahar		Carrying loads in kanvars–RCM Bal 300/167, Ayo. 193/293; CV 54/31. Carrying dolas etc.-Vp. 189/198; Sur 5-4; Ch 51/109; MM 465/410; A.K. 29/5.
Dai	Dhagar	Ch 26/90, 251/222; Sur 10-15, 16, 18; MM 310/265 mentions Bari in this group.
Mali	Bhaghban	KV Sundar 31/63; K-G I K 6/183, 23/200; Pd
	Fulhari	15/15; Sur 10-32, 40, 1075, 3109; Din 36-5; Nand 119, 336; Ch 439/327; MG 165/120, 348/189; MM 380/331, 384/334, 385-86/336, 388/338, 392/342; MMV 65, 67; A.K. 29/5; BM 47, 123. Malin sent as messenger–Ch 275/237.

Nai	Hajmana, Vratti	Ch 26.90; K-G iii VC 2/525; MG 387/202; A.K.
	Chhatisa, Napit	29/5; BB 109/43; Akbari 7/313, 160/442; BM 147,
	Nau	148. (i) Cutting the hair; (ii) Massaging–BM 147, (iii) Doing sundry works in marriages and other ceremonies–Rln T-G ii 8-18/4-5. (iv) Carrying marriage proposals–Ch 37-38/ 100, 151/165/260/228, 393/298, 397/307; A.K. 102/12.
Bari		Rln T-G ii 8/4; RCM Bal 319/177; Ch 151/ 165; MG 387/202; Pd 8/21; K-G I R 1/68; Sur 10-19; A.K. 29/5; Rahim 13-14/353; Cp 55, 57, 58, 59, 100. Sent as messengers–MM 283/240, 400/349. Holding respectable position–MM 425/372.
Khawas		K-G i R 2/61, iii VC 13/256, 21/526; BM 158, 177.

(ii) The Business Groups

Bania		Kabir 149; Pd 3/81; KRV 186-7; MMV 70, 72-74, 79, 90; KL 118/191; Akbari 76/356, 167/444;Rahim 17-18/353-54; A.K. 75/10; BM 273, 277.
	Agarwal	Ch 26/90; A.K. 75/10.
	Mahur, Mathur	
	Mahaur	A.K. 119/14.
	Dhani	DV 207/65.
	Banwara	Ch 26/90
	Sahu	DV 148/46; Kabir 99; BM 79, 213, 218.
	Banik*	DV 398/136; KV Uttar 96/162; K-G i K 50/ 126, iii VC 20/478, 17/495; BG 61/18; MMV 54, 56, 57, 71, MMR 291, 292, 299; BM 96, 282. *Also used as a socio-economic group, being a term for businessmen in general-Cf. RCM Bal 3/20, Uttar 28/544; KL 90/64; Senapati 96/39.
	Modi	SS ii 36.
Banjara	Baipari	Pd 2/59; MG 298-99/172-73; Kabir 379, 420, 490, 496; Pd 30/33, 2/94; GB 15/104; Vp 151/ 341; MG 275/164, 289/169, 298/172; MM V 50; VP 92/49, 129/67, 180/92; Rahim 25-26/ 354; BM 73, 143, 185, 256. (i) Generally traders going from place to place for business. (ii) Appears to be a socio-economic group, including traders of other castes as well–Ch 432/323; Pd 1/30.
Bajari		KV Lanka 5/68.
Dalal		Rahim 104-5/363.

Gandhi	Gandhai	Ch 26/90; Pd 15/15; BB 663/242, 676/246; Rahim 57-58/358.
Bisati		Ch 26/90.
Sahni		RCM Ayo. 272/330.
Bajaj		PR 101; RCM Uttar 28/544; Akbari 166/443; BM 281.
Sarraf		Akbari 31/423.
Mahajan	Vyohariya	Pd 13/14, 2/30; Kabir 282; KL 28/75; RCM Uttar 28/544; KR 132; MG 171/121, 328/182; VP 454/231, 849/425; Senapati 10/4, 96/39, 14/6, 24/10, 6/11; BM 110, 154, 273.
Jauhari		Kabir 184; A.K. 40/6, 111/13, 145/17, 148/17, 327/37; Akbari 99/433; Rahim 7-8/352; Senapati 28/12.
Kalar		Kabir 47, 312; Pd 3/81; RCM Uttar 99/582; A.K. 29/5;Rahim 31-32/355.
Teli		GB 42/137; Kabir 496; RCM Uttar 100/581; A.K. 29/5; Rahim 41-42/356; BM 145.
Bhadbhunja		Ch 260/228; A.K. 29/5; Senapati 15/75.
Tamboli		Rln T-G ii 6/31; K-G i R 20/80; Kabir 126; MG 387/202; Akbari 166/443.
Kachhi	Sakbanik	RCM Bal 3/20; A.K. 29/5; Rahim 35-36/355.
Marijiya		Pd 4/63, 9/93, 18/100, 21/101, 23/184, 5/295. Special type of businessmen who undertook great risks for procuring rare supplies.

(iii) The Artisans

Sunar	Soni, Svarnakar	Ch 26/90; Pr 25/101; Pd 3/81; KV Uttar 24/120; GB 6/91; K-G i R 1/68, K 16/178, 6/188, iii VC 20/475; A.K. 29/5; MG 208/139; Rahim 15-16/352; Akbari 15/396; Senapati 37/15, 44/18, 79/32; BM 73,201, 303.
Patuva		Pd 3/81; K-G i R 2/68; VP 13/463-64; A.K. 29/5; Rahim 43-44/356.
Kori	Julaha, Patbunia	Kabir 348, 391, 405, 406, 417; KV Uttar 106/169; A.K. 29/5; Rahim 98-99/362; BM 134, 205-06.
Badhai	Suthali, Khati Kathariya	DV 536/188; Vp 189/394; A.K. 29/5; MG 208/138; Rahim 122-23/365; BM 172, 196.
Lohar	Lohkar	Pd 2/286, 5/288; Rln T-G ii 5/3; Kabir 175, 177; VP 545/274; A.K. 29/5; MG 208/138; Rahim 29-30/355; Senapati 43/57.
Darji		Rln T-G ii 6/3; A.K. 29/5.
Mochi	Chamar	Kabir 496; Pd 3/200, 2/267; A.K. 29/5; Rahim 139-40/366; Akbari 63/354, 83/357; BM 144, 188, 206, 244.
Kansera	Thathera	KL 101/72; K-G iii VC 19/478; A.K. 29/5; Rahim 106-7/363.

Pakhandi		Pd 15/15.
Dhadhi		Pd 15/224; K-G i K 57/170; Nand 336; Cp 157.
Shilpi	Raj	K-G i R 1/68; A.K. 29/5.
Churihar	Manihar	K-G i R 1/68.
Bihna	Dhunia	K-G iii VC 39/480; A.K. 29/4; Rahim 96-97/362.
Bedin	Kanchani, Pature	Pd 14/46; Ch 203/197; K-G ii RC 13/255; Rahim 75-76/360, 81-83/360-61.
Chuni	Chunhara	Ch 26/90; MG 208/138.
Sisgar		A.K. 29/4.
Dhinwar		A.K. 29/5; Senapati 19/131;Cp 100.
Rangbal	Rangrez	A.K. 29/4; Rahim 19-20/354.
Sangtarash	Patharia	A.K. 29/4; MG 208/138.
Kandoi		A.K. 29/5.
Kundigar		A.K. 29/5; Rahim 94-95/362.
Kagadi		A.K. 29/5; Rahim 108-9/363.
Masikari		Rahim 110-11/363.
Kisan		A.K. 29/5.
Chitera		A.K. 29/5; MG 208/138; Rahim 11-12/353.
Thabai		MG 29/75, 208/138; Rahim 92/93/361-62.
Kudera	Unhera	MG 25/75, 26/76.
Bindhera		A.K. 29/5.
Lakhera		A.K. 29/5.
Chhappanbandh		A.K. 29/5.
Siklligar		A.K. 29/5; Rahim 53-54/357.
Hawaigar		A.K. 29/5.
Dhanva		Rahim 21-22/354.
Chhipi		Rahim 51-52/357; BM 75.
Khatik		Rahim 86-89/361; BM 203.
Kasai		Senapati 4/41; BM 196.

(iv) Miscellaneous

Kayastha	Munshi	KL 121/80, 116/190; Pd 3/81; K-G i K16/178, iii VC 30/594, 33/596; Kabir 105, 106; Akbari 76/356; Rahim 9-10/353; BM 166, 290.
Bhat	Badi, Sut Magadh Baital Charan Bansh Prasansak, Jaga, Dasaundhi	KL 226/127; Pd 20/17, 4/112, 6-7/113; K-G i R 21/62, 57/170, ii RC 17/420, 9/235, 19/240 8/254,13,255, iii VC 23/611; KV Uttar 96/162; RCM Bal 316/175. 319/177; KR 8/9; GV Bal 1/2, 2/6, PR 28/61, 34/67, 8/79, 21/120; Jm T-G ii 180/51; Nand 326; Akbari 102/431; Rahim 65-66/359; Senapati 1/1, 46/111. Acting as envoys-Senapati 53/144-45.
Bajigar	Chharhanta Chetaki Indrajali	Ch 29/93; KV Uttar 96/162; RCM Lanka MMR 285; Rahim 118-19/364; BM 111.

Vyadh	Paradh, Baheliya	Vp 208/430; Pd 15/15, 8/21, 4/27, 5/31, 2/76;
	Chairhanta Chairhari Vadhik, Aheri	Kabir 32; VP 175/90, 392/200; Ch 338/272; CV 14-15/15; MG 158/117, 178/125; Akbari 115/331; 20/422; Rahim 77-78/360; Senapati 19/131; BM 288.
Bhand		DV 63/21; K-G ii RC 34/242, 13/255; MM 535/478; BM 125.
Sut		RCM Ayo 153/274. Chariot-driver.
Od		BB 675/245.
Gadariya		MG 199/135, 233/148.
Jangam		Sur 657.

APPENDIX-C
The Tribal Castes

Ahir	Gop, Ghoshi Gwal Jadav, Gopal, Pohiyo, Dauva	(i) Quite a prominent tribal group, descended from the Abhirs of old, and renowned and celebrated due to Krishna's connection with them. (ii) Regarded by some as a branch of the old kshatriyas and the medieval rajputs. (iii) Generally engaged in animal husbandry, specially cows, and selling milk and curds. (iv) Figure very prominently in the medieval Hindi poetry, especially of the Krishna-Bhakti School. For general references–BB Vp, Ch, GB, KRV, Sur, Nand, T-G ii KV, GV, VP, KL, Pd, K-G i & iii. Akbari, Rahim, Senapati, Cp, BM. (v) Banarasidas refers to a special type of courtesan, Ahiri-505/56.
Kevat	Karia, Gundhara Nishad, Guh	BB 687/249; Ch 418/313; Pd 3/63, 4/173; KV Ayo 8/25; KV Uttar 21/117; BR T-G ii 25/18; GV Ayo 68/181; RCM Ayo 88/244, 193/293; K-G ii RC 13/280; MG 126/106; Akbari 10/320, 180/446; BM 51.
Nat	Natva	MG 210/139; Ch 29/93; KV Uttar 96/162; RCM Bal
	Nrityakari	319/177; GV Bal 225/6; Kabir 273; Jm. T-G ii 180/51; K-G i R 1/68, ii RC 3/235, 13/255; BM 262, 301. (i) A tribal occupational caste of dancers-RCM Bal 348/194, Ayo 241/315; PR 6/293, 20/306; K-G ii RC 13/255; BM 172. (ii) Giving performances–PR 24/267; Pd 15/1, 6/251; BM 28. (iii) Practising magic–RCM Uttar 104/584; Pd 15/15, 6/251; Rahim 71-74/359-60.
Jat		K-G iii VC 9/489, 18/490, 36/508.
Gujar	Badgujar	K-G iii VC 18/490, 53/497, 5/99, 105/505, 36/508. The jat and Gujar were both considered as branches of the rajputs.

Khasia		CV 18/41.
Rajput	Gaharwar	Ch 26/90; K-G i K 7/94, iii VC 3/476.
	Chauhan	Ch 26/90; PR 3/14ff; Pd 22/119; K-G iii VC 15-20.516l BM 112.
	Parnar/Panwar	PR 11/49; 1/74, 27/201, 31/236; CV 15/63, 26/111; K-G iii VC 15-20/516. .
	Rathor	PR 1/74, 16/225; BG 100/31, 134/41, 259/74; K-G iii VC 15-20/516; BM 234, 238, 282.
	Solanki	PR 13/114; BG 2/134; K-G iii VC 15-20/516.
	Pundir	PR 1/74.
	Guhil	PR 1/74.
	Badgujar	PR 1/74; 14/224, 15/225; BG 19/115; K-G iii VC 15-20/516.
	Kurambh	PR 1/74.
	Rohilla	PR 1/74.
	Jangara/ Jagara	PR 1/74; K-G iii VC 11/489, 18/490, 53/497.
	Dahima	PR 20/196.
	Chandel	PR 27/201; Pd 3/81; K-G iii VC 15-20/516.
	Bhatti	PR 27/201; BM 205-6.
	Bhagari	PR 31/204-5, 4/211.
	Jadav	PR 31/204-05, 4/211; K-G iii VC 15-20/516. Also identified with the Ahirs.
	Parihar	PR 31/204/5, 4/211; K-G iii VC 15-20/516.
	Mori	PR 31/204-5, 4/211.
	Chalukya	PR 29/235, 12/282.
	Baghel	PR 32/237; BG 12/115; K-G iii VC 15-20/516.
	Tomar/Tonwar	PR 34/238; K-G i K 12/100, iii VC 36/508, 15-20/516; BM 301.
	Kachhwaha	K-G iii VC 2/476; BG 134/45.
	Sisodiya	K-G iii VC 8/494, 15-20/516; BG 5/2, 10/4, 315/88.
	Bundela	K-G iii VC 25/495; BG 19/115.
	Shekhavat	BM 285.
	Sikarwar	K-G iii VC 36/508.
	Bhadauria	K-G iii VC 53/497, 15-20/516.
	Hada	K-G iii VC 36/508, 15/516; BG 134/41.
	Khichi	K-G iii VC 36/508.
	Gaur	BG 134/41.
	Gujar	K-G iii VC 15-20/516.
	Maru	K-G iii VC 15/20/516.
	Bais	K-G iii VC 15-20/516.
	Chandawat	BG 292/83, 19/115.
	Banafar	K-G iii VC15-20/516.
	Kanaujia	K-G iii VC 15-20/516; Ch 26/90
	Pavaiya	K-G iii VC 15-20/516.
	Kaikeya	K-G iii VC 15-20/516.
	Naishadh	K-G iii VC 15-20/516.

	Bikavat	BM 301.
	Vidavat	BM 207.
Rajput		Reference as a separate caste–KV Uttar 106/169; BM 258.
Thakur		As an equivalent of rajput. K-G iii VC 15/516.

APPENDIX–D
The Sectarian Caste

Saravag	Saravagi	Ch 26/90; Kabir 93; BM 107. The Jains ultimately came to be recognized as a particular caste, and most probably they themselves regarded them to be the same with distinct kula and gotra-A.K. 9-10/2.

APPENDIX–E
The Untouchables

Pachvanan		Ch 26/90.
Chandal	Mor	KL 110/76; VP 725/363; KRV 59/31;
Dom	Hela	Pd 9/195, 8/263,5/295; SS i 183; BM 125, 209.
Svapach		K-G ii RC 20/289, iii VC 37/480; BM 165, 238.
Pasia		K-G iii VC 19/478. The hangman.

APPENDIX–F
Outside the Pale of Society

Kol		BR T-G ii 54/21; KV Uttar 15/112, 19/115, 20/116; RCM Ayo 224/307, 250/319, 251,320, 276/331; GV Ayo 45/160.
Bhil		KV Uttar 18/115; RCM Ayo 28/216; PR 191; GB 26/119; K-G i K 6/132; BM 51, 53.
Kirat		KV Uttar 19/115, 169/213; GV Ayo 42/157, 45/160, 47/165; RCM Ayo 60/.231, 135/266.
Sabar		DV 11; KV Uttar 15/112; GV Aran 17ff/382 ff.
Dhangad		KL 86/244. A wild tribe in the Vindya and Kaimor regions (Referred to as plunderers).
Gond		DV 559.
Mima/Maina		BB 104/41; K-G iii VV 9/489, 18/490, 36/508. A wild predatory tribe of Rajasthan. General remarks: (i) Generally looked down upon RCM Ayo 194/293; DV 5. (ii) Called ban manush and banchar–CV 45/76, 47-49/76-77. Also called ban samaj–GV Ayo 40/166. (iii) Used as terms of abuse–RCM Ayo 13/209, 159/277.

3

Widows and Fallen Women : Gleanings from the Nineteenth and Early Twentieth Century Bengali Literature

Chhanda Chatterjee

Of the various changes introduced in Indian society in the wake of colonial rule the most widely debated and the most far-reaching were the reforms concerning the status of women. Although inequalities were not unheard of in the western societies, colonial sensibilities found female infanticide, child marriage, *kulin* polygamy, widow burning or the sexual exploitation of surviving widows almost verging on the barbaric. They found their ally in one section of the western educated Indians who felt a natural urge for reform under the inspiration of European Enlightenment. The strident attack of the Christian missionaries on the social anomalies of the country provoked them to an immediacy in order to be able to save the jurisdiction of the orthodox religion by purging it of some of the more obnoxious customs and to acclimatize it to the changing times. One way of achieving this purpose without seeming to stray too far from Indian traditions and allowing the reforms to become a shameless mimicry of the west, was to search for precedents and sanctions within the Indian social code, as embodied in the scriptures and religious texts. Both Rammohun and Vidyasagar had therefore to delve into the Hindu religious texts in order to authenticate norms, which had risen out of the novel needs of the day. But while *sati* could be nearly forced out of existence by a legal ban in 1829, a mere permissive legislation allowing widows to get married could not bring back widows into the mainstream of life very easily. The inhibition against widows persisted beyond the legislation of 1856 and as Sumit Sarkar has put it, 'tradition refused to be reformed'. The purpose of this paper is to trace the transformation of the initial state of shock to a gradual arousal of sympathy for the deprivation of young widows through a study of the literary works of three Bengali novelists spanning a period of more than fifty years. A beginning is made with Bankimchandra, who had not yet succeeded in getting over the orthodox society's reservations against the admission of the widow's right to sexuality and then proceed to Rabindranath Tagore and Saratchandra who had softened this rigidly towards the sexuality of widows and yet had not, as yet gone beyond a sublimation of this sexuality in virtue and self sacrifice.

Literature, when it is at its best, is often a true mirror of life. The function of literature is not exactly the same as history and it has no responsibility to portray only what has happened. And yet while spinning a satisfying tale, powerful literary works conjure up the sentiments and aspirations of a period much more successfully than is possible for a dry as just dust historian[1]. It is easier to peep into the silent changes taking place in the outlook of society concerning the treatment that women should get, the place to be accorded to them in the household and the accommodations to be made for their security and dignity from the pages of a narrative than from the collection of inanimate data from a book of history. Literature can compensate for the inarticulateness of women, their hesitation to pen their secret aspirations and their sense of shame at the possibility of being 'discovered' for aspiring after what is not to be, for cherishing what is natural to the desires of the flesh and yet labelled as sin by the moral dictates of the age-in short it can, to borrow a phrase from Dipesh Chakravarty, "narrate the private in public"[2]. The use of fictional recreations to gather women's experiences was also common in women's studies in Britain.[3] A familiarity with the evolving pattern of such 'culture specific' novels can open up new perspectives on the emotional voyage of a culture[4] from one set of ideals to something completely different.

Status of Bengali Women

In the nineteenth century people still believed that marriages were made in heaven and a girl was predestined for marriage to her spouse by divine ordination. This relationship would not even be broken by death. Therefore those who were truly devoted to their husbands would accompany the husband even in death and burn themselves in their funeral pyres *(sahogaman)*. The less virtuous would remain alive even after she was widowed and live a life of austerity *(brahmacharya)* to be united to her husband at the decay of the body.[4] Hindu scriptures like *Taitiriya Upanishad*, the *Vedas and Mahabharata* insisted on a strictly monogamous relationship for women.[5] "Families displayed", as pointed out by Malavika Karlekar, "an almost obsessive concern with the chastity of widows in order to ensure the parity of lineages"[6]. The prospect of widows developing new liaisons with a second husband struck the social conscience of nineteenth century Bengal as a profanation of all that had been held dear to their heart as pure and sacred. Of the three options offered to a widow in the scriptures-*sahagaman* (death with the dead husband), *bramhacharya* (austerity) and *punarbhaba* (remarriage), the third one was a taboo. Only low caste women could contemplate it[7]. Widow remarriage had first been proposed in Bengal long before the English could consolidate their grip over the province. In 1756 Raja Rajballabh Roy of Dacca wanted to get his widowed daughter married. He had employed a number of pundits who had spotted the sloka (hymn) in *Parashar Samhita 'Nashte, mrite, prabrajite, klibe cha patite pratau pancham apatsu narinang patiranyo bidhiyate'–i.e.*, women whose husbands have either died or taken to asceticism, or are impotent or visit prostitutes may be allowed to have another husband. However, the opposition of Maharaja Krishnachandra of Nadia did not allow the prospect to make much headway.[8] Rammohun's Atmiya Sabha had touched upon the idea but could not carry it very far.[9] The idea was revived by Derozians in July 1842 issue of the *Bengal Spectator*. The stalwarts of *Brahmo Samaj* like Ramchandra Vidyabagish and Debendranath Tagore took up the idea. The Maharaja of Nadia nearly succeeded in persuading the *pundits* but in the end the erratic behaviour of his young supporters shocked the pundits and they were forced to retreat.[10] Ishwarchandra, although not the first, was the most stubborn of a long line of reformers and it was his tenacity of purpose which saw the proposal of widow remarriage codified as a law.

Ishwar Chandra Vidyasagar

Vidyasagar, as Sumit Sarkar would have us believe, was not inspired by western models. He wanted to gain acceptance for what he thought was right by an appeal to the *shastras* and posed the *Parashar Samhita* as against the *Manu Samhita*[11]. He wanted widow marriage to redress the evils of child marriage and kulin polygamy which often resulted in the marriage of several innocent children to a mature person. This kulin brahmin often maintained a long list of his spouses living with their parents.

Visits to the in-laws' places became a sort of a profession for such a man who could earn sumptuous meals and even cash presents for spending a night with the wife. Girls had to be married young *(Gauridan)* before they reached puberty and if a kulin failed to get his daughter married to a matching family of kulins then he risked losing his ritual status. Having unmarried daughters at home beyond the permissible age might lead to social ostracism and even to exclusion from the village services of shaving and washing. Therefore girls were sometimes married as a token gesture to some absentee husband much older to them in age. Such husbands often remained a stranger in their lives because in those days of poor medical facilities he often died even before the girl had reached puberty. But even if marriage remained a vague dream for the child widow, she was made to undergo the rigours of asceticism like fasts on certain days of the lunar calendar and prohibition of all kinds of nutritious or energising food that might rouse her natural physical urges. She was thus confined at home and made to while away her youth in austerities and deprivation. "Her voluntary abdication of an earthly life is a form of *sanyas* within the household," as Tanika Sarkar has tried to demonstrate, not only providing moral and spiritual energy for the widow herself but also ensured "a reservoir of spirituality in each home and for the Hindu order as a whole."[12]

In a curiously liberal way, far in advance of his age and contrary to his Sanskrit *pundit* origins, Vidyasagar displayed a realistic awareness of the problems haunting child widows.[13] In his tract against child marriage *(Balyabibaher dosh)* he had argued for 'compassionate conjugality based on adult mutual love (*pronoy*)' as an alternative to the subjection of innocent child brides to the lusts of their much more aged husbands who were sometimes widowers and sometimes polygamous kulins. Arguments against child marriage were also informed with a compassionate recognition of the natural physical urges of a young widow or a young wife of a polygamous kulin with rare opportunities of visiting their husbands. Such a state of affairs was extremely prone to immorality and sexual exploitation of the widows by their corrupt male relatives. This often resulted in destitution, suicide, abortion and infanticide.[14] Vidyasagar could only think of a legitimate marriage as the only way for a young upper caste widow to be restored to an honorable existence. Mary Carpenter's proposal to train widows as teachers to enable them to have an independent living came as a bit too premature and Vidyasagar could not conceive of upper caste widows from conservative homes in the role of teachers. He thus continued to pay lip service to the ideas of a patriarchal domination of society. Widows according to his notions of modernity could at best seek a new master in place of a deceased one but they were still not thought to be competent to live on their own.[15] A renewed matrimony was their only hope of rehabilitation.

Bankim Chandra Chattopadhyay

The naked exposure of the sexual aspirations of the widowed female population implicit in the Widow Remarriage Act came as a gross violation of the orthodox Indian's sense of privacy. The shame and shock of the contemporary Indian at this interference of the state in their private domain was mirrored in the writings of Bankimchandra Chattopadhyay.[16] In two of his famous novels-Bishabriksha (The Poison Tree) and Krishnakanter Will, he had chosen two young widows as central characters. The progress of the narratives demonstrated through the meanderings of the various characters how the unbridled sexuality of the two widows resulted in their own destruction as well a turmoil in the lives of all those who came into contact with them. *Bishabriksha* was the story of an orphaned girl who had found shelter in a rich *zamindar* (landlord) family and who had then been married to another orphaned boy who had also been brought up in the family. The boy died soon after marriage leaving the girl a widow. The girl's beauty had earlier drawn the attention of the owner of the household the rich landlord Nagendra Datta. While the girl Kundanandini remained in the married state, Nagendra had not fully recognised his own passion for Kunda. On his first meeting with Kunda he had written in a letter to his friend "Tell me, then, at what age is a woman beautiful? ... The girl called Kunda ... is thirteen. Seeing her, I think that this is the time of beauty. The sweetness and simplicity which precedes the first transition to adolescence diminishes afterwards.... It is not that Kunda is beautiful without flaw. In comparison with others, her appearance would probably not be praised; yet it seems to me that I have never seen anyone so beautiful. It seems that there is in Kundanandini something beyond this earth, as if she is not made of flesh and blood; as if moonlight fashioned her by embodying the beauty of the flowers... If you imagine the rays of an autumn moon falling on a clear lake, you will have some idea of what she is like."[17] But when Kunda was widowed and came to live in Nagendra's household then Nagendra found it impossible to control his passion for her. The state of his mind is brought out in a letter of his wife to her sister-in-law.

If Kundanandini was as other women in his eyes, why would be so eager not look at her? Why would he be so careful not to say her name? Because of Kundanandini he feels himself to be guilty. That is why he sometimes rebukes her without reason. His anger is not at her but at himself. He rebukes himself, not her ... Sometimes absent mindedly, his eyes seek here and there–do I not understand that? Seeing, he becomes confused again and turns his eyes away; do I not understand? At meal times with food in his hand, he turns his head to hear the sound of her voice. The rice in his hand stays in his hand, he can not get it to his mouth, but he turns his head to listen-why ? Then as soon he hears Kunda's voice he starts to cram food into his mouth".[18]

The matter became serious that Nagendra's wife arranged his marriage with Kundanandini and left the house herself. Suryamukhi's departure suddenly awakened Nagendra to a realization of the sinister effects of his passion. He left home and Kunda in search of his wife Suryamukhi. When the two of them finally became reunited Kunda felt utterly lonely and left out. She had no more attraction in life and she sought peace in death.

Bankim's depiction of Kundanandini and her woes was not devoid of sympathy for the young widow. And yet he could not conceive of a young widow in the midst of a peaceful household except as a *femme fatale* wreaking havoc in the family, had the widow been tonsured, half starved, emaciated and made to look ugly in a shabby dress as prescribed by Hindu family customs then probably the household could have been saved from the evil occurrences that followed. But Suryamukhi's lenience towards the widow and bringing her to stay in the family "sowed the seeds of the poison tree" as Bankim would have it. In this he was merely reflecting the sentiments of his age which, inspite of all its sympathy for the suffering of widows could not bring itself to accept the persistence of normal sexual urges in a widow and its fulfilment in a happy union with her beloved.

The same superstition against widow marriage seemed to recur in Bankimchandra's *Krihsnakanter Will.* Rohini, the young widow of this novel was not as innocent as Kunda. Kunda had been unaware of her sexuality and made no particular effort to entice Nagendra into the net of her attraction. The unhappy incidents at Nagendra's household were not at all of her doing. She herself had been the victim of her destiny and an instance of what evil shape female sexuality might assume unless absorbed within the conjugal household or suppressed under the rigours of a life of austerity. But Rohini was representative of the unsatiated, aggressive widow seeking to burn the male in the fire of her lust. So, Bankimchandra had from the very beginning introduced Rohini as a restless soul aggressively vaunting her sexuality to trap the unaware in her net.

"Rohini was then in the full bloom of youth and overflowing with beauty like the harvest moon in autumn. She had become a widow in her early youth, but had acquired some improper habits for a widow; she wore a black bordered dhoti; bangles on her wrists and took up chewing betel leaves".[19]

The very language in this paragraph exudes Bankimchandra's disapprobation of a young widow's interests, dressing herself and attempts to look attractive. Soon the reader discovers that such emphasis on the widow's fondness for cosmetics was a mere preliminary to further expositions of her evil inclinations when she actually bargains with Haralal for marriage.

"why are you laughing"? Haralal asked.

Hearing you speak of your wife reminded me of your proposed widow marriage. Do you still intend to marry a widow?

I do, but where can I find a widow to my liking?...

You see Rohini, widow marriage is allowed by our sacred books, Rohini said, 'so they say now'.

'you can also marry again, and why shouldn't'? Rohini pulled her dhoti over here head and turned round.[20]

Rohini was so keen for marriage that she went to the length of stealing Krishnakanta's will to please Haralal. But when she understood that Haralal was not really willing to marry her then she refused to surrender the stolen will to him. While she was crying her heart out beside the lake near Krishnakanta's nephew Govindalal's garden, she met Govindalal and could quickly switch her affection to Govindalal. This fickleness in Bankim's imagination was characteristic of a widow shamelessly seeking a married life. Bankim's contempt for such greedy and fickle characters is obvious in the subsequent events of the novel.

Rohini finally attempted suicide, was rescued by Govindalal and their mutual attraction intensified and culminated in their elopement to some unknown destination. When they appear once again in the pages of the novel we find Rohini as a courtesan trying to entertain Govindalal. It seems that Bankimchandra could not think of any other denouement for such profligate people.

"As we enter the large room on the first floor we notice the pictures. Some are beautiful while others are so offensive as to be indescribable. We see a bearded Muslim music teacher, sitting on a clean soft cushion, tuning a tambura, while a young woman, sitting next to him is playing a tabla... Through the open doorway we see a young man in the next room, reading a novel and occasionally looking at the young woman to see how she is getting on with her lesson. The young man was Govindalal and the young woman was Rohini"[21]

Rohini's fickleness did not end with leaving Haralal for Govindalal. She later tried to meet another man without Govindalal's knowledge and was murdered by Govindalal when caught in the act. Thus both young widows in Bankim's narrative met death, ignominy and destruction. Bankim could see nothing more than impurity and profanation in the marriage of widows and the assertion of sexuality in a widow who had lost her husband and with him had lost the passport to happiness and a normal life. Widows were nothing more than a symbol of austerity in the household and the attempt to impose any other identity on them was unacceptable to the social conscience of the age.

The worst specimen of Bankimchandra's impatience with widows straying from the path of virtue is the character of Hira in *Bishabriksha*. Hira had been an upper caste widow eking out a living in the landlord household. Bankimchandra depicted her as greedy and crafty. But he would tolerate these minor vices in Hira till she fell for her landlord's talented and handsome but lecherous and drunkard cousin Devendra. Her infatuation was so great that in spite of being aware of Devendra's interest in Kunda. Hira surrendered to Devendra when the latter pretended to have a soft corner for Hira to make use of her services in gaining access to Kunda. It was Hira's intrigues which created a misunderstanding between Nagendra and Suryamukhi and brought about the situation in which Suryamukhi had to leave home and Kunda was forced to commit suicide. Nemesis followed fast in the shape of a cruel rejection from Devendra and the attack of a deadly madness and Hira had to end her days in suffering and ignominy.

Through all these fictional characters Bankimchandra tried to convey the apprehension of his age at the possibility of an arousal of sexuality in widows, the threat posed by their insatiable lust to happy conjugality and the unfastening of the lid to a Pandora's box of an inconceivable variety of complication arising out of the widows' aspirations for new liaisons.

Although contemporary society was peculiarly indulgent to upper caste men maintaining a roster of their many wives lest they would forget their names and addresses, for a deviant widow they would not feel psychologically vindicated without anything short of death, suicide or madness. While both Govindalal and Nagendranath could be restored to life of honour and dignity once they realised their mistakes the partners in their deviations had to fade out of existence.

The cruel fate meted out by Bankimchandra to the three widows in his novels probably represents, as Ashis Nandy had put it in connection with the previous generation's commitment to Sati and prohibition of widow marriage, "the culture's deepest fears of–and hatred towards–woman and womanhood"[22]. The Bengali pantheon, because of its local tribal slant, had always been dominated by the mother goddess or *shakti* and all women were believed to have a hidden strength or energy deriving from this *shakti*. Good women were able to protect their families and their husbands from destruction and death by an activation of this hidden force through sacrifice and piety. Death of the husbands on the other hand, represented a failure of this "ritual potency" and widows were associated with evil and revived the fear that "woman will betray, aggress, pollute or at least fail to protect" [23]

Rabindranath Tagore

The harshness and distrust typical of the 1870's when Bankimchandra was writing had probably somehow mellowed down by the time Rabindranath Tagore penned his 'Chokher Bali'. The central character in this novel is that of Binodini, a widow in her late teens, who had wrought havoc in a household where she had been brought to stay with a newly married couple, a glaring contrast to her own sad and lonely life. Initially she had pretended to train up the young wife for her new life, but gradually it turned into a proxy love affair with her husband. The poignancy of the widow's frustration has been captured in Tagore's sympathetic pen when Binodini is addressing a letter to Mahendra.[24]

There is no place for me to love or to get love in the whole world. That is why I quench my thirst for love by false play. When you had leisure, you too had joined that game. But playtime also comes to an end. Now you have been called inside the house, why do you peep into the playroom now! Now you must wipe the dust and go home. I don't have a room, I will play alone in my mind and won't call you.[25]

The young Mahendra is a contrast to this picture of deprivation and futility. He already had an indulgent mother, a loyal wife and now he was after the beautiful young widow. In his conscience there was no conflict between love for his wife and attraction for the other woman. Then Mahendra consoled himself with the thought that few women could get the love which he still could feel for Asha. Why can't Asha be happy with that! His heart was large enough to accommodate both Binodini and Asha, he became happy at the thought that without giving up either Binodini or Asha, he could carry on like a planet served by two moons.[26]

However, Tagore was aware of the dignity of women and that was why he did not allow Binodini to settle for anything cheap and mundane. When blamed by Mahendra's mother, she left the house with Mahendra. And yet she never surrendered to Mahendra. Intelligent as she was, she could distinguish between Mahendra's shallowness and the depth and rectitude of the feelings of his friend Bihari in contrast and her affections went to Bihari instead of to Mahendra. Yet she respected Bihari's deep admiration for Asha and that is why when Bihari proposed marriage to Binodini, not out of love for her, but to save Asha and Mahendra's conjugal life, Binodini refused marriage and opted for destitute Bengali women's last refuge in the pilgrimage centre at Benares.

Binodini could find a haven of peace in Benares, but not all widows were so lucky to retain their places of honour in society even after having given way to passion and strayed from the path of virtue. In *Vicharak* a short story in *Galpaguchchha*, Tagore had shown how a widowed girl had left home for the boy she loved and how she was deserted by that boy after the initial phase of enjoyment was over and how she had been left no other option but to earn her living through prostitution. Years later she became involved in a murder case in the brothel and the judge was the same person who had seduced her from home. Tagore perhaps wanted this story to underline the cruel irony of fate by which men who were responsible for women's calamities were allowed to sit in judgement on those women. Once a girl had committed a mistake she was doomed forever. But when the same aberrations were committed by men, society was indulgent enough to condemn their offence and elevate them even to the honoured position of a High Court Judge. Tagore's sympathetic pen had deftly captured all the confusion of a young widow at her ignorance of the ways of the world and her subsequent disillusionment.

"The forest clad greenery of the shores appear to be a beautiful painting in a dream from the depth of the sea, but they look different when the shores are actually approached. As Hemshoshi had been distanced from family life through the barriers of widowhood, the distance made the world appear like a mysterious garden of pleasure on the far away shores. She did not know that the mechanism of this world is very complicated and harsh and mixed with joys and sorrows, weal and woes and beset with doubts, problems, despairs and regrets. She used to think that life was easy like a free flowering, crystal clear waterfall; all the ways of the beautiful world were straight and wide, pleasure was waiting outside her window and she alone had her soft, little heart palpitating with insatiable desire. Mohit's illuminated room overflowing with its songs, dances and other kinds of enjoyments used to draw Hemshoshi with false visions of a heaven as the fire tempts the insect with images of a star world. She did not know that beyond the window in the mansion in front of her own there was a terrible fatigue, dirtiness, frightful hunger and morbid burning. The widow could not detect from afar that a heartless cruelty played with a crude grin within that sleepless illumination of the night."

Sarat Chandra Chattopadhyay

Prostitutes are present in all societies and the way women are forced to sell their bodies due to poverty might arouse compassion everywhere. In Contemporary Europe the weak legal status of women, their lack of rights and their weak constitutional position might have been responsible for frequent persecution of poor, working class women even when sometimes they had nothing to do with prostitution.[27] But the way women of good family background were often seduced away from home and then deserted or actually sold to some brothel owner-was something unique in Indian society. The story of Hemashashi in Vicharak was the writer's imagination. But such imagination was very close to reality as found in the diary of a prostitute.[28] The life of prostitutes is reprehensible. But how does she became repugnant and blemished? She did not became blemished from her mother's womb? You have to think who spilt this life for the first time ? Many suffer eternal hell and get the blemish by trusting men and getting deceived. Who are those men? Are not some of them worshipped and honoured in society and sometimes those deceitful men became the guardian of public morals for crushing these distressed women at every step.[29]

Prostitutes were elevated to heroines in many of Sarat Chandra Chattopadhyay's novels. Sarat Chandra had a genuine affection for women and he therefore always found some inward goodness in women even if they sometimes appeared to be wicked. In *Devdas* Sarat Chandra has spoken of Chandramukhi, the prostitute:[30] "Oh ! The epitome of tolerance! You are an example of how much a woman can tolerate-harassment, rebuke, insult, torture and disturbance." [31]

In Shrikanta, Sarat Chandra made Rajlakshmi his heroine. But this Rajlakshmi had became Peary, the dancer, by the time the story unwinds. Behind each Peary there was a sweet and innocent Rajlakshmi who had been driven to this misfortune by a wicked turn of events. Rajlakshmi's story reveals how child marriage, Kulinism and the dowry system were driving many child widows to prostitution– "Piari said, 'ghost indeed! Those who die and even then do not die those are called ghosts, this is what you want to say'. After a brief pause she again started saying, 'in a sense it is true that I have died. But whether it is true or false, I have not spread the news of my death myself. My mother had done it through my maternal uncle... My maternal uncle was very worried that the nieces were not able to get married. Accidentally it came to his knowledge that the Brahmin cook of Birinchi Dutta was the son of a person of kulin heritage. Mr. Dutta had brought this person of kulin origins when he had been transferred from Bankura. My maternal uncle approached Birinchi Dutta with his entreaties–he must do something to help a Brahmin to maintain his caste status. Until then people knew that the Brahmin cook of Dutta family was a simple and good natured person. But at the hour of need it was found that the cook was not lacking in experience in the ways of the world. When offered rupees fifty one as dowry he retorted with a vehement nod-you can not get it cheap sir, you might as well see for yourself in the marriage market. For fifty one bucks you cannot even get a good pair of goats and you are looking for a son-in-law! Give me one hundred and one, I will only once sit as a groom with one girl and then with the other and make some ritual offerings of flower to complete the marriage rites. You will get rid of both nieces at once. Whatever, if you have to pay a hundred bucks, won't you give me the money to buy a pair of bullocks? His arguments were not unreasonable yet after prolonged haggling the amount was lowered to rupees seventy and both Rajlakshmi and Suralaskshmi got married on the same night. Two days later the son-in-law, a kulin for two generations, collected his seventy rupees in cash and left for Bankura. No one had seen him ever since. After one and a half years Suralakshmi died of fever and an enlarged spleen and after year and a half Rajlakshmi died in this Benares and attained salvation. This in brief is the history of Piari, the courtesan."[32]

The most popular of Sarat Chandra's novels based on widows was *Charitraheen*. Here Sarat Chandra has portrayed the heroine Savitri with all his sympathy and respect for widows. Savitri was the personification of an ideal dignified Hindu widow observing all the austerities laid down in Hindu rituals for widows and eking out her living through the sweat of her own brow in a mess. There is a faint suggestion of her having been betrayed by some Bhuban Mukhopadhyay and being driven to destitution in spite of her high caste. But even then she did not stray from the path of virtue and sold her labour rather than her body to keep body and soul together. He had met the wayward and emotional Satish in a workingmen's mess in Calcutta and had developed a deep attachment for him. She had closely guarded Satish from the various evil temptations of city life by playing on Satish's emotional dependence on her and yet she withdrew at the right moment for Sarojini to step in. Selfless as she was, she did not desire any further involvement with Satish which might embroil him into controversy. Like the guardian angel of his life, she appeared in moments of distress and disappeared when the need was gone.

But not all could be as self-effacing as Savitri. Sarat Chandra could also feel the retaliatory urges of Kironomayee who had been widowed after a loveless marriage with her husband and wanted to worship the honest dutiful and compassionate Upendranath. But when Upendranath distrusted her sisterly affection for Divakar whom Upendranath had left at Kironmoyee's place to study in Calcutta, Kironmoyee wanted to pay him back in his own coin by eloping with Divakar to Burma. But then repentance soon followed and Kironmoyee brought back Divakar from Burma guarding him like a sister and herself became a reformed soul ready to be bundled off to Benaras to spend her life in austerity like a chaste widow.

These meanderings through the nineteenth to the early twentieth century Bengali emotional upheavals reveal the slow journey of the middle class Bengali mentality from regarding the Bengali widow as an evil force, who having failed in her protective "ritual potency", as Ashis Nandy has suggested, is out to destroy happy conjugality and the peace of orthodox Hindu households-to a destitute and deprived person at the fringe of society deserving care and consideration. Bankim Chandra Chattopadhyay was unable to come to terms with the arousal of sexuality in widows, which according to his analysis, might pose a serious threat to all civilised norms of society without benefiting the widow in the least. After the lapse of a generation, with Tagore, the Bengali mind had woken up to the fact that widows too were human beings with all the physical and emotional needs to live a normal life. Tagore saw no reason to censure a widow's desire to love like Bankim Chandra and he know that this problem of deprived widows lurking on the fringes of happy conjugality could not simply be wished away. If the happiness of the household was to be ensured then there must be some way of seeking a fulfilment for the lingering emptiness of the widows' lives. While Peary Chand Mitra and Vidyasagar had touched upon the subjects of infanticide and abortion as a cruel upshot of forced widow asceticism, Tagore and Sarat Chandra showed an awareness of the pathetic fate awaiting deviant widows outside the limits of decent society at the brothel. It was through Sarat Chandra's pen that society was brought to think of the prostitute as the girl next door, a person lost to decent society through the deception of some of its erring men folk.

Historians have noticed a waning in the nineteenth century spate of social reform with the onset of the awakening of nationalism and the beginning of the freedom struggle in the twentieth century. Till the first partition of Bengal in 1905 Bengali intellectuals had been reconciled to a life of coexistence with British rule in India. The moderate policy of prayer and petition had received its first jolt in the Bengal Tenancy Act of 1859 tightened in the second Tenancy Act of 1885. It slowly undermined the Bengali renter's power to squeeze the surplus resulting from increasing cash crops cultivation from out of the cultivators' hands. This probably awakened the Bengali intellectuals from their complacency with political and economic matters. While in the earlier generations, they had been trying to answer missionary criticism of their society by purging it of some of its evil practices and trying to link up their household to the global imperial model of modernization. In the later phase we find that they displayed an increasingly orthodoxy about their traditional social modes. The questions of improvement in the status of women later became a subject for economists following the impulses and pressures on society resulting out of the development and distresses in the economy.

References

1. Joyce Moss and George Wilson, *Literature and its Times*, 4 Vols, U.S.A, 1997.

2. Dipesh Chakrovarty, 'The Difference-Deferral of a Colonial Modernity: Public Debates on Domesticity in British India' in David Arnold and David Hardiman, *Subaltern Studies*, VIII, pp. 50-88.
3. Judy Giles, *Women Identity and Private Life in Britain*, 1900-50, Macmillan, 1995, p. 9.
4. Rajat Kanta Ray, *Exploring Emotional History Gender*, Mentality and Literature in the Indian Awakening, O.U.P, 2001, p. 7
5. Peary Chand Mitra, 'Marriage of Hindu Widows' in Alok Ray (ed), *Society in Dilemma* Nineteenth Century India, Riddhi, Calcutta, 1979, pp. 50-70.
6. Malavika Karlekar, *The Voices Within*, p. 38
7. Peary Chand Mitra, *Society in Dilemma*, pp. 50-70.
8. Ashok Sen, *Vidyasagar and His Elusive Milestones*, Riddhi, 1977.
9. Amales Tripathi, *Vidyasagar: The Traditional Modernizer*, Longman, 1974, p. 58.
10. Tripathi, *op. cit.*, p. 59.
11. Sumit Sarkar, 'Vidyasagar and Brahmanical Society', *'Writing Social History'* OUP, 1998, pp. 216–281
12. Tanika Sarkar, 'Hindu Wife, Hindu Nation : Domesticity and Nationalism in Nineteenth Century Bengal' in *Hindu Wife, Hindu Natiion : Community, Religion and Cultural Nationalism*, Permanent Black, 2001, p. 42.
13. S. Sarkar, 'Vidyasagar and Brahmonical Society' *op. cit.*
14. pp. 50-70 Peary Chand Mitra, 'Marriage of Hindu Widows' and Ashok Sen, *Vidyasagar and His Elusive Milestones.*
15. pp. 216-281 S. Sarkar, Vidyasagar and Brahmanical Society.
16. The idea of examining the evolution of the Bengali literary mind since Bankimchandra down to Tagore and Saratchandra concerning the problem of widow remarriage came to my mind while leafing through the pages of Amitrasudan Bahttacharya's 'Bankimchandrer Bangla Sahitya Chinta' in his Bankim Bidya (Dey's July 1986) where Bhattacharya has drawn attention to Bankim's aversion to the idea of Vidyasagar's project for widow remarriage in the dialogue of Suryamukhi, a character of his novel Bishabriksha as well as in some other of his tracts.

17. Bankim Chandra Chatterje, *The Poison Tree*, Three Novels, Translated by Marian Maddern and S.N. Mukherjee, Penguin Books, 1996.
18. *Ibid.*
19. *Ibid.*
20. *Ibid.*
21. *Ibid.*
22. Ashis Nandy, 'Sati : A Nineteenth Century Tell of Woman, Violence and Protest' in *At the Edge of Psychology : Essays in Politics and Culture*, O.U.P; 1980, pp. 1-31.
23. Ashis Nandy, 'woman versus womanliness in India' in *Ibid.*, pp. 32-43.
24. Rabindra Rachanabali, Vol.-2, Visva-Bharati, 1986.
25. Translation mine.
26. Translation mine.
27. Jill Harsin, *Policing Prostitution in Nineteenth Century Paris*, Princeton, 1985.
28. Sumanta Bandyopadhyay, *Asruta Kanthaswar*, *Subarnarekha*, 2002, p. 145 Bandyopadhyay had quoted from Binodini Dasi 'Amar Katha O Ananya Rachana.
29. Translation mine.
30. Sarat Chandra Chattopadhyay, Devdas in *Sulabh Sarat Samagra*, Ananda Publishers, 1989.
31. Translation mine.
32. *Sulabh Sarat Samagra*, *op. cit.*

4

Emergence of Seditious Literature and its Social Impact in the French Colony of Pondicherry (1908-1915)

Ajit Neogy

At the beginning of the Twentieth Century Pondicherry had been passing through a period of political turbulence and it was twofold in character. The first one was centered around the election of a Deputy to the French National Assembly in Paris and the other one had emerged out of a situation created by the anti-British group in Pondicherry by way of dissemination of seditious literature and pamphlets received from foreign countries in British Indian territories. The election of the Deputy in Pondicherry could be traced back as early as to the establishment of the Third Republic in France under a decree dated 1st February 1871 wherein we find the male population of the French possessions in India had been conferred with the right to elect a Deputy to the National Assembly in Paris. According to French records, since 1875 the inhabitants of the French colonies had been participating in the election of the Deputy, but unfortunately the election to the Deputy in French India, more particularly in Pondicherry had never passed off peacefully. It was invariably attended by large scale violence, rioting, intimidation, false voting and booth capturing on the day of election. This violence had also continued for some more time and during the subsequent election in 1906 it had very much wide spread. Further, the situation had reached its climax during April-May 1910 in the wake of the election, in which both the *Pierrists* and the *Lemairists* had participated. This election had created so much panic that the people had to keep their "doors closed".[1] Beating, breaking of heads and cutting of hands were common sights. Thus, while Pondicherry, the capital of French India, was passing through this tumult, it also had become a big headache to the British Indian authorities for the other reason stated above.

Pondicherry: An Asylum of Anti-British Groups

During the first decade of the Twentieth Century, Pondicherry, in the opinion of the Criminal Intelligence Department of the Government of India, was a place of the anti-British activities and functioned as a centre for the distribution of seditious literature from outside India.[2] The main object of the anti-British party was the production and dissemination in British India of inflammatory literature. Revolutionary parties abroad had attempted to utilise this French port as a fairly safe and reliable means of introducing seditious pamphlets into British India in order to assist the anarchical parties and inspire the people through them. The vigilance of the customs officials in British ports had rendered such attempts very unsafe, while there was reason to believe that Pondicherry, by the nature of its situation and the presence of a friendly and sympathetic party there, could serve as a launching pad. They believed that production and dissemination of seditious literature and pamphlets could be done in 'Pondicherry without fear of prosecution'.

Pondicherry had also attained notoriety for offering a safe retreat to those political and criminal offenders who had made British India too hot for themselves by their sayings, doings and writings, and this led the Director of Criminal Intelligence Branch to observe : 'Pondicherry is becoming an Altatia to which political and criminal offenders in trouble resort....'. The Director of Criminal Intelligence of the Government of India reported that they did not have any reliable definite information that arms were being smuggled into Pondicherry by the revolutionary parties abroad with a view to their introduction in French India. But the D.I.G. Madras said in December 1908 that he did not rule out the probability of guns and revolvers being imported occasionally into Pondicherry in vessels coming from Singapore, sometimes in passengers' luggage and sometimes by the crew of the vessels, but there was no evidence of any large scale importation of arms in Pondicherry.[3] The Bengal Government had a different reading of the situation and it believed that it was in Pondicherry that Vanchi Aiyar had received lessons in revolver shooting and acquired there the Belgian revolver with which Ashe, the Collector of Tirunelveli district, was assassinated.[4]

Growth of Various Printing Press and Publications

The agency for this anti-British activities was taken by the "India Office" group which had its office at 58, *Rue de Mission Etrangeres*, Pondicherry, and it was this India Office group which was receiving literature from Paris and New York in packets marked "By French Steamer".[5] The anti-British party was headed by M.M. Srinivasa Aiyengar, the registered editor of the *India* (Madras). The tone of the *India* had all along been violently anti-British and it had spread so much poison and disaffection that the Madras Government had to proscribe it under Section 12 (1) of the Indian Press Act and its editor was arrested in July 1908 for sedition and subsequently sentenced to a long term of imprisonment. The Madras Government had been keeping a vigilant watch on the activities of other staff of the paper. These included Subramania Bharati, S. Srinivasa Achari, M.P. Tirumala Acharya and S. Nagaswami Aiyar etc., who found Madras unsafe for them, and considering the French territory a safer refuge, transferred the whole of the press plant to Pondicherry and set it up there. In the middle of September they had applied to the French authorities of Pondicherry for permission to start the paper *"India"*. This was refused by the French authorities when their antecedents were known, but subsequently the paper was registered in the name of one Lakshmi Narayan Aiyar, a French subject, and it made its appearance on 10th October, 1908.[6] M.P. Tirumala Acharya, who was then in Paris and for whose arrest a warrant had been issued in connection with the *India*, transferred his ownership in November 1908 to Srinivasachari.[7] These people who shifted to Pondicherry after the Madras Government had cracked down on the *India* actually formed a nucleus known as the Indian Office group.

The *"India"* which continued to be printed and published in Pondicherry had an extensive circulation in the port town as well as in British India. In May 1909 it had a circulation of 1600 and in October of the same year it rose to 1830. With the increase of circulation and popularity as well, there took place a considerable addition to the staff employed. Beside *India*, there were other papers which had indulged bitterly in anti-British propaganda. They were:

1. The *Vijaya*, a Tamil daily printed in the same building and press as the *India*.
2. The *Bala Bharati*, an English monthly journal edited by Subramania Bharati.
3. The *Karma Yogi*, a Tamil monthly.
4. The *Suryodayam* (or L'Aurore), a Tamil weekly, which was started in April 1908, but later proscribed under Section 12 (1) of the Indian Press Act.

5. The *Dharmam*, a Tamil paper, edited by Nagaswami of Ettyapuram (Tirunelveli district), published irregularly.

But the *"India"* could not maintain its circulation and popularity for long and according to Intelligence Department Report, it ceased to appear from 30th April, 1910. Internal dissensions among the staff were rife and in June 1909 Subramania Bharati severed his connection with the India Office group and threw in his lot with the *Suryodayam*. In October of that year, however, he again joined the *India* as editor of the *Vijaya*.

In the opinion of the Intelligence Department based on documentary evidence, the India Office group was in touch with the revolutionary parties in London, Paris and New York and for reasons stated above they used Pondicherry as a safe centre for disseminating seditious literature in British India. In fact, Pondicherry functioned as a centre of seditious literature and pamphlets from outside had caused considerable alarm to the British Indian authorities. Between March 1910 and February 1911 packets of seditious literature and prohibited periodicals received in Pondicherry included 456 copies of *Bande Mataram*,[8] 162 copies of *Talvar*, 124 copies of *Gaelic American*,[9] 109 copies of the *Indian Sociologist*, 70 copies of the *Liberator* and 47 copies of *Free Hindustan* besides many seditious leaflets. Apart from newspapers Pondicherry was also known to have received 417 copies of Savarkar's book on *The Indian War of Independence of 1857*, 100 copies of the *Social Conquest of the Hindu Race* by Har Dayal and 100 copies of *Pagans and Christians or the Black Spot in the East* by W.N. Strickland, the importation of which publication had been prohibited under section 19 of Sea Customs Act. At first these seditious papers and books were only locally distributed to a small extent-a large number was kept in stock by Nagaswamy in the office of *Dharmam* newspaper, but later copies of *Bande Mataram*, *Talvar* and *Free Hindustan* were sent by post from Pondicherry to other parts of India.[10]

The object of all this literature was primarily to make them available to anti-British militant group or groups for the subversion of the British administration in India. It also aimed at challenging French rule in India which was no less odious to the India Office group than the British authorities. This is evident from a Tamil leaflet addressed to the citizens of French India[11] which was pasted in different places of Pondicherry and distributed to the people after the violent election of the Deputy during April-May referred to above. The translated version of the leaflet runs as follows:

"It is a known fact that our success in the recent election of the Deputy is due to our *"Swadeshis"* of British India. Therefore, we should gain an upper-hand over the French European party in French India and try to root them out as soon as possible just as our brethren in British India are working with a desire to see that the British do not govern them.... Truly, we should have been defeated by these Whites, had it not been for the help we received from people from Palayamcottah, Trichinopoly, Madura and Tinnevelly who worked for our cause with about 3, 000 at Karikal, 1000 at Odaya Narakkarai village and 1000 at Vamba Keerapalayam. All these outsiders being the real sons of our *Bharat Matha* worked and helped us without caring for their lives in the least and won success for us. We should be grateful to them for ever.... We should work with them and drive away the Whites of this place also".

It is difficult to ascertain how far the anti-British party in Pondicherry was influenced by the *Swadeshi* movement of Bengal. *Swadeshis* did not preach sedition. Probably being far away from Bengal, they could not distinguish one from the other and wrongly identified sedition with *Swadeshi*. But still the Englishman wrote, "Since the outbreak of sedition in Bengal the defeated party in French India have openly professed the most advanced views of the Bengal extremists, and Pondicherry is now influenced from Chandernagore".[12]

The French colony of Chandernagore, between 1907 and 1909, was passing through a period of political excitement. Young men of the town under the leadership of Charu Chandra Roy had been actively working for undermining the French authorities there. The situation in Chandernagore had taken a very unpleasant shape and attempts were made on the life of Tardival, the French Mayor of the town and to derail the train of Lieutenant Governor (Sir Andrew Fraser) as he was proceeding to Ranchi.[13] An active secret society existed in Chandernagore at that time, and on 24th April, 1909 the Bengal Government wrote to the Government of India that Chandernagore was a source of greater trouble, actual and potential, to the British authorities.[14]

Pondicherry: A Meeting Place of Several Leaders

Between 1907 and 1910 some prominent nationalist leaders had taken refuge in Pondicherry and the most important among them were Aurobindo Ghosh, who had to flee from Chandernagore in order to escape an arrest of warrant, and Subramania Bharati. V.V.S. Aiyar, who was wanted in the Ashe murder case was also staying in Pondicherry. Further, Paingala Lakshmi Narayan Rao of Bezwada (Presently Vijayawada) had also undertaken shelter at Pondicherry who was wanted by the British Government for writing some articles published in a Telugu paper called *Swaraj*. Subramania Madaswami Pillai was also believed to have taken shelter in the same town who belonged to the group of men responsible for the murder of Ashe. Another rabid extremist who had taken shelter in Pondicherry too was Nagaswami Aiyar who had close contacts with Aurobindo Ghosh.

In early 1910, Aurobindo Ghosh had arrived in Pondicherry and men like V.V.S. Aiyar and Subramania Bharati and others paid him frequent visits. His presence in Pondicherry and his contact with these persons gave rise to many wild speculations in the British official circles. Some were of the opinion that the anti-British forces in Pondicherry were drawing inspiration from him and he was connected with the India Office group. Even Minto believed that Aurobindo during his stay in Pondicherry had developed some 'undesirable French connection' and he was eager to go to France in order to assist Swamiji Krishna Verma in his plan of assassination[15] and a member of Hardinge's Executive Council thought that the anarchist movement in Pondicherry had sprung up 'very probably from the recent advent to Pondicherry of Aurobindo Ghosh'.[16] At this time Aurobindo Ghosh tried to dispel their wrong impressions and he wrote in *The Hindu*, "I left British India in order to pursue my practice of Yoga undisturbed either by my old political connections or by harassment of me which seemed to have become a necessity of life to some police officials".[17] He also wrote that he was 'in retirement' and 'see none but a few local friends and the few gentlemen of position who cared to see me when they come to Pondicherry'. But in spite of this, in the opinion of the Intelligence Branch of the Government of India, V.V.S. Aiyar, Subramania Bharati against whom a warrant was out for complicity in the murder of Ashe, and few other revolutionaries met him frequently even in 1912. It is difficult to explain the reasons which impelled them to meet Aurobindo. But there was no doubt that the presence of the nationalist exiles in Pondicherry helped to organise an anti-British party there.

Banning Seditious Literature

The activity of the India Office group and the network of its contacts in and outside the country considerably unnerved the Government of India. The continued activity of this gang in Pondicherry is as much a menace to the French as to the British Government. It would be to the advantage of the French Government to break up this organisation by seizing and destroying the seditious literature stored in the '*Dharmam*' office and by preventing the further importation of this class of literature through the French Post Office at Pondicherry.[18] However, the Government of India could not remain blind to the fact that the little parcels of French territory scattered through the Empire threaten to become breeding ground of discontent, if not of overt sedition. And sensing that such seditious activities should not be allowed to continue in the French headquarters, Hardinge wrote to Alfred Martineau, the Governor of French Settlements in India, for his co-operation 'to break up this dangerous organisation'. He further added, "I am sure that if you could see your way to seizing and destroying any seditious literature now stored in *Dharmam* office, and prevent the further importation of this class of literature through your post office, a valuable step would have been taken in this direction".[19]

The Pondicherry authorities were not unaware of the circulation of seditious literature to other parts of the British Indian Empire through this port-town and between October 1910 and February 1911 they had, on their own, seized a large number of objectionable literature. The operation for the seizure of such seditious literature intensified after Hardinge had written to the Pondicherry Governor, and on 1st October 1914 the latter wrote to the British Minister of Colonies assuring him that "my active desire to co-operate in our common task by taking all necessary measures to prevent the political refugees from abusing the hospitality which they received in our territory, and I immediately ordered the Commandant of Police to depute an European officer to assist at the opening of mail bags at the French post office, to take note very discreetly of all communications from outside addressed to the refugees in question or to their friends, and to take back all newspapers published in foreign languages".[20] Actually a thorough examination of foreign papers was made in concert with deputed British officers before their entry into the French territory of Pondicherry. On 29th October 1915 the French Governor again wrote to the British Minister of Colonies that the French Police had intercepted a packet of newspapers from San Francisco addressed to Swaminatha Mudaliar and Chinnaraja Mudaliar, sons of retired Police Inspector in British India, then residing in Pondicherry.[21]

To conclude it may be said that Indian literature with the establishment of the British and French rule in India (then known to have classified broadly into sacred and secular) came to be newly called as seditious and what was seditious to Europeans was not so in the case of the Indians. While the above said measures had the effect of largely restricting the ingress of seditious literature and newspapers into Pondicherry, the local papers which had once preached and propagated sedition against the European powers in India either discontinued or were in a low profile. Already the *India* and the *Suryodayam* had sunk into a moribund condition-rather they were on the verge of extinction. This also led to the break-up of the India Office group. There were other factors too. Aurobindo was on his way to embracing the life of a recluse and some of the suspects in the Ashe murder case were arrested. Meanwhile the outbreak of First World War brought England and France closer together and as a member of the Entente powers the French authorities in Pondicherry extended their co-operation in foiling the Germans and their Indian revolutionaries to carry on propaganda campaign by the circulation of the *Ghadr* in Pondicherry and Madagascar.

References

1. *Amrita Bazar Patrika*, 30th April, 1910.
2. National Archives of India, (hereafter NAI) New Delhi, *Home Political (Deposit)*, 12th March, 1911, No. 12.
3. *Ibid.*, Note prepared by the Director of Criminal Intelligence Department.
4. NAI, *Foreign and Political, Confidential B (General)*, 1914, No. 2.
5. NAI, *Home Political (Deposit)*, 12th March, 1911, No. 12.
6. *Ibid.*
7. *Ibid.*
8. The usual of seditious literature, *Bande Mataram* and the *Indian Sociologist* etc., was imported partly from Europe and partly from America through the agency of George Freeman of the Gaelic American in New York.
9. *Ibid.*
10. NAI, *Home Political (Deposit)*, 12th March, 1911, No. 12.
11. *Ibid.*, Circulated around 5th June, 1905.
12. *The Englishman*, 16th May, 1910.
13. NAI, *Home Political* (A), May 1908, Nos. 112-150.
14. NAI, *Home Judicial* (B), August 1910, No. 154.
15. *Minto Papers*, 26th May, 1910.
16. NAI, *Foreign General (Confidential A)*, 1910, Nos. 31-41, Office Note by A. Earle, 20th June, 1910.
17. *Amrita Bazar Patrika*, 25th July, 1911.
18. NAI, *Home Political (Deposit)*, 12th March, 1911, No. 12, Hardinge's letter dated 17th March, 1911.
19. *Ibid.*
20. NAI, *Home Political (Deposit)*, January 1915, No. 45, French Governor's letter dated 1st October, 1914.
21. *Ibid.*

PART-II

FROM EUROPE TO INDIA: THE SPREAD OF IDEAS AND KNOWLEDGE IN LANGUAGE, LINGUISTICS AND LITERATURE

5

Portuguese in Bengal : A Literary and Linguistic Interaction

Sovon Sanyal

Portuguese travellers and chroniclers like Antonio Galvão, João de Barros, Tomé Pires and Duarte de Barbosa since early sixteenth century have mentioned Bengal as *Os Reynos de Bengala* (the Kingdom of Bengal) or *A cidade de Bengala* (the city of Bengal) in their writings.[1] Affonso de Albuquerque, the second Portuguese Viceroy of India was the one to realise the good prospects of trade and commerce of Bengal and Camões, described her in his epic Os Lusíadas:

> "Águas do Gange, e a terra de Bengala
> Fertile de sorte que não lhe iguala."[2]

Scholars have pointed out that the official presence of Portugal was minimum in the Bay of Bengal during the Sixteenth century and the private traders dominated the maritime trade here.[3] The last quarter of the sixteenth century witnessed tremendous growth of the various Portuguese settlements of private traders, deserters from different garrisons and adventurers along the Bengal coast. Important among these settlements were Satgão (Saptogram), Bandel of Hugli (*Porto Pequeno*), Dianga, Sripur, Loricul and Chatigão, (*Porto Grande*). António Viera a contemporary of this period has mentioned that there soon had arrived at these centres Portuguese missionaries to spread the message of Jesus Christ. In the first instance, there was a small number of Augustinian Friars, the then largest religious order of the missionaries of Goa. Joseph Sicardo in his work *"Christianidad del Japon y dilatada perscucion que padecio"* published in 1698 from Madrid has referred to the names of some more centres of missionary work in Bengal where the Portuguese missionaries had done commendable service in the second half of the seventeenth century. At this time there has been interaction between both the two cultures of Bengal and Portugal. Therefore in this paper an attempt is made to survey the linguistic reality that emerged through the contact of the Bengali and the Portuguese. Emphasis is laid here on some factual data regarding the books written and printed by the Portuguese missionaries. The study is chiefly based on the manuscripts in Portuguese and Spanish besides published works in English and Bengali.

In the history of Bengali literature, Portuguese phase of the missionary literature needs to be adequately treated as a subject of research. Modern scholars of Bengali, until very recently, had no access to the original works, or to the information about them. Khondkar Ahamed, a renowned scholar of Bangladesh had made an interesting study on the Portuguese contribution to Bengali prose, grammar and lexicography.[4] This pains-taking work has also dealt with the various aspects of the texts composed by the Portuguese missionaries.

Language being the most powerful instrument for creation, destruction and modification of the society, it is at first necessary to survey the exact socio-linguistic role that the Portuguese language had played, since its early contacts with Bengal. It is indeed, a difficult task in the absence of sufficient documentation on the Portuguese presence in Bengal. We know for certain that in language contact, how much one language could influence the other naturally depends on the social status of the language and its speakers. Further we also find that other factors like the power relationship with different language communities and language domain which play a key role.

On the basis of the available information found in the different travel accounts and official documents, we shall trace out the social conditions of the Portuguese in Bengal and their language during the seventeenth, eighteenth and the nineteenth centuries. The first group consists of Portuguese pirates, runaway soldiers, outlaws, *degredados* who lived in lower Bengal. One of the earliest recorded visitors of this region was John Van Linschoten (1583-1589) who described them as "savage and untamed horses" in his work. To the natives of Bengal, these dauntless settlers were known as "harmad" (word originating from "armada" fleet used for attacking sea pirates to control raiding the coastal region (word deriving from *bombardeiro* meaning bombarding). This group of Portuguese settlers and their descendants were also known as *galinhas do mar* (Hens of the Sea). It was a group considerably big in number, and was hardly subjected to any local authority. This large group of Portuguese though mostly were illiterate had created significant linguistic and cultural miscegenation, mainly in the coastal areas. They were condemned for their *unportuguese* way of living.

The missionaries from Portugal who were doing pastoral work in the Eastern Bengal formed the second group of Portuguese speakers. The number of these Augustinian Friars never increased to more than thirty at no point of time until the beginning of the nineteenth century. The Jesuits were much fewer in Bengal. According to Joseph Sicardo, the Christian missionaries commenced their ecclesiastical works in 1599 and founded a Church probably in Bandel.

The third group consists of the *mestiços* and the converts who lived at various settlements with their Portuguese co-religionists. These settlements had stretched from the Chittagong Hill to coastal Orissa. Churches were established to offer strictly spiritual and social protection to the inhabitants there. They were also not in large number. These churches were not only served as the source of spiritual learning but also acted as centres of cultural and linguistic miscegenation.

Merchants and traders of different communities began to use Portuguese for their commercial transactions. It would be logical to think that these merchants therefore introduced many Portuguese terms to the interior parts of Bengal and Tripura. The fragmentary pieces of information that are available from different travel accounts and documents of the sixteenth, seventeenth and the eighteenth centuries, provide us some suggestive glimpses of the life of the Portuguese in Bengal. In different islands and coastal villages of the lower Bengal region, they had maintained very low level of culture and profession for their livelihood. In Terry's *Voyage to East India*, 1655, we find an interesting reference to these Portuguese settlers. "The truth is that the Portugals, especially those which are born in those Indian colonys most of them a mixed seed begotten upon those natives are a very low poor-spirited people, called therefore *Galiinas del Mar*, the Hens of the Sea. These Portuguese were known to the locals as "*methe firingue*".

Some of the Portuguese settlements in Bengal were without churches and the religious life of these Portuguese had also not been well defined. Portuguese who lived in Bandel, Hugli, Dacca, Sripur, Loricaul and Chottogram had a higher level of culture and occupied respectable professions. Thomas Bowrey who visited the region is ungrudging in his appreciation of good features of these Portuguese of Hugli. He mentions that "A great Multitude of Portugals inhabit the Kingdom of Bengala, Especially in Hugly... They have a very large towne… They are for the most part very poore, but are much to be commended for their industrie, in acquireing a livelyhood by honest means, much more commendable and honourable for the Christians to begge in a heathen country. They knitt stockins of silke and cotton; they bake bread for the English and Dutch Factories and particular dwellinge houses, and for their ships and vessels; they make many sorts of sweetmeats... Many of the men use the Sea in English or Moors ships and vessels, soe that these people live very happily, better then in most places in Asia."[5]

Some Portuguese (perhaps their descendents) were known as filhos de Lisboa (sons of Lisbon) since they proved their loyalty to their country. A section of the population in Bandel was certainly bilingual, that is, they used to speak Portuguese and Bengali. Perhaps it would not be an exaggeration to say as trilingual since Hindustani was widely spoken then for their normal social interactions.[6]

Bengali vocabulary became enriched with Portuguese words during the seventeenth and the eighteenth centuries. Importance of Portuguese language in Bengal was not only felt in the commercial domain, as it happened along the Asian coasts, but also in the administrative circle of the English East India Company as late as in the nineteenth century. We find that Portuguese language was almost indispensable for the English missionaries who worked then in Bengal. The nineteenth century church records of Calcutta show that Portuguese language was chiefly used for sermon preaching and at other congregations along with English language. Even legal documents were continued to be written in Portuguese language.

Among the Portuguese speaking linguistic groups the missionaries and the converts who lived in Eastern Bengal had played a special role to develop some steady cultural activities that can be marked as the instance of Luso-Bengali interactions. A conversion always presupposes some dialogue between the locals and the missionaries. The Portuguese missionaries had not only learnt the language of the converts, but also their religious and social customs to draw them closer to their religious fold. In this respect, it would be incorrect to say that the other groups had played less significant role in the cultural interactions. It is perhaps because of their particular social positions, they acted as an important vehicle for introducing Bengali words, which are names of objects and ideas of a material culture. Suniti Kumar Chatterjee mentions the extent of the material culture which Bengal and India owed much to the adventurous Lusitanians. In this respect, the Church had played though steady but restricted role. The missionaries in Bengal prepared prayer books, booklets on Christian doctrine, catechism, vocabularies and grammar for initiating dialogue between them and the locals, i.e., their prospective converts. This body of literature in Bengali is known as *kristang Sahitiya*. In the history of Bengali literature this *Kristang Sahitya* is divided into two phases-the first by the Portuguese and the second by the English. We come across two different policies in the use of Portuguese language by the Portuguese authorities in their expansion process. The first one is by the state and the other by the Church. For the state, Portuguese was a vehicle for imposition not only their authority, but also culture and ideas. Whereas for the Church in spite of its dogmatic position its concept of other language was not an obstacle. It is because of this situation, we find that Portuguese creoles or bilingualism in some centres where officials and administrative presence was weak.

From the letter of Fr. João de Beira, written on 20 November 1554 to Rome we find that at the *Casa de Santa Fé*, a seminary in Goa, there were sixty students of nine different languages at that time. There were two Bengali speaking students in that group. Fr. Beira asked for permission to prepare prayer books in these nine languages. Some eight years before this, the report of *Colégio de São Paulo* of Goa shows the presence of six Bengali students.

Some scholars think that the credit of writing books in Indian languages by the missionaries should go to the Franciscans. It is because that the Franciscans had come first to propagate and the Jesuits had not yet well established and we have some famous works like Cartilha[7] in Tamil in the year 1554 (the first book in Indian language printed in Lisbon), Konkani grammar and vocabulary. With the permission granted to the Jesuits, the missionaries of Goa set to write books in local languages. But we do not find any work in Bengali. This is because the Portuguese missionaries had not yet established their mission stations in Bengal at that time.

From the records of the missionaries, we find that the Bengali converts were given formal religious education at Bandel since it became the main centre of Christian activity the early seventeenth century. As in Cochin and Goa, *Santa Casa de Misericordia* (the Holy House of Mercy) in Hugli served as an institute where the rich and the poor alike received the benefits of Christian charity.

According to sources, Fr. Francisco Fernandez and Fr. Domingo de Souza were the first Jesuits to start preaching the Gospel in Bengal. In a letter written on 17th January 1599 from Sripur Francisco Fernandez states that he composed a small treatise explaining the tenets of Christianity and also confuting the superstitions of the Hindus. He also wrote a small catechism in the form of dialogue. Fr. Domingo de Souza translated both the works into Bengali and he too wrote a book in Bengali on the defects of Hinduism in dialogue form. In fact it is to be noted here that this is the first book written in Bengal by the Portuguese (Europeans).

The mission of São Nicolas de Tolentino established by Dom Antonio after 1663 is associated with many books composed by Dom Antonio and Padre Manuel da Assunção. Almost after eighty-five years, [8] Fr. Marcos Antonio Santucci, the chief of the Jesuit mission in Bengal (from 1679 to 1684) informed in his letter written in 1683 that the Jesuits were actively preparing missionary literature in Bengali language for facilitating evangelization process. Unfortunately none of these works composed by the Jesuits are traceable nor do we know whether they were printed at all.[9]

Brahman-Roman-Kayatholic Smabad

This famous work is written in the late seventeenth century, in the form of dialogue between a Brahmin and a Roman Catholic priest, on their respective faiths. The purpose of this dialogue initiated in the work is by a Catholic priest, obviously to prove the superiority of Christianity over Hinduism and its uniqueness as the path of salvation for mankind. The manuscript of the original work in Bengali did not reach us. What is preserved today in the Evora Public Library, in Portugal is the manuscript of padre Manuel da Asssunção who not only translated this work, but also transliterated into Roman script.[10] The manuscript does not contain any title, at the first page it is written as follows: *"Argumento e disputa sobre a Ley entre hu Christão, ou Catholico Romano, e hu bramneé ou Mestre dos gentios, em que se mostra na Lingua bengala a falsidade de seita dos gentios, e a verdade infalivel da nossa Santa Fee Catholica em que so ha o caminho verdadeira Ley da salvaçao e o conhecimento de Deus. Composto por grande cathequista Christao que converteo tantos gentios, chamado Dom Antonio, filho do Rey do Busna.*"[11] In the prologue of Assunçao's manuscript it is mentioned *"foi dotado e bem conhecido entre os bengales cristao e gentios*" and seems that the author was not aware of Dom Antonio's book. Certainly he gained considerable fame in his lifetime as a catechist. The earliest reference to Dom Antonio is found in a letter of the King of Portugal to the then Viceroy of India, Conde de Alvor in Goa who in his reply informed that what His Excellency has heard was false and Fr. Santucci had only complaint against Dom Antonio.[12] No matter how one chooses to interpret Santucci's letter against the fellow missionaries then worked in Bengal. Joseph Sicardo was attracted by the zeal of this new convert for propagating the Christian faith among his countrymen.[13] Dom Antonio had a chequered life–prince to slave, slave to monk, perhaps later caught in the missionary intrigue. His life can only be compared to that of Dom Martinho, Prince of Arakan. The content and the language of Dom Antonio's work are, in a number of ways, very important, particularly for cultural studies and to know the use of late medieval Bengali of a person grown in different cultural environment.

In the course of argumentation to refute various thoughts of Hinduism, Dom Antonio has displayed considerable knowledge of his earlier faith, particularly its "defects". He has vehemently attacked *"Avtarbad*", that is, the Hindu theory of reincarnation of God. A careful study of Bengali used by Dom Antonio would reveal that of his considerable knowledge and acumen in using literary and colloquial language, though the diction is predominantly literary. It was the time when Bengali prose was freeing from the clutches of Sanskrit and being used for literary prose. There was hardly any model of Bengali prose to be followed by Dom Antonio which perhaps led him to shape his Bengali prose in Portuguese model. This work has, two effects–at first freeing the *gentios* from the influence of the Brahmins and secondly their language which is Sanskrit though the latter may not be perhaps intended by the author. Dom Antonio's text is considerably free from the influence Persian vocabulary. Thus text was written during the second half of the seventeenth century. Pedre Manuel da Assunção translated Dom Antonio's dialogue. It is evident he was aware of the distinction between *Sadhu bhasa* and the local dialect. His knowledge of *Sadhu bhasa* seems to be limited. One possible reason may be that the Portuguese missionaries, under inquisitional laws, avoided theological discussion with the Hindu *Pundits*.

In the process of transliteration of the text, several words remained beyond recognition and it is an invaluable specimen of Bengali prose language of the late seventeenth century. At the end of the work, readers would find a fairly long glossary of mainly mythological terms used in the text. This glossary seems to have been prepared not by the author, but by the translator who intended to publish it for the benefit of the Christians. For obscure reasons, Dom Antonio's text was never published. Nevertheless, in all probability, it was in the knowledge of other Augustinian missionaries who worked in Bengal. Only after the arrival of Padre Manuel da Assunçao in Bengal it was translated in 1725 and the prologue of the translation suggests that Dom Antonio had already died.

Crepar Xaxtrer Orth, Bhed

Written in dialogue form, the *Crepar Xaxtrer Orth, Bhed* is a religious conversation between a catholic priest and a Bengali convert. Padre Manuel da Assunçao, translator of Dom Antonio's work, composed this catechism in 1734 at Bhawal near Dacca, and it was published in Lisbon in 1743. Jacobus Franciscus Maria Guerin, a missionary had edited and published this work in Bengali script in 1836, from Chandannagore entitled "Kripar *Shaster Orthoved*".[14] My study of the original work of Assunção, i.e., the Portuguese version led me to accept the Guerin's translation of the title as correct. In fact, Assunção used in his work the word 'Bhed' as scripture in general. Though we do not know if the religious authority easily accepted use of such term of heathen religion. According to Franciscus Guerin that a native has done the Bengali translation of Assuncão's work. But he could hardly justify his claim. His words suggest that Assunção did not have sufficient knowledge required for Bengali rendering. But on examining the patterns of mistakes in the work like syntactic order, placement of verbs with nouns, nouns with adjectives, one would certainly conclude that the Bengali rendering of Assunção's work was done by a Portuguese, in this case Assunção himself. This argument also can be substantiated by the fact that Dom Antonio's work was translated by Assunção himself.

Certainly this fact was not in Guerin's knowledge as the work was unknown to the scholars.

Crepar Xaxatrer Orth, Bhed had a third edition from Margao in 1869. A copy of this third edition is preserved in the National Library, Lisbon, Portugal. This third edition maintains the title *Catecismo Da Doutrina Cristaa*, i.e., the title is in Portuguese, and it is without Bengali version. Nowhere in this edition it mentions its Bengali edition or translation. The third edition was shortened by leaving out some of the deductive stories and portions of the original dialogues. In the title page we find that the work is reprinted– "*Reimpresso com um pequeno additamento*". In the short prologue, Assunçao tells the readers that he has composed *"em terra de infies"* and what clearly emerges from this is that Assunção had published in his lifetime the original Portuguese version which he composed in Bengal. The language of *Crepar Xaxtrer Orth, Bhed* is literary prose interspersed occasionally with some East Bengali local colloquial words along with words of Persian origin. The Bengali version of the dialogue often shows the influence of Portuguese in syntactic order. Jacobus Franciscus Maria Guerin who edited and published it in Bengali script in 1836, from Chandannagore. Assunçao worked as a monk of the Augustinian order in Bengal from 1725 to 1735 near Dacca. He was very conversant with local language and composed poems in the language. The value of this text of Assunçao is due primarily to the phonology as well as document of dialectal Bengali.

Portuguese-Bengali-Hindustani Vocabulary

There is a manuscript which is incomplete and it is a vocabulary of ninety eight pages in total, preserved in Portugal. It contains nearly 2000 entries. This work occupies a special place in the history of Bengali lexicography. A remarkable character of this work is that it gives the user the idea of colloquial as well as literary use of the Bengali vocabulary, arranged in two separate columns, very practical for the use of the missionaries. Unfortunately, in the column for Hindustani, many entries are left blank. Perhaps he did not possess sufficient knowledge of Hindustani to complete. Further a careful study of this vocabulary reveals the fact that the compiler had an extraordinary acumen in transcribing the local sounds using Portuguese alphabets. The author has accurately transcribed some local words and name of places. Many Portuguese expressions have been just literally translated into Bengali, instead of collecting its equivalents. This was the period when the colloquial language used by the educated along the Hugli river, emerged as the language of the literate for entire Bengal. The use of the word "Hindustani" disproves hitherto accepted notion that the term was coined by an Englishman, John Gilchrist, the then first president of Fort William College of Calcutta. From this work what emerges is that the Hindustani had already emerged as *lingua franca* in the Mughal Empire and the importance of it was felt by the Portuguese, and again half a century before the English who settled in Bengal. About the compiler of this vocabulary, we come to know nothing. From his manuscripts and some personal papers it is evident that he came to Bengal as a missionary and stayed there for nearly ten years.

The main purpose of these bilingual works in Roman scripts in the form of dialogue, together with grammar and dictionary composed by the Portuguese missionaries were to attract the Hindus to embrace the Christian faith, also to facilitate literary works composed to facilitate the evangelization process of the missionaries from Portugal, and also to bring back shepherdless Portuguese flock of South Bengal continue to follow the true Christian path. In spite of the favourable and liberal atmosphere for the missionaries in Bengal, the limited aims and objectives left the first phase of *Kristang Sahitya* without any followers and did not produce intended result. All these works written in Bengali are mainly translations from Portuguese, not originally written in Bengali, as some scholars have pointed out earlier. The use of Roman script in these works suggests an attempt to segregate the new converts from their heathens and their scriptures. In Bengal, the Portuguese power and their success had remained considerably limited. There was no printing press set up in Bengal and so the circulation of such works was unthinkable, as a result, it could not produce any great impact on Bengali language or literature. The influence of the English missionaries in the later period is due to the fact that they had set up a printing press and were successful to have an impact on Bengali language and literature.

References

1. Duarte Barbosa, *The Book of Duarte Barbosa*, 2 vols, New Delhi, 1989 ; João Barros *Da Asia*, I to IV, 8 Vols, 1777-78, Lisboa, 1973 ; Tome Pires, *The Suma Oriental of Tome Pires and the Book of Rodrigues*, 2 Vols, New Delhi, 1990.

2. Luis de Cameos, *Os Lusiadas*, Lisboa, 1998.
3. Sanjay Subrahmanyam, *Improvising Empire : Portuguese Trade and Settlements in the Bay of Bengal, Delhi*, 1990. S. Jeyaseela Stephen, *Portuguese in the Tamil Coast: Historical Explorations in Commerce and Culture, 1507-1749*, Pondicherry, 1998.
4. Khondkar Ahmad, *Portuguese Contribution to Bengali Prose, Grammar and Lexicography*, London, 1958.
5. Thomas Bowrey, *A Geographical Account of the Countries Round the Bay of Bengal, 1669-1679*, Cambridge, 1905.
6. Jorge da Presentaçao confirms this fact in his manuscript and it is also referred in the preface of *Vocabulario da Idioma Bengalla e Portuguez* of Pe. Manuel da Assunçáo. The author with a decade's experience in Bengal, says for the missionaries interested in working there, "*nos Bandeis a onde pertendes parroquiar, a mayor parte da gente falla Portuguez; te respondo, que esta mayor parte tambem entende Bengalla; e que a manor parte, que naõ sabe Portuguez, tambem saõ tuas ovellas...*".
7. S. Jeyaseela Stephen, *op. cit.*, pp. 327-328.
8. The text runs as follows. "*Nao faltarao os padres nada a sua obrigaçao, assym aprenderem muito bem a lingua, como em fazerem vocabulario, oraçoes verteram na lingua de terra doutrina crista, etc; que nada havia disto athe entao*".
9. C.R. Boxer *A Tentative Check-list of Indo-Portuguese Imprints, 1556-1674*, London, 1958.
10. The text runs as follows. "*Os Missionarios poderem disputar na ditta lingua* (*bengalla*) *com os bramanes e gentios*."
11. Surendra Nath Sen who edited and published its Bengali version from the Calcutta University in 1937, gave the title *Brahman-Roman-Kayathalic Sambad.*
12. The text runs as follows. "*Tenho noticia do muito que Antonio do Rossario com seus companheiros tem trabalhado pela salvaçao das almas em Bengala, Dacca, Taliate e outras terras, e que chega o numero dos baptizados a quarenta mil*."
13. The text runs as follows. "*En Loricul...y otros Lugares circunvenzenos donde asiste Don Antonio del Rosario, hijo*

del Rey de Busna, a quien no solo convertiera nuestros Religiosos, sino que le redimio del cautiverio el padre Pe. Manuel de Rosario, siendo Vicario de nuestra Iglesia de Catigan, o Dianga: y en reconocimiento de verse libre de la esclavitud que padecia Don Antonio en tanto en la propagacion de la Fe, que se referie aver reducido a ella mas de trienta mil Almas."

14. There lies some confusion regarding the title "Crepar Xaxtrer Oreth, Bhed". Sukumar Sen in his work "*History of Bengali Literature*" published in 1960 gives the title as it is given in the original work, and as the meaning of the title is given as "The Meaning and Implication of the Scripture of Mercy". Sukumar Sen did not raise any doubt regarding the meaning of the title of Assunçao's work.

6

European Impact and Paradigm Shift in Tamil Development

L. Rama Moorthy

Thomas Kuhn in his monograph on 'The Structure of Scientific Revolutions' coined the term paradigm to refer to accepted examples of actual scientific practice which provide models from which a coherent tradition of scientific research subsequently springs. Later he modified his definition and distinguished between disciplinary matrix and paradigm. The entire constellation of beliefs, values, techniques shared by the members of given community he referred to as disciplinary matrix and the exemplary past achievements, he continued to call paradigm.[1]

The notion of paradigm has been applied to the entire history of the study of language from antiquity onwards. Other historians of linguistics have seen the early nineteenth century as the watershed which established the first genuine paradigm in linguistics and have accordingly applied the notion of paradigm only to the 19th and 20th centuries but have disagreed on the question of how many paradigms must be recognized. But in the case of Tamil development, though many paradigms at different periods exist, there are evidences to show a clear-cut paradigm before and after the European contact. In this context, this paper, after analyzing the contribution of European scholars during 18th and 19th centuries, tries to explain the shift in the paradigm of Tamil development due to the European impact.

Modernization and Society

Development of a language is mainly designed/decided by the use of it in various domains of activity. The use is determined by the demands made by the society on language. The development of a language is therefore shaped by the social forces and social philosophy. The understanding of the development of Tamil paradigm, therefore, needs the study of social paradigms in the Indian society, especially in Tamil society. Sociologists are of the view that the traditional societies are organized on the ideologies of societies based on religion, mythology and individuals with unequal rights etc. Indian society experienced the ideologies of western countries from the 19th century as a result of European contact. The ideology of European society is organized on the principles of equality, freedom of individuals and the advancement of the society through knowledge based on reason. Implementation of this European ideology in Indian society resulted in a social process called modernization.

Modernization generally refers to the process of change towards a particular state of existence. The main forces behind this process during the 19th century were industrialization, education etc. Modern forms of education and industrialization yielded a modern society which was ideologically seen to be opposed to a traditional society. This being the era of globalization, there have been changes in the perception of people and society. The driving forces of globalization are information revolution and free trade explosion. There is a shift in the entire constellation of beliefs, values, etc in this society due to this social process. Hence, one can say that there are many paradigms available such as traditional paradigm modern paradigm and now global paradigm in Tamil society.

Language Modernization

When the whole society is undergoing modernization, language, which is part and parcel of the society, cannot escape from it. Any change that takes place in the society is to be reflected on language. Language being a social and cultural institution, it is not only modernized but also functions as an instrument of modernization. A language that exists in the era of modernization or globalization, could not be called the language of modernization/globalization. It must have certain characteristics that are derived from the kind of society in which it is used.[2] Modernization of language in this ideological framework means attaining inter-translatability with languages of industrialized countries by developing new vocabulary for new areas of knowledge and new styles.[3] A scholar has added another process called simplification as a part of modernization and explained it as the conscious efforts to simplify language in the areas of script, *sandhi* and syntax.[4]

As far as the society is concerned, the shift in social paradigms is effected by the social forces like industrialization, technology, free trade, information revolution etc at different periods. Languages also have to equip themselves adequately to cope with these social changes. They do develop in the course of time. But all the changes due to historical evolution could not be considered as real language development. The changes in the language, suitable for expressing the changing social paradigms, are considered the development of language. Conscious planning or continued use in new domains achieves this type of language development. When languages are introduced for expressing new concepts or functioning in new paradigms, they are developed in such a manner that they express those concepts adequately. The engine of language development lied in its use.[5] Thus the paradigm shift in the society is caused by the social forces whereas in the language development, the shift is caused by its use.

Paradigm in Tamil

The paradigm shift in Tamil development cannot be examined without reference to the history of its use, which has not been well documented. Tamil has the oldest literary tradition. The written history of Tamil is almost 2500 years old. The literary evidences show that Tamil was used for creative literature, grammatical treatise, commentary, etc. The *bhakthi* literary tradition shows that Tamil was used to codify philosophical and moral discourses. It is evident from inscriptions that Tamil was used to some extent for administrative purposes such as recording decrees. Thus Tamil was a developed language even at that period. The modernization of Tamil society due to the impact of industrialization and science and technology during the 20th Century created a demand for Tamil modernization. The introduction of Tamil in the new domains of activity and the creation of technical terms, etc., are some aspects of modernizing efforts which were consciously planned. When we compare the use of Tamil in the present context with earlier use, we could notice a paradigm shift.

There are evidences to show a paradigm shift in Tamil development during the 17th and 18th centuries as well. This paradigm shift was the result of European contact and direct contribution of the Christian missionaries. The availability of Roman coins and the references about *Yavanar* 'the Greek and the Romans' in the ancient Tamil literature, established the trade links between Europeans and Tamils during the *Cankam* period. The loan words from Greek source identified in the

Cankam literature also bear testimony to this trade contact. The European contact initially started through trade, missionary work and politics ended in colonization. Even though the European contact had been there since *Cankam* period, the major impact of it took place only from the 17th century. The role of Christian missionaries during 17th and 18th centuries is very important to study the paradigm shift.

The main purpose of these missionaries was to spread the message of the Gospel. As Panikkar has noted, "the Portuguese came first to India with a cross in one hand and sword in the other and the conversion of the inhabitants of the lands was to be one of the objects of Portuguese policy".[6] In the records of the Church, there are many references to the Apostle St. Thomas who must have visited and done some missionary work in the beginning of the Christian era.[7] Fr. Henrique Henriques seems to be the first missionary in the sixteenth century, who is now considered the first European Tamil scholar.[8] From then onwards, many missionaries from different nations like Italy, Portugal, Spain, France, Denmark, Holland, England and Scotland came to Tamil Nadu to undertake missionary work. The way the missionaries preached the Gospel could be understood from the plans of Roberto Nobili.[9] K. Meenakshi Sundaram records that "He (Roberto Nobili) openly dissociated himself from Fr. Fernandez proclaiming that he was a Roman Brahmin. His original plan consisted of three features such as the adaptation of the life of missionary to that of the people (i.e., the Brahmins), the appropriation of harmless (Hindu) customs and ceremonies for Christian use and through the study of the vernacular (and Sanskrit, the language of the sacred books of Hinduism) with a view to achieving fluency of speech and writing and accurate knowledge of the literature of the people. We find that the French missionaries also followed the life style of locals".[10] So Missionaries irrespective of their nationality background mingled with the people to spread Christianity. Tamils while writing the names of missionaries they used the titles *Aiyyar* and *Munivar* which clearly indicate their life style and their close identification with the local people. Though the title 'Aiyyar' indicates the Christian priest, we can think of the influence of then prevailing Sanskrit Paradigm on them. They studied Tamil and contributed to the development of Tamil language and Tamil linguistics. Their works spread over four centuries viz. the 16th to mid 20th century. Before attempting to explain the paradigm shift in Tamil development, the contribution of Europeans, especially, the Christian missionaries could be studied first.

European Contributions

S.V. Shanmugam classified the missionary works in Tamil into two types viz., religious work and intellectual work.[11] In order to refute the statement of Venkatasamy that the missionaries had not done Tamil development works intentionally, Shanmugam mentions their contributions in the fields of Tamil religion, culture and history.[12] Their religious works are of two kinds such as works relating to conversion of locals to Christianity and works relating to helping the co-workers to do conversion. The translation of the Bible into Tamil, writing of Tamil grammars in other European languages falls under religious works.

The contribution to Tamil by Christian missionaries can be said as follows. (The works cited here are not complete and exhaustive but selective.) The first contribution of missionaries intended to spread Christianity is the translation of the Bible into Tamil. David Prabhakar elaborately discusses the styles followed in various Biblical translations viz such as the ones by Ziegenbalg, Fabricius, Rhenius, Nobili and Pawar.[13]

The bilingual dictionaries can be considered as another important work done by the missionaries apart from the monolingual dictionary viz. *Caturakarathi* by Beschi. They wrote bilingual/trilingual dictionaries in order to facilitate the other missionaries and co-workers to learn Tamil and to mingle with the local people. There are bilingual/trilingual dictionaries including languages like Latin, Portuguese and French. The following bilingual dictionaries are worth mentioning:

Antão de Proença - Tamil-Portuguese Dictionary
Ziegenbalg - Tamil-Latin Dictionary
Ziegenbalg - Latin-Tamil Dictionary
R.P Gury - Tamil-Latin Dictionary
Dupis - Tamil-French Dictionary (1855)
Dupis - French-Tamil Dictionary (1895)
John Philip Fabricius - Malabar and English Dictionary

One of the first French-Tamil Dictionaries was completed at Pondicherry by Fr. Dominique de Valence. This contains 12, 450 entries alphabetically changed with their Tamil equivalents. There are also a few trilingual Dictionaries compiled by these missionaries such as Portuguese-Latin-Tamil Dictionary by Zieganbalg and Latin-French-Tamil Dictionary by Dupis.

Another important area in which the Europeans contributed significantly is on Tamil Grammar. The grammars written by European missionaries could be classified into three such as grammars written in

European languages like Latin, English, Dutch and French, the grammar written in Tamil and the comparative grammars.

S.V. Shanmugm has elaborately studied and classified the contributions on the grammatical side.[14] According to Meenakshi Sundaram, the first grammar of Tamil Language by a foreigner available is that of Rev. Philip Baldeus, a Dutch Missionary in 1672.[15] We know the existence of the Tamil grammar by Fr. Henrique Henriques, (1520-1600) on the models of Latin grammar. S. Jeyaseela Stephen has unearthed the Tamil grammars composed by Portuguese missionaries like Fr. Gaspar da Aguilar (1588-1648) and Balthazar da Costa (1610-1673) during the 17th century.[16] Hence the view of K.Meenakshi Sundaram that the grammar of Philip Baldeaus was the first needs to be reconsidered. Then we find Ziegenbalg's grammar in Latin published in 1761 under the title 'Grammatica Damulica'. In the later period we find Portuguese-Tamil grammars were also written by Paulo Francisco de Noronha (1780-1848) and Benjamin Francisco Amaranate (1812-1879) as pointed out by S. Jeyaseela Stephen in his study.[17] Many more grammars were written by the missionaries during the 18th and early 19th centuries.

We find that Fr. Joseph Constantius Beschi who wrote "The grammar of common dialect of Tamil" (in Latin), "A grammar of High dialect of Tamil Language" (in Latin) and "Tonnul Vilakkam" (in Tamil). J.P. Fabricius wrote "A Grammar for learning the principles of the Malabar language, properly called Tamil or the Tamulian Language" (in English).

The following were also very important Tamil grammars which were written during the 18th and 19th centuries.

Przirkyl	–	"*Principia linguae Brahmanica* (Czech)"
Robert Anderson	–	Rudiments of Tamil Grammar combining with the rules of Kodum Tamil or the ordinary dialect, an introduction to Shen Tamil or the elegant dialect of the language.
Rev Karl Graul	–	"Outline of Tamil Grammar"
G.U. Pope	–	"A Hand book of the ordinary dialect of the Tamil language"
	–	"A Larger grammar of the Tamil language in both its dialects".
C.T.C. Rhenuis	–	"A Grammar of the Tamil Language with an appendix.
Robert Caldwell	–	"Comparative Grammar of the Dravidian or South Indian Family of Languages".

There are also comparative grammars like Tamil-French grammar written by Louis Saviniene Dupis. Arokiasamy believes that before Caldwell wrote his monumental work about the comparative grammar of Dravidian languages, a French man called Milliett had evolved one".[18]

A very important dimension of European contribution to Tamil is their creative writings in Tamil. They chose Indian and religious themes and wrote creative pieces in a style and manner which was very distinctive. The few examples of such creative writings include Beschi's *Tempavani, Tirukkavalur Kalampakam, Paramartha Kuru Kathai, Veta Vilakkam, Vetiyar Olukkam,* besides Dupuis's *Veta Tarkkam, Deva Cineka Muyarci, Turavara Utayanam* and *Illara Uttayanam.*

The Christian missionaries also embarked on translating some of the precious native literature into the western languages, adding to the dimension of Biblical translation. T.P. Meenakshi Sundaram states that "the study of Tamil language inspired them to give the best of their knowledge to their countrymen in their translation of Tamil classics."[19]

They also translated Biblical literature into Tamil. Roberto Nobili's *Gnanopatesam, Attuma Nirnayam, Mantira Viyakkiyanam* and *Tiviya Matirikai* are note worthy. J.P. Fabricius translated the prayer book into Tamil under the caption *Pirarttanai Pustakam*. Rhenius translated several works into Tamil viz *Gnanopatesam Vinaa-Vidai, Veta Sastira Curukkam* and *Motca Markkam*. L. Sapaudling translated John Bunyan's Piligrims Progress into Tamil is 1853. S.Winfired translated the songs of David as *Taavit Arasan Ammanai* in 1885.[20]

Many Tamil works were rendered into Latin, French, Spanish, German and English. French missionaries did mostly translation work of Tamil literature into French. Barrique de Fontaine undertook Thirukural translation and Abbe Dubois translated *Panca tantirams, Paramartha Guru kathai* (written by Beschi). A few of the translations rendered up to the 19th century are listed below:

H.Stokes	–	*Nithi neri Vilakkam* (1830)
Charles Graul	–	*Kaivalynavanita Ca vendanta*, (in German, 1853)
Karl Graul	–	*Der Kural des Tiruvalluvar* (1856)
Charles Graul	–	*Ku0ral* (in Tamil and Latin, 1865)
T.Foulkes	–	*Cacivarnapotam* (in German 1861) *Civa prakasa kattalai* (in German, 1863)
P.Percival	–	*Avvaiyar's Aphorisms* (1870)
G.U. Pope	–	*Kural* (in English, 1886)

Apart from the translation of literature, they also brought out books on science, medicine and other informative literature. The following are a few chosen examples:

Rhenius	–	*Pumi sastiram* (from English to Tamil, 1882)
B.Schminal	–	*Ulaka Caritira malai* (from English to Tamil, 1830)
William Robertson	–	*Nutana vivasayam* (1843)
L.Theron	–	Science book on Steam and the Steam Engine (1868)
Sonnerat	–	Tamil Alphabet system (in French, 1806)
La Flolte	–	Travaloque (payana tinacari) (in French, 1769)
Foucher d'obson ville	–	Flora and Fauna of Tamil Land (1783)

It is to be noted that the translations, which came up during the 19th century, were plenty in English and French.

Paradigm Shift

From a comparative study on the overall contributions of the Europeans and the status of the Tamil language before 17 and 18th centuries, we could suggest certain shifts in the developmental Paradigm of Tamil. The shifts were caused at form, content of Tamil and attitudes of people. These three constitute the Paradigm of Tamil. At the form level, the phonology, script, grammar, arrangement of words, and the styles and structure of Tamil shifted to a new Paradigm due to the impact of European scholars. At the content level also, Tamil assumed different functions, and expressed new contents, which were not there before the European contact. The European impact also brought changes in the values of Tamil and attitudes of Tamils towards their language. We shall discuss these shifts one by one.

Shifts in the Script

The earliest written evidence for the Tamil script goes back to the third century B.C. The form of writing is called Tamil-Brahmi, evidently a variety of Brahmi script used in the sub-continent. The Tamil Brahmi script underwent changes and took shape similar to the modern writings of Tamil language.

During the period of *Tolkappiyam*, the vowel scripts e, o were written with dots to differentiate long and short. The Placement of dot over the vowels and vowel combination indicated them as short forms. Similarly, the forms Kurriyalikaram, Kurriyalukaram, ie. the phonetic values of i, u, were also indicated by dots. The first paradigm shift with respect to script occurred when Beschi made certain modification in the script. He removed the dot over the vowels and vowel combinations and introduced minor changes, which had major consequences. Beschi in his book on Kotuntamil described how he brought about a change in the secondary symbol of e, o, vowel combinations. To denote the length or to differentiate the short from long, he used two secondary symbols.

Another change that he introduced was to replace the dot over the vowels with-the symbol to denote length markers. This is the marker used by linguistics to denote length even today. These changes added new dimensions to palm-leaf writing. This reform in the script by Beschi led to further reforms in the modern period to suit the printing and typewriting technology.

At the phonetic level also Europeans were the pioneers to give of the phonetic value to the alphabets. Most of the grammars written by Europeans discuss the phonetic value of the Tamil graphemes. Even though modern linguistics could give phonetic values to alphabets now a days, this had its roots in the writing of foreigners. There is no other source for this except the foreigner's grammar. The famous law given by Caldwell on the convertibility of surd (voiceless sound) into sonants (voiced) is now considered to be more ancient in a point to cite. This fact is not noticed by any native grammars.[21] Beschi and Rhenius compared Tamil sound system with the sound system of other languages like Latin, German and Portuguese. The Comparative study revealed the peculiarities and different pronunciations which existed.

Another important graphemic change was the evidence of conjunct consonants especially in the case of germinated consonants. These consonants together with the following vowels were formerly written as one letter. The introduction of printing press and the practice of writing letters separately in Europe modified the Tamil graphemic system.

The European printing technology effected many changes in the form of Tamil language. Papers and books would have been still unknown, had the press not found its way to India. Due to the impact of press large numbers of copies were made later. Most of the works in Tamil were in manuscript forms. No two manuscripts were identical and making multiple copies was difficult and time consuming.

Shifts in Style

Apart from the phonological level, there are shifts in the styles of writing Tamil. Tamil words were not spaced when written. Several words were joined together and written as one large single word. The missionaries began to introduce changes in this manner also. In order to understand the meaning of the words clearly they gave space between words. It is worth mentioning that in the older days, there were no established practices of using punctuations in Tamil. The European introduced punctuations in Tamil.

Another style due to the impact was the authorship of the work. The authorship of a work was usually omitted and often the original work was never obtained. We had to be satisfied with the commentary only. There are many instances in Tamil literature where the author of the work is still debatable. The Europeans had the system of mentioning numerous references in their works and for comparative purposes they listed authors and titles. Giving authorship and citing reference etc., were systematically followed due to this impact.[22] The responsibility for the script reform and the introduction of punctuation marks including space between words rested on Europeans. According to Annamalai these two innovations helped to greatly simplify the task of reading by eliminating reflection and back tracking and thus increasing speed and comprehension.[23]

Shifts in Tamil Grammar

Tamil language had possessed a great grammatical tradition. The European scholars have mostly written grammars with specific purpose in their languages like Portuguese, Latin, French and English. S.V. Shanmugan classified these grammars under three major heads from the linguistic point of view, such as descriptive grammars, comparative grammars which means the comparison of the genetically related languages and the reconstruction of Proto language and comparative study of grammar which means the comparison of grammars of languages belonging to two different periods.[24] He is of the opinion that the last two areas of research introduced by the European, are new to Tamil Paradigm.

All the grammars written in foreign languages can be considered pedagogical grammar because they were written for the co-workers with specific purpose of language learning. This is yet another aspect of Paradigm where the native grammars were of descriptive type. In the descriptive study of grammar also, the western impact paved the way for the theoretical improvement in the conjugational class. Shanmugam identified points at grammar which the traditional grammar had not noticed and later descriptive grammars developed from it as follows:[25]

1. Classification of nouns on the basis of variant of empty morphs (declensional class) and the classification of verbs on the basis of the allormorph of the tense suffixes, verbal participal (conjugational class) were first noticed by foreign grammars.
2. Classification of pronoun as a sub-class of nouns is found in these grammars along with nouns whereas the native grammars grouped the pronouns as part of common noun.
3. New structural facts about Tamil Language have been observed by them.

With regard to the grammar written by Europeans in Tamil i.e *Tonnul Vilakkam*. Shanmugam stated "it has shown many new insights in the organisation of the phonology and grammar. Really it is nearer to the modern descriptive linguistics than to the native Tamil grammar. In more than one way, it has anticipated the birth of the descriptive linguistics in this century."[26]

The comparative-historical linguistics, yet another aspect of grammar paradigm was introduced into India through Europeans. Robert Caldwell's, *Comparative Grammar of the Dravidian or South Indian Family of Languages* was the first comparative grammar for the Indian languages. Indian Linguistic study got a boost when William Jones in 1786 declared about the genetic relationship between Sanskrit and many European languages. This resulted in the birth of comparative-historical study, which was vigorous in Europe. This gave importance to the study of Sanskrit.[27] But the main contribution of Caldwell's book is the discovery that South Indian languages are not genetically related to Sanskrit. This was the common prevalent opinion among the European and Indian Scholars. As for the Tamil language, this aspect of paradigm shift aid the foundation for many socio-political awakenings in Tamil Nadu.

Shift in the Style and Prose

The important shift in the aspect of form in Tamil is the shift from, i.e.; verse form to prose form. There were no separate Tamil Prose books in Tamil before the advent of Europeans. Books on literature, medicine, astrology and astronomy were written in poetic Tamil, which could be understood by the elites only. Though there was the prose form, it was restricted to commentaries in the early period. It was not developed as a separate genre in Tamil Literary tradition. Sakthivel observes that there existed three styles of prose before European contact, such as Commentator's Style, Manipravala Style and Epigraphical style.

The missionaries found that Tamil poetry and literary writings were not intelligible to a large number of people. Tamil was of course dominant in the oral domain as bilingualism was restricted to the elites only. The oral tradition supported continued use of poetry for all purposes. The establishment of printing press and publication of series of books and pamphlets in Tamil to disseminate Catholic doctrines among the people, shifted the trend in oral tradition and contributed to the use of prose instead of poetry. The missionaries like Nobili and Beschi wrote books both in verse and prose forms. His books viz *Tempavani, Tirukkavalur Ammanai* and *Caturakarati* are in verse form.

The style followed by Europeans in prose writing is totally different from the earlier styles. Since their aim was to propagate Christianity, they adopted a style close to the colloquial Tamil. The verse style was the symbol of high caste and educated people at that time. Introduction of prose style and propagation of education among the down trodden shattered the symbolic function and thus created a shift in the paradigm.

Shift in the Literary Tradition

At the literature level, we could note shifts in both form and content. Tamil development was conceptualized as the development of literature alone during the early period. This is self evident from the use of Tamil throughout the period for creative literature, grammatical treatise, commentaries, philosophical and moral literatures and discourse. These literatures and art forms were in verse and these could be said to be one aspect of Tamil development. The major part of the development constitutes the non-literary development only. The non-literary development consists of making dictionaries, translations, travelogues etc.

The Europeans used Tamil for religious purpose, but also added a new dimension to Tamil by their creative works like short stories, articles, etc. They also contributed to the development of modern dictionaries and translations, which were new to Tamil. The translation works mentioned earlier are clearly a new diversion. The Europeans translated the Tamil Literature in other languages and thus propagated the richness of Tamil. They also brought in new contents from other sources through translation such as science, medicine and other informative literature.

Dictionaries are a rich addition to Tamil development due to European impact. The Tamil *Nigandus* used metrical tradition and were of use to those who composed verses. The modern feature of the dictionary is the alphabetical arrangement of words and graphic cues are used for retrieval. The modern dictionaries are used by all sections of people as reference materials. The contributions cited earlier by Europeans followed this alphabetic system which was new to Tamil tradition. The bilingual and trilingual dictionaries mentioned earlier were also a new trend, set by Europeans.

Travelogues and recording the events of daily things in a diary form are also a valuable gift from Europeans. The diary tradition was known to sailors and missionary officials. The habit of maintaining private diaries was adopted by the natives who came in close contact with these people. As a result of this practice, diaries in Tamil came into existence. S. Jeyaseela Stephen mentions that the diary of Guruvappa Pillai in Pondicherry happens to be the first known diary in Tamil.[28] There are also diaries maintained by Ananda Ranga Pillai,[29] Rangappa Thiruvengadam Pillai,[30] Muthu Vijaya Thiruvengadam Pillai,[31] and Vira Nayakkar[32] which are considered to be a new dimension of Tamil Prose development.

Shifts in the Attitudes

So far we have seen the paradigm shift in the structure, form and development aspect of Tamil. The scientific approach of Europeans gave new insights not only to the Tamil language but also created a new awareness among Tamils. There were certain attitudes among the scholars and people of that period such as, (a) They thought that Sanskrit was the mother of all languages and Tamil evolved from Sanskrit. (b) Between the two varieties of Tamil (viz. written and spoken), the written variety was given superior status and spoken variety was considered inferior. (c) Literature was the site for elites and verses were the language of literature.

The contribution of European scholars shattered all these attitudes. It was only after Caldwell's contribution, the natives and other scholars believed that Tamil was not genetically related to Sanskrit. It had its own independent existence. Each and every European scholar had registered his opinion about the richness of Tamil language and literature. These authentic and systematic analyses not only brought shifts in the attitude but also paved way for the creation of new attitudes. The later scholars and purists, taking clues from these writings, elevated Tamil to such heights that it is the mother of all world languages. Even though Caldwell has praised Tamil for its antiquity and richness of lexicon, he never equated Tamil with proto Dravidian.[33]

The diaglossic nature of Tamil was the identification by the Europeans though it falls under the 20th Century. The long literary tradition in Tamil over centuries created two types of varieties. Among the varieties, literatures were composed in High Tamil and the spoken variety was always looked down upon since it contained dialects of so many caste people. Any written form was associated with verse and the elite. It was only after the European contribution, these attitudes changed. The missionaries adopted a separate style, which was in between literary and spoken Tamil, and printed many books. Beschi had written grammar for spoken Tamil which gave new status to spoken variety. Though he has written grammar for spoken Tamil, the title of the book called 'Kotuntamil' shows the attitude prevalent in those days. Modern linguistics gives importance to the spoken variety because of its vitality and historicity. Writing of grammars for spoken Tamil, had some specific purpose but it created a shift in the attitude of the people. By adopting prose style, using colloquial form, simplifying Tamil *sandhi*, etc, the Europeans had freed Tamil from the clutches of the elite and hence set a trend for new paradigm.

To conclude it may be said that the comparative study of the development of Tamil during the period from the 18th to the 20th century provides many new insights. Though the 20th century Tamil development is due to western/global impact, there are certain social forces and social changes (industrialization, free trade explosion etc.) that lay behind the development. The main emphasis of this period is to adopt Tamil for new domains of activity and shape Tamil to suit global technology. These developments are done by natives for the benefit of the Tamil society.

The earlier Tamil development was limited mostly refining, structuring Tamil and identifying uniqueness of Tamil. Through the technological development, they brought about changes and they structured the form of Tamil. The intellectual developments of the European countries also helped to systematize Tamil. When the Europeans began to study Tamil, they were able to identify the uniqueness of Tamil. Their main aim was to preach the Holy Gospel and they used Tamil as a tool for the spread of Christianity. They refined the tool with their intellectual and technological background. Their contributions such as the adoption of prose style, adoption of colloquial form and making of dictionaries were due to their lack of fluency in Tamil and to their own needs such as learning Tamil and to propagating the message to the non-elite. If we take into account the rich literary tradition, their contributions were made during the 16th-19th centuries, but it took Tamil to greater heights. They were the path breakers in Tamil for new development paradigm.

References

1. R.E Asher, et.al., *The Encyclopedia of Language and Linguistics*, Pergaman Press, p. 2926.
2. E. Annamalai, "Modernization of Language :The case of Tamil", *Standarisation and Modernization: Dynamics of language planning* (ed.,), Imtiaz Hasnain, Delhi, Bahri Publication, 1995.
3. Ferguson, *Language Development in Language problems of Developing nations*, (ed.,) Fishmen, J.A et.al. New York, 1968.
4. E. Annamalai, "Simplification as a process of Modernization", in *Socio-linguistics and dialectology* (ed), Agastialingam and Karunakaran, Annamalai Nagar, 1995.
5. E. Annamalai, "A New Paradigm for Tamil development" A Paper presented at the *Eight International Conference-Seminar of Tamil Studies*, Tamil University, Thanjavur, 1993.
6. K.V Panikkar, *"Malabar and the Portuguese"* Annamalai Nagar, 1979, p. 183.
7. S. Innesi, *Kritkvaram TamileKanwer*, Madras, 1990, p. iv.
8. *Ibid.*, p. :9.
9. K. Meenakshi Sundaram, *A Contribution of European Scholars to Tamil*, Madras, 1974, p. 18; See S. Jeyaseela Stephen, *Portuguese in the Tamil Coast: Historical Explorations in Commerce and Culture, 1507-1749*, Navajyothi Publishers, Pondicherry, 1998, pp. 349-350.
10. S. Jeyaseela Stephen, *Ibid.*, p. 351.
11. S.V. Shanmugam, *"Kiruthava Arinarkalin Ilakkanappani"*, Madras, 1993, p. 10.
12. Venkatasamy, *Krittuvamum*, *Tamilum*, Madras, 1936, p. 15.
13. David Prabhakaran, *Kiruthak Arinarkalin Ilakkanappani*, Madras, 2002.
14. S.V. Shanmugam, "Christians and Tamil". Innasi (ed), *Christian Contribution to Indian language and literature*, Madras, 1994, p. 147.
15. T.P. Meenakshi Sundaram, *A History of Tamil Language*, Poona, 1961, p. 160.

16. S. Jeyaseela Stephen, *Portuguese-Tamil Grammar : Modernisation and Democratization of Tamil*, Institute for Indo-European Studies, Pondicherry, 2001.
17. *Ibid.*, pp. 23-26, 26-27.
18. Meenakshi Sundaram, *op. cit.*, p. 13.
19. *Ibid.*
20. R. Balakrishnan, *Directions in Translation*, Annamalai Nagar, 2002, pp. 29-30.
21. S.V. Shanmugam, *Christians and Tamil...op. cit*, p. 149.
22. K. Meenakashi Sundaram, *op. cit.*, p. 82.
23. E. Annamalai, *Simplification...op. cit.*, p. 4.
24. S.V Shanmugam, *Christians and Tamil op. cit.*, p. 146
25. S.V. Shanmugam, *Christians and Tamil op. cit* p. 147.
26. S.V. Shanmugam, *Christians and Tamil op. cit* p. 157.
27. S.V. Shanmugam, *"Noun Morphology Studies since Caldwell"* IJDL, Vol. XX, (14), No. 2, 2002, p. 20.
28. S. Jeyaseela Stephen, *Thamizhil Natkurippugal: Pathinettan Muttrandu, Seythi Ithalgalin Munnodigal*, Pondicherry, 1999, p. 32.
29. H. Dodwell and K. Rangachari, *The Private Diary of Ananda Ranga Pillai, 1736-1760*, 12 Vols, Madras, 1904-1928.
30. S. Jeyaseela Stephen, *"The Diary of Rangappa Thiruvengadam Pillai 1761-1768, Translated from original Tamil with Notes*, IIES, Pondicherry, 2001. See also his two volumes of the diary in Tamil, *Rangappa Thiruvengadam Pillai Natkurippu*, Pondicherry Institute of Linguistics and Culture, 2000.
31. S. Jeyaseela Stephen, *Muthu Vijaya Thiruvengadam Pillai Natkurippu, 1794-1796*, Pondicherry, 1999.
32. Orsay M. Gopala Krishanan, *Irrandam Viranayakkar Natkurippu, 1778-1792*, Chennai, 1999.
33. S.V. Shanmugam, *Christians and Tamil*, *op. cit* 1994, p. 146.

7

Advent of the Europeans and Emergence of New Literary Genres in Tamil

B. Ravi Kumar

It is well known that among the Indian languages, Tamil has a rich and fertile tradition. Its heritage is more than two thousand and five hundred years old and had undergone so many changes in its long and chequered history due to social, religious and political conditions prevalent. Various forms of ancient and medieval texts (such as *Sangam* literature, devotional literature and epics) in Tamil exist and these came to be classified by scholars like Mayilai Seeni Venkatasamy, K. Meenakshi Sundaram, Chengalvaraya Pillai, Rajamanickam, T.P.Meenakshi Sundaram Pillai, K.Sivathamby and Kailasapathy who have done commendable research.[1] These classical works in Tamil were composed only in poetic form, right from the pre-Christian era to the fifteenth century. Among these ancient texts, *Purananuru*, *Agananuru* and *Silapadikaram* speak about the overseas commercial contacts between the Tamils and the Greeks. Strabo states that in B.C. 22, the Pandya king of Madurai had sent ambassadors to the court of Augustus Ceaser in Rome. Pliny mentions overseas trade contacts. It may be noted here at this juncture that these encounters did not last beyond the third century B.C. due to the decline and fall of the Roman empire.[2] After a very long gap, overseas trade with Europe again came to be developed with the arrival of the Portuguese, the Dutch, the Danes, the English and the French which resulted also in the development of Tamil literature with innumerable changes. In this paper an attempt is made to analyze the emergence of various new forms of literature like the diaries, novels, short-stories and new verses in Tamil literature by conveying some new ideas and presenting new arguments.

European missionaries who came to India at first began to learn Tamil grammar. Scholars who have written so far about the contribution of the Europeans to Tamil did not write much about this. The contribution of Portuguese to Tamil grammar is worth noting here as they were the pioneers. In modernizing and democratizing Tamil language, the Portuguese missionaries who preached Gospel in the Tamil Coast have played a major role and this fact is pointed out by S. Jeyaseela Stephen in his recent work.[3] These Portuguese learnt to speak Tamil in order to spread the tenets of Christianity in the Tamil soil and in course of time wrote Tamil grammar in Portuguese language for the use of their fellow missionaries. For the first time Tamil grammar in verse form came to be written in the prose form. This Tamil grammar was helpful and suitable for the purpose of conversation. It is surprising to note that several Portuguese missionaries such as Henrique Henriques, Gasper da Aguilar, Balthazar da Costa, Paulo Francisco de Noronha and Benjamin Francisco Amarante had seriously taken the study of Tamil grammar in the absence of learning aids to a considerable degree of perfection.[4] These Portuguese missionaries evolved their own method of learning Tamil and authored Portuguese-Tamil grammars by understanding the rich grammatical tradition besides comparing it with Latin. Scholars like Meenakshi Sundaram[5] who made attempts to study the contributions of the Europeans to Tamil had not touched upon such contributions of Portuguese missionaries, especially Tamil grammars written in prose form.

Development of Tamil Prose

It has been generally stated that only after the arrival of the Europeans Tamil prose developed. Was there no prose in Tamil before the fifteenth century?. *Tolkappiyam* speaks about prose and in *Cheyyuliyal* it is mentioned *"thonmaitha Uraiyodu Punarntha Pazhamai*" and here urai refers to prose. *Silappadikaram* has been called *"Urainadaiyitta Paatudai Cheiyul*", an epic in poetry form with prose interludes. Another Tamil work called *Iraiyanar Kalaviayal Urai* is an adequate evidence to show the prose talents of the Tamils. We also find many commentators (*Urai Asiriyargal*) like Ilampooranar, Nachinarkiniyar, Parimelazhagar, Adiyarku Nallar and Deivachilaiyar who were well known for their commentaries in prose form.[6] Therefore in the light of the above, the view that before the advent of the Europeans, Tamils did not know prose need to be reconsidered. Further, scholars while writing the Tamil literary history have failed to take into account the inscriptions composed in prose form. Those who wrote the history of Tamil literature had thus given much importance only to Tamil poetry. The truth is that the Europeans developed

Tamil prose writing, which already prevailed. The introduction of the printing press was a major development in this direction. Henrique Henriques and Roberto Nobili had composed several works of Christian literature in Tamil prose and it has been pointed out by scholars.[7] However, the Tamil literary history is yet to be written in a complete form by analyzing all these prose works of the missionaries.

Thambiran Vanakkam, the first book in Tamil was published at Kollam on 28 October 1578. A Tamil printing press was established in 1712 at Tharangambadi by the efforts of Ziegenbalg and books were also printed. Some works dealing with subjects such as astronomy, geography and history composed in prose were published by the *Mission Etrangers de Paris* at the Mission Press in Pondicherry later. Thus the advent of the Europeans contributed towards the growth of Tamil. Veeramamunivar in his work *Thonnul Vilakkam* brought out some reforms in Tamil alphabets and made certain marks to differentiate between them.[8] Division of paragraphs and punctuation marks were also introduced into Tamil only by the Europeans and the introduction of the printing press helped and changed the course of the history of Tamil literature to a large extent. While reconstructing the Tamil texts in palm leaf manuscripts for printing several critical editions were also undertaken. The possibility of interpolation in the texts of the palm leaves had almost become impossible when the texts were printed. Literature also reached the masses after printing, and the palm leaves and writing nails came to disappear from the hands of the Christian missionaries. In the Hindu circles it continued, while the epics, devotional literature, and other forms could not see the light of printing. Many *Puranas*, *Pillai-Tamils*, *Kovais*, and *Kalampagams* continued to be composed by the Hindus.

Diaries

Scholars who have written Tamil literary history so far have failed to understand the importance of diaries in Tamil, written in prose by the natives during the eighteenth century. These Tamil diaries help to analyze the development of Tamil prose after the advent of the French in Pondicherry. Further it has been argued that these diaries were precursors to Newspapers.[9] Guruvappa Pillai was the first to write a diary in Tamil.[10] Ananda Ranga Pillai had maintained a diary in Tamil and this became popular since it was translated and published in English.[11] The little known other diaries in Tamil such as The diary of Rangappa Thiruvengadam Pillai[12] and Muthu Vijaya Thiruvengadam Pillai[13] were published by S. Jeyaseela Stephen, while the diary of Vira Nayakkar[14] by Orasy. M. Gopala Krishnan need to be mentioned in this connection. A thorough analysis of the text of these diaries of eighteenth century is still awaited to understand the growth and development of Tamil prose.

Novels

The first Tamil novel, *Prathapa Mudaliar Sarithiram* composed by Vedanayagam Pillai was published in 1876. It is pertinent to ask the question why should Tamil novel for the first time appear in the nineteenth century. It is to be stated that some turning points occurred at that time and in the year 1835, Sir Charles Metcalfe gave the right of using the printing press to the *Swadeshis*, which had been earlier under the control of the English East India Company. Further by establishing the universities in Madras, Bombay and Calcutta, the British attempted to spread English education. On Macaulay's report William Bentinck declared that "the great object of the British Government ought to be the promotion of European literature and science among the natives of India and that all the funds appropriated for the purpose of education would be best employed on English education alone". At this time, the English schools and colleges not only introduced teaching of English language, but also they began to introduce the writings of Charles Dickens, Oliver Goldsmith, George Elliot and Scott. In those days, most of the educated Tamil people had an opportunity to study English novels and against this background a new literary genre, the novel appeared in Tamil. Thus the Tamil world accepted novel which was totally an alien form. These novels in Tamil are seen just as an extension of the prose. British have created a situation in which the Tamils have to speak their social problems of the then world and it became the right medium of expression.

Vedanagayam Pillai in his first novel states that it was an "epic in dialogue". Similarly the names of the novels which appeared in Tamil during the nineteenth century had the word *charitiram* which meant history. Novels like *Kamalambal Charitiram* and *Padmavathy Charitiram* clearly show the mental attitudes of the Tamils those days. Besides Vedanagayam Pillai, scholars like Rajam Iyer, A.Madhavayya and others wrote novels in Tamil. In the opinion of R.E. Asher we find that "Tamil renaissance may have started quite well with the early novels, but there was a considerable period of stagnation before others showed signs of consolidating their work". Novels gained a new direction and within this 125 years, more than 5000 novels in Tamil had been published. But there is no record for the annual publications of such novels as per the historical order till today and an in depth study of tracing the historical development of such novels is very important. With the establishment of the printing press, the number of reading Tamil public, particularly the educated middle class increased during the nineteenth and twentieth centuries. We can clearly state therefore, that only after the advent of the English, Tamil prose began to expand well its horizon when compared to the previous periods.

Short Stories

In the year 1913, V.V.S. Iyer wrote a short story called "*Kulathangkarai Arasamaram Sonna Kathai*" in the journal entitled "*Viveka Bodhini*". After this A.Madhavayya published his short story book "*Kusikar Kuthi Kathaigal*" in 1924. Later in 1930s, with the advent of the *Manikkodi* writers like Puthumaipitthan, P.S. Ramaiah, Mouni, L.S Ramaamirutham, K.J.P.Rajagoapal and K.Azhagiri Samy we find many short stories and tremendous development in this direction. Since the story-telling tradition was already in vogue among the Tamils, these short stories were accepted. Hence in the nineteenth century, *Mariyadai Ramam Kathaigal*, *Tenali Raman Kathaigal*, *Dravida Kakla Poorna Kathaigal*, *Boologa Vinodha Kuthaigal* and *Pancha Thanthra Kathaigal* were published. But the critics did not accept the above said for being indigenous in nature but accepted the short stories written in the European themes. The *Manikkodi* writers who have read the English and French short stories took the Tamil short story to the forefront. Subramania Bharati's comment on the short stories is worth mentioning in this context. He says, "In our (Tamil) stories the protagonists birth, growth, race, caste, creed and all other details are available. In the European style just as in the dramas, we find that they start the story in the middle." V.V.S. Iyer's short story, in which the tree narrates a story itself is totally a new form in the arena of Tamil literature. Today we find that the Tamil short story writers have strong influence of the European style. Undoubtedly it is chiefly because of the European influence on Tamil society.

New Verse

New verse was another literary genre. It is possible to say that the birth of novels and short stories paved the way for the emergence of new verses in Tamil. Subramania Bharati had written *Vasana kavithai* (free verse) in 1920. However new verses developed only after 1950s. After Bharati, N. Pichamurthy had tried this new form. The journal "*Yezuthu*" (word) started by C.S. Chellappa was the first one to publish a number of new verses and encouraged the writers who belonged to the same period. The journal *Yezuthu* primarily focused attention on this style under the influence of the European writings. Though the new verse has established its present form very well recently, it had a long struggle to establish itself among the public with the disliking by the Tamil Pundits for the language being colloquial. But after the 1970s when the *Vanambadi* and *"Ka Sa Da Tha Pa Ra"* movement gained momentum, the influence of the European prose literature gradually began to disappear.

To conclude it may be said that the new genres like diaries, novels, short stories and new verses gave ample scope for the growth of Tamil prose. Certainly European literature had much influenced Tamil writers as well. It paved the way for the use of new criticism like Marxism, modernism, post-modernism and deconstruction theory which emerged in the later half of the twentieth century.

References

1. Mayilai Seeni Venkatasamy, *Krittuvamum, Tamilum*, Madras, 1936; T.P. Meenakshi Sundaram, *A History of Tamil Language*, Poona, 1961; K. Kailsapathy, Tamil Heroic Poetry, Oxford, 1968.
2. K. Karttunen, *India and Early Greek Literature*, Helsinki, 1989, See also, Vimala Begley, *Rome and India*, Wisconsin, 1997.
3. S. Jeyaseela Stephen, *Portuguese-Tamil Grammar : Modernisation and Democratization of Tamil*, Institute for Indo-European Studies, Pondicherry, 2001.
4. *Ibid.*, pp. 21-28.
5. K. Meenakshi Sundaram, *A Contribution of European Scholars to Tamil*, Madras, 1974. In this monuemental work the author deals with the contributions of more than fifty Europeans to Tamil and some of the important names include Roberto Nobili (1577-1656), Constantius Joseph Beschi (1680-1742), Bartholomeow Ziegenbalg (1683-1719). Charles Theophilus Edward Rhenius (1790-1838), G.U. Pope (1820-1903), Robert Caldwell (1814-1891), Francis Whyte Ellis, J.P. Rotler, Winslow and others.
6. S. Jeyaseela Stephen, *Portuguese-Tamil Grammar*, *op. cit.*, pp. 18-19.
7. S. Jeyaseela Stephen, *Portuguese in the Tamil Coast: Historical Explorations in Commerce and Culture, 1507-1749*, Navajyothi Publishers, Pondicherry, 1998. On Henrique Henriques, see, pp. 335-339, 343-345; On Roberto Nobili see, pp. 349-350; For details see also, S. Rajamanickam, *The First Oriental Scholar*, Tirunelveli, 1972.
8. V.M. Gnanapragasam, *Contributions of Fr. Beschi to Tamil*, Ph.D. Dissertation, Univeristy of Madras, 1965.

9. S. Jeyaseela Stephen, *Thamizhil Natkurippugal: Pathinettan Nuttrandu, Seythi Ithalgalin Munnodigal*, Pondicherry, 1999.
10. *Ibid.*, pp. 30-33.
11. H. Dodwell and K. Rangachari, *The Private Diary of Ananda Ranga Pillai, 1736-1760*, I-XII vols, Madras, 1904-1928.
12. S. Jeyaseela Stephen, *"The Diary of Rangappa Thiruvengadam Pillai 1761-1768, Translated from original Tamil with Notes*, IIES, Pondicherry, 2001. See also two volumes of the diary in Tamil, *Rangappa Thiruvengadam Pillai Natkurippu*, Pondicherry Institute of Linguistics and Culture, Pondicherry, 2000.
13. S. Jeyaseela Stephen, *Muthu Vijaya Thiruvengadam Pillai Natkurippu, 1794-1796*, Pondicherry, 1999.
14. Orsay M. Gopala Krishnan, *Irrandam Viranayakkar Natkurippu, 1778-1792*, Chennai, 1999.

PART-III
CONSTRUCTION, DIMENSION AND MANIFESTATION: SOCIETY IN INDIA

8

Tamil Society and the Military in the Age of the Medieval Cholas

Shouvik Mukhopadhyay

There was a persistent tendency among the scholars to characterize the Indian society as a changeless one without assigning any good reason. However now the scholars have pointed out that the South Indian society had witnessed several sharp changes in its recorded history of two millennia and during the thirteenth and fourteenth centuries we especially find the decline of the *nadu* assemblies and the subsequent rise of the *periya-nadu* assemblies. This was not simply a shift in the political geography but a result of major socio-political changes that occured. The coeval or related social development was the waning of the *brahmin-vellalar* alliance whose domination was also challenged by the establishment of 'warrior regimes' during this period. Martial communities like the *Maravars* and the *Kallars* were creating a niche for their own through mechanisms like *patikaval* (protection fees) and donations to the temples. A contemporaneous phenomenon was the reemergence of thc Murugan cult. The Tamil god par excellence in the Classical period, who had gone for a historical hibernation for almost five hundred years or more was again coming back with vengeance. In this paper an attempt is made to show these significant changes in the South Indian society were the manifestations of the changing dynamics of 'Inner' and 'Outer' communities due to some historical reasons in the thirteenth-fourteenth centuries. The terms Inner and Outer (to substitute 'Core' and 'Periphery' as their usage has some serious epistemological problems) are used as *Akam* and *Puram* being used by the Classical Tamil literary traditions. In this paper I endeavour to look into the interactions between communities living in the agrarian heartland of South India and those communities living in areas inhospitable for sedentary agriculture and naturally dependant on pastoral activities. These later people were also militarily active. In Tamil classical literary conventions the heroic deeds are known by the generic term '*Puram*' and also has prompted me to choose the terms 'Inner' (*Akam*) and 'Outer' (*Puram*) for agrarian heartland and non-agrarian zones respectively.

At the outset I want to make clear, what I mean by such terms like 'Inner' and 'Outer' communities. These are eco-cultural phenomena. Ecology-the alternations of seasons, the monsoons and the characteristics of soil and topography had more implications on the making of Indian history. Until the most recent times, scholars failed to accept it except the *Sangam* (*Cankam*) literature where the 'time-space' continuum (*tinai*) is considered to be the most basic (mutal) in explaining the human experience. Combining this *tinai* (primarily in spacial context) concept with *Akam* (inner) and *Puram* (outer) we get *akattinai* (interior or inner landscape) and *purattinai* (exterior or outer landscape) which has an all encompassing schematized formula to understand different 'love' and 'war' situations. Though primarily *akam* and *puram* were meant to describe love and war but these meanings expanded to encompass larger context. Here I quote from the observations of A.K Ramanujam: "The meanings complement each other systematically. As we move from context to context, for each meaning of akam, there is a corresponding sense of puram. It is characteristic of this poetry and its poetics that the meanings seem to expand and contract in concentric circles, with the concrete physical particular at the centre, getting more and more inclusive and abstract as we move outward. The context picks and foregrounds one or another of these circles of meanings."[1] Though the Tamil literature takes the external reality more into account, we find in Sanskrit literature too a dichotomy between established settlements/regularly ordered land/established social system on the one side and the jungle/forest dwelling on the other.

In South India the physical diversity had deeper historical implications too. There is a complex interplay between the Deccan plateau and the riverine deltaic regions which had affected the settlement pattern. 'We find fertile lands capable of supporting relatively dense population, besides isolated nodes of prosperity and civilization being surrounded by forest clad uplands capable of supporting small and often predatory population.'[2]

O.H.K Spate has delineated a group of perennial nuclear regions consisting of Kalinga country (Orissa) Telugu country, (Andhra) Chola and Pandya regions of the Tamil country, and the isolated littoral of the Kerala (Malabar) in South India. Further subregions can be discerned where sedentary people lived amidst forest and hill people. This pattern of isolated settlements had critical historical importance in South Indian history.

A large region, starting from Belgaum in Karnataka-Maharastra border in the west, Rayalaseema in the east and the entire upland complex of Coimbatore, southern Salem, northern Salem not only shares the general topographic characteristics but climatic ones as well. This is the dry area with a rainfall pattern neither resembling the classic monsoon of the west coast nor the retreating south-west monsoon. Precipitation ranges between 27-35 inches and highly unreliable. Raymond Allchin referred to the concentration of neolithic pastoralist settlements in this area which, with its scanty vegetation and low rainfall but good pastures provided a suitable area for neolithic cattle herders. I consider these regions, with unreliable precipitation and naturally unsuitable for sedentary agriculture to constitute the 'outer' and the riverine deltaic region like the Cauvery to constitute the 'inner' regions. It is the highly variegated relationship between this 'inner' and 'outer' regions, which moulded the South Indian society in the medieval period.

The Land and the People

South India in its recorded history saw many battles being fought. Particularly between the Deccan and the deep south, there is a tradition of almost one and half millennia of almost regular political struggle. Despite the vicissitudes of individual dynasties this tradition of struggle persisted. Warfare needed detailed man management as well as logistic support and because of the continuous warfare the 'outer' areas became a very good 'military labour' catchment area.

There is an almost consensual feeling among the strategic thinkers and the historians that 'peripheral' people (who in our view constituted the 'outer' communities) had a great advantage in martial activities and the political leadership recognized their martial superiority. In Arthasastra, one of the most important ancient Indian political treatise we find the six 'limbs' of the army (*Sadanga balam)-maula, bhritaka, sreni, mitra, amitra and atavi balam*. This categorization was done not only according to the sources (from where the particular army was recruited) but also according to the value judgement of the author regarding the degree of the trustworthiness of the particular 'limbs'. The author cautions the reader about the unreliability of the last two arms i.e. *amitra* and *atavi*. "...yet these wild tribes were often employed for military purposes by the Hindu kings, in the same manner as the Red Indians were employed by the English and the French in their wars in North America. They brought their own war apparatus to the theatre of war but they fought for pay and plunder. Their services were considered specially helpful when a king's army had to pass through forests and defiles, morasses and mountains, or when it was the intention of the invader to ravage or devastate enemy's country".[3] Marc Bloch quotes from the observations of the Arab historian Ibn Khaldun that 'When two sides were equal in number and strength, one more accustomed to the nomadic life gains victory'. He adds that '...in the ancient world it had an almost universal validity-atleast till such times as the sedentary people should call to their aid the resources of an improved political organization and of a really scientific military machine'.[4]

In the South Indian context the role of 'peripheral people' in organized warfare is well attested in both literature and inscriptional evidences. In *Cankam* literature we find the *marava* or *kanava* community (kanavar-people of the forest) associated with *palai* landscape (the so-called desert land among the fivefold *tinai* divisions. As there are no deserts in the Tamil country it has been stated in the grammatical treatise that when rain failed in *kurinci* (hill) *mullai* (pastoral tracts) they resembled the characteristics of *palai* (desert). The inhabitants of the *palai* region were actively associated with killing people who passed through the area. In the later stages of Classical literature it seems that they were absorbed as warrior servants (*sevakar*) by the local leaders or village heads to protect their cattle. Another dominant feature of the 'Heroic society' (as the society of the Cankam literature is sometimes called by some scholars) was the importance attached to the cattle raids (in fact cattle raid-*vetchi* was a signal for actual engagement/war according to Tolkappiam-the earliest extant Tamil grammar). In Cankam literature nat*ukal*s or hero-stones (memorial stones were raised in memory of fallen heroes who lost their lives in the course of the raids) are mostly found from the *mullai* (pastoral) tracts.

Hero Stones

This fact is further corroborated by the actual provenance of the hero-stones (*natukal/virakal*) dating between fifth and thirteenth centuries A.D. Almost ninety percent of the extant hero stones in this period are found from a triangle formed by Mysore plateau, pastoral zone of Rayalaseema region in Andhra pradesh consisting of four major districts namely Kurnool, Cuddapah and Chittoor and Pennaiyar river basin in Tamilnadu covering mainly Dharmapuri and Tiruvannamalai districts. Within the last mentioned region it was mostly concentrated in the Cengam taluk of Tiruvannamalai and Harur and Uttangarai taluks of Dharmapuri district.

The heavy incidence of hero-stones in the areas characterized as 'outer' region shows that the population was militarily active. The continuous feuds helped these 'outer' communities honing their military skills. Thus we find evidences of '*itaiyan*' (shepherds) acting as military leaders-*pataitalaivan*.[5] Naturally the large scale military activities during the eleventh century A.D, launched by the Chola emperors gave a chance to exploit the military brilliance of these peripheral people and actually there are inscriptional evidences to prove that the Chola kings tapped this 'military labour market' for good results. Many regiments of bowmen (*villi*) were formed in these outlying areas.[6] James Heitzman notes that the men of the dry zone of Thanjavur long retained a reputation as good warriors. These places were noted for the martial traditions which were also predominantly pastoral regions.[7]

Warfare and Soldiers

Additionally before the advent of the mechanized warfare, to carry the provisions, articles of the army, draft animals, pack oxen were needed in large quantity. The pastoral regions were famous for breeding good quality oxen. In Hosur we find the famous Amritmahal breed while in the south-western Mysore up to the forested hills of Salem district is found the famous Alambadi breed. Oxen of this breed were preferred as draft animals. So not only for 'military labour' but also for logistical necessities, the pastoral areas had been of extreme importance for the warring parties in the medieval period. Thus the 'outer' communities because of their military superiority and logistic necessities were held at premium by the established kingship form the period of transition from 'Lineage' to 'State' society onwards. The integration of the 'outer' communities with the 'inner' took an altogether new dimension in the medieval period as the former penetrated the later and changed their own identity and in the process wrought important changes in the identity of the 'inner' society.

It has been pointed out by Noboru Karashima that the imperial expeditions of the Chola kings in the eleventh century brought enormous wealth in the Chola country and its utilization was one of the important factor for the emergence of the private landholding in Cauvery delta. Karashima examined seven inscriptions from Uttatur which belongs to the period of Rajaraja III.[8] These inscriptions, all recorded within three years of the reign of Rajaraja III show land transaction (selling and buying) by several *Surutiman* fellows in the Tiruchirapalli district. The *Surutiman*s seem to be closely related to the *Palli*, *Vanniya* or *Agambadiyar* castes and claimed Kshatriya origin. We find the earliest reference of the *Surutiman* community in an inscription dated 1015 AD where a *Surutiman* lays down his life as a vanguard soldier in the battle of Katakkam.[9] Another *Surutiman* is referred to in 1141 AD as a member of the Urattur-nadu and as landholding was an important qualification for being a *nattar*, we can presume that this person was a *kani* holder.[10] In the next one referred to in 1150 AD we find the person mentioned as a landholder (*udaiyan*) and *natalvan*.[11] So here we find an erstwhile non-peasant, martial community slowly transforming itself and becoming substantial landlords in the lower Cauvery basin in the thirteenth century.

A somewhat similar trajectory can be traced about the *palli* people. They were martial people like *maravar*s and *kallar*s. In an inscription dated 1122 AD the *palli* people were described as *kani* holders in the village situated in the northern dry zone.[12] Here they were described as *palli-nattar* or *pan-nattar*. Incidently this inscription was an address to *palli*s over a large area, Viranayanan tank on the east, the Paccai hills on the west, the Cauvery on the south and the Pennai river on the north. So this gives us a picture of social integration over a large area.

In another inscription from Varanjuram dated on 1227 AD we find *Nattaman* and *Malaiyaman* to be considered as the eyes and hands of the left hand group called *idangai*.[13] In *Cankam* corpus we have seen the *Malaiyaman*, chief of Mulurmalai going for cattle raid during the night.[14] The name *Malaiyaman* itself suggests that these people were the residents of the hills or *kurinci* region. The non-peasant background of the *Nattaman* was emphasized in an inscription from Valikandapuram which refers to the *Nattaman* as the leaders of the *Yadava-kula* or the pastoral communities.

So from the above evidences we find that in the twelfth-thirteenth centuries the non-peasant people were being absorbed in the society as the land-holding peasants. This obviously would bring them into opposition with the old *kani*-holders. Possibly this was the reason behind the growth of *periya-nadu*, a supra-local integration which was noted in twelfth-thirteenth centuries. Interestingly the references about *periya-nadu* come from the peripheral areas or the dry-zones where these non-peasant people were transforming themselves as land-holders. However this conflict seems to have ended in the subsequent Vijayanagara period when we find the *idangai-valangai* communities were joining hands to oppose the increased revenue pressures of the government officials.

It has been argued by different scholars that it was because of these new entrants that caste (*varna/jati*) system got strengthened.[15] With the strengthening of the caste norms in an erstwhile nebulous situation these new groups jostling for an elbow-room started producing caste/community hagiographies and we find works like *Itti elupatu* or *Silai elupatu* (with dubious authorship).

Another important development was the establishment of warrior regimes by martial, non-peasant communities like *maravar*s or *kallar*s. In some places like Pudukottai they succeeded in establishing kingships in the seventeenth century. However the process started during the thirteenth and fourteenth centuries. In the last phase of the Chola regime, the wide spread disturbance prompted people to buy protection in lieu of money and we find spawning of a system called *patikaval*. There are numerous instances of these strongmen donating the dues to the local temples (the example of Magadaiperumal Ponparapinnan during the reign of Kulottunga III comes to one's mind. The name itself suggests that he donated money to guilt a temple pinnacle with gold).

A vital question is, why did these local strongmen donate their protection fees to the temple or undertook to protect the temple itself. One simple answer can be devotion, which was obviously there. On the other hand whatever information we have received regarding *patikaval* these are solely from the temple inscriptions. So it is quite natural that they will speak about the temple devotion only. Another alternative suggestion can be said that this opportunity provided to those strongmen, mostly from the 'outer areas' an opportunity of gaining respectability. David Ludden says regarding the *Marava*s that these 'marginal people' particularly in the unsettled conditions of the period between fourteenth and the sixteenth centuries and even after that found their skills very lucrative. However they found that their martial skills did not bring them unqualified success. Where they were thinly settled, they were poor agricultural servants selling protection for fees. But where they could muster the strength of protecting something really big they also became rich. Thus he finds that the *Arapangu Marava*s established a protectorate over the great Vaishnava temple and sectarian centre (*matam*) at Nanguneri which brought them rich rewards.[16] Hence we find in these cases 'outer communities' through the route of donating *patikaval* dues to the temple secured a niche for themselves without transforming them into agriculturists as in case of the *Surutimans*, and the *Pallis*.

The Murugan Cult

Further it is proposed that there is a correlation between the assimilation of the 'outer communities'/martial communities and the revival of the Murugan cult. '...a god at the least, is the commentary on the nature and conditions of man. The ways in which the people apprehend divine is in a large measure a statement about the way in which they see themselves and their context in a given moment. It follows that the gods which are most persistent are those that have been adapted to the changing cultural and historical situations and are in some measures understood in terms of that change.'[17]

Murugan in the Cankam literature was the reigning god of the *kurunci* (hill) *tinai*. He was the war god and in *Tirumurukarrupadai* which is considered to be a relatively later composition, we find his cult sites to be spread over all the four *tinai*s. So in this method he was being universalized. Moreover *Tirumurukarrupadai* is considered by some scholars to be the precursor of *bhakti* literature. However in the subsequent period the importance accorded to the Murugan cult ceased. In the Pallava period Somaskanda became the leitmotif of the Pallava art. Though Skanda and Murugan became finally related in *Tirumurukarrupadai*, the Sanskritized version Skanda, who gained popularity in the Gupta period in North India, is quite different from the primeval force personified as Murukan as depicted in the Cankam literature. In the Chola period the Thyagaraja cult became important. We know that Thyagaraja is the processional form (*utsavabera*) form of Somaskanda and shares some characteristics with Murugan (the red colour, bigamy etc.)

In the context of the interrelation between the reemergence of the Murugan cult and that of the martial communities, the medieval text *Ittiyelupatu* composed by Ottakuttar provides relevant information. *Ittiyelupatu* is a poem in the praise of *Cenkundars*. *Cenkundar*s are a class of weavers known in the epigraphs as *Kaikkolar*s. They played a very important role in the temple administration as well as military matters. *Kaikkolar*s are known to have been granted *ruttirapatti* lands and are referred to by the title *senapati*.[18] Even the ninth century lexicon Divakaram refers to *Cenkuntarpatai* or the army of the *Cenkundar*s. Infact the *Kaikkola* regiments formed an important portion of the Chola army, with different denominations. Ottakuttar, the poet belonged to that community. The *Cenkundar*s or the *Kaikkolar*s were referred as *Ekangaviras*.[19] In *Ittiyelupatu* it is stated that the Chola king Muchukuntan won favour from Murugan after completion of penance.[20] Lord Murugan bestowed upon him nine of his personal bodyguards, with the help of whom he established a world wide empire. It was this warrior-weaver and the close confidante of the king who was credited with the bringing of Thyagaraja to the earth.

Another important body of soldiers i.e. *Virasolanukkar* was possibly built up by Chola king Parantaka I. It was possibly a band of soldiers dedicated to look after the personal safety of the king.[21] This class of soldiers has been referred to in inscriptions from Thiruvarur, Thiruvottiyur and Vedaranyam. An inscription[22] refers to *Virasola-anukkan* Katan

Melvayil, who donated ghee costing 100 ilak*kasus* to light lamps in the temple in the year 937 AD. Another record in the 31st regnal year of Parantaka I registers a gift of land by a member of the body called Nitta-Virasola-anukkar of Arinjigai-Isvaram in Itaiyarru-natu for burning a perpetual lamp in the temple of Tiruttavatturai-Isvarabhattaraka. It was purchased from the *sabha* of Nityavinita-chaturvedi-mangalam of Koyil Tavatturai of Murramam.[23] Parantaka I had the epithet Virasola and the earliest reference to this regiment is found from mid-tenth century. So it is quite possible that he built up this regiment. The inscription dated in the twenty-ninth regnal year of Kulottunga III, which corresponds to 1208 AD, refers to a regiment of the same name[24] which records the gift of money by a person who is referred to as a member of *Virasolanukkar*. This proves that this regiment formed possibly during the reign of Parantaka I continued to function for a long time. This *Virasolanukkar* has been fondly mentioned as *"Nam-makkal"* (Our sons) by Vitivitankar i.e. Thyagaraja who himself is said to have granted land to one Punkoyil Nambi, a dramatist for composing an eulogistic poem, *Viranukkavijayam* in honour of *Nam makkal Virasolanukkar*. The close connection between this body and Thyagaraja and the fact that Parantaka I and Virarajendra both held the epithet Virasola tempts one to equate either of these two with the myth of Muchukuntan.

Actually *Ittiyelupatu* explains the backdrop of the revival of Murugan cult. Though Murugan was so powerfully represented in *Tirumurukarrupadai* which has been viewed as the precursor of the '*bhakti*' literature by the literary historians, he is virtually forgotten in the 'Bhakti' literature. Murugan cult was subsumed under the Sanskritic Skanda cult for a larger part during the second half of the first millennium AD. In the twelfth and the thirteenth centuries Murugan cult comes back. *Kanthapuranam*, the authoritative Tamil text for the myth of Murugan was composed by Kacciyappa Civachariyar probably around 1400 AD. By this time Arunagiri was spreading the fame of Murugan and Valli, his bigamous partner with whom he enjoyed secret love (*kalavu*) outside the nuptial bond. However the seeds seem to have been sown just in the preceding years and the martial communities that we have examined appear to be breaking forth through the 'inner' communities and in this period the revival of the Murugan cult seem to have played a very important role. Thus it is concluded that the 'outer communities' had played an important role in restructuring the 'inner society'. However in the process they also changed their own identity.

References

1. Ramanujan, A.K., *Interior Landscape*, 1985.
2. Burton, Stein, *Peasant State and society in Medieval South India*, OUP, 1994, p. 36
3. P.C. Chakrabarti, *The Art of war in Ancient India*, 1989, Delhi, p. 9.
4. Marc Bloch, *Feudal Society*, 1975, Vol. I, p. 54.
5. Natana Kasinathan, 'The Role of shepherds through the ages (from first to the fifteenth century AD) in *Hero-stones of Tamilnadu*, Madras.
6. *Epigraphia Indica* (hereafter E.I.) Vol. VII, No. 19(1); *South Indian Inscriptions* (hereafter S.I.I, Vol. XVII, Nos. 204 and 209.
7. James Heitzman, *Gifts of Power*, OUP, 1997, p. 142.
8. No. 500 (RJ III :15; No. 493 (RJ III : 16) ; No. 497 (RJ III : 16); No. 499 (RJ III : 16); No. 501 (RJ III 16); No. 495 (RJ III : 18); No. 496 (RJ III : 18).
9. *Annual Report on Epigraphy*, (hereafter *ARE*) 515 of 1912.
10. *ARE*, 523 of 1912
11. *ARE*, 502 of 912
12. *ARE*, 35 of 1913
13. *ARE*, 276 of 1943-44
14. *Narrinai*, 291.
15. M. Arokiaswamy, 'Social Developments under the Imperial Colas' in *TASSI* 1956-57; Y. Subbarayalu, 'Social change and the valangai and idangai Divisions', *Studies in Cola History*, Chennai, 2001.
16. David Ludden, *Peasant Society in South India*, Princeton University Press, 1985.
17. Clothey, Fred, *The Many faces of Murugan: The History and Meaning of a South Indian God*, The Hague, 1978, pp. 8-9.
18. *ARE*, 163 of 1916.
19. *ARE*, 5 of 1944-45, 7 of 1944-45
20. *Ittiyelupatu*, v. 31.
21. *SII*, Vol XVII, intro p. V.
22. *SII*, Vol. XVII no.466.
23. *ARE*, 1928-29, Appendice.B, No.103.
24. *SII*, Vol. XVII No. 446.

9

Civil Society Under the Sultanate-Mughal Rule: The Role of the Sufis

Syed Ejaz Hussain

The concept of civil society is modern. In layman's language the term civil society refers to the autonomous social organizations which resist arbitrary exercises of power by the state. In other words, civil society is a society wherein the social institutions enjoy certain liberties and by this method the power of the state is restrained or controlled. This conception goes back to the eighteenth century, when philosophers like Montesquieu and Thomas Paine argued that the despotic tendencies of Europe's absolute monarchs could be checked if 'intermediate powers' such as the nobility, the bourgeoisie, the Church, and the press united to assert their independence.

Hegel, a noted modern Philosopher, who believed in a rational state based on individual liberty, has advocated a mutual dependence of state and civil society. The society, in Hegel's opinion, will be governed by mechanical laws formed, directed and regulated by the state, and in this way, civil society will depend upon the state for intelligent supervision, while the state will depend upon civil society for accomplishment of its aforesaid task. But this theory of mutual dependence attributes a superior position to the state and gives an inferior status to the civil society. The authority of the state thus remains absolute and supreme. However, Hegel's theory of individual liberty comprises the individual's right of property which is considered an essential condition of human personality and without which people will become only a formless mass. This gives added strength to the civil society. Hegel's concept of civil society, therefore, guarantees certain liberties and empowerment to the social institutions like guilds, corporations, local communities and other such autonomous organizations. Later on, growth of labour unions, chambers of commerce, corporate bodies, press and other voluntary associations began to be considered as strong elements of civil society. The level of internal organizations and assertiveness of these autonomous bodies determine how they control (and collaborate with) the state power[1].

Today, the canvas of civil society and its elements has become wider. The conditions for a society qualifying as civil are now searched generally within the ambit of democracy, liberalism, human rights, individual's liberty, civil justice as well as other social institutions which are immune from the state tutelage. India, with its pluralistic pattern of society for centuries and now being the largest democracy in the world, enshrines a long tradition which provides conditions for qualifying her as a civil society. During the period of six hundred years of the Sultanate-Mughal rule, India had witnessed many collisions and conflicts. In spite of this, the country forged a realm of harmony between the ruler and the ruled on the one hand, and between the two principal socio-religious groups i.e., the Hindus and the Muslims, on the other hand. This harmony largely qualified India as a civil society. A study of the Indian experience of civil society demands a wider analysis of social forces operating as determinant of civil society. In the context of the Sultanate-Mughal rule in the medieval period, we find one strong social force which was sufism that worked not only for harmony among different segments of the society but for a harmony between the state and the society too.

Sufism

The mystical tradition or *tasawwuf* in Islam is known as sufism. Those who belong to or practice this mystical tradition are called sufis. The term sufi is derived from the Arabic word *sûf* (course wool) in honour of the coarse woolen garments worn by the first sufis, resembling the garb of Christian monks and mystics in other faiths. Like other mystical movements in different religions like Christianity, Judaism, Buddhism and Hinduism, the sufi path seeks to discipline the mind and body, in order to experience directly the presence of God. Sufism also began as a reform movement in response to the growing materialism and the wealth of Muslim society that accompanied the expansion and growing power of the Muslim kingdoms. Sufism emphasized on seeking the purity and simplicity in life. Sufis concentrated in developing practices of intense devotion and lived ascetic lives[2]. Abul Fazl, in *Ain-i-Akbari*, has given a list of all sufi orders that existed during his time, with some details of leading sufis[3].

The studies of sufism has till now emphasized the esoteric dimension of different sufi orders. The role of sufism in social reconstruction or as an element in constituting civil society in India is yet to be paid attention. Sufism eschewed violence and respected pluralism in the society. It often resisted tyranny and promoted civil rights by its role as mediator between the rulers and the ruled.

Two Groups of Sufis

India witnessed broadly two groups of Sufis-one who abstained from having any direct links with the state, denying honour, title or even grants and preferred a spartan life-the other who collaborated with the state. They not only accepted honour, title and grants but shared power and held honourable posts in the government[4]. Both the groups, either by adopting a separatist outlook or by collaborating with the rulers, influenced the state in some way or the other, and restrained its arbitrary power though in a limited sense.

The *Chishti* sufis were such saints who maintained aloofness from the state. They avoided the political authority and refused to accept any kind of favour from the rulers. But this attitude of the early *Chishti* sufis did not deter the rulers from having connections with them. The *Chishti* sufis were very popular and revered among people, both Muslims and Hindus. They in their *khanqahs* or hospices cultivated contacts with people from all strata of the society and developed a mass-base behind them. They could, if they so desired, endanger the political security of a ruler. Hence, the rulers in order to get mass-base support as well as moral support desired to gain the favour of the sufis. This gave, though indirectly, political stability to their rule. Since the *Chishti* sufis did not accept any grant or favour from the state; the rulers were keen not to do such an act which might hurt their sentiments. In this way, the *Chishti* sufis indirectly influenced the rulers and restrained them from arbitrary use of their power.

Qutbuddin Bakhtiyar Kaki (d.1235) and Baba Fariduddin Ganj-i-shakar were great sufis of the *Chishti* order. Qutbuddin Bakhtiyar Kaki lived in highly impoverished condition but did not accept any gift from the contemporary rulers like Qutbuddin Aibak or Iltutmish. Once he enjoined the king Iltutmish: 'O ruler Of Delhi, it is incumbent on you to be good to all poor people, mendicants, *darveshes* and helpless folk. Treat all men kindly and strive for their welfare'[5]. Iltutmish wanted him to be the spiritual head of the state (or *Shaikh-ul-Islam*) but the saint declined.

Baba Fariduddin Ganj-i-shakar popularly known as Baba Farid (1173-1265) became so popular in Punjab that the Sikhs long after his death included a portion of his teachings known as *Farid Bani* consisting of 112 *slokas* in *Guru Granth Sahib* when it was compiled by (the 5th Sikh Guru), Guru Arjun Dev. He was much respected by the Delhi rulers. Once he wrote a letter to Balban on behalf of a needy person. His disciple, Mian Mir Shah (1550-1636) of Lahore was a personal friend of Guru Arjun Dev on whose invitation he came to Amritsar and laid there foundation of the Golden temple[6].

Nizamuddin Awliya (1236-1325), the most outstanding *Chishti* saint lived in Delhi for about seventy-five years from the age of sixteen and witnessed the rule of seven sultans on the throne of Delhi. He followed the teachings of his mentor Khawja Moinuddin *Chishti* (d.1236) who said, 'If anyone has these three qualities, you may know that God holds him to be His friend : First, a generosity like the generosity of the river; secondly, a benevolence like the benevolence of the Sun; and thirdly, a hospitality like the hospitality of the earth'[7] Zia-ud-din Barani writes, 'He made no distinction between the nobles and the plebians, the rich and the poor, the learned and the illiterate, the villagers and the towns fold, the soldiers and the warriors, the free-people and the slaves'[8]. His disciples were spread all over India. He and his contemporary, Shaikh Nasiruddin (also known as *Chiragh Dilli*) and Shaikh Fakhruddin Zarradi often admonished the rulers for their anger and high-handed policy. Shaikh Fakhruddin Zarradi asked Muhammad Tughluq to control his anger. 'What anger ?' the Sultan asked. 'The anger of wild animals'[9], replied the Shaikh. Nizamuddin Awliya also admonished the Sultan in the same tone for the proposal to coordinate missionary activity with political expansion.

The other group of sufis were those who collaborated with the state and accepted government jobs too. Prominent among them were *Suharwardis* and *Shuttaris.* Bahauddin Zakariya (1182-1269) of Multan was the founder of *Suharwardi* order in India. He was appointed as the spiritual head of the state by Iltutmish. He remained linked with the rulers and had the fortune of witnessing the rule of first eight *mamluk* sultans of

Delhi. This office of the spiritual head or *Shaikh-ul-Islam* continued in his family till AD 1535.

The State, Society and the Sufis in Medieval India

Suharwardis believed that they could perform their function more effectively if they cultivated relations with the political authority. Shaikh Bahauddin Zakariya once complained in writing to Iltutmish against Qubacha, the governor of Sindh and Multan. When the Mougols attacked Multan during the reign of Nasiruddin Mahmud in AD 1246 and besieged Multan, the saint played an important role in pursuing the invaders to raise the siege and thus the city was rescued, and citizens were saved from hunger, death and killing. *Suhawardis* believed in living good life and accumulating wealth. Bahauddin Zakariya felt for the society and its welfare. He emphasized that for a decent living, men must work hard. With this end in view he encouraged them to apply their labour to productive activities such as cultivating lands for good harvest and running trade and commerce for profit. Whenever opportunity came, he cleared off the forests and brought unused lands under cultivation. Wells were also renovated by him for providing water facility. Once when there was a famine in Multan, Bahauddin Zakariya not only asked the governor for distributing relief to the famine-stricken people but he helped the tide over the calamity with considerable amount of grains supplied from the stock of his *khanqah*[10]. One of the eminent *Suhawardi* sufis, Shaikh Samauddin Kambo, became the patron saint of the Lodi dynasty in Delhi. His son-in-law, Shaikh Jamali, was elevated to the status of poet laureate at the court of Sultan Sikandar Lodi. Several other Kambo saints held important ranks and positions in the Lodi Empire. A sufi saint remonstrated Sikandar Lodi against his prohibition of pilgrimages. 'Wretch', cried Sikandar Lodi, drawing his sword, 'do you defend idolatry!' 'No', replied the sufi, 'but I maintain that kings ought not prosecute their subjects'[11]. Once Sikandar Lodi, stationed ins Delhi as the deputy of his father, thought of looting the Hindu temples at Kurukshetra. Before taking action, he however consulted Mian Abdullah Ajudhani who advised against it. This enraged the prince so much that he charged the saint with supporting idolaters and threatened to begin by killing him. The sufi said that he was prepared for it. This silenced Sikandar Lodi and he bowed to the Sufi's advice[12].

Some sufis restrained the rulers by writing letters to them either on their own or by way of reply to a correspondence begun by the rulers. Alauddin Khalji wrote to Nizamuddin Awliya and sought his advice on some political-administrative matters. Muzaffar Shams Balkhi, a disciple of Hazrat Sharfuddin Yahya Maneri wrote letters to Firuz Shah Tughluq, the ruler of Delhi as well as Sikandar Shah and Ghiyasuddin Azam Shah, the rulers of Bengal. He gave personal opinions on some government matters as sought by these rulers. This was also a way to control the arbitrary use of power by the kings.

Sufis wielded some control over the state and its ruler through their *murids* or devotees also. The *murids* spread the message and teachings of his *pirs* in other regions and this widened the mass-base of the sufis. Many disciples of the sufis were members of the ruling elite in different regions. Shaikh Husain Nagauri, a *Chishti* sufi of Nagaur in Rajasthan had several such disciples. Ahmad Khan Lodi Sarangkhani, the governor of Jaunpur was one of his *murids.* Through the agency of *murids* the sufis laid some control over the rulers. Another advantage of this was that the poor *murids* of an eminent sufi could get help from the richer *murids* of the same *pir*.

Among the sufis of later period Shaikh Bayazid of Punjab was noted for his ungrudging manner in which he took up himself the burdens of all who needed his help whether Muslims or Hindus. When Sidi Yahya was appointed *kotwal* of Delhi by Aurangzeb, he decided to employ some more persons on his staff. A group of people came to the *Shaikh* and asked him recommend their appointment. The *Shaikh* took them all along with him to the *kotwal* and made the recommendation. The *kotwal* said, 'Everyone comes to you and you do things for everyone. But I am a person with three defects. First, I am a purchased slave; secondly, I am an Abyssinian, uncouth in appearance and harsh in speech, the worst kind of man. Thirdly, I am a *kotwal*, whose business and profession is to disregard persons. Now that you have come for the sake of these people, I shall employ them. But if you take the same trouble again, I shall not oblige you'. The *Shaikh* said, 'If I come again, you may shave my head, seat me on an ass, and have me taken round the town'. Those people were immediately appointed on some posts. After two or three days, a few more people came to the *Shaikh* and besought him to get them (also) appointed. First he excused himself, but on insistence by them he went to the *kotwal*, taking a barber and an ass along with him. He said, 'As I had accepted the condition that if I troubled you again, you could shave my head and take me round the town, I have brought this ass and a barber with me. I am willing to undergo the punishment at once, but you must employ these people'. Sidi Yahya smiled when he heard this and fulfilled the demand of the sufi[13].

The sufis thus stood on the side of the people and had the courage to criticize and persuade the rulers to act fairly and justly with their subjects. Rulers accordingly sought their cooperation in ensuring the smooth running of their administration. Thus, having a harmonious dialogue with the state they balanced the power between the state and the society by restraining the first from tyranny on the other. They eschewed violence and respected pluralism in the society. By comprehending god devotionally instead of intellectually, the sufis minimized the areas of collisions and conflicts between the two major faiths. On the one hand, the sufis laid a restrain on the arbitrary use of power and by cultivating harmonious condition avoided stifling communalism and forged tolerance between different segments of the contemporary society. The sufis stressed on the need of adopting greater *jihad* i.e., striving for the just and fighting one's animal tendencies and shunning the lesser *jihad* or militancy. Sufis cultivated moderate minds in the society and attempted to refrain the rulers from the use of the power arbitrarily. In fine, the sufis acted as a strong factor in creating a civil society during the rule of the Delhi Sultanates and the Mughals in medieval India.

References

1. George H. Sabine, *A History of Political Theory*, London, 1964, pp. 658-67.
2. John L. Esposito, *What Everyone Needs to Know About Islam*, OUP, New York, 2002, pp. 56-8.
3. Abul Fazal, *Ain-i-Akbari*, (Trs.) H.S.Jarret, Vol. III, pp. 254, 361-2, 402.
4. Muhammad Muzammil Haq, *Some Aspects of the Principal Sufi orders in India*, Dhaka, 1985, pp. 1-22, 182; M. Mujeeb, Indian Muslims, New Delhi, 1985, pp. 113-67, 283-315.
5. Vivek Bhattacharya, *Famous Indian Sages–Their Immortal Message*, Sagar Publications, New Delhi, 1982, p. 397; Ajeet Jawed, *Heritage of Harmony : An Insight into Medieval India*, Gyan Publishing House, New Delhi, 2002, p. 16.

6. Muhammad Muzammil Haq, *op. cit.*, pp. 43-56; Ajeet Jawed, *op. cit.*, pp. 12-14.
7. Amir Khurd, *Siyar-ul-Awliya*, Muhibb-i-Hind Press, Delhi, 1309 A.H., p. 46.
8. Ziauddin Barani, *Tarikh-i-Firuz Shahi*, Calcutta, 1862, p. 343.
9. M. Mujeeb, *op. cit.*, p. 140.
10. Mufti Wali Hasan, *Tazkirat-ul-Awliya-i-Hindo-Pakistan*, Karachi, n.d., p. 83; Muhammad Muzammil Haq, *op. cit.*, pp. 84-91.
11. Thomas Keightley, *History of India*, London, 1847, p. 17, Ajeet Jawed, *op. cit.*, p. 25.
12. Fathullah Mujtabai, *Aspects of Hindu-Muslim Cultural Relation*, New Delhi, 1978, p. 100; Ajeet Jawed, *op. cit.*, p. 25; I. H. Siddiqui, 'The Composition of the Nobility under the Lodi Sultans', *Medieval India–A Miscellany*, Aligarh, 1977, Vol. 4, pp. 20, 23, 62; *idem*, 'Social Mobility in the Delhi Sultanate', *Medieval India* (ed.), Irfan Habib, Delhi, 1999, pp. 42-44.
13. M. Mujeeb, *op. cit.*, pp. 312-13.

10

Caste and Dynamics of Society in Andhra (1600-1750)

M. Krishna Kumari

The social change and the new social order that pervaded the pre-colonial Andhra society has not gone unnoticed in the Telugu inscriptions and the literature of the Seventeenth and Eighteenth Centuries. The changing occupations of people during medieval times is indicated by the fact that during the period under survey some of the *Sudras* had become the rulers and the Brahmins took to the profession of arms. It is observed that the tribals and non-Hindu people in the peripheral regions were admitted to the Brahmanical system mainly as *Sudras*.[1] As a result, a wide variety of social groups or sub-castes in the *Sudra* community have come into existence. Several early *Puranas* have ascribed the changes in the society to *kaliyuga*,[2] and so also the Telugu literary works in Andhra. The extinction of an old social order is always a matter of great concern as it inaugurates the beginning of a phase of uncertainty. From the descriptions of the *Kali* age, one can perceive that the social crisis was manifested in terms of breaking up of the erstwhile social relationship which weighed heavily in favour of the *Brahmins*. Further, some of the castes and communities found no mention at all in the epigraphs due to their state of economy and religious ideology. On the other hand, some of the literary compositions provide ample information about the different sub-castes among the *Sudras*. Besides these literary works and epigraphs, sources such as the oral traditions, ballads and the songs sung by some of the dependent communities and the place names of the villages contain useful information about the social groups of the late medieval times. With the help of these historical evidences, an attempt is made here to critically analyse the dynamics of society including the information and proliferation of new castes due to their occupation/profession, religion and language, the changed social order and the social mobility.

Hamsavimsati

The major changes during the period are the growth of caste system into its mature form and the proliferation of *Sudra* caste into innumerable sub-groups. The caste system which is a form of social differentiation is very much intimately connected with changes in material life and thereby the study of the growth of the caste system can be made with the social processes and social changes. The proliferation of castes during the medieval times was mainly due to the land grants in tribal areas and bringing each tribe into the Hindu system as a *Sudra* caste. The temple and agrarian land expansion and the spread of iron-plough agriculture encouraged the absorption of tribal people into Brahmanical fold, who were ultimately ranked as *Sudras*. As a result, not only more number of castes emerged but also we find a number of sub-castes within each caste in the medieval Andhra society. For example, the Telugu stone inscriptions of the Sixteenth century refer to *Dommaras*, the professional jugglers and acrobats as of having twenty-four castes. The fourth caste comprising large number of sub-castes can be known from the Telugu literary work, *Hamsavimsati*, written by Ayyalaraju Narayanamatya. The importance of this rare piece of literary evidence in this context can be emphasized as it provides a large list of people who belonged to different castes and communities that have gathered to participate in the celebration of a *Tirunallu* (festival) of the village God.[3] About one hundred and eleven castes and communities are mentioned in the work in addition to the traditional castes such as *Brahmins*, *Kshatriyas*, *Vaisyas* and *Sudras*. Further, it may be pointed out here that sixty-one groups or communities are mentioned in a later chapter of Manu and more than one hundred castes in the *Brahmavaivarta Purana* mostly consisting of tribal people converted into castes. The list of castes mentioned in *Hamsavimsati* includes agricultural communities, artisan and industrial communities; mercantile and trading communities; pastoral communities, dependent communities, entertainers, forest tribes, religious and foreign communities. Since these different communities of groups are not mentioned in an order according to their occupation/nature of work, they have been arranged on the basis of the knowledge derived from the other historical sources. (See Table 1)

Sukasaptati

Though this list appears to be exhaustive and lengthy, for some reasons some of the important castes in the society are omitted. However,

Table–1

List of Castes and Communities Mentioned in Hamsavimsati, Canto III, pp. 140-141

Sl. No.	Agricultural	Artisanal/Industrial	Mercantile/Trading	Service Communities	Dependent Communities	Entertainers	Forest Tribes	Pastoral	Religious Communities	Foreigners	Miscellaneous
(1)	(2)	(3)	(4)	(5)	(6)	(7)	(8)	(9)	(10)	(11)	(12)
1.	Kamma	Kummara	Komati	Rajaka	Vaitalika	Parihasakulu	Poya	Golla	Janagalu	Parangulu	
2.	Velama	Kammari	Balija	Kshauraka	Vamdimagadhulu	Sufa	Eruku		Teranatakapu Jangalu	Ingillsulu	Nasidavaka
3.		Vadrangi Kavalla varu	Kamchi	Katika	Bhattu	Nataka	Chenchu (fisherman)	Jalagarl[13] Jogulu	Talakrimdu	Parasulu	Malneri
4.		Vadasale		Kati Papalu	Chandala Matangulu[9] (of Mala caste)	Bogam Varu	Enadi		Ramagovindulu	Turaka	
5.		Agalasa		Medara	Pichchuguntilu	Dommari	Venkarl[11] (a gypsy tribe)	Besta[14] (fisherman and Palanquin bearer)	Gorada Jogulu	Odde	Piddemvaru
6.		Kanchari		Idige	Mamdapichchulu	Bommalatavaru	Patra[12] (akin to Boyas)		Pairagulu	Ghurksra	
7.		Gamdla[1] (oil monger)		Talari	Kommuri Dasallu	Vipravinodinulu			Jatadharulu	Gauda misra	
8.		Pinjari[2] (Cotton cleaner)		Bheri Dasallu	Taviru	Palanativirulu			Avadhutalu		
9.		Battulu		Charma Karmulu	Suddulu Kamallu	Indrajatika			Paramahamsalu	Chatiki	
10.		Tellakoka battulu		Mashti		Mahendra jatika			Sannyasulu		Srugalaka
11.		Chitrakara		Jetti		Hastalaghava			Valandulu		
12.		Uppara		Chippe[8] (tailor)		Konangulu[10] (buffoon)			Ekadamdulu		Jatikarta

(Contd.)

(Table-1 Contd.)

Sl. No.	Agricultural	Artisanal/Industrial	Mercantile/Trading	Service Communities	Dependent Communities	Entertainers	Forest Tribes	Pastoral	Religious Communities	Foreigners	Miscellaneous
(1)	(2)	(3)	(4)	(5)	(6)	(7)	(8)	(9)	(10)	(11)	(12)
13.		Jogata[3] (weaver) Jandra[4] (a certain tribe of weaver Vane[5] (Baman caste) Vannegattu[6] (engaged in painting) Satuni[7] (who weave sack cloth)							Tridamdulu Vanaprasthulu Digambarulu Gomukhulu Niyamasthulu Urdhvabahulu Satani sivasttulu Tambala Yogulu Jaina Viramushti Kall Mallari Parasalu		Sevaparulu Padigevaru Valagamda

Note : The meaning/explanation of some of the castes and communities provided in C.P. Brown, *Telugu-English Dictionary* (2nd edition, Deihi, 1992) are given within the brackets for a better understanding of the caste/community.

Source : 1. C.P. Brown, *op. cit.*, p. 362; 2. *Ibid.*, p. 755; 3. *Ibid.*, p. 557; 4. *Ibid.*, p. 469; 5. *Ibid.*, p. 1159; 6. *Ibid.*, p. 1136; 7. *Ibid.*, p. 1327; 8. *Ibid.*, p. 417; 9. *Ibid.*, p. 977; 10. *Ibid.*, p. 326; 11. *Ibid.*, p. 1225; 12. *Ibid.*, p. 703; 13. *Ibid.*, p. 463; 14. *Ibid.*, p. 905.

information about them can be gathered from the same work in different contexts and also from the other literary evidences like *Sukasaptati* written by Palavekari Kadiripari. They are the *Kapus* or *Reddis*, *Madigas* and *Vettis*, who belong to the agricultural communities, *Bavanilu* or *Bainindu*, *Pambalavaru* and *Kommulavaru* of the dependent communities. While describing a *Kapu*, his house and the names of the crops grown by him, Narayanamatya states that *Siranka* is the best among the eleven sub-sects of the *Kapu* caste flourishing on this earth.[4] In this context, the sub-sects of *Kapu* caste are stated as *Patna*, *Motali*, *Pedakamti*, *Pakanati*, *Are*, *Kamma*, *Velama*, *Konda*, *Adi*, *Gona* and *Konide*.[5] To this list of the sub-sects of the *Kapu* caste, few more can be added from the information provided by the folklore literature. The stories of Komirelli Mallanna, Kunti Malla Reddi and Anumala Brahma Reddi refer to the names of fourteen sub-sects of *Kapu* caste as well as their formation.[6] This includes *Motati*, *Gudati*, *Pakanati*, *Pedakanti*, *Kongakoyya*, Mukkamattu, *Mumjuru* and *Valugonda*. The *Jamba Purana* contains a list of low castes like *Mala*, *Madiga*, *Dakkali*, *Kanikudukulu*, *Gampa*, *Dimpula*, *Bolli* and *Kayala* besides mentioning the other castes in the society as *Kapu*, *Munnuru Kapu*, *Bomdili*, *Bogamu*, *Muttarasi*, *Vadramgi*, *Mamsali*, *Kamchari*, *Komati*, *Atkari*, *Kammari*, *Medari*, *Gaundla*, *Pichchuguntla*, *Balasamta*, *Turka*, *Tambala*, *Kummari*, *Mangali*, *Pinjari*, *Marvadi* and *Arvakula*.[7] *Bavanilu* or *Painindu* or *Bainedu* are the *madiga* musicians performing the rituals to the goddess.[8] Some of them known as *Pambalavaru* used to play music on an instrument called *Pamba*, praising and singing about the goddess. They sing the stories of *Ankalamma*, the origin of the *Mata*, etc. Another sub-sect is *Kommuvaru*, who used to sing Katamaraju Kathalu and Ganga Kathalu. *Mala Dasaris* used to narrate the stories of Pandavas.[9]

One of the remarkable features of this period is the emergence of several groups of entertainers and dependent communities, who led a semi-nomadic life and depended for their livelihood on the others. They used to sing and praise the family histories and *prasasti* of certain sub-castes of the *Sudra* caste besides entertaining the people. For example, the *Bhattu* or *Bhattrajus* had special attachment to the *Velama*, *Kamma* and *Kapu* castes.[10] The *Pichchuguntas* are known for being learned in family history of *Kapus*, *Kammas*, *Gollas* and others.[11] Similarly the *Viramushtis*, who were the professional acrobats and mendicants are attached to the *Devangas* and *Komatis*.[12]

Because of the specialisation of the craft works and other activities in this period, certain groups might have emerged as *Battulu*, *Tellakoka*, *Jandras* and *Pinjaris* (cotton cleaners), all belonging to the weaving community. The Telugu region had witnessed the immigration of many foreigners, who integrated themselves into the Andhra society during this period. People known as *Parangulu*, *Ingilisulu*, *Parasulu*, *Turaka*, *Odde*, *Ghurjara* and *Gauda Misra* are mentioned participating in the village festival, though they belong to the different religious faiths.

Telugu Inscriptions and Andhra Society

Although the idea of caste and caste regulations were explicitly mentioned in the inscriptions of the early medieval times, solidarity of the caste became an important feature of the society during this period. This can be said on the basis of the imprecatory verses of the inscriptions ranging from the Sixteenth Century onwards.[13] Several epigraphs registering the donations made by the caste groups like *Viramushtis*, *Dommaras* and others mention in clear terms of the social ostracism and denial of certain caste privileges for those who violate the stipulations made in the grants belonging to their communities.[14] Sometimes, it is also mentioned that those members of the caste groups who defy the stipulations made in the inscriptions should be considered as those of the low castes like *Malas*, *Vetti*, Barbers, *Chandalas*, *Upparas*, *Dommaras*, *Boyas*, *Vaddevaru*, etc.[15] These instances suggest that even among the dependent castes who were nomadic in nature, the identity of caste is sharply defined and the different castes are consciously ranked with the land holding and that the agricultural castes naturally getting the top ranks. The *Brahmins* have been given the highest respect due to their Vedic knowledge, spiritual leadership and land power. While describing the activities of the *Brahmins*, it is stated in an inscription of the Sixteenth Century that the *Brahmins* having been born from the face of Lord Vishnu will always become the *Acharya*; *Vaidikis* and *Niyogis*. And that, even if they write the accounts and become the *karanams* of the village they will not become the *Sudras*.[16] In this context it may be mentioned here that the *Vipravinodins*, a dependent caste was considered to be the descendents of a *Brahmin* by a *Lingayat* woman according to the tradition.[17] It is interesting to note that almost all the epigraphs registering the gifts made by the *Vipravinodirs* refer to their *Gotras*, *Sutras*, and *Sakhas* which are like those of *Brahmins*.[18] But it is not clearly known whether they really belong to the *Brahmin* lineage or that they assumed the *Gotras*, *Sutras* and *Sakhas* in their records to exalt their social status.[19]

It can be seen from the literature of the period that the land holding castes like *Reddis* or *Kapus* were accorded great respect in the society, while the artisan castes were accorded only subordinate status. The lower-most place was given to the *Malas*, *Madigas* and *Vettis* working as the agricultural labourers. The dependent castes became prominent by virtue of their activities and attracted the people of the times. This is mainly due to the changed socio-religious situation in the region.

Telugu Literature of 17th and 18th Centuries and Society

Visvagunadarsamu written by Venkatadhvari of the Seventeenth Century contains a very good description of the contemporary social conditions of India in general and South India in particular. The changes in the social status of the *Brahmins* and their activities are mainly attributed to the *kaliyuga*. While describing the situation in Andhra, it is stated that the *Sudras* became the lords in every village and the *Brahmins* became the *karnamas* (accountants) under them and if at all one or two *Vaidikas* were found they will be entrusted with the task of preparing the leaves used for dining.[20] All the practices and vices like inter-dining with the people of other castes, eating the food seen by the dogs (*sunulu*) and foreigners (*mlechchas*), wearing the clothes after bathing brought by the washer-men with the help of the donkeys (*rasabhamulu*), going out to the market places several times for purchasing the provisions, engaged in trade activities, acting as village accountants leaving aside the *Sastras* and mingling freely without any inhibitions with the *Sudra* caste people and other social groups by the *Brahmins* are considered by Venkatadhvari in his work as the evils of *kaliyuga* and not as virtues to be followed by of the *Brahmins.*[21] On the whole, it can be said that the *kaliyuga* is characterised by *Varnasamkara*, i.e., intermixture of *Varnas*, or social orders which implies the changed social order and a deep social crisis.

Kuchimanchi Timmakavi of the Eighteenth Century explained the social conditiбns of Andhra region very humorously in his work *Kukkutesvara Satakam*. From this work as well as *Chandrasekhara Satakam* by an anonymous author, we can get the picture of the emergence of several new social groups, their popularity and prominence and how it was resented by the people of the *Brahmin* caste. The social crisis is clearly reflected in the descriptions of *Kali* age in the Telugu works of Kuchimanchi

Timma Kavi and others. It is stated in his work that the money earned by a person would easily reach the prostitutes, thieves, *Dommaras*, deceitful persons, physicians, *Mala Dasaris*, entertainers, (*Atapatalavaru*) and kings, by way of the payment of penal fee, i.e., *Tappu, Danduga* and towards the bad vices of the people, such as intoxication and drugs (*Ganjayi, Kallu, nallamandu*), small eats (*nanjudlu*) and cock matches rather than good poets, *Brahmins* or temples.[22] He further observed in another poem that in this '*Kaliyug*', the people patronise and appreciate the skills of the entertainers, the stories narrated by the *Gollasuddulu*, the sayings of the Persians (*Parasikoktulu*) and non-brahmanical religions rather than *Vedas, Sastras*, Puranic learnings; prose, poetry and *Vichitra Kavitas*; divine languages and *Saiva* and *Vaishnava* religious traditions.[23]

The traditional occupations of the different castes how became interchangeable in the society can be known from another verse in the same work. It refers to the prominence of the poets of *Kapu* caste, *Yogis* or mendicants of Kanchara, Vaishnavas of Satani, soldiers of Salle, donors of *Komati*, *Pauranikas* of *Golla*, physicians of *Mala*, *Veyas*, slaves and kings of foreign origin (*Yavana dharadhisvarulu*), ministers of *Vaidikis* (*Brahmin* caste) elephant riders of *Boya* and fortune tellers from the villages (*Palle Daivagnulu*).[24] Likewise there are verses describing how people have favoured the songs and stories of the *Mala Dasaris*, *Gollas*, *Satani Jiggar* and *Jangamas* rather than the Puranic stories narrated by the Brahmins.[25] Another work, *Sri Giri Mallesa Satakamu* of Ramalingaraya refers to the changed social scenario and the evils of the period. It states that the *Mala* who kills and eats the cows became the kings; the prostitutes became the mothers of great warriors, people of low status became the learned scholars and those who polluted the *Varna* system (*Varna Sankarulu*) were felicitated by the kings while the upper caste was set aside.[26] Likewise, it is stated in *Sri Syamalamba Satakam* of Mallampalli Mallikarjuna Panditaradhyulu that the people will not hesitate to resort to any harm to the others on this earth due to *kaliyuga*. Further, the deviations in the behaviour, life styles of the people and certain social evils are described as the results of the *kaliyuga*. It states that the people used to eat meat and drink liquors claiming that their religion was different, accept even the donations of buffaloes and cats stating that it is not strange on this earth to sacrifice the animals with the view that it would bring the merit of the attainment of heaven for them, and roam in the village only begging for food being clad in the dress of the asceties.[27]

Raghavabhyudayam of Chintalapalli Chayapati of the Seventeenth Century throws a welcome light on the state of social crisis and anarchy in medieval Andhra. Like the other Telugu literary works it refers to the importance attained by the *Sakta* and *Vamachara* religious sects than the *Smarta*, *Saiva* and *Vaishnava* traditions. It specifically mentions *Varnasamkar* decline in the moral and *dharma* values and the state of anarchy in the kingdoms due to the changed social conditions. It is mentioned in the work that due to the impact of *kaliyuga*, rich men became misers, philanthropic persons became stingy, rulers became immoral and the people became jealous while injustice prevailed among the *Jatis*.[28] All these literary references clearly indicate that *Varnasramadharma* was passing through a social crisis and that there was upheaval among the various sections of the society.

Rise of Innumerable Sub-caste

Since the medieval times several sub-castes of the *Sudra* caste tried to exalt their social status by assuming a *Brahmanical* or supra-*Brahmanical* status through constructing long family p*rasastis* tracing mythical origin of its own and sometimes even deriving its origins from the celestial beings to excel the *Brahmins*, who trace their origins from the immortal sages.[29] This can be viewed as the legitimising mechanism invented by the certain dominant castes to win popular recognition and to foster. It appears from the literary sources of the period under study that the *Sudras* of different sub-sects seem to have been satisfied by the eulogies and family *prasastis* construed and sung by some of the dependent caste groups. Such attempts made by the sub-sects of the S*udra* caste people for the exaltation of their caste indicates the processes of upward social mobility taking place in the Andhra during the late medieval times. Exaltation of caste by way of adopting a person belonging to a higher caste is evidenced from an instance in a copper plate grant about the adoption of a *Vaisya* by the *Panchalamvaru* (artisan) caste during the time of Ibrahim Qutub Shah of Golconda.[30] It is clearly stated in the record that the adopted son loses both his original and acquired caste status in the event of violation of caste regulations.[31]

Another interesting feature of the medieval Andhra society is the harmony and the coordination among the sub-castes of the *Sudra* community. Unlike the neighbouring Tamil Nadu and Karnataka regions which witnessed the social conflicts for the rights and privileges between the artisans and agricultural caste groups, [32] the Andhra society was totally free from such conflicts. A few stone records of the Sixteenth Century refer to the grants made by the *Dommaras* to the temples along with the *Vipravinodins*.[33] It is also known from a copper plate record of the Seventeenth Century that communal donations were made jointly by artisans and agriculturists.[34]

Thus it can be deduced that the number of the newly formed sub-castes and communities of the *Sudra* caste had out-numbered those of the early medieval times. The formation and proliferation of new castes in the late medieval Andhra society is viewed in terms of the changed socio-religious and political conditions of the country besides the occupations of the people. The evidences drawn from *Hamsavimsati* and *Sukasaptati* bring to light a detailed picture of the different sub-castes that existed in the Andhra society during this period. The changed position of the upper castes especially the *Brahmins* and the *Sudra* ascendancy in Andhra society indicates the social dynamics and social change. Although these descriptions suggest a social crisis and that it was not a peaceful society where every one did his prescribed duties. The Andhra society did not experience any communal conflicts or struggles for rights and privileges. Donations made by the caste groups or by the heads of the community for the merit of all the members of their caste emphasises the solidarity pact of the castes. The other remarkable changes in the society were the conscious ranking of different castes and the exaltation. It appears that during this period the emergence of the dependent castes, who composed and lamented the family *prasastis* of different sub-castes in hyperbolic terms tracing their mythical origins had substituted the inscriptional passages of the early medieval times.

References

1. R.S. Sharma, *Social Changes in Early Medieval India, (C.A.D. 500-1200)*, Devraj Chanana Memorial Lecture, Delhi, 1969, p. 19.
2. R.S. Sharma, "The Kali Age : A Period of Social Crisis" in S.N. Mukherjee (ed.,) *India : History and Thought*, Delhi, 1982; B.N.S. Yadava, "The Accounts of the Kali Age and the Social Transition from the Antiquity to the Middle Ages", *Indian Historical Review*, Vol. V, 1-2, 1978-79, pp. 31-63.
3. *Ayyalaraju Narayanamatya's Hamsavimsti* (Published by) Vavilla Ramaswamy Sastrulu and Sons, Madras, 1964, Canto, III, pp. 140-141.

4. *Ibid.*, Canto IV, V. 136, p. 237.
5. *Ibid.*
6. M. Krishna Kumari, *Telugu Janapada Geya Gathalu* (in Telugu), Hyderabad, 1990, pp. 319-320.
7. *Ibid.*, B. Ramaraju and N. Krishna Kumari (eds.,) *Janapada Geyalu-Samghika Charitra* (in Telugu), Hyderabad, 1974.
8. *Ibid.*, Palavekari Kadiripati, *Sukasaptati*, Canto, V, 414, 415, pp. 209-210.
9. *Ibid.*
10. Edgar Thurston, *Castes and Tribes in Southern India*, Madras, 1909, Vol. I, p. 226.
11. *Ibid.*, Vol. VI, p. 195.
12. *Ibid.*, pp. 406-411.
13. *South Indian Inscriptions*, (hereafter S.I.I) Vol. XVI, No. 193, 197, 300.
14. *Ibid.*, *Inscriptions of Andhra Pradesh : Cuddapah District*, Vol. II, No. 46, pp. 53-54.
15. Butterworth and V. Venugopala Chetty, *Inscriptions on Copper Plates and Stones in the Nellore District*, Nellore, No. 124, 5, 9, 52, 115; Ongole, No. 114, Rapur, 26, 28, 29, 30, 43, 5, 51, 53, 54, 59, 62, 63; Kavali 49, 50; S.I.I., Vol. XVI, Nos. 227, 133, 135, 136.
16. *Inscriptions of Andhra Pradesh : Cuddapah District*, II, No. 23, dt. A.D. 1549; pp. 250-251, 1.21-25.
17. Edgar Thurston, *Op. Cit.*, p. 406.
18. Although it is difficult to state clearly which *Gotra*, *Sutra* or *Sakha* was considered superior or inferior to the other, references to *gotras*, *sutras* and *sakhas* by the Brahmins in the epigraphs indicates the hierarchy of Brahmins.
19. *S.I.I.*, Vol. XVI, Nos. 182, 186, 190, 195, 203.
20. *Visvagunadarsamu of Venkatadhvari* (Translated by Venkata Ramakrishna Kavulu), Madras, 1917, p. 40, V.2.
21. *Ibid.*, pp. 24-25, V.8, 9, 10, p. 35, V.3.
22. Kuchimanchi Timma Kavi, *Kukkutesvara Satakamu*, Vavilla edition, Madras, 1919, V.19, p. 11.
23. *Ibid.*, V.21, p. 12.
24. *Ibid.*, V.22, pp. 12-13.
25. *Ibid.*, V.24, 25.

26. *Sataka Samuchchayamu*, Part II, Andhra Sahitya Parishad, Kakinada, 1933, p. 125, V.60.
27. *Ibid.*, p. 60, V.56.
28. Chintalapalli Chayapati, *Raghavabhyudayam*, (ed.) By B. Ramaraju, Andhra Pradesh Sahitya Academy, Hyderabad, Canto I, V.67, 68 and 69.
29. Vijaya Ramaswamy, *Textiles and Weavers in Medieval South India*, Delhi, 1985, p. 112.
30. M. Krishna Kumari, "A Deed of Adoption and its Beliefs : A New Interpretation", *Proceedings of the Indian History Congress*, 54th Session, Mysore, 1993, No. 169, pp. 869-873.
31. *Ibid.*, p. 871.
32. Vijaya Ramaswamy, *Op. Cit.*, pp. 109-112; *Annual Report on Epigraphy* (hereafter *ARE*, 1913, No. 39, *Ibid.*, 1921, No.185; *Epigraphia Carnatica*, (hereafter EC) Vol. V, B 1.5.
33. M. Krishna Kumari, *Studies on Medieval Andhra History and Culture*, Delhi, 1994, p. 44.
34. *ARE*, 1918, Part II, para 84-1.

11

The Social World of the Weaver in the Northern Coromandel (1775-1817)

P. Swarnalatha

Following the acquisition of the Northern *Circars* by the English through the Mughal *farman* in 1765, the colonial State attempted to create and consolidate its power structures that ultimately shaped the political, economic and social conditions of the region. Till the end of the Eighteenth Century, the Colonial state tried hard to give a political cohesion to the conflict-ridden society of the region. By the adoption of various mechanisms, the Company in fact penetrated more deeply into the hinterland social activities, intertwined with the agrarian economy, textile economy and trading world; thereby the company paved the way for its consolidation in the region. As Robert Eric Frykenberg suggested, the Company was able to establish its colonial hegemony over the region because it comprehended its role, "within the inner logic and dynamics of traditional society".[1] In this paper an attempt is made to study the social world of the weaver during the end of the Eighteenth Century; and to find out the extent to which the intervention of the new political power transformed its character, especially through its trade policies.

Various Weaving Castes of the Region

The social structure of the weaving community of the Northern Coromandel region, like that of many other similar communities elsewhere, was many layered and complex. A number of castes in the region were engaged in or otherwise were related to the weaving profession, although only a few dominant traditional castes virtually monopolized the work. A significant correlation between caste and the production of specific varieties of cloth could be discerned in this region. While the *Padma Sales* specialized in coarse. weaving, the *Pattu Sales*, as the name indicates, confined their activities to silk weaving and superfine cloth weaving.[2] The *Devanga* weavers specialized mostly in producing pure cotton cloths.[3] The *Togatas* specialised in weaving the coarsest kind of cotton cloth catering to the needs of lower classes.[4] Traditionally, this group specialized in the production of red cloth.[5] The *Jandra* caste weavers as the name indicates, specialized in weaving long cloths.[6] The evidence from the Guntur and Masulipatnam districts reveals that the non-traditional weavers specialized in producing ordinary cloth meant for local consumption.[7] Even the popular forms of expressions such as proverbs indicate the specialization of the weaving carried on by the *Pariah* weavers. If the cloth was not woven perfectly, a common form of expression was *'Sagamu Sale Neta, Sagamu Mala Neta'*, meaning half the weaving was done by *Sales*, the other half by *Malas*.[8] Generally speaking, the finer varieties of cloth were produced by the castes higher in the social hierarchy.

In the Visakhapatnam district for instance, the principal weaving communities were *Devangas, Sales, Pattu Sales, Kaikalavallu, Dasarivallu* and *Goni Perikalu*: while in the Godavari district the great majority of the weavers belonged to the *Devanga* caste, although *Pattu Sa!es* and *Padma Sales* determined the production process in certain impotant textile centres.[9] In contrast, in Masulipatnam and Guntur districts, along with the traditional weaving castes like *Padma Sales*, there were also *Pariah* weavers, *Jandra* weavers, *Togata* weavers and even a few looms had been set up by barbers.[10]

One of the most important weaving castes of the region was the *Pattu Sale* community, The *Pattu Sale* community was an endogamous section of the *Sale* community the other being the *Padma Sale* community. The traditional customs of the *Sales* demonstrate three well marked points of difference between *Padma Sales* and *Pattu Sales*. First, the *Pattu Sales* wear the sacred thread, whereas the *Padma Sales* did not. Second the *Pattu Sales* do not take food or water at the hands of any other social group except Brahmins, whereas the *Padma Sales* could enter into the houses of *Kapu, Golla, Telaga* and *Gavara*. Thirdly, the *Pattu Sales* weave super-fine cloths, and in some places work in silk, whereas *Padma Sales* weave only coarse cloths. Each section is divided into a number of exogamous sects or *intiperulu*. Both speak Telugu, and are divided into

Vaishnavites and *Saivites*. These religious distinctions were no bar to inter-marriage and interdining.[11] The geographical limits of this *Pattu Sale* community in the early Nineteenth Century was virtually limited to a few villages in Visakhapatnam and Godavari districts.[12] This community continued their specialization by turning out silk cloths or super-fine variety cloths, for instance Uppada Silk cloths in Visakhapatnam district.

The *Togata* caste weavers were another important community of weavers mainly found in the districts of Masulipatnam and Guntur. They manufactured coarser fabrics especially a variety of thick white cotton cloth with red borders, and handkerchiefs and *romals*, which were mostly consumed by the poor.[13] Although their primary occupation was weaving, the other weaving castes did not participate in the rituals of the *Togatas*.[14] Other weaving groups in the region were the *Perikas* essentially weaving tape cloths, *Coorap* people who produced blankets or *combalies*, *Jungamas* weaving *jida* cloths, and others weaving gunny bags.

The existing studies on the weavers and the economy of the region, suggest that the presence of 'low' caste weavers was a Nineteenth Century development. For instance, the Report of the Fact Finding Committee (Handloom and Mills) held that the entrance of low class non-weaving castes into the handloom industry was a Nineteenth Century phenomenon.[15] Again Joseph Jerome Brenning has suggested that "as demand for export quality textiles increased, caste weavers ceased to produce coarser domestic fabrics to produce for export, opening opportunities at the bottom of the weaving industry for non-weaver castes".[16]

For instance, in the later half of the Eighteenth Century; the weavers of the Guntur district were categorized essentially into three groups, depending on the variety in which they specialized. There were weavers weaving for the company, weavers weaving for the natives and the *Pariah* weavers weaving for the Natives, and in total they had in their possession nearly fifty per cent of the looms of the entire Guntur district. In the district records, the term used to refer to them was *'Mala Maggalavallu'* that is, *Mala* weavers.[17] The *Malas* constituted the major weaving community in the village economy of the Guntur district and they contributed a considerable revenue towards *Moturpha* taxes in villages like Amrithaluru and Modukuru. Even in the districts of the Guntur *Circar*, the *Mala Maggatavallo* played an equally prominent part in the weaving economy, especially in Kondapalli Haveli, Vallur Samut, and Inngodroo *Parganahs*.'[18]

Loom Tax

The annual report of Fasly 1204 and 1205 (1794-95), mentions the principle on which tax was levied. In the *Moturpha* tax collection structure, a separate rate was fixed on *Pariah* weavers' looms in the region.[19] Further, the position of the *Mala Maggatavalloo* within the tax collection structure of the society, was alongside four major ccmmunities,-*Salavallu*, and *Jandravallu*, *Komativallu*, *Govaravallu*, and *Gollavallu*.[20] And they paid an amount equal to that paid by the traditional weaving and *Bania* caste people. Thus from the *Moturpha* collection list it appeared that *Mala Maggatavalloo* was one among five main groups in the society.

Besides the loom tax which all the weavers paid, the *Mala* weavers had to pay additional taxes, levied on them because of their social position. One such was the tax called *'Boota paraster'* referred to as '*Pallaputtada*' in the southern districts. This tax was paid by the various low caste groups of the village, including *Pariah* weavers.[21] "The nature of this tax was that the groups included in this tax had to pay a certain amount per house to the government."[22] It is also the custom to receive from the people by way of fine when any of them be found guilty of working contrary to the custom of the caste. These groups were *Chakalivallu* (washermen); *Mangalivallu* (barbers); *Cummara vallu* (pot makers); *Malavallu* (Pariahs); *Gollavalloo* (cow-keepers); *Pammulavallu* (Tom-tom beaters before-the Gods of the Pariahs); *Medaravallu* (workers in bamboo); *Buta Caummaravallu* (country ironsmiths); *Bogumvallu* (dancing girls); *Pamlillavallu* (snakemen); *Yaraculavallu* (basket makers,); and includes five professions-ironsmiths, carpenters, goldsmiths, brass-smiths and stone cutters.[23]

The large scale participation of the *Mala* weavers in the weaving world of the Masulipatnam and Guntur districts, therefore, was not a sudden phenomenon of the early Nineteenth Century. The place accorded to them along with other weavers and other social groups in the taxation structure of the society, as well as the maintenance of their group identity as a left hand faction of the society recognized in the levy of *Boota Parashee*, thus provide clear indications to argue that *Malas* entered the weaving world of the region much before the arrival of the European powers in the region. Besides the English records, the presence of the *Malas* during this period was supported by the evidence available in the Mackenzie collections of the Cuddapah district. In 1813, in the report submitted by *Mutasiddi* Narayanan Rao to Colonel Mackenzie entitled *"Gandipeta Kaifaiyat*", a detailed description of the textiles produced in various villages, and their prices, was found. Here, a mention is made to one of the coarser variety of cloth produced by *Malas* and *Madigas* along with *Sales* and *Mangalivanllu* (barbers).[24]

The major weaving castes in this region, relatively prosperous by virtue of their industry, had various groups attached to them as dependent castes. These groups were supported by giving alms, and their dependent status was continually underlined by a variety of rituals which emphasized their inferior status.[25] It would appear that marginal groups (of weavers or others) were traditionally attached (and traditions invented to legitimize and justify this attachment) to the probably more prosperous elements of the weaving community as a means of protecting the less well off.

Groups like *Sadhana Surulu*, *Samayamuvaru*, *Padiga Rajulu* or *Koonapilla Vallu* and *Inakamukku Bhatrazus* were various marginalised itinerant dependent groups attached to the *Sale* caste. From the evidence, it appears that *Sadhana Surulu* were attached to the *Padma Sale* section of the *Sale* caste. The *Sadhanasurulu* prayed to goddess *Renuka*, who is identified with the goddess *Yellamma* whom the *Padma Sales* revere, on behalf of the *Padma Sales*, and in turn, the *Padma Sales* paid an annual contribution of four *annas*, and helped to perform their marriages.[26]

Samayamuvaru were another group of mendicants attached to both sections of the Sale caste, and who trace back their origins to *Bhavana Rishi*, the patron saint of the Sale caste. This group wander from place to place like a single family, and whenever they reach a halting-place, dress up in the ritually prescribed clothes, and visit the house of the *Pedda Senapati* (Headman) who fed them for the day. The *Senapati* thereupon gave them a note showing the amount paid by him, perhaps to indicate that the Sale community of the locality had discharged its responsibility to the *Samayamuvaru*. On their visit to Sale houses, the *Samayamuvaru* praised *Bhawana Rishi*. The *Samayamuvaru* married in the presence of, and with the aid of the *Sales*.[27] While the *Sale* community thus had as their dependents, members of their own caste, the case of the *Devangas* was rather different. They too had a sub-caste attached to them as *kulabhikshuvulu* or caste mendicants.[28] These were the *Singamavallu*, who were paid a small sum annually by each *Devanga* village for various services rendered such as carrying fire before a *Devanga* corpse to the burial ground, acting as messengers and for cleaning the weaving instruments.[29]

Another dependent caste linked to the *Devangas* as well as other castes like *Komatis*, was the *Veeramushitivallu*, literally meaning the warrior beggars.[30] This group, mostly resident in the Godavari district area; received alms from the *Devangas* as well as the *Komatis* of the region. The most distinctive of the mendicant communities which revolved satellite like around the weavers of Northern Coromandel was that of *Jangamas*. The *Jangamas* who belonged to the *Virasaiva* sect, were traditional priests of *Lingayats*, and were disciples of *Basava*. *Saivites* regard them as incarnations of *Siva*. Most of the *Jangamas* were religious itinerant mendicants who moved from village to village and undertook preaching of the principles of the Lingayats.[31] It appears that these *Jangamas* mostly depended on *Devangas*, who essentially belonged to the *Saiva* sect, and who sustained the *Jangamas* through giving alms. This is illustrated in an Eighteenth Century verse which indicated that the *Jangamas* had a right to the wealth of the *Devangas*.[32] These mendicant groups associated with various castes were provided with land grants, specially for their maintenance. For instance, at Agiripalli village of the Krishna district, a piece of land was allotted as *Veeramushtivalla vritti*, along with other social groups like *chakalis*, *mangali* and *vetti*.[33] This was a long standing tradition and it is indicated by the land grant made to *Jangamas* recorded in a Nellore inscription.[34]

Caste Rules and Regulations

How did the weaving world of the region perpetuate itself, despite the complexities generated by the caste rules and regulations? It would seem that the formal regulations and the entire ideology of the caste system, particularly as manifested in the left hand and right hand divisions helped to maintain order in a society riven by caste. These divisions and their attendant rules and codes of behaviour prevented tensions from surfacing and destroying the social fabric.[35] During the late Eighteenth and early years of the Nineteenth Centuries many disputes at Madras arose from conflicts between Left (*Idangai*) and Right (*Valangai*) castes.[36] In the existing left and right hand division of the social fabric, the *Devanga* was placed within the left hand faction, while *Padma Sales* were placed under the category of the right hand division.[37] As per the customary practices associated with these factions, *Devangas* and *Padma Sales* never lived in the same street, and did not draw water from the same well. Like other left hand faction castes, *Devangas* had their own dancing girls called *jathi biddalu* (children of the castes), whose male off spring did *Acchhupani* (printing work on cloth) and occasionally went about begging from *Devangas*.

Paradoxically, however, this traditional division of the weaving communities into left hand and right hand castes was itself a source of serious conflict because in reinforcing caste identity, the prescriptive codes also heightened caste rivalry. The coming of the new economy did not extinguish these conflicts. On the other hand, it may have precipitated such conflicts. Their recurrence disrupted textile production and alarmed company officials ever conscious of protecting their precious investment. For example George Maidman, the Commercial Resident at Ingeram in 1803 reported with alarm about an incident in which the refusal of the *Sale* caste weavers to honour a custom of giving alms to the *Veeramushitivallu*, led to a violent conflict between the *Sale* on one side and the *Devangalu*, *Kameelu* and *Kaikalavallu* on the other, the latter taking upon themselves to champion the *Veeramushitivallu*.[38] The *Sales* argued that they were not required by customs to give alms to this groups. The *Veeramushtivallu* on the other hand, encouraged and supported by the *Devangas*, and other weaving communities like *Kameelu* and *Kaikalavallu* harassed the *Sale* community and disrupted their work by disturbing the thread markets, destroying their looms and otherwise creating tension by aggregating in large, menacing members. The *Devangas*, *Kameelu* and *Kaikalavallu* also joined them and attacked the *Sales*. The Deputy Commercial Resident of Ingeram, worried about the effect of this conflict on textile production, instructed the Collector to arrange for the suppression of the disturbance.[39] The Company was, at this juncture, caught in a dilemma, for perceiving the conflict to be essentially a religious one, it was reluctant to interfere; at the same time however, it was compelled to restore peace as quickly as possible.[40]

There were clear grounds for believing that the conflict was primarily a religious conflict. The *Veeramushtivallu* being *Saivites*, were necessarily supported by the *Devangas* and others who were also *Saivite* weaver communities, while the Sales were predominantly *Vaishnavites*. Besides, the conflict was rooted also in the deep ideological rift represented by the left hand and right hand castes division, the Sale falling into the right hand, while the *Devanga* fell into the left hand category. At the same time, we must note that this division, originating in or legitimized by ideology, was also reinforced by or even derived from economic rivalries which must have existed between weaving communities.

Social Disturbances and the English Company

The English Company's law and jurisdictional structures which were created to maintain the production, producers and to tighten the control over the groups were not extended to cover those issues that fell under the realm of religious and social customs. It was this demarcation of the company's jurisdiction that ultimately might have kept in tact the rigidity of the Hindu caste during this period. In 1802, the Collector of the Rajahmundry district reported to the Board of Revenue "with reference to the religious issues, there followed different methods altogether. In all cases relating to the rights, privileges and immunities of the respective caste, the higher orders or each one are either consulted, or the most learned *Brahmins* whose wisdom and piety may have raised them to public estimation of confidence are resorted to, who are supposed to possess a thorough knowledge of their divine institutes and to decide accordingly".[41] The emergent colonial state with its changes in production relations and structural arrangements did not immediately produce a stable economic and political systems. Towards the end of the Eighteenth Century as the Company was consolidating its control, the Northern Coromandel was disturbed by various kinds of disruptions. Many of these affected the economic life of the weavers.

One such disturbance occurred in 1798 in the Godavari district, when the '*Mahanauttee* people', disrupted the markets at Nellapalli and Yanam, and sent orders to different villages asking the people not to pay revenue to the company.[42] These *Mahnauttee* people were obviously very powerful and so their orders were obeyed and this adversely affected the company's textile investment in the region.[43] The company officials suspected that some "designing persons" were behind these disturbances. The *Zamindars* of Cotah and Ramachandrapuram in fact suggested that the merchants, *Dubashees*, and other rich men of the region were supplying *Mahanauttees* with money. Besides, it was believed that the conflict might also be led by a right hand caste group and the *Yanadees* being belonged to left hand faction.[44]

The occasional recurrence of the traditional schisms during the period 1794 to 1817 did not mean that there were no instances of co-operation among these categories in opposition to other elements in the society. Indeed, the same weavers of the Godavari district had expressed their co-operation, and organized their revolt in 1796 mainly against the conditions related to the tightening of control over the production processes of their economy. The company's officials had to take the views of the four major castes of the weaving community represented by their heads, in order to bring in some solution to their problems and grievances. Other instances of co-operation among them were seen, when the weavers revolted against the company or the *Zamindar* or the *Copdar* which are a part of the broader contradiction with in the society, subsequent to the coming of the new political control in the region.[45] Weavers unrests in the Godavari district in 1775 also featured remarkable unity among the various weaving castes (*Salegar*, *Devanga* and *Kaikalavallu*) who combined to form a *samaja* (association); they also received support from other weaving castes through the territorial assembly of the *mahanadu*. Again in 1798, weavers of the Daglooroo village organized themselves and lacked by the strength and solidarity of their caste issued orders to their caste members not to undertake work for the East India Company.

How far did the changes wrought by the East India Company in the production processes or those emanating from other pressures affect the social structures that were based on caste? How did the weavers react to these shifts? To some extent, the system of registration of the weavers introduced by the Company to acquire greater control over the production process may have contributed to the blurring of the finer nuances of caste distinctions. That is, the caste based specialization of production broke down, since the weavers were required by the Company to produce specific types of cloth, and not necessarily those which they wove traditionally. The company's demand for textiles revolved around the cotton goods; still the weavers were required to produce specific varieties meant for external markets. For instance, *Sales*, *Devangas* and *Pattu Sales* from Rajam village of Visakhapatnam district were specialized in manufacturing a fine variety of cloth called *Sanna Baju* meant exclusively for the Hyderabad market and huge quantities of sarees called locally *Kokalu* which were marketed at the *santas* (weekly markets) of Vizianagaram, and then re-exported to Hyderabad. But when the Company's demand for long cloth increased greatly, these weavers were forced to give up their earlier specialization and produce only long cloth.

An important factor that appeared to have prompted the weaver to give up his caste specialization and brought him out of the limits of his village was the attempt of the Company to induce the weaver to register for their factories. Since the beginning of their consolidation process in the region, the Company provided allowances and privileges to attract them to join the Company's service; sometimes by changing their place of residence also.[46] Moreover, the Company many a time utilized the caste hegemony for the maintenance of the newly created structures in the region. And it was through these caste elites that the Company met its commercial needs and relegated to the background the active primary weaver.[47]

The effect of the colonial economy on the socio-economic life of *Pattu Sale* caste was hardly perceived perhaps because the Company's textile demands were confined essentially to coarser ones. The *Pattu Sale* community as may be conjectured followed the traditions associated with their cultural patterns. For instance, the tax which they paid was the same for all members of their caste in respective villages.[48] *Pattu Sales* of Seyedem village agreed to pay some *annas* per year as *Moturpha* tax as per the *Kattubadi* Settlement, agreed by the *Koolah Karnev* or caste head. The verdict of the *Koolah Karney* was final for deciding issues related to the socio-economic life of the community. And, in case of any complaint against any intrusion into their economic life, the *Pattu Sale* community received the support of other well off members of weaving castes, like *Senapatis*.[49]

At the village level, the weaver castes maintained their socio-economic identities by the acceptance of certain norms and traditions related to the organization and control of village resources. For instance, among six *Cheruvu Kuntas* one was allotted to Sales exclusively in Yaduvuru village of Guntur district.[50] These identity reinforcing mechanisms and institutions strengthened the boundaries of each caste and sub-caste among the weavers, thus apparently making the world of the weaver impermeable to outsiders. Yet, the caste specialization barriers appear to have been flexible enough to allow the intrusion into the textile economy of castes not usually associated with weaving, such as the *Mala* weavers.

Notes and References

1. R.E. Frykenberg, "Company Circar in the Carnatic, 1799-1859: The Inner Logic of Political System in India", in Richards G. Fox (ed.,) *Realm and Region in Traditional India*, New Delhi, 1977, pp. 117-159.
2. Edgar Thurston, *Castes and Tribes of Southern India*, 4 vols, 1909 (reprint 1975), entry under *'Sales'*, pp. 265-278.
3. *Ibid.*, Vol. II, entry under '*Devangas*'.

4. *Ibid.*
5. Potukuchi Subramanya Sastri, *Achha Telugu Kosamu*, Vol. 2, Tenali, 1979, pp. 170-172.
6. *Ibid.*, pp. 170-172.
7. G.A. Ram, Collector of Guntur to the Board of Revenue, 13 January 1796, *Proceedings of the Board of Revenue*, (hereafter PBOR), 143, Tamil Nadu State Archives, Chennai, p. 43.
8. P. Narasimha Reddy, *Telugu Sametalu: Jana Jeevanamu*, Tirupati, 1983.
9. F.R. Hemingway, *Madras District Gazetteer: Godavari*, Madras, 1907, pp. 102-104; P.F. Carmichael, *A Manual of District of Vizagapatnam in the Presidency of Madras*, Madras, 1869, p. 65.
10. G.A. Ram, Collector of Guntur to the Board of Revenue, 13 January 1796, PBOR 143, Tamil Nadu State Archives, p. 473:
11. Edgar Thurston, *Castes and Tribes*, Vol. VI, entry under *Sale*, pp. 265.
12. F.R. Hemingway, *Madras District Gazetteer: Godavari*, Madras, 1907, pp. 102-104; P.F. Carmichael, *op. cit.*,
13. Francis Buchanan, *A Journey from Madras Through the Countries of Mysore, Canara and Malabar*, London, 1807, Vol. 1, p. 21.7.
14. Edgar Thurston, *Castes and Tribes*, Vol. VI, entry under *Togatas*, p. 265.
15. *Ibid.*, under '*Perikas*', pp. 191-194.
16. J.J. Brenning, 'Textile Producers and Production in Late Seventeenth Century Coromandel', *Indian Economic and Social History Review*, 23, 4, (1986), p. 347.
17. G.A. Ram, Collector of Guntur to the Board of Revenue, 13 January 1796, *Proceedings of the Board of Revenue*, 143, Tamil Nadu State Archives, pp. 474-89.
18. G.A. Ram, Collector of Guntur to the Board of Revenue, 13 January 1796, PBOR, 143, Tamil Nadu State Archives, pp. 474-89.
19. Guntur District Collector's letter to the Board of Revenue, *Guntur District Records*, (hereafter GUDR) 978/B, p. 482.
20. G.A. Ram, Collector of Guntur to the Board of Revenue, 27th March, 1796, PBOR, 143, Tamil Nadu State Archives, pp. 469-474.

21. G.A. Ram, Collector of Guntur to the Board of Revenue, 27 March 1796, PBOR, 143, Tamil Nadu State Archives, p. 43.
22. A. Stokes, Collector of Guntur to the Board of Revenue, 25 May 1843, GUDR 5402, pp. 34-37.
23. *Ibid.*
24. 'Gandikota Kaifiyat', 30th April 1813, Mackenzie Collections in N. Venkataramanayya (ed.,) *Cuddapah Sila Sasanamulu*, Madras, 1971, pp. 1-39.
25. Louis Dumont, *Homo Hierarchicus : The Caste System and its implications*, Chicago, 1970, He discusses this concept. But he uses this as signifying the *jajmani* relationship between dominant castes and others. The terms used here are in a different sense, as referring to those castes which are entirely dependent on charity for their livelihood.
26. Edgar Thurston, *Castes and Tribes*, Vol. 6, entry under *Sadhanasurulu*', pp. 261.
27. Edgar Thurston, *Castes and Tribes* Vo1. 6, entry under *Samayamvaru*, pp. 290-291.
28. Edgar Thurston, *Castes and Tribes* Vo1. 6, entry under *Simgamvaru*, p. 389.
29. Edgar Thurston, *Castes and Tribes*, Vo1. 2, entry under *Devangas*, pp. 154-166.
30. For a discussion on the mythological sanctions that led to the creation of such a custom, see entry under *'Viramushitis'*, in Edgar 'Thurston, *Castes and Tribes* Vol. 7, pp. 406-411.
31. P. Narasimha Reddi, *Telugu Sametalu Jana Jeevanamu*, Tirupati, 1983, pp. 233-34. Edgar Thurston, *Castes and Tribes*, Vo1. 2, p. 450-51.
32. Adidamu Surakavi, "Ramalingeswara Satkamu: A Dwipada Kavya, c.1600-1750 "in Suravaram Pratap Reddi, *Andhrula Sangheeka Charitra*, 1949, (reprint) Hyderabad, 1982, p. 346.
33. *Agiripalli Kaifiyat* June 1815 A.D, Mackanzie Collections, Andhra Pradesh State Archives, *Grama Kaifiyatlu: Krishna Zillah*, Hyderabad, 1990, pp. 1-12.
34. Nellore Inscriptions, Ongole 85, (A.D.1350) in *Inscriptional Glossary of Andhra Pradesh*, Hyderabad, 1967, entry under *'Viramushitis'*, p. 112.

35. For a discussion on this right-left hand divisions, see E.K. Brenda Beck, 'Right-Left Division of South Indian Society', *Journal of Asian Studies*, 29 (1970), pp. 779-798; Arjun Appadorai, 'Right and Left hand castes in South India', *Indian Economic and Social History Review*, 11, 2. (1974), pp. 216-259; Burton Stein, *Peasant State and Society in Medieval South India*, Delhi, 1980; Vijaya Ramaswamy, *Textiles and Weavers in Medieval South India*, New Delhi, 1986;
36. Francis Buchanan, *A Journey from Madras, op. cit.*, Vol. 1, pp. 77-80; Mattison Mines, *The Warrior Merchants: Textiles, Trade and Territory in South India*, 1984, chapter 3. He traces the position of Kaikolars in the Idangai-Valangai schisms.
37. *Ibid.*
38. George Maidman, Deputy Commercial Resident at Ingeram to Collector 1st Division in Masulipatnam, 26th March 1803, Andhra Pradesh State Archives *Godavari District Records*, 946/B (hereafter GDR), pp. 617-19.
39. *Ibid.*
40. R. Fullerton, Commercial Resident at Ingeram to Collector, 1st Division in Masulipatnam; 2 April 1803, GDR 946/B. pp. 635-37.
41. G. Balmaid, Collector of Rajahmundry to BOR, 21 December, *1802*, GDR 931/A, pp. 73-86.
42. Letter to Benjamin Branfil, 9 May 1798, GDR 917, pp. 102-03.
43. John B Travers, Deputy Secretary BOR to Benjamin Branfil, 24 May 1798, GDR 919, pp. 138-40; Benjamin Branfil, Collector of Rajahmundry to BOR, 13 May 1798, GDR 917, pp. 105-07.
44. Benjamin Branfil, Collector of Rajahmundry to BOR, 13 May 1798, GDR 917, pp. 105-07.
45. Proceedings Relating to Enquiry into the conduct of Sadlier while Resident at Ingeram, 28 November 1775 to 30 March, 1776, *Public Department Sundries*, Tamil Nadu State Archives, pp. 112-115.
46. V. Corbett, Commercial Resident in Masulipatnam to Charles Hynox, The Acting-Collector, Masulipatnam, 19 July 1797, *Masulipatnam District Records*, 2974/B, Andhra Pradesh State Archives, Hyderabad, p. 664.

47. R. Fullerton, Deputy Resident to James Taylor, Acting Secretary to the Committee of Reform, 14 March, 1799, GDR 831, pp. 41-42; Letter addressed to Benjamin Branfil, Collector 3rd Division of the Masulipatnam District, 17 February 1802, GDR 9401/B, pp. 239-246.
48. J. Smith, Collector of Vizagapatnam to the Commercial Resident at Vizagapatnam, 6 November, 1817, *Vizagapatnam Districts Records*, 3771/B, Andhra Pradesh State Archives, pp. 388-391.
49. *Ibid.*
50. 'Yadavuru village Kaifiyat" *Mackenzie Collections*, Andhra Pradesh State Archives, *Grama Kaifiyatlu: Guntur Zillah*, Vol. 5, Hyderabad, 1990, pp. 144-146; 'Peddanandipadu Kaifiyat', Mackenzie Collections, Andhra Pradesh State Archives, *Grama Kaifiyatlu: Guntur Zillah*, Vol. 3, Hyderabad, 1990, pp. 78-79.

12

Society and the Identity of the Santals : The'Other' Way of Interpreting the Subalterns

Suchibrata Sen

The debate over the colonial construction of 'tribe' is well known, but the subaltern construction of the 'tribe' remains uncontested and the social categorisation of the Santals, the most important tribal community in Eastern India, into subaltern group is almost an accepted phenomenon till now. Indeed the colonialists, the nationalists and the subaltern historians have a consensus at least on one ground that the Santals belonged to the lower strata of the society. Bankim Chandra Chattopadhyay while writing *Anandha Math* (1882) had taken the description of 1770's famine from Hunter's *Annals of Rural Bengal.* (Published 1868). Interestingly, he never bothered about the Santal Rebellion of 1855 vividly described in the same annals as an anti British movement. K.K. Datta's *Santal Insurrection* came out in 1940 and in 1947 R.P. Datta in his *India Today*'[2] referred to the Santal Rebellion as a "primitive and spontaneous forms of isolated acts of revenge and violence." Before that however, in his *Notes on Indian History* Karl Marx had mentioned it as a revolt of half savaged Santals. Later on the nationalist historiography included the Santal rebellion as a part of the national movement, where of course the movement had been described as a spontaneous one. In 1983 Ranajit Guha's *Elementary Aspects of Peasant Insurgency* brought about a new dimension in the history of the peasant movement of colonial India and there too Guha put the Santals into the same rank of the other lower as well as dominated sections of the society. So from the colonialists to the Subaltern historians we find a strange unanimity in locating the social position of the Santals, the only difference being discovering a separate political consciousness among them. The various facets of this subaltern consciousness during the Santal Rebellion had, however, been uniquely dealt with by Guha.

Methodological Problems

In this connection it is necessary to have a look into some of the methodological problems in writing the history of the tribals. The people of the various tribes have no written documents of their own, so one had to depend much on their oral evidence which has survived through the ages. Needless to say, it includes their language, songs, tales, customs etc., which taking together, form the tribal culture. Ranajit Guha has admitted that "The information on some of these is not accessible to us either because it has not being recovered from the primary sources or because it is available only in a language not known to the author."[3] But actually there is no dearth of evidence about the language and culture of the Santals. The British officials and the Christian missionaries contributed a lot in understanding the Santal way of life. So even without being an expert in the Santali language one could have derived some idea about the Santal psyche from the above mentioned sources. Indeed Guha had used it extensively while dealing with the insurrectionist mood of the Santals. Knowingly or unknowingly Guha had not paid much attention to the other interpretation of the same folklores "oral as well as written." Contradicting Guha it may be argued that there is enough evidence in the 'songs, rhyme, ballads and anecdotes' of the Santals to prove that the Santals world view differed from that of the subalterns' view.

The Subaltern historians devoted much energy, time and intelligence to understand the insurgency and thereby totally branded the Santals as subaltern ignoring the other aspects of their life which tried to speak a different story. Revolt is but an occasional episode in the general drama of life and this total life pattern determine the real attitude of the tribe towards the world as well as their level of consciousness. During the period of revolt certain uncommon acts take place no doubt, but those acts alone cannot be regarded as the only criteria to understand a tribe and moreover these acts also could be interpreted in another way which were consistent with the general life pattern of the Santals. It is not violence which alone speaks, silence also speaks some thing and this unheard message of silence could be found in the collective psychology of the Santals and this feature of the Santals completely rejects the notion of subalternity imposed on them.

From Marc Bloch, E.H. Carr and Fernand Braudel we have come to know that economic factors alone do not construct the history of man.

Certain hidden forces along with the mind of man need due consideration in reconstructing any history. Indeed to quote Marc Bloch, "Historical facts are in essence, psychological facts… Even where the intrusion of these external forces seems most brutal, however, their action is weakened or intensified by man and his mind."[4]

E.H. Carr in his famous book *What is History* has written, "History can not be written unless the historian can achieve some kind of contact with the mind of those about whom he is writing."[5] This idea, if we can call it the idea of mentality, was further developed by Fernand Braudel. "In every period, a certain view of the world, a collective mentality, dominates the whole mass of the society. Dictating a society's attitudes, guiding its choices, confirming its prejudices and directing its actions, this is very much a fact of civilisation. Far more than the accidents or the historical and social circumstances of a period, it derives from the distant past, from ancient beliefs, fears and anxieties which are almost unconscious-an immense contamination whose germs are lost to memory but transmitted from generation to generation. A society's reaction to the events of the day, to the pressure upon it, to the decisions it must face, are less a matter of logic or self interest than the response to an unexpected and often inexpressible compulsion arising from the collective unconscious… what isolate and differentiate them most sharply. Any such habits of mind survive the passage of time."[6] This is particularly true for writing the history of the tribes, because the archival records do not correctly represent the psyche of the tribe.

Reconstructing the Santal Society

The Santal society had its own rhythm which is to be understood through their myths, customs, folk songs, village system and other cultural aspects and this understanding can tell us whether they could be categorised as subaltern. Actually the phase of insurrection and the common life style of a people are not quite independent of one another. In the distant past the Santals had no superior authority to acknowledge where as the lower class Bengali Hindu caste peasants had accepted the *chaturvarna* system as a natural condition of their existence. They were fully conscious of their lower position in the society and had hardly dared to become equal with the higher caste Hindu society. On the other hand the strong sense of Santal ethnic identity had always regarded itself as a superior race. The term tribe or Santal had not been acceptable to them. It meant to them sub national or sub-caste. The Santals call themselves *'Hor Hopon'* or true sons of mankind. By identifying them as *'Abo do Hor Jati'* (we are her folk) they had regarded themselves as a special people and their claim to speciality was not without reason. The egalitarian character of their society speak much of this speciality. The absence of caste system, the equal position of the women with men in Santal life are some of the traits of this egalitarian society. Even the headman or *Manjhi* who had been a functionary of central importance in the political order of the society, was the first among the equals. This was fully consistent with the Santal idea of *'Sanam hor hopon'* (All Santals are alike). Closely associated with the *hor hopon* is the geographical concept of *hor disam* (Noa da hor disam kana) this is Santal country. The term was used by the Santals to distinguish between the areas occupied by them and those occupied by other people.[7] The *hor hopon* and *hor disam* are the two concepts which were intimately related in their emotional context. The *Manjhi* was the pivot of these two concepts. When *hor disam* had fallen into the hands of the Non-Santals, with it there came a threat to the Santal cultural identity.

It is necessary to mention here the Santal's excellent sense of ecological balance and the indigenous preparation of the medicine by them was not altogether unscientific. The Santali language received high praise from the scholars concerned. By the test of language the Santals reveal a high degree of social cohesion. J.H. Hulton's judgement can not be gain said. The extent of the survival of the tribal language is a better cohesion of the tribe, since the test of language is easier and more definite than that of religion, where the border land of Hinduism is often vague and obscure. "The Santals have been more tenacious of their language than many of the other peoples to whom they are racially allied. They are the largest tribe in India to retain an aboriginal language to the present day."[8] P.O. Bodding in his preface to Santal Dictionary he had mentioned the high standard of Santali art facets which are preserved in Oslo. That the Santals had a civilisation of its own can hardly he doubted and here in lies the strength of a strong sense of Santali identity. With this back ground of rich cultural heritage, the Santals can justly claim, *"Dekhu Khonang abu geban Saresha"*-we are a higher caste than the Hindus. This feeling of the Santals had been corroborated by the Christian Missionaries and the British civilians who had worked among them. Bodding had mentioned in one of the folk tales of the Santals that they regarded that the so-called high castes souls are that of animals and human and beautiful souls reside in the body of the Santals'[9] Culshaw, a Christian Missionary who had worked among the Santals of Bankura, had also experienced, "A Santal once said in reply to a direct question as to whether any other race was superior to his; "no, there are no others who are greater than us. You can see that from the fact that even today our womenfolk will not eat rice that has been cooked by

Brahmins. Formerly, when our men folk ate Hindu rice they were made to sleep outside for one night; they could not sleep with their wives. When they brought rice from outside to the house they were made to eat it in the courtyard and clean up the place where they had eaten and then wash their own eating utensils ... and so by refusing to acknowledge the supremacy of the Brahmins they hold themselves aloof from the Hindu social structure."[10]

This feeling of aloofness had a historical perspective. The first interaction of the Santals with the Hindus was not a happy one. Socially speaking, the first attitude of the Bengali Hindus was a great challenge to the Santal concept of Identity. From Walter Hamilton description of Hindustan (1820) it is known that the Santals had been "despised on account of their low caste by the inhabitants of the plain country, who would on no account allow any of them to fix himself in their village,"[11] or would they live among the Santals. They seemed to think that their castes disqualified them for the atmosphere of the jungles and for the task of reclaiming land there. On the other hand, the Santals were regarded as unfit for the enjoyment of *'abadi'* land. They scarcely admit the Santals within the pale of humanity.[12]

What an irony indeed! The 'true sons of mankind' were to be regarded as sub-human creatures. This two divergent attitudes remained unresolved and as a result the Santals had become more and more aloof from the so called mainstream. The later historical events only confirmed the cause of aloofness. This silent withdrawal of the Santals was also a protest and it had nothing to do with subalternity. The Santals' pride for self-identity was so strong that they had never cared for any rank concession syndrome and in every action of theirs was present the Santal concept of cultural superiority.

The Rebellion of the Santals, 1855

The revolt study of the Santals in 1855 may be interpreted in the light of the above. The Santals rebelled only when the *Hor Disam* had been occupied by the Non-Santals or the *Dikus.* Rent question was not the prime cause of the movement.[13] The Santals had migrated from *Jungle Mahals* to *Damin-I-Koh* and there they had found a place free from the domination of Hindu cultural hegemony. Bradley Birt had given a poetic description about the Santal settlement in *Damin-I-koh.* "It seemed that as if the Nature had reserved this land from all time for the Santals in their hour of need, and no race could have been more fit and worthy so great an inheritance. Repeatedly driven out of the lands they had made their own by the oppression of Hindu and Musulman Zamindar and money lender, they hailed the *Damin-I-koh* as a veritable promised Land, where the oppressor might not come."[14] Virgin soil of Damin-I-Koh was upturned by the Santals but the virginity of the Santals was lost in the long run. It was not in Jungle Mahals but in Damin where they had found an opportunity to re-establish their superiority of socio-cultural ethos. Initially the treatment they had received from the colonial government was also congenial to them. During 1823-27 the Government had regarded the hilly tract from a political point of view. But from 1837 onwards the area acquired a financial significance. The good treatment of the Santals began to yield increased revenue.[15] In 1831 Mr.Ward, the officer entrusted with the charge of demarcating the area, informed the Commissioner of Revenue at Bhagalpur, that the Santals were in possession of lands granted to them under *pattas* and he was looking after them so that in no way they were molested by the *Zamindars* or the *Paharias*.[16] In this connection it may be mentioned that the Santals of Jungal Mahals had never been given pattas.[17] It was here in *Damin* that the Santal social structure and their spiritual ethos got its full satisfaction. It is to be remembered that the Santals attitude to land differed to that of the other so called lower class Hindus of Bengal. The Santal land is *noa da hor disam*-This is Santal country. A Santal would never settle alone in an uncultivated area. When they would find a suitable place for settling, they used to go there in a body and settle under the leadership of the *Mondal* or *Manjhi.* The clearer of the jungle would become the owner or co-owner with his original associates. In *Damin*, land had at last become a permanent feature in the life style of the Santals. Land had become a part of their soul so to say.[18] W.G. Archer has analysed, "No motive is so strong in a tribal people as the preservation of the life of the tribe and it 'moves' albeit the motive works for the most part at the unconscious level, and a Santal's land not only provides economic security, but is a powerful link with his ancestors, and this applies to newly entered areas no less than the old, for he will not take possession till the spirits approve. The land is a part of his spiritual as well as his economic heritage. Hunger drove them to despair, but their attachment to land provided also an emotional basis without which the rebellion might not have taken place."[19] This also explained why the Santals had a great aversion to work as *coolies* in rail roads or any other corners. They even refused to live on the side of the high road lest they might be induced to work as coolies, even on higher wages. They preferred to live in the land of their birth, on a much lower wage than they might earn elsewhere.[20] Even under dire necessity, they could not be induced to work as *coolies* in Mauritius while large number of *Bauries* and other lower castes of Bengal were regularly taken to Mauritius by the English.[21] It was a question of dignity which is not a general characteristic of the so called subalterns. Incidentally an emotive remarks of an aboriginal leader of Australia may be recalled," My land is my backbone. I only stand straight, happy, proud and not ashamed about my colour because I still have land."[22] This mental attitude of the 'tribes' is something different form that of the ordinary lower caste peasants. It demands a footing of equality along with the elites.

The gradual *Diku* infiltration in *Damin* and their subsequent encroachment of Santal land was a direct threat to the dignity of the Santals. What the Santals had abhorred most was the *kamiotee* which was the direct result of *Mahajan's* exploitation. Slowly, but surely the Santals soon found themselves in a state of bondage which was nothing but a form of slavery, a complete antithesis of their cultural identity.[23] The question which had perplexed the British administration of the time was why a tribe who was known for "honesty of purpose and purity of word" and "by nature a quiet race and averse to quarrelling" resorted to violence?

Neither the British mind nor the *Diku* moneylenders had the least idea about the radical change that was undergoing in the psychological level of the Santals This is because "at the abstract psychological and sociological levels, he (Diku) is an 'outsider' with the difference that he is not the original insider, who gradually gets estranged or alienated due to differences in cross-cultural perspectives and levels of ideology.[24]

W.G. Archer's methodology for understanding the 'tribe' is very clear when he says "that only through its songs do the attitudes of a tribe or caste become clear and it is not until the poetry has been understood that a tribe is understood."[25] Indeed these songs and poems supply ample evidence about the motive, purpose and ideology of the Revolt of 1855. The action of the Santals during the period of Revolt was neither primitive nor subaltern. It can be interpreted as assertion of tribal identity, not as appropriation of elite practices.

First of all revolt for what? Let us listen to the voice of the Santals.

janam Disam Lagite Ho
Delan pathar koh Taben pe,
for my land, we will go forward.

Again the English rendering of another song is as follows

The Trader thieves have robbed us of our land.
Saheb rule is trouble full
Shall we go or shall we stay?
Eating drinking clothing
For everything we are troubled
Shall we go or Shall we stay?

This is not at all on ordinary peasant consciousness which even in 1850s could perceive the link between the trader Mahajan and colonial power.

Secondly, revolt by whom?

Nusousabon, Nowarabon chele Hon
Bako Tengan
Khanti gebon Hul gea ho
We will fight our own battle,
No body will help us,
Only the headman and other Santal country will help us,
No body will be on our side
Yet we will revolt

Thirdly, what had been the objective of this revolt? Starting from W.W. Hunter to Dhirendra Nath Baske all have agreed that they had wanted to establish a Santal Raj. About the subaltern consciousness, Gramsci is very clear when he says, "The peasant hates the civil servant, does not hate the state, for he does not understand it." But the Santals, as revealed through their songs, not only had the clear understanding of the state character but had a vision of an alternative government. This is certainly not a common feature of other peasant insurrections. Indeed at a conceptual level the Santals had a distinct shape of thinking which is not consistent with the theoretical proposition of subalternity.

Fourthly, the revolt had been planned and organized initially by the Santals alone. The circulation of *Salgira* had been the medium of information for the assembly. One can draw an analogy between it and the circulation of *chapattis* during the 1857 Revolt. "That the Santals had an elaborate preparation before the Rebellion is also evident from the fact that about 5, 000 to 7, 000 Santals came from Birbhum, Bankura, Chotanagpur and Hazaribagh in Damin in early 1855 for the purpose of avenging the punishment inflicted on their comrades in the last years' dacoities."[26] Perhaps there was no recorded evidence in the historical past of the colonial rule where such a big gathering took place in an organized way and hence no question of appropriation of elite practice arose at least on the point of solidarity.

Fifthly, the ideology of the Revolt had been supplied by the idea of the appearance of *Thakur*, It was needed to have a sanction for the Revolt and Sidhu and Kanhu had perhaps consciously invented it to mobilise their fellow men. Following Paul Radin's *Primitive Man as philosopher* it can be argued that the thinking process, in the Santal society, was fairly sophisticated compared to other tribal groups. Though it had been propagated that *Thakur* would fight, Sidhu, Kanhu would not fight. In reality, however, Sidhu, Kanhu did fight and died and even after their death the Santals had continued fighting without becoming disheartened.

Sixthly, how the Santals had looked at their imprisonment? To quote another song in translation.

"I have killed Rup Sing Tamboli by the order of Sidhu and with the strength of Kanhu,

I am now going, to Suri jail with handcuff in
My hand and chain in My feet,
as if these are flute and dancer's anklet
and I am going to visit the
fair in Suri."

Here one does not find any reference to *Thakur* and there was no repentance.

Finally, mention may be made of a strange behaviour of the Santals during the revolt. They were expert in hunting and in that case they used poison in their arrow heads as a result the victim was sure to die within half an hour. But the Santals had never used poisoned arrows in their fight against the British troops. E.H.Man did not find any explanation for it,[27] but this act of the Santals was fully compatible with their strong sense of moral ethics. They had a clear distinction between sin and virtue. They wanted to establish a reign of virtue but not through an action which would be sin or *pap* to them. In fine it may be said that the elite historians of Subaltern school have spoken on behalf of the Santals, but the Santals speak otherwise. So why impute subalternity to another equally valid way of life?

References

The songs used in this paper have been collected from Man in India, Vol. XXV, December, 1945; Dhirendra Nath Baske : Saontal Gana Sangramer Itihas, Calcutta, 1980 and Surhid. K. Bhowmick, Saontali Gan o Kabita Sankalan, Sahitya Academy, New Delhi, 1996.

1. *Bankim Rachanabali*, Sahitya Sansad, 3rd edition, Vol. II, 1969, Calcutta, p. 44.
2. Quoted in Sumit Sarkar, *Marxian Approaches to History of Indian Nationalism*; Calcutta, 1990, p. 9.
3. Ranajit Guha, *Elementary Aspects of Peasant Insurgency in Colonial India*, OUP; 1994, p. 13.
4. Marc Bloch, *The Historian's Craft*, Manchester University Press, 1979, p. 194.

5. E.H. Carr, *What is History*, Penguin Books; 1967, p. 24.
6. F. Braudel, *A History of Civilisations*, Penguin Books, U.S.A., 1993, p. 22.
7. George. E. Somers, *The Dynamics of Santal Traditions in a Peasant Society*; New Delhi; 1977, p. 57.
8. W.J. Culshaw, *Tribal Heritage: A Sudy of the Santals*, London, 1949, p. 2.
9. P.O. Bodding, *Santals Folk Tales*, Reprint, New Delhi, 1990, Vol. III, No. 74.
10. W. J. Culshaw, *Ibid.*, p. 16.
11. *Parliamentary papers*, Vol. 9, Part–II.
12. *Ibid.*
13. Narahari Kabiraj, *Santal Village Community and the Santal Rebellion of 1855*, Calcutta, 2001, p. 75.
14. Bradley Birt, F.B., *The Story of an Indian Upland*, London, 1905, pp. 10-11.
15. MC Pherson, H., *Settlement Report : Santhal Parganas*, Calcutta, 1910, p. 35.
16. Bhagalpur Commissioner Records, *Damin-i-Koh Correspondence*, Vol. 108. Letter from Mr. Ward to the Commissioner of Revenue, Bhagalpur, dared 5th September 1831.
17. B.S., Das, "Agrarian Relations in South West Bengal" *Journal of Asiatic Society of Bengal*, Vol. XV, 1973, p. 117.
18. R. K. Mukherjee, "Race Elements in Village Constitution" *Man in India*, Vol. III, 1923, p. 1.
19. *Man in India*, Vol. XXV, 1945, No. 4, p. 219.
20. O' Malley, L.S.S, *Bengal District Gazetteer: Bankura*; Calcutta, 1908, p. 74.
21. *Parliamentary Papers*, (H of C) Vol. 30, 1842, pp. 17-18
22. Victor Das, "Jharkhand Movement: From Realism to Mystification" *Economic and Political Weekly*, 28 July 1990.
23. Suchibrata Sen, *The Santals of Jungle Mahals*, Calcutta, 1984, p. 113.
24. Sitakant Mahapatra, *Modernisation and Ritual*, OUP, 1986, p. 11.
25. *Man in India*, March, 1943, Vol. XXIII, No. I, p. 1.
26. P.C. Roy Chaudhury, *Santal Parganas District Gazetteer*; Calcutta, 1965, p. 79.
27. E. G. Man, *Sonthalia and the Santhals*, Delhi, 1983, p. 121.

PART-IV
EUROPEAN ENCOUNTER AND SOCIAL INTERACTIONS IN INDIA

13

Crime, Social Ramifications and the Portuguese Diaspora on the Coromandel Coast (1538-1695)

S. Jeyaseela Stephen

"All history is the history of thought, for the object of history is to discover not the mere event but the thought expressed in it. The cause of event means the thought in the mind of the person by whose agency the event came about. Man is swayed by ideas and these prompt his actions pre-eminently in the matter of his relations with his fellow-men and determine his conduct as a social being".

-R.G. Collingwood

Society in India came into contact with various other civilizations of the world societies such as the Romans, Arabs, Persians, Jews, Armenians and the Chinese through maritime trade in the ancient and the medieval period. The Portuguese, the Dutch, the Danes, the English and the French had extensive cultural contacts with the Indians between AD 1500 and 1800 and as a result of this Indo-European interaction, we find very many small groups of people through mixed marriages living in coastal India identified as Luso-Indians, Anglo-Indians and Franco-Indians who formed part of the Indian society in minority. Their social life is not yet adequately explored and it is necessary to relate the boundaries of the Indian society to these various social groups that emerged with diverse features at that time. Hence the social history of India between AD 1500 and 1800 is an interesting but intricate task for the historian. Writings on this topic will also definitely help in knowing them better as these people had a place in history and the historians are not concerned so far with the manner in which this Indo-European society changed with the passage of time, although the particular literature on society of the period is available.[1] Hence there is a need to examine the Portuguese society in the Eastern Coast of India and study the changes in social institutions like marriage, family and caste. The present paper aims at bridging the gap by expanding the coverage of topics published earlier by me.[2] Some important questions are raised in the context of this paper. Were the Indo-Portuguese community been accepted by the natives as a social group? Did these people have any distinct cultural traits? Did they adopt any indigenous customs and manners? How far they were accommodative or assimilated into the Indian social environment? Did the families of the Indo-Portuguese have many traditional functions to perform besides existing as the basic unit in the then society? Was there joint family system and eradication or decline among the Indo-Portuguese? Did there arise a situation in which there existed no effective or meaningful interaction among the various members? In the newly emerged nuclear families at that time did several social problems arise? How did the Indo-Portuguese men and women actually live at that time? We shall cull the information from the travelogues and Portuguese documents and try to examine and interpret them very well in order to understand the Indo-Portuguese community and society during the Sixteenth and Seventeenth Centuries.

I

The stratification of the Portuguese society into various identifiable social groups is possible on the basis of certain characteristics such as military, commercial and religious which are very important elements of the Portuguese presence in India. The various sections of population include *soldados*, *casados*, *mercadores* and *fidalgos* They brought Portuguese (Iberian) culture of Europe with them. These men in the beginning had hesitation to blend Portuguese habits with Hindu influences. They never had a thought to mix rightly or wrongly and colour was a barrier in each step forward. We find that Portuguese women were not allowed to undertake voyages from Portugal to India because of the hazards of travel and as well as moral problems involved during the voyage which normally took six to eight months. An extremely small number of Portuguese women used to sail annually in the company of their husbands such as Garcia d' Orta who brought his wife to India. It is mentioned that on the Cape route there were at least 2000 Portuguese going to Asia each year.[3] The life of these men in India must have become a problem without families in India or with families in Portugal. Hence mixed marriages were slowly encouraged by Affonso de Albuquerque, the (second) Portuguese Viceroy in India after the conquest of Goa in 1510. This policy of miscegenation introduced by Albuquerque encouraged Portuguese to marry local women and he assumed that the progeny of such marriages would remain loyal to the Portuguese Crown. Many Portuguese sailors, soldiers and merchants in the Bay of Bengal took the Indian women and lusitanized them to serve their interests. Thus the population of the Portuguese in the Eastern Coast of India increased and the women who got married to Portuguese men had to get converted to Christianity where they experienced a relatively upward mobility.

On the Tamil Coast, those Portuguese merchants who came to trade had settled down at the various flourishing ports by marrying the Tamil women and this mixed population known as *mestiços* had increased from time to time. It is recorded that the population of Nagapattinam settlement owing to Portuguese social interaction in 1577 was with sixty *casados*, 200 Eurasians and 300 Indian Christians.[4] According to Antonio Bocarro's report in 1635 there were 140 white *casados* 360 black *casados* called *topasses* (artillery men) 700 Indian Christians at Nagapattinam.[5] The Portuguese Viceroy in his letter dated 22 March 1663 requested the Danes at Tranquebar to give shelter to the Portuguese who came from Nagapattinam owing to Dutch occupation of the settlement.[6]

Further, the population of the Portuguese settlement of Santhome of Mylapore had increased steadily from sixty families in 1538 to 100 in 1543. The Portuguese population in 1545 was around 500.[7] Francis Xavier in one of his letters dated 10 November 1545 mentioned that there were more than 100 married Christians in Santhome.[8] After a year (1546) there were 500 Portuguese in Santhome with their slaves.[9] By the end of the year 1559 the population rose to 2000 including the Portuguese and natives.[10] In 1563 as many as 4000 Christians lived there besides sixty war veterans with their families.[11] In 1635 there were 120 white *casados* (Portuguese families) and 200 black *casados* (Tamil Christians).[12] According to a Jesuit report in 1644 we find that 1700 Christians lived there.[13] In 1661 sixty Portuguese settlers migrated from Nagapattinam to Santhome of Mylapore.[14] There were 200 *topasses* and 600 Portuguese *mestiços* in 1669 who continued to live there.[15] Thus we find large mixed population and it is very difficult to define the social organization of these groups. Of the Eurasians, certainly there could be broad distinction such as *fidalgos*, (nobles) *soldados* (soldiers) *casados*, (married settlers) and *mestiços* (half-blood).

II

Jesuit letters written in 1559 and 1563 mention several corrupt acts and unlawful behaviour of the Portuguese in the Tamil Coast.[16] There were few missionaries in the early period to attend to the spiritual needs of the Portuguese and the Indo-Portuguese community. Further, it is to be noted that only in the later period when the number of missionaries increased in the coast they took active steps to give really a new shape to the lifestyle of the converted Indians by administering the sacraments. They also noted in their letters and reports about the Portuguese and Indo-Portuguese community which had various social problems that have special and anti-social dimensions. We cannot close our eyes to these hard realities and these issues in criminology have not attracted the attention of sociologists or historians in Europe and Asia and so we shall deal with them here.

Pen-Picture of Murders and Death

Portuguese records throw light on several instances of murder. Symão de Britto who lived in Santhome of Mylapore was stabbed by one *mestiço*, a relative of Francisco de Freitas. The Portuguese captain of Mylapore therefore arrested the culprit and confined him in a church. An enquiry was later held when Symão de Britto, the injured had died.[17] Similarly, there was a man in Santhome of Mylapore married to a rich and influential lady of good connections. He misbehaved with the servant girl in his house and She became conceived. The landlady found the occasion that she needed to deal with her husband and the servant properly. Hence she managed to kill the maid servant with the help of some paid agents. After mutilating the body, she ordered it to be buried in the garden at the backyard of the house. The flesh removed from the body was taken into the kitchen and a dish was prepared under the direct supervision of the lady. When her husband came home for dinner the dish was served to him and told that she had herself specially prepared it for him. The husband ate and praised very much for its exquisite taste. Then the woman lifted the dish and flung the contents in his face, saying that it was not enough to have enjoyed the maid servant while she was alive; even in death she was of good savour. Her anger overflowing, she gave her husband plentiful abuse, and quitting the house went to live with her relatives. She did not consent to meet husband for the rest of her life.[18]

Evidences suggest that the Portuguese merchants were very brutal to their slaves both male and female. Learning from the reports sent from India to Portugal, the King of Portugal issued a royal order on 26 January 1559 stating the Portuguese merchants should not be brutal to their slaves both male and female and prohibited them from mutilating or slaying slaves.[19] However, instances of murder and death we find in the Portuguese settlements. An instance is worth mentioning. There was a slave girl in the house of Cosmo Lourenco Madeira, a Portuguese in Santhome of Mylapore. His wife name was Dona Escolastica, the daughter of João Pereira de Faria who had imprisoned the slave for having stolen something in the house. By reason of severe punishment meted out by her and deprivation of food that slave died and was buried in the dunghill. No one in the town dared to ask any question about the death of the slave. If the native rulers of the region had known they would have definitely chastised the husband and wife.[20] Thus instances of cruelty were found common among the Portuguese and it continued. The earlier said two crimes committed were with a definite purpose of assault and murder.

Records do mention that the Portuguese soldiers had committed murders. A Antonio Miranda who lived in Santhome of Mylapore had wounded a Dane at a tavern in Madras and he killed an English soldier who had come there to quell the tavern brawl. During his imprisonment Antonio Miranda, the soldier revealed that in the previous year he had killed another person at Santhome of Mylapore and it was found out that the English soldier whom he killed was the seventh murder that he had committed.[22] Further we find that Manoel Branden Lima a Portuguese soldier of Madras was arrested on the charge of murdering a fellow Portuguese. A jury comprising of six Englishmen and six Portuguese conducted the case. Finally he was found guilty and on 25 September 1678 he was sentenced to death.[23]

III

Disclosing the Dimensions of Adultery and Sex

Portuguese in the Tamil Coast seems to have acculturated and fitted into the Indian environment. There appears to have been copious sexual interactions and hence reproduction between Portuguese men and Indian women had taken place as gleaned from the increasing population details mentioned earlier. The result was the creation of a very large *mestiço* population in the Tamil ports. We also find damsels (*donzellas*) born in India and wives whose husbands were away on duty. The fundamental questions about civil liberties and the power of the Portuguese *Estado da India* can be raised since plenty of crimes are noted. Crime as a social phenomenon is an important area of scientific research, debate and historical study because it helps us to understand the human behaviour in general. Cause behind the rise in crimes against sex, women and youth is important to note and the behaviour in violation of the legal code, the activity that offends the social code and different aspects of behaviour that violates crime law is mentioned in various documents.

A report mentions that the Portuguese and *mestiço* women were very luxurious and unchaste, for there were very few among them, although they be married. They had besides their husbands, one or two soldiers, with whom they took their pleasure, and they used all the slights and practices. They devised plans by sending out their slaves by night, and at extraordinary times, over walls, hedges, and ditches, how narrow lie so ever, they were kept and looked unto. They had likewise an herb called *Deutroa*, which bore a seed, where of bruising out the sap, they put it into a cup or other vessel, and gave it to their husbands, either in meat or drink. When presented therewith, the man was as if he were half out of his wits, and without feeling, or else drunk, doing nothing but laughed. Sometime it took him to sleeping, whereby he was like a dead man, so that in his presence they did what they wanted. The women took their pleasure with their friend's and the husband never knew of it. In this manner they continued for long hours, but when they washed the feet of the husband for long with cold water he revived his senses and knew nothing thereof, but thought he had slept.[24]

It is mentioned that in 1594 Lopo Alvares da Moura, a rich merchant had abducted the wife of another settler in Santhome of Mylapore as he was interested in sex. Therefore he was punished by the Portuguese captain of the town. Earlier the merchant's house was attacked by the women's relatives.[25] Another incident happened in 1695 and it is said that there was a Portuguese called Antonio Pinto, married to Isabel Rapoza who lived in the town of Santhome of Mylapore. He went the evil way with another married woman called Antonia de Torres, who allowed this Portuguese man at any time to enter her house publicly. Isabel Rapoza who often heard about this affair kept silence. One day when she heard of this, not being able to cool down her passion, found an opportunity in the afternoon. She came out of her house followed by four strong and stout slaves. She proceeded to the house of her adversary, dragged her to the streets, attacked physically and the bones were broken by a good thumping, and the face had disfigured also by shoe-beating. The aggrieved wife retired with all dignity to her own house. The wretched Antonia de Torres went off to Madras to be healed. Thus Antonio da Torres and Antonio Pinto were branded with infamy all over the town. The man by way of restoring his credit, assigned a reason that his wife was impotent and left for Madras to live with Antonia da Torres.[26]

Further, another incident happened. There was a wealthy and honoured Portuguese called João Perreira de Faria married to Dona Maria de Souza who migrated from Nagapattinam upon the loss of the town from the hands of the Portuguese to the Dutch in 1658 and settled in Madras. One of the slave-girls of the house was much favoured by him and he had given such an authority to her in order to gratify his own desires in an illicit direction. The maid servant wanted to kill the mistress by magic arts. For this purpose she stole some money from her master and resorted to a young Hindu servant to take measures to put an end to her mistress's life. Her idea was to become the head of the house when the landlady was dead and at that time she would reward the Hindu servant. The youth who accepted the task tried to do what the slave-girl wanted, and not succeeding, had to finally recourse to a magician. This man directed him to bring some hair, nail-clippings, and a piece of defiled cloth belonging to the land-lady. The youth reported to the slave-girl, and she sent what was required. When some days had passed, the youth brought one pin, the point of which reached nearly to the stomach, and another pin which was stuck into the navel coming half-way down the legs as given by the magician. The slave girl was told that at midnight she must go entirely naked into the middle of the house-garden, holding up in one hand a doll, and in the other a piece of burning wood. Orders as to what she was to do were added. She was warned that while acting as above, there would appear a black cat, but she must not be afraid. The wretched woman did as instructed. Going to the centre of the court-yard, she set fire to the doll's feet and hands. At that moment there appeared to her the awe-inspiring cat, with eyes which looked like two flames of fire. On seeing such an apparition the slave-girl was in terror. At this time, there also arose in the house loud cries and commotion. Being frightened, the girl went into her mistress's chamber as if she wanted to help, carrying with her the doll, which she hid in the sacking of the lady's bedstead. In her hurry and agitation, she did not thrust it well in, and it remained half-hanging out. The land-lady of the house was in mortal anguish, complained that she felt on fire from her head to stomach, and from the navel down to her lower limbs, besides her hands and feet burning with insufferable heat and agony. They called in the doctors, who could not determine what ailment it was, and the remedies given her did not take effect. For several days the land-lady suffered in the same way.[27]

After a few days, then it chanced that a child of three years old, playing about in the house, went under the bed and saw a doll half-projecting. It pulled it out with a cry of delight, and played with it showing it to the nurse. When the woman saw it she recognized at once what it was, and showed it on the spot to her mistress and the rest of those present, said that it was a piece of magic and through which she had suffered. Upon making sure of this, she called in a Hindu magician, who as soon as entered the house went to João Pereira de Faria, and told him that he was the cause of his wife's sufferings. He was ashamed, and hung his head. Upon seeing the image, the magician told the wife that in short time she would be restored to health, but the people of the house must not be alarmed when they saw her lie without senses or any movement. For his work, the magician retired into a room and very slowly drew out the pins, and unstitched the image bit by bit. Finally he opened up the abdomen, from where he found the nail-clippings, the hair and the cloth spoken of above, with other mixed items put in earlier by the magician. When the image had been entirely pulled to pieces, he threw it into a vessel of milk and after making his incantations, he threw that vessel also into the sea. After twelve hours Dona Maria de Souza came back to her senses and lost all her pains, but she was so weak that it took nearly three months for her to recover strength. The magician immediately fixed upon the slave-girl who had done the mischief and on confessing it, she was punished and banished for the rest of her life. The originator of the trouble was João Perreira de Souza, the master of the house, who had enjoyed sex illegally with the servant.[28] The above said three crimes were committed chiefly because of sexual and economic motives.

IV

Voices from Dowry

According to official Portuguese reports many orphan girls were sent from Portugal to be married in India, the daughters of the Portuguese soldiers and sailors killed in various expeditions held in Europe and Africa. The King of Portugal had taken special interest relating to the affairs of such women in Portugal and so he passed an order in 1623 which stated that these young girls should be given in marriage between fifteen and twenty years. The King also passed another order in 1627 that any Portuguese granted to orphan girls as the marriage settle was to be fixed for a term of three years. Further, the King of Portugal issued a royal order dated 27 June 1684 wherein he allowed widows to remarry unmindful of the caste to which they belonged before. It also sanctioned punishment to the parents and close relatives who forbade a widow for remarrying through the penalty of confiscation of property.[29]

In the beginning of the Sixteenth Century, Portuguese became rich through overseas trade and so they lived in great pomp and show in India. But this was no longer the case in the Seventeenth Century with the decline of Portuguese trade, arrival of the Dutch and the Luso-Dutch rivalry which brought misery. They had barely enough for food. At this time they married any girl after obtaining almost everything on loan that is needed for the wedding. The day after the marriage and feast, everybody came and carried away whatever had been lent out. The greater part of the house also stood empty and the bride was without jewels. As for dowry, the bridegroom did not even receive really the half of what was promised to him.[30]

Though ritual and ceremonial elements were usually present in marriages the material valuation was always dominant. It happened in Nagapattinam that a young man from Portugal came to get married with a recommendation letter to a resident who had a daughter. After reading the contents of the letter, the father of the girl stated the dowry that he intended to give. The young man had also agreed to the amount. When a few days had elapsed, a married man told that young man that he should not marry anyone from that house and family but he himself offered his own daughter instead of the previous one with a larger dowry. The young man accepted this proposal also and spoke no more to the first man. The latter, on learning the facts was very much annoyed. The girl, seeing that the new arrival was governed by his interests, fcnd of her money and not of her, advised her father to promise him the double of what the other had offered. The self-seeker, being an ambitious fellow, came back to the house, and in a few days their marriage was arranged. On the day of the marriage they went to church for the wedding ceremony. The priest asked the groom if he was willing to marry this lady. He replied most confidently in the affirmative. The same question was put to the bride, and she, in place of saying 'Yes,' lifted her hand and gave him a smart smack on the face and said: 'With this big rogue, I have no intention of marrying. He wanted the money, and he is not worthy of being my husband'. The man, put to shame, hurried out of the church. When this happened, at that time, there was present at the same wedding a rich youth. Seeing this noble action of the bride, he took a fancy to her, and asked if she would marry him. He added that he would accept her without any money benefit. The bride lifted her eyes and had a look at him. Then she accepted him as husband, and the feast was held for him. To no one's imagination this had happened.[31] Thus we find an example that happiness depends on the choice of a girl upon whom one's heart and eyes are set, and not on any other which ultimately helps the husband and wife to be deeply smitten in love. The decision of the girl to marry one in whom she finds a heaven of happiness is shown in this case.

In the year 1694, in Madras, there was an incident related to dowry and love which is interesting. There was a young man born of humble parentage but lofty thoughts. His name was João da Cunha. He became enamoured of a young girl, and, as it seemed to him, fortune could not favour him better than by making her his wife. As the father of the girl never gave it a thought nor could the young girl imagine such a thing, he did not have the courage to declare his concealed feeling. He came to the house every day, nursing a mystic passion, and anything required to be done at the house was carried out by him with exactitude. But time and again he said that many marriage proposals were made to him, though he would not accept any one of these proposed brides, except one whom he strongly desired. Seeing the little progress he was making, he went one day to the father of the girl and said: 'This morning they bribed me to make a marriage by offering a dowry of (Rs. 2000) one thousand *patacas'*. He added that the person was of some position and of good fame and the name of the girl was Catharina da Silva. He asked for advice from the father of the girl. The man replied that it was quite certain that God had come to his help and he must accept the proposal. They talked with such secrecy that the whole household heard of it so loud. Everybody congratulated him. He went on to say that he never meant to marry, if the girl were not to his liking. Some days elapsed, and they were continuously asking him, only way of joke, when the wedding was to be. The man was put out, and not wishing to be counted a liar, made out a paper for the banns, showed it to them, and said he was going to the Priest to have the marriage banns published. He delivered the paper to the vicar, who published the banns on two Sundays. The bridegroom, his sisters, and all his parents received everybody's congratulations. Everyone asked about the bride, and he said that she was away from Madras and lying ill. Under this pretext he borrowed jewels from his relatives and from the young girl's parents.

The following Saturday he went to confession, and during the mass on Sunday, when about to receive the host, he fell to the earth in a swoon just as if he were dead, and thus remained nearly two hours before recovering his senses (a just chastisement for his evil deeds). At night he left secretly, and made off to Santhome of Mylapore, and then sent word to his relatives that he was now married, that his wife was ill, and growing always worse. After a few more days passed, he moved to St. Thomas Mount and there he hired a house, and lived with great secrecy being shut up in one room, and said that, it was his suffering wife, whom he had brought to St. Thomas Mount to recover health. From Madras his relatives asked whether they might come and see his wife. He replied not to trouble and he would send necessary transport when the proper time arrived, for his wife was delirious, and it was not good for them to see her in that state.

One day the inhabitants of St. Thomas Mount, with the two hermits went to visit him. He gave a welcome, to which he in a very despondent tone answered: 'Cursed be the hour when I married, and cursed be the dowry paid me, for greed of money made me take a wife troubled with a thousand ailments, so that I was forced to transport her to this St. Thomas Mount to get her well, and I expect that here she will find a sepulchre'. They asked him as to what was the matter with her, to which he said not a word, but burst into tears and lamentation. At this time a woman servant arrived and he had brought her with him on purpose. She said that the lady was very weak and it was two days since she had eaten anything. He told the maid to see if his wife could take some broth or medicated drink. The woman went inside before everybody with the bowl of food, and said such words from within that those outside imagined the wife to be really very ill. After a few days, he made a figure of straw and enshrouded it so that it looked like a real corpse, and set up many candles which he had brought for the purpose. Then he sent a message to the Priest to have the bell tolled for his wife Catherina da Silva, she being dead. In great haste he dispatched an advice to his relatives in Madras that his wife had died, and they must all come to attend her funeral. The vicar descended to the house very angrily and said that they had not sent word to him, so that confession and extreme-unction could have been administered. The man answered that she had already been confessed at Santhome of Mylapore. The excess of grief he displayed over the bundle of straw very much affected the attention of everybody present, and the whole night long the two hermits sat on vigil over the dead body, in company with the people of St. Thomas Mount and some other devout persons. From time to time, an old woman whose name was Bernarda, bribed beforehand with a small sum, asked João da Cunha, 'What of the lady Catharina da Silva? The day before yesterday I saw her with these very eyes alive, and today she is already dead! During this time the servant woman cried: 'O my mistress! How could you yield yourself to this wretch who had so long followed you? When I supposed that I was to see you happy, you were going to your death'. João da Cunha frequently fell upon the corpse of straw, and emitted such cries that all present were moved to compassion. Fearing a fit, the hermits and the other guests present there wanted to carry him away and place him on a bed. The cheat, suspecting that those surrounding him might go and inspect the pretended corpse, wrested himself out of the arms of the hermits, and once more threw himself upon the sack of straw and renewed his exclamations. Very early in the next day morning his relatives arrived, and they wailed greatly. With a considerable number of persons following the cortege, the burial took place at the foot of the hill of St. Thomas Mount, and each man retired to his own home. On that day he distributed much alms, and ordered very many Holy Masses to be said. But as the secret lay among some poor women, it soon began to be said that what had been interred was a straw figure. The rumour spread, and it came to the ears of the Bishop of Mylapore. He sent orders to open the tomb, and they lighted upon the straw figure, buried there eight days before. But a month afterwards João da Cunha came to pray pardon for his offences, and he was then given absolution. Thus we find in this incident that all activities had been undertaken because he could not get the old man's daughter in marriage and also to embezzle ornaments and cash.[32] *Stridhana* (women's personal property in the legal Indian literature) was prevalent very common and it was restricted to jewels and other such moveable goods. Property of land was considered as an inappropriate possession for women in the Indian context. It seems that the Portuguese had not picked up the practice of dowry from the Hindus since grants had been made available for marriages of the orphan girls as dowry by the King of Portugal himself.

V

Women and the Social Universe of Superstitions

The social and economic affairs of the Portuguese settlements in the Tamil Coast were looked after by the Portuguese captains appointed by the King of Portugal. All matters relating to military were decided by the Portuguese Governor in Goa. Law and order problems were handled by the judges appointed in the settlement. In the Indian port settlements near the Portuguese settlements all matters were governed by the *adhikari* appointed by the *Nayaka* ruler.[33] The Portuguese established inquisition in 1560 in Goa to prevent recourse by the converts to non-Christian customs and its range of prohibitions covered a number of socio-cultural practices but it was absent on the East Coast of India. Therefore social evils such as superstitions, sorcery and magic were widely prevalent among the Portuguese and converts in the Coromandel Coast.

A rich Portuguese woman who lived in Madras had a married daughter who was pregnant. The mother wanted to know whether it would be an easy delivery or not. To this intent she asked for an old woman who lived as a diviner to get her to pray. The woman placed herself for prayer near the door to the street at nine o'clock at night. This she did for two nights. The third night while praying she heard a voice saying: 'We shall die and leave no remembrance.' On hearing this, the woman was disconsolate, and said nothing to the widow, so as not to lose the payment promised to her. She produced other reasons to pacify her, and the mother, to maintain her own credit, went about saying what would happen to the pregnant daughter. After some time, it was learnt that the latter had died in child bed.[34]

Similarly, a Portuguese woman who lived in Madras being married to a merchant being delayed in his voyage, and no news came of him, she wanted to know about him. So she went to the old woman directing her to pray, and ask that in a dream she might see what had become of her husband. While asleep she saw the ship wrecked, when several persons died of drowning, including the husband. The news was disclosed to the wife, who mourned and was unable to keep the secret (ordinarily there are few secrets kept by women). She communicated it to her neighbours, and thus the news passed through the whole town. At length it came to the ears of the vicar, who made efforts to abolish such an abuse by preaching and admonishment. None the less the practice persisted, faith was still placed in the old woman and the advice of the vicar was disregarded. Some months had passed and news came of the husband's death that he had been drowned. The old woman earned much money through her sooth-sayings and lived as a diviner.[35]

In another case, we find that a rich Portuguese widow in Madras who became anxious to know whom she would marry and so she had sent word for the old woman. She gave a reward to the old woman and commanded her to perform rites in her presence. For this purpose, the old woman sent word to fetch for her a clear glass phial. When it was brought, breaking some eggs she poured them into and prayed into the mouth of this bottle. Slowly the eggs formed into a human shape with some letters showing the name of the person who was to become the widow's spouse. After some time, there appeared a man who bore the name announced by the phial. When the widow saw him, she declared that he resembled the man whom she had seen and so later she married him. In the entire region there was no old woman like her who bore such fame and name after this incident.[36]

In Santhome of Mylapore, there was a lady who sent word for one of the women diviners and requested her to pray in her house in favour of a certain intention which she recommended to her. For the purpose a special chamber was set aside. After ten o'clock at night the old woman took her seat at a window, and engaged in prayer. Fancying she would hear a voice, according to her intention, there appeared instead in the middle of the room a face surrounded by white. On seeing it the old woman became speechless and was in a state of terror, sitting motionless, while the face remained stationary for some time. Finding that no question was put, it went out again by the same window. The old woman then fell down. The people of the house, hearing the fall, ran into the room, where they found the woman extended on the ground in a swoon. They raised her up, and with the help of medicine she came to senses by herself in the next morning. But she was unable to move one of her legs. Asking her what had happened she explained that as the face passed out of the window, she felt it touch her on that leg. On inspection, they found the leg withered into a mere stick, and its flesh all shrivelled. Remedies were applied, but were not effective, and for the few years she survived and it remained in the same condition. She repented herself of her deeds, for no one could fully understand an evil that has not actually experienced.[37] It is often found how people foolishly behaved without applying their mind and reasoning in their daily life and such events make this study particularly rewarding.

In Santhome of Mylapore there was a lady who asked an old woman of a confraternity to inform her on some questions she wanted to be answered. In the depth of night, when the old woman was performing her ritual in the lady's house, there appeared an awe-inspiring monster that seized the old woman by the hair and forced her out of the house, leaving her in the street half dead from the blows it applied. At the same time a ball of fire fell upon the house and all it contained was burnt. The inhabitants escaped with great difficulty. The old woman found herself in the street, and on recovering her senses she repented herself, and decided never again to perform such rites. It took her a considerable time to recover health, and for the few years she lived she seemed to be in a state of right, and trembled at the recollection of what had happened to her. It was a merited punishment for meddling in things that did not concern her. Even by this example people have not mended their ways, for they continued to act as before without any compunction and many of these old women died in misery.[38]

There was an old blind Portuguese woman in Madras called Androza and she lived with the reputation of a saint, many women resorting to her to discover matters similar to those already stated. They bestowed liberal alms on her, by which she lived comfortably. Through her fame for holiness, the whole village of fisher-folk had recourse to her, presenting to her good fish and some money. They enjoyed hearing her conversation and did not go to church. The vicar noticed their absence, while the alms that they usually brought to church at the time of mass and their other offerings were also missing. On his taking up the question, he discovered the pretensions of the blind Androza, who had imposed this superstition upon the whole village. She was admonished and expelled from the town. After these events Androza moved to St. Thomas Mount (*Monte Grande*) where she continued her practices and lived on the alms given to her by the devout. [39]

VI

Men and the World

A Portuguese called Manoel Macedo de Azevedo lived in Santhome of Mylapore and this man dreamt several nights running inside his house, a treasure being buried in a godown, close to a pillar on which the house rested. To find out whether the dream was true or not he called in a sorcerer, to whom he set forth what he had dreamt. The sorcerer asked for three days to inquire and see if things were as he had dreamt. To find out by experiment whether the sorcerer knew how to divine what had been buried, the Portuguese placed some money and jewels in the earth at four places in his garden. When the three days had passed, the sorcerer came, back and going into the garden, drew forth a small paper from his pocket, and took from it certain black powder and anointed his eyes. Then the Portuguese led the sorcerer to the places where he had buried the things already referred to. The sorcerer halted, and described minutely what had been interred. The Portuguese then believed in the sorcerer through the proof that he had put him to, and took him to the middle of the godown of which he had dreamt. The sorcerer came stood there and displayed great astonishment, saying that in that spot was a large caldron full of gold; but it was down seven cubits deep near the water-level. The caldron had two rings, and each ring was placed on the horn of an ox which upheld the caldron. On hearing this, the Portuguese was delighted, and wanted to order the pot to be excavated. The sorcerer advised him that it was inexpedient to touch it without having performed a sacrifice. In obedience to his counsel, goats and cocks were sacrificed. Then men were set to work to dig while the master stood by. As soon as they had dug down about four cubits and when the work was still in progress, an announcement was made that the Portuguese captain had come to call on him. Therefore the work was suspended, the labourers were turned out, and the door was locked. Then the master went to greet the captain at his gate, and conducted him to the garden. While they were in conversation, the house fell down owing to the removal of the foundations of the pillar. Thereby the man saw how the good God had been to him, and the net in which the Devil had tried to catch him. Repenting himself, he abandoned his attempt. All the people in the town heard of this case, and to the unholy rites the sorcerer had performed. The Portuguese man was compelled to appear before the inquisition in Goa to defend himself but he came out free.[40] The Portuguese seems to have followed the local tradition, customs and manners of the natives in the Tamil coast and it is also possible to say that that superstitions were prevalent in Portugal and this enabled the Portuguese to follow the same in India too.

There were many notorious men and criminals who lived in the Tamil Coast. In a letter of 1612 we find a complaint sent to the King of Portugal about Antonio de Sous a who had thrown dead things in drinking water wells from which water was drawn.[41] It is to be borne in mind that the sequences of action of men and women in society were essentially historical phenomena involving persistence and change in time. A scientific study of society must therefore necessarily include a historical method and the absence of this would mean an insufficient understanding of the nature of the facts being studies, a falsification and superficial treatment of them and so the great possibility of error would occur in the findings.

VII

Slavery, Immorality and Disorderly Conduct

Slaves were owned by the Portuguese for domestic purposes in the Tamil Coast. But there was no active slave trade as such conducted by the Portuguese between 1507 and 1662.[42] In the later period we find some stray evidences. According to a report, there was a married Tamil who came from Madurai to Nagapattinam exploring the possibility of finding some means of livelihood and employment to support his family. Having found some job at Nagapattinam he asked leave of absence after a month from the person with whom he was serving to go to Madurai and fetch his wife and children. After obtaining leave and necessary permission he reached Madurai. There he learnt the news that the neighbour in Nagapattinam to whom he had confided his family had abducted them, telling his wife that the husband had sent word. When the man returned to Nagapattinam he learnt that his wife and sons were already taken to Tranquebar, and were sold treacherously to the Portuguese priest for thirty *pagodas*. His family members were not aware of it. In the end he came to Tranquebar, and made efforts to recover them. The vicar resisted and reported the matter to the Danish Governor. Further, the man himself was captured so that he could make no further attempts for his own release. Later, when he was delivered away from the prison, the poor man lodged a complaint to the Bishop of Mylapore, but a hearing was refused out of regard for the said priest. He submitted a petition then and prayed that he might at least have permission to re-marry, since the said priest had already bought his wife and sons. In the mean while, he learnt that his family members were sold again for sixty *pagodas* and were ready to sail from Madras to Manila. At this time, the whole of his caste members assembled and undertook to pay the sale price of his wife and sons within one month notice, since this Tamil was a poor man. Even this did not avail. The

English Governor of Madras had since earlier decided that resold slaves should not be embarked in the ships leaving for Manila, thereupon the priest was forced to take away the wife and sons. The priest had again managed to send them for re-sale elsewhere into the hands of the Hindu traders. The husband in desperation changed his faith and returned to Hinduism, since he was unable to secure justice from the Portuguese.[43] Thus we find crimes committed against public decency, morality and disorderly conduct and these crimes were against justice and breach of trust.

It is not possible in this short paper to list or to describe all the important aspects of Portuguese society. The Portuguese had introduced a regular administration of justice through *relacão* (highcourt) and *ouvidor* (judge) to guard and control the society in the settlements of the Tamil Coast. The assembly of the elders (*Os Eleitos de Negapatao*) had controlled the social affairs of the people according to Tamil customs.[44] The crimes committed by individuals taken here for examination show that the presence of criminals was destructive to the society. The social life of the mestiços by tracing instances of slavery, adultery, murder, dowry and marriage in the society and an analysis throws new light on the mixed culture by outlining the distinct characteristics. Pleasing tales (*manoranjan Itihas*) had been widely prevalent in Indian literature but travellers like Nicolau Manucci had indulged this talent narrating upon the mysterious activities of the Portuguese in Tamil Country is noteworthy. Whether the ridiculous event he relates proceed from that common partiality which he had from a judgment formed upon as an Italian or some external ceremonies and superstitious activities of the Portuguese is very difficult to determine. But this travel account has thrown disgrace upon a system of Portuguese living which they did at that time. Portuguese had followed a life of licentiousness amidst luxury and plenty in the Sixteenth Century. They were also not free from practising the extravagance and vain glory in the daily material life than a very high spirituality as the medieval Christianity and missionaries expected from them. The Indo-Portuguese were also subjected to some of the evil practices such as robbery, adultery, theft and murder. The absence of a strong political leadership in the social organization helped the Portuguese in the Eastern Coast of India to behave as they liked.

It is enjoyable to talk about women and we are able to view a range of life styles concerning Portuguese women. The varied possibilities of identity are not open to Portuguese women in the familial, professional, religious and royal contexts. Conventional historiography that perceives women as silent voices of history because they had little or nothing to do is not applicable in this context. Events and moments are made the central theme and the Portuguese men and women who once walked on the stage of history in flesh and blood are depicted in the historical stage. The Indo-Portuguese community was not a homogenous social group and it was considerably stratified in terms of race and status. The *castizos* or the Portuguese of purer blood were less in the Coromandel coast and thc descendants of mixed parentage or thc *mestiços* were more in numbcr. The wayward life style and lawlessness were found common and it created unusual social pressures. It may be concluded that the crimes committed by Portuguese and Indo-Portuguese community could be classified generally into three groups on the basis of their motives, i.e., economic, sexual and miscellaneous. These crimes could also be further classified according to different purposes such as (a) against women (assault and murder) (b) against property (theft and robbery) (c) against public decency or morality (disorderly conduct) (d) against public justice (embezzlement and breach of trust). Blood feud was another practice in society in which the family of a murdered person sought vengeance on the murderer or murderer's family. In sum it is to be mentioned here that good and bad people had existed in that age and society. Various social problems and crimes mentioned in this paper had a harmful impact on social interests and detrimental to the well-being of the society of the Sixteenth and Seventeenth centuries in Portuguese India.

Notes and References

1. For details see, Dejanirah Silva Couto, "Some Observed Portuguese Renegades in Asia in the 16th Century" in *Vasco da Gama and the Linking of Europe and Asia* (eds.,) Anthony Disney, Emily Botham, New Delhi, 2000, pp. 178-201; Maria Augusta Lima Cruz, "Exiles and Renegades in Early 16th Century: Portuguese in India", *Indian Economic and Social History Review*, Vol. 23, No.3, 1986, pp. 49-62; Jurrien Van Goor, "European Exiles, Renegades and Outlaws and the Maritime Economy of Asia, 1500-1750" in Anthony Disney, *Historiography of Europeans in Africa and Asia, 1450-1800*, London, 1998; K.S. Mathew, "Indian Ocean and Cultural Interaction" *Indica*, Vol. 35, No.2, 1998, pp. 97-132.
2. S. Jeyaseela Stephen, "Social Life of the Portuguese and the Luso-Tamils in Mylapore and Nagapattinam during the 16th and 17th Centuries", *Bharata Vidya*, Vol. II, 2003, pp. 7-14; See also another paper, "Societal Changes: Portuguese and the Native Christians in Tamil Country (Cir 1537-1759) in (eds.,)

K.S. Mathew, Teotonio R. Desousa and Pius Malckandathil, *"The Portuguese and the Socio-Cultural Changes in India, 1500-1800*, Tellicherry, 2001, pp. 479-513.

3. See, Vitorino Maghalaes Godhino, *Os Descobrimentos e a Mundial*, Lisboa, 1981-84.
4. George Winius "The Shadow Empire of Goa in the 16th Century" *Itinerario*, Vol. VII (2) 1983, p. 92.
5. Antonio Bocarro, "Livro das Plantas de Todas as Fortalezas, Cidades e Povaçoes do Estado da India Oriental" in A.B. de Bragança Perreira (ed.,) *Arquivo Portugues Oriental*, Bastora Goa, 1937-38, pt. II, p. 8.
6. *Bolteim da Filmoteca Ultramarina Portuguesa*, Vol. 11, pp. 176-179. The Dutch reported the Golconda authorities that the English Council in Madras would not refuse shelter to fellow Christians during the war in 1661. See. William Foster, *The English Factories in India*, 1618-1669, 13 Vols, Oxford, 1906-1927, (henceforth EFI), 1661-1664, p. 145n.
7. Antonio da Silva Rego, *Documentação Para a Historia das Missões do Padroado Portugues do Oriente, 1499-1582*, 12 Vols, Lisboã, 1947-1958, Vol. II, pp. 252-54; Vol. III 165; See for the statistics of Portuguese residents in Coromandel, *Arquivo Nacional da Torre do Tombo*, (henceforth ANTT,) Mss. *Corpo Cronologico*, (henceforth CC) CC-III-9-94 (1521). See also Elaine *Sanceau, Colleção São Lourenço*, (henceforth CSI), Lisboã, 1973-83, Vol. III, pp. 64-65.
8. Jose Wicki, *Documenta Indica*, (henceforth D.I.) 18 Vols, Rome, 1948-88. see Vol. II, 16; Antonio da Silva Rego, *Documentação*, *op. cit.*, Vol. III, p. 165; *Monumenta Xaveriana*, 2 Vols., Matriti, 1899-1912, Vol. II, p 549.
9. Georg Schurhammer, *St. Francis Xavier: His Life, His Times*, 2 Vols., Rome, 1977, Vol. II, p. 549.
10. *DI*, *op. cit.*, Vol. V, p. 181.
11. ANTT, *Gavetas*, 11-8-19-7; See also *D.I*, *op. cit.*, Vol. V. p. 743.
12. Antonio Bocarro, *Livro das Plantas*, *op. cit.*, pt. II, p. 8.
13. S. Jeyaseela Stephen, *Portuguese in the Tamil Coast: Historical Explorations in Commerce and Culture*, Pondicherry, 1998, pp. 243 and 252.
14. Antonio Bocarro, *op. cit.*, pt. II. p. 8.
15. *Dagh Register Gehouden int Casteel Batavia van het Passerende Daer teer Plaetse als over Geheel Nederlants Indie*

(1624-1682), 27 Vols., The Hague and Batavia, 1887-1931, (henceforth DR) 1661, p. 42.

16. Cunha Rivara, *Archivo Portuguez Oriental*, (henceforth APO-CR) 6 fasciculos in 9 Vols., Goa, 1857-76. See Decree 18, p. 20 and Decree, 40, p. 30.
17. *D.I, op. cit.*, Vol. VI, pp. 89-93. S. Jeyaseela Stephen, *The Coromandel Coast and its Hinterland: Economy, Society and Political System, 1500-1600*, New Delhi, 1997, see pp. 182-186.
18. Niccolao Manucci, *Storia do Mogor*, (tr.,) William Irvine, 4 Vols., London, 1907-08, Vol. III, p. 112.
19. *APO–CR, op. cit.*, fasciculo 4, Decree 12, pp. 12-16.
20. Niccolao Manucci, *op. cit.*, Vol. III, p. 113.
21. *EFI, 1642-1645, op. cit.*, p. 44.
22. *Ibid.*, p. 59.
23. Records of Fort St., George, *Diary and Consultation Book. 1672*, Madras, 1918, pp. 165-66, See also p. 110.
24. John Van Linschoten, *The Voyages of John Van Linschoten to the East Indies*, 2 Vols, London, 1885, Vol. I, pp. 209-210.
25. Annual letter of Francisco Caral at Goa dated 17 December 1594 in *Documenta Indica*, Vol. XVI, pp. 750-751.
26. Niccolao Manucci, *op. cit.*, Vol. III, pp. 112-113.
27. *Ibid.*, Vol. III, pp. 206-207.
28. *Ibid.*, Vol. III, pp. 207-209.
29. See, Vitorino Maghalaes Godhino, *Os Descobrimentos e a Mundial*, Lisboã, 1981-84.
30. Niccolao Manucci, *op. cit.*, Vol. III, p. 118. He says that "I will relate these stories by various old inhabitants, natives of the place of Santhome of Mylapore. Formerly it was richer than all the other towns held by the Portuguese in India, owing to its great trade with China Java Melaka etc. The merchants gained more than a thousand percent but this was before the Dutch came to India. They received goods and paid for them by the para which is a measure used in Europe to measure corn and vegetable. Nowadays (1653-1708) they measure in those measure rice lime and other products. The coins for which these goods were exchanged are called pagodas which are still current. These coins which are of gold and weigh a drachem are small and circular, stamped only on one side with symbol of some idol. The ancients must have thought little of gold from the way they used it in painting and adorning various

unnecessary places such as beams doorways, windows in their houses, and for various purposes such as on chests, chests of drawers, benches, chairs etc., adding nails and fastenings of gold and silver or putting gold feet and other ornaments to their bedsteads of aloes wood or sandal wood, also to the chairs and benches of the same woods".

31. Niccolao Manucci, *op. cit.*, Vol. III, pp. 177-178.
32. *Ibid.*, Vol. III, pp. 187-191.
33. S. Jeyaseela Stephen, *Portuguese in the Tamil Coast*, *op. cit.*, p. 244.
34. Niccolao Manucci, *op. cit.*, Vol. III, p. 210.
35. *Ibid.*, Vol. III, p. 210 and 254.
36. *Ibid.*, Vol. III, pp. 210-211.
37. *Ibid.*, Vol. III, p. 211.
38. *Ibid.*, Vol. III, pp. 212-213.
39. *Ibid.*, Vol. III, p. 212 and.255.
40. *Ibid.*, Vol. III, pp. 213-214, p. 256
41. R.A. Bulhão Pato, *Documentos Remettidos da India ou Livros das Monções*, 5 Vols, Lisboã, 1880-1935, (henceforth DRI) Vol. II, p. 226.
42. S. Jeyaseela Stephen, *Portuguese in the Tamil Coast*, *op. cit.*, p. 158.
43. Niccolao Manucci, *op. cit.*, Vol. III, pp. 128-129. See, for details of the nine forms of slavery during the Dutch and French expansion in the Bay of Bengal, S. Jeyaseela Stephen, "Slavery and Society: Experiences of the Dutch and the French Trading Companies in Coastal Andhra, AD 1600-1800", in (ed.,) R. Soma Reddy, *Social Evils in Andhradesa: 17th and 18th Centuries*, Osmania University Publications, Hyderabad, 1999, pp. 75-96.
44. S. Jeyaseela Stephen, *Portuguese in the Tamil Coast*, *op. cit.*, pp. 237.

14

French Missionaries, Tamil Catholics and Social Changes in Pondicherry (1674-1793)

K. S. Mathew

A serious study of the social changes in India is vast and complex, and an adequate understanding of it will require the collaboration, for many years, of a number of scholars in such diverse fields as economics, social and cultural history, law, politics, education, religion, demography and sociology. This becomes all the more difficult in the case of the society of the peninsular India, multi-racial, multi-lingual, multi-cultural and multi-religious in nature which came into contact with the Europeans hailing from a social milieu embedded in principles of equality and unity of Christian religion. Scholars working on social changes in India experimented several conceptual frameworks to explain the process in the modern period. Sanskritization and westernization are the two concepts put forward by one of the leading Indian sociologists to explain social changes in India with emphasis on religious and cultural aspects. "Sanskritization is the process by which a 'low' Hindu caste, or tribal or other group, changes its customs, ritual, ideology and way of life in the direction of a high, and frequently, "twice-born" caste. Generally such changes are followed by a claim to a higher position in the caste hierarchy than that traditionally conceded to the claimant caste by the local community"[1]. This concept includes both sacred and secular elements of culture. Being unaware of the changes that had taken place in Hinduism in the haste to imitate the life of Brahmins in the process of sanskritization, the lower castes gave up animal sacrifice and consumption of liquor (Soma) though the Vedic Brahmins consumed liquor and ate beef.[2] They adopted vegetarianism and teetotalism and sanskritized-the ritual and pantheon. Some studies recently conducted buttress the fact that there were attempts on the part of lower castes to imitate customs of the *kshatriyas* and not those of Brahmins.[3] Similarly, tribes who do not come under the caste system of Hinduism imitated the customs of caste Hindus.[4]

On the other hand some scholars have proved that the higher castes have been found imitating the tribal customs in some place, which leads to "tribalization"[5]. Hence sanskritization is not confined to Hindu castes but also prevalent among the tribal and semi-tribal groups as conceded by eminent Indian sociologists.[6] In certain cases the upper and lower castes in Hinduism seem to have adopted some cultural styles of Islamic tradition totally exogenous to the Hindu tradition, which prompts one to underline the role of economic and political domination in sanskritization. Hence undue emphasis on Brahmanical model of sanskritization and the neglect of other models *Kshatriya*, *Vaishya* and *Shudra* were considered insufficient to explain social change in India.[7] Another concept employed by the eminent sociologist to explain social change was "westernization" entailing emphasis on humanitarianism and nationalism, which brought about considerable institutional and social reforms in India.[8] Westernization according to him implies humanitarianism, which in its turn includes egalitarianism and secularization. He makes mention of the westernization of eating meals at table as a point of secularization vis-a-vis the traditional practice of considering it among the upper caste Hindus a religious act squatting on the floor.[9] The concepts like sanskritization and westernization explain social change in structural terms, but only in cultural terms as admitted by the proponent.[10] To a good number of sociologists the concept westernization has pejorative meaning account of its association with colonial domination and so it has not been widely used in explaining social change in India. Others used a set of concepts such as Little and Great Traditions[11] having broader coverage than the concepts of sanskritization and westernization in explaining social changes in India. These too are considered to be suffering from culturological bias to the neglect of structural aspects of social change. Hence, another concept of multiple traditions is suggested to be a useful tool in analyzing social change.[12] A few other sociologists recommended structural approach towards social changes. This is based on functional and dialectical models. Functionalism takes for granted that the society is a relatively persisting configuration of elements and consensus is an ubiquitous element of the social system. French and the British social scientists made use of functionalism in their study of ethnography of caste, custom and culture. Dialectical model on the other hand treats change or tension ubiquitous in society. Hence major sources of change are immanent in the system itself.[13] Louis Dumont put forward cognitive historical viewpoint for the study of social change in India. According to him the focus of the study of social change, "should be on the reaction of Indian minds to the revelation of western culture such as individualism, freedom, democracy, etc., the cognitive system of Indian tradition is reacting with rejection or acceptance."[14] The Indian cognitive system is holistic in character while western cognitive system is individualistic posing the natural tension between tradition and modernity in India. Ideas of inequality, pollution-purity and priest-king alliance to enforce social order through charismatic authority followed from this principle. Here too we find emphasis on the basic themes of Indian culture, but not on social structure. Unsatisfied with this approach recently an Indian sociologist has proposed an integrated approach expressed in a paradigm formulated on two dimensions namely, a) sources from which the social changes may begin and b) the nature of social phenomena undergoing such changes. The social phenomena consist of 'tradition' and 'social structure'. He categorizes tradition into 'little' and 'great' and social structure into 'micro' and 'macro' structures. He is of the opinion that basic changes in the micro and macro structures of Indian society began to take place only after it came into contact with the West. He affirms: "... the orthogenetic sources of change in the social structure of Indian society did not have the potential for real structural changes which have been set into action through the heterogenetic form of the contemporary processes".[15] We shall examine how the major source of change immanent in the social system paved the way for the changes in micro and macro structures of the society in French Pondicherry when the Tamil society came into contact with the missionaries from France imbued with the principles of equality, freedom and democracy which in course of time got crystallized into the triple watchwords of equality, liberty and fraternity.

The rites, customs and manners followed by the different strata of society in India were inextricably associated with the social groupings or *varnas;* the four divisions of the society namely, *Brahmans*, *Kshatriyas*, *Vaisyas and Sudras* and those outside this grouping or *jatis* (castes) and were indicative of their affiliation to a particular stratum of society. Hence, adoption of some of the rites, customs and manners followed by those in the higher stratum of society and at the same time abandonment of those practised by the members of the lower stratum of the society by the same group of people would definitely indicate a conscious aspiration towards upward mobility in the social stratum. The French missionaries who worked in Pondicherry had to grapple with nuances of the local rites, customs and manners and on this score forgetting their basic and common commitment they faced inter-congregational conflicts in which sometimes the Roman Pontiffs had to intervene. The three important groups of missionaries who worked in Pondicherry during the period under review from France consisted of the Capuchins, the Jesuits and the Association of the Foreign Missionaries of Paris.

French Capuchins in Pondicherry

Father Ephraim, a native of Nevers in Auxerre, in the northern part of the province of Burgundy, on the banks of the Yonne born of a distinguished family and a member of the order St. Francis of Assisi was the first French missionary to come to Pondicherry along with the French expelled from Madras by the English.[16] He was the brother of M. De Chateau des Bois, counsellor of the Parliament of Paris. These Capuchins were of the Province of Touraine. They, accompanied by Deltor reached Gingee on 22 June 1674. At the orders of François Martin, three horses and twenty lascars were placed at their disposal for their safe journey to Pondicherry. Father Ephraim, Father Zenon reached Pondicherry on 29 June 1674 along with Deltor, Sieur Villedor, the protestant officer and two other French men.[17] They started a friary in Pondicherry in 1676 and worked chiefly among the Europeans and the Eurasians. Lazzaro de Motta, otherwise known as Thanappa Mudali donated the Church of St. Peter in Pondicherry to the Capuchins in 1686. Lazzaro de Motta built this church "for the glory of God, for the benefit of my soul and also for the consolation of the Gentiles, who have embraced our Holy Faith by the zeal and exemplary life of the said missionaries".[18] This donation was done through a letter signed by Lazzaro de Motta on 1 October 1686. These Capuchins did not make any serious effort to learn any languages since their nature of work did not demand it. As a result their interaction with the local people was very little and their understanding of the local rites was negligible. They worked in Pondicherry till the Dutch capture of Pondicherry in 1693, and returned to Pondicherry only after 1699 in view of the Treaty of Ryswick. The Capuchins obtained their mandate from the Bishop of Mylapore-the bishopric was in existence since 1606. In 1707 they built a new church attached to the official church St. Louis within the fort under the patronage of Our Lady of Angels. They frowned at the indigenous rites, customs and practices and found fault with the other missionaries from Europe who had developed contact with the local people of different religious avocations and learned their own mother tongues and got themselves acquainted with their way of life intimately. The attitude cherished by the Capuchins towards such practices can be well understood against the backdrop of the activities of the Jesuits who had come to the Eastern coast of India prior to the arrival of the French Capuchins and initiated a novel method of making Christian religion take shape in the oriental tradition. They continued to be in Pondicherry side by side with the Foreign Missionaries of Paris and the Capuchin Apostolic Prefect even in 1780's had a sort of jurisdiction that overlapped with that of the latter. In 1778, The Sacred Congregation of the *Propaganda Fide* made it clear that their Apostolic Prefect had ecclesiastical authority only of the Europeans and the Creoles, while the Eurasians like any other Indians were under the Foreign missionaries of Paris.

French Jesuits in Pondicherry

In view of the Siamese embassy to Paris in 1684, Louis XIV organized an expedition in which six Jesuit fathers, namely, Frs. Fontenay (Superior), Gerbill, Le Comte, Bouvet, Visdelou and Tachard were included. They were asked by the Royal Academy of Sciences to prepare maps, study navigation in the Indian Ocean, and devote themselves to astronomical studies in the East. Palace intrigues compelled them to leave Siam and so fourteen of the Jesuits from Siam left the place. Some of them took refuge in Pondicherry in 1689 and a few in Chandernagore.[19] They were hoping to go back to Siam later. But seeing that the return to Siam was rather difficult they decided to work among the natives of Pondicherry and two of them, namely Fr. Venantius Bouchet and Fr. Mauduit put themselves under the Jesuits working in Madurai to learn Tamil and the missionary methods followed in the interior parts of South India. Rome was informed of the developments and sent Father João de Britto, a Jesuit to Pondicherry. He met François Martin, the founder of the French Settlement in 1681. He had been recently to Rome. He had been following the methods of Roberto Nobili in Madurai. Thanappa Mudaliar, a Hindu of *Vellala* group offered the Jesuits a piece of land outside the fort where François Martin himself laid the foundation for a church and a house. Between 1691 and 1693 they obtained a vast garden and built a chapel along the present day Mission Street. But the Dutch capture of Pondicherry in 1693 compelled the Jesuits to go back to France.

In the meantime, Louis XIV of France was in the process of negotiating with Rome and Lisbon for the establishment of a French mission in India. He entrusted the evangelization of the French territories in India to the Jesuits and in due course of time the Carnatic or Coromandel Mission came into existence. Father Tachard reached Surat in 1696 with royal letters patent to start a Jesuit Mission for "the advancement of religion and the progress of scientific studies". The Jesuits came back to Pondicherry when it was restored to the French in 1699. An agreement between the Jesuits of Madurai and Pondicherry was reached at that time according to which the Jesuits residing in Pondicherry were supposed to work in the area north of Madurai called the Carnatic Mission with Pennaiyar as its boundary and Pondicherry as its headquarters.

The Jesuits had to face stiff competition and resistance on the part of the Capuchin missionaries who were working in Pondicherry under the Bishop of Mylapore, their Ordinary. They did not welcome the return of the Jesuits to Pondicherry and considered it an encroachment on their presumed exclusive right to work in Pondicherry. François Martin who had already helped the Jesuits on the occasion of their first visit and also met Father João de Britto directed the Capuchins to work among the Europeans and the creoles and the Jesuits to work among the Indians. Though the Capuchins contacted the Congregation of the *Propaganda Fide* (Established in 1622) against the Jesuit intervention, the Bishop of Mylapore too approved the suggestion of François Martin especially on account of the lack of linguistic expertise on the part of the Capuchins. But the Capuchins sent Father François Marie de Tours to Rome to plead their cause. He presented on 17 March 1703 a memoir to the Pope in which he accused the Jesuits for allowing the converts to follow the Hindu customs and manners. Charles Thomas Maillard de Tournon who was sent to India in 1703 as Apostolic Visitor issued a decree on 13 March 1704 confirming the Jesuits in their parish in Pondicherry for Indians even on the face of the opposition from the Capuchins. The Jesuit methods of carrying the message of Jesus Christ to the Indians were taken with great disgust by the Capuchins who did not have the knowledge of local language nor of the indigenous ways of life. Two disgruntled Hindu officers were dismissed from the service of the French Government in Pondicherry, and Teissier, the procurator of the Foreign Missionaries of Paris helped the Capuchins to prepare a manuscript consisting of three parts, with 195, 215 and 141 pages respectively covering the methods of conversion in India, social customs, castes, theatrical performance and refutation of Hindu doctrines. This was circulated anonymously to Pope Clement XI and various prelates and laity in Europe. The conflict between the Sacred Congregation of the *Propaganda Fide* and the Portuguese *padroado* rights over the missions in India accentuated the conflict between the Jesuits and the Capuchins working under the Bishop of Mylapore.

The Jesuits obtained the chapel at Ariyangkuppam, which was under the Armenian Bishop Mgr. D'Adda since 1690 and later Archbishop who retired to the neighbourhood of the Church of Our Lady of Angels.[20] By 1703 there were in Pondicherry five fathers and two brothers. They built a new church in Ariyangkuppam in 1714. The Jesuits in Pondicherry followed the missionary methods initiated by Father Roberto Nobili in the Madurai Mission. By 1771 the Carnatic Mission of the Jesuits covered the entire Coromandel Coast from Karaikal to Masulipatnam and the district of Cuddapah, the area under the Nawab of Arcot and the eastern province of Mysore. The French Jesuits were still found in Pondicherry in 1767 as noted by Rangappa Thiruvengadam Pillai.[21] Even after the suppression of the Society of Jesus, they had been inducted by the Foreign Missionaries of Paris society into their mission areas on account of their experience in various parts of India.

After the restoration of the Society of Jesus, their missionaries came to Madurai in 1837 and started their work. Father Joseph Bertrand, the superior was happy to know that the principal church in Madurai was still called Jesuit Church. He approved the design of the church in the shape of a Roman Cross. This was useful to pay attention to the caste distinctions by reserving the nave from the side arms by little walls. Mindful of the oppositions faced by the Irish Bishop Daniel O'Conner at Mylapore, he did not want to make any changes and so he decided to follow Indian tradition. He and his colleagues appreciated the marvelous work of Roberto Nobili who followed the life style of Brahmins and avoided the society of low castes. They admired the large number of conversions made by him from among the Brahmins. The Jesuits of Madurai were following a strict vegetarian life. Slowly taking into account the changed circumstances, they suggested adding some non-vegetarian dishes, but no beef at all, in their menu.[22] The Bishop of Pondicherry advised Father Bertrand to tolerate the existing separation of the Indian society in the church according to which the people of lower stratum of society like *Pariahs* had to remain in the arms of the cross-fashioned church and the high castes in the nave of the church. Fr. Bertrand considered it a social distinction as in Europe where the nobles were separated from the peasants in the church even by walls. One can witness the extant partition in the Cathedral church of Xanten, in West Germany. The above mentioned attitude of the Jesuits was discussed in the synod held in Pondicherry in 1844 by the French priests of the Foreign Mission of Paris

Rome and the Indigenous Customs of the Converts to Christianity

Pope Clement XI appointed Charles Thomas Maillard de Tournon as Apostolic Visitor to India in addition to his duty as Apostolic Legate to China. He was consecrated Bishop in 1701 and reached Pondicherry on a French vessel on 6 November 1703. He spent about eight months in Pondicherry. He is reported to have been influenced by the Capuchins, the disgruntled Hindu officers and Teissier who prepared a manuscript on various aspects of missionary work in India especially in Pondicherry. Hence, on 23 June 1704 he issued a decree preventing the missionaries and the new converts to Christianity from following some indigenous customs and introducing a few which were considered extremely odious to the caste Hindus. This decree was handed over to Father Guido Tachard, the superior of the Jesuits on 8 July 1704 with the implication that the Jesuits should desist from permitting such customs.[23] The decree was examined by the committee of Cardinals in Rome in the presence of Pope Clement XI on 7 January 1706. The decision was that the decree should be observed until further orders from Rome. There were several representations made to Rome by various groups of people in India. The prelates of Goa, Cranganore and of Mylapore made it very clear that the use of saliva as a sacramental in the administration of baptism was not acceptable to the converts. Because the Indians regard it with the same disgust as the Europeans regard the "sacred urine" or the "holy cow dung" of the Hindus. Similarly they cautioned Rome about meddling with the *thali* (pendant) and ashes used by Indians. Father Venantius Bouchet and Father Francisco Laynez of the Society of Jesus in India reached Rome in July and November 1706 respectively and argued before the Pope in defense of Indian customs and manners followed by the missionaries and the converts. Since Father Laynez was nominated Bishop of Mylapore,

Father Bouchet alone remained in Rome discussing the details of the missionary methods with the Cardinals and submitted a *memorial* for the consideration of the authorities. But no final decision was taken. Jesuits seem to have continued their missionary methods observing indigenous customs in Pondicherry and surrounding places. Monsignor Visdelou, a Jesuit working in China for twenty years, was made Vicar Apostolic by Charles Thomas Maillard de Tournon, on 12 February 1708.

Monsignor Visdelou moved to Pondicherry and settled down there fighting against the Jesuits.[24] Jesuits sent their representatives to Rome as desired by Pope Innocent XIII, the successor of Pope Clement XI. Father Brandolini, in place of the late Father Peter Martin represented the Jesuits and reached Rome in 1720, while Fr. Maria Lucino represented the Capuchins. Unfortunately the new Pope also expired shortly and could not settle the question of following the local customs and manners in Pondicherry disputed among the Capuchins and Jesuits. His successor Benedict XIII took up the matter and permitted the representatives of the Capuchins and the Jesuits to present their opinions regarding the decree of Cardinal Tournon on the matter. After a long-drawn out attack and counter attack,[25] Pope Clement XII, the successor of Pope Benedict XIII issued the famous decree *Compertum exploratumque* on 24 August 1734 modifying, the decree of De Tournon. The Jesuits in India were instructed by their Superior General in Rome to see that the provisions of the decree were taken into consideration and adhered to especially since the Society of Jesus was facing problems from the conspiracy of Jensenism, Erastianism and Libertinism. The successor of Clement XII who died in 1740 was Benedict XIV who, as cardinal Lambertini, had been aware of the problems of the Malabar and Chinese rites in the capacity of assessor of the Congregation of Rites since 1712. Therefore, he decided to take firm steps to end controversy of Malabar rites for which he issued the famous Bull *Omnium Sollicitudinum* on 13 September 1744. It was ordered that all Catholics, whatever their birth, should attend the divine liturgy and receive communion in the same church at the same time. The Jesuits who provided separate entrances to the Church for *pariahs* and small walls to separate them from the people of higher stratum of the society would hold that their practice was not disturbed by the Pope's order. The Pope reconfirmed the decrees of his predecessors and approved the proposal of the Jesuits to start a *pariah* mission. Non-Jesuits considered it tantamount to the constitution of two churches, which would hold each other in perpetual horror. This was in fact against the spirit of the decrees of the previous Popes whereby it was forbidden to assign separate places to the Brahmins and the *pariahs* in the churches. The Pope seems not to have disapproved the puberty feast according to which a girl was purified with water on reaching puberty. Rice was thrown at her. She was to drink a beverage of milk, butter, cow-dung and urine. The Jesuits permitted this. The Sacred Congregation of the *Propaganda Fide* permitted some of these practices to avoid greater evils. But the situation posed additional difficulties when in the Nineteenth Century the missionaries had to face the ambitions of the upwardly-mobile groups of lower strata of society, like the *pariahs.*

Missions Etrangères de Paris

The Fathers of the Foreign Mission of Paris after the revolution in Siam shifted the *Procura* from Ayuthya to Bengal and finally to Pondicherry where the French Jesuits of the Carnatic Mission had its headquarters. Monsignor Gabriel De La Vigne established a *Procure* in Pondicherry in 1688. He was the first procurator till 1698. Maria Dias, a Christian Lady offered a piece of land to the missionaries for their house.[26] He was expelled from Pondicherry when the Dutch captured it in 1693. He returned to Pondicherry only in 1699. His successor, a certain Tessier or Texier de Queralay reached Pondicherry in 1699 as Procurator of the Foreign Missions.[27] He was a man with his bias against the Jesuits in view of the anti-Jesuit views prevailing at that time in Paris. He therefore naturally sympathized with the Capuchins who had their grievances against the Jesuits in Pondicherry. He left Pondicherry in 1720 on his appointment as Co-adjutor Bishop of Siam in 1717. He was succeeded by Father Guety as Procurator in Pondicherry while Father De Loliere-Puycontat as Assistant Procurator from 1722. A certain Pootchiammal gifted a piece of land to the missionaries in 1730 at the big Bazaar Street, where they erected the Church of the Foreign Missions dedicated to the Presentation of the Blessed Virgin Mary. This was adjacent to the land given by Maria Dias and just in front of the house of Ananda Ranga Pillai. De Loliere was appointed Vicar Apostolic of Siam in 1738, and consecrated Bishop at Mylapore in 1740. Father Mathon was Procurator in Pondicherry since 1742. He was asked by the British in 1761 to withdraw to Ariyangkuppam. When he returned to Pondicherry from Ariyangkuppam in 1765, the *Procure* was razed to the ground. But he courageously rebuilt it. The French

Governor M. Law used to visit the priests of the Foreign Mission as it is learnt from the entry on 24 February 1767 in the diary of Rangappa Thiruvengadam Pillai.[28] The M.E.P Fathers who had a *College Generale* for the training of indigenous clergy in Siam since 1666 had to shift it to Cochin-China and finally to Virampattinam where they purchased a piece of land in 1771. Fr.Mathon became the Rector of the *College Generale* of Virampattinam in 1774. Pope Pius VI approved the *College Generale* in Virampattinam in 1775 and put it under the special care of the Holy See. Father Mathon continued to be the Rector till 1778. The College was closed in 1781 on account of the lack of candidates.

After the suppression of the Society of Jesus by the order of Louis XV, the Government of France discussed the matter of inviting the MEP Fathers to look after the mission so far under the Jesuits in India. After a series prolonged negotiations, Louis XVI, the King of France issued an order in March 1776 entrusting the missions which were managed by the extinct Society of Jesus in several places on the Eastern coast of India and particularly the one known as the Malabar Mission to the priests of the Society of the Foreign Missionaries of Paris. Monsignor Pierre Brigot, the superior for India with the team of fifteen priests took charge the mission on 18 September 1777. Since there was a Capuchin Apostolic Prefect in Pondicherry besides the superior of the MEP Fathers, there were several occasions of conflicts of jurisdiction even though all of them were under the Bishop of Mylapore. These missionaries had the privileges enjoyed by the Jesuits and had to look after the Indians and Eurasians of all kinds in Pondicherry, and the whole population of Karaikal, Chandernagore and of the Carnatic Mission. The Capuchins had jurisdiction only over the Europeans and creoles of Pondicherry. The former Jesuit fathers working in the French settlements of Pondicherry and Karaikal were taken into the M.E.P. society and were asked to work with the latter though the society was suppressed. The property of the Jesuits was transferred by the end of 1777 to the Fathers of M.E.P. including the former Jesuit community house located in the place where the present Archbishop's house in Pondicherry is situated. As part of their original plan, Mosignor Brigot started a seminary in Ozhugarai to train Indian priests in 1778. In 1783 Mgr. Brigot reaching seventy years of age asked for a co-adjutor. The Foreign Missionaries proposed the names of Father Magny and Father Champenois working in the *College Generale* of Virampattinam. Father Champenois, co-adjutor of Mgr. Brigot was nominated Bishop of Pondicherry and consecrated

Bishop in 1786. Father Magny formerly working in *College Generale* of Virampattinam assisted him. After the death of Mgr. Brigot in 1791, the co-adjutor took full charge. The M.E.P. Fathers had to face the problem of the Malabar rites.

Onc of the important problems was that of the caste distinctions. The Sacred Congregation of the *Propaganda Fide* had already issued on order in 1779. "The separation in church, and the entrance into church, as well as the distinctions of graveyards may, for the present, be tolerated in order to avoid greater evils". Again in 1783 the Sacred Congregation wrote: "... while permitting for the present to tolerate the division, in order to avoid a greater evil, makes clear enough, by that restriction, how far she is from approving such a discrimination, and is longing, the Christian Religion progressing day by day amongst Malabars, for the complete disappearance of such a lamentable abuse". Father Magny raised his objection to the following three customs such as the painting of string of the *thali* of women with saffron, use of *pottoo* or red spot on the forehead of women and ceremonial baths.

Mgr. Champenois brought these points to the notice of the Sacred Congregation of the *Propaganda Fide* in 1790 at the insistence of Father Magny. The congregation instructed the Bishop to consider it licit if the prevalent custom was permitted by all missionaries. In other words, the matter was left to the local missionaries to decide.[29] The Missionaries conducted the training of local priests in the seminary at Ozhugarai and the first local candidate was ordained priest in 1788. The Cathedral, which was begun by the Jesuits in 1770 on the same foundation of the Church of 1736, was completed in 1791 and was christened as the Church of Immaculate Conception by Mgr. Champenois. The Seminary (*Seminaire-College*) was shifted in 1846 to the premises near the Cathedral.

The Missionaries of the Paris Foreign Mission convened the synod of Pondicherry in 1844 in which the general policy on v*arnas* and *Jatis* was discussed. The synod recommended to extend schools and facilities for the training of priests. All Indians belonging to the four v*arnas* including *Sudras* could be eligible for priesthood. But the polluting groups or *jatis* were excluded. The resolutions were taken to the Sacred Congregation of the *Propaganda Fide.* Further references were made to the deference paid by the Jesuits to the caste feelings. Authorities in Rome instructed the Bishop of Pondicherry not to discriminate any body on grounds of birth. But the Jesuits did not yield. Even when they established a college at

Nagapattinam in 1845, they admitted only youths of high caste. Father Bertrand of thc Society of Jesus stated in the same year that the Jesuit policy was necessitated by circumstances. Here it should be remembered that even the decree issued by the Second Republic of France on 5 May 1848 regarding the election of representatives from Pondicherry based on universal suffrage could not be implemented on account of *varna* and *jati* consciousness. The egalitarian ideals of French Revolution (1789-1799) could not be accepted by the Hindus of the upper strata of the society. Even the decree issued by the Third Republic in 1871 for cultural assimilation could not be successful. The conflicts among different *varnas* and *jatis* did not permit the cultural assimilation to strike root in India on the face of the distinctions based on *varnas* and *jatis*.[30]

Towards an Upward Social Mobility

The converts from Pondicherry sometimes tried to accept the customs and manners followed by the members of higher *varna* irrespective of their previous affiliation to any of the *varna* or *jati.* A Venetian who had been in Pondicherry in the eighth decade of the Seventeenth Century narrates some instances vividly and picturesquely. He took them as great affront to Christianity and holds the Jesuits responsible for this innovation which in some sense evinces the tendency towards an upward social mobility.

One is the nocturnal procession conducted on the eve of the feast of the Assumption of Blessed Virgin Mary with the paraphernalia of a procession conducted in South Indian Hindu temples of the upper stratum of the society. This was on 14th August 1700 and the procession started at nine o'clock at night.[31] The statue of the Blessed Virgin Mary, surrounded by parasols and fanned by several persons, was taken in the procession led by a person holding the cross adorned with flowers. Christian piety turned into cries amidst fireworks and illuminations.[32] Both Christians and Hindus took part in the procession. Celebration of this nature was approved by the French Jesuits working in Pondicherry and so the Venetian writer accuses them of following Hindu customs and manners. But he compliments the Capuchin fathers who worked in Pondicherry for twenty four years but did not adopt these practices. He adds that no Christian outside Pondicherry was allowed to retain the Hindu customs and manners because they were under the strict supervision of the Inquisition. In other words, he asserts the fact the Christian converts in the French territories were allowed to follow these practices only because of the presence of the Jesuits and the absence of Inquisition.[33]

Another Hindu practice retained by the converts under the instructions given by the Jesuit missionaries was the use of ashes made out of cow-dung. They were purchased from the market and later blessed by the missionaries for the Christians. The Christians were asked to use the ashes in the way the Hindus of the higher stratum of society employed them, but without invoking the names of Hindu gods.[34] Manucci finds fault with the Jesuits permitting these customs to be followed by the Christians.

An eyewitness[35] account of the celebration of marriage in August 1701 in Ariyangkuppam, approximately six kilometers south-west of Pondicherry refers to the attempt made by the Christians in the line of sanskritisation, if one may use the expression side by side with the western custom. Both the contracting parties were from among the natives Christians. The first ceremony in connection with the marriage took place seven days before the actual marriage. A branch of pipal tree *(ficus religiosa)* or *arasa maram* in Tamil was planted in the middle of the courtyard of the house where the proposed wedding was to take place. A pit was made to plant the branch. Then it was filled with a gallon of cow's milk and a gallon of water. The branch of the pipal tree was besmeared with sandal, red lead and saffron. Flowers were hung all round. This ceremony according to the eyewitness was some thing usually performed by the Hindus in connection with their God *Vishnu* and *Savitri.* The Hindus believed that *Vishnu* lived in pipal tree and his spouse in the form of breeze came as gently as possible to remain united with him. That inseparable relation between the god and the goddess was wished for the newly wed. The leaf of the pipal tree has been considered to be representing the genital part of woman by the Hindus according to the eyewitness. The use of red-lead put on it indicated something still unpleasant in the view of the Venetian reporter. Saffron and flowers are offered as sacrifice to the tree venerated by the Hindus. A tent *(pandal)* adorned with leaves of mango tree was erected. After the ceremonies of the first day, seven small pots filled with earth and sprouts of rice and country peas were brought and placed round the foot of the tree. Besides, a stone was also placed so that on the day of the wedding a coconut could be broken on the stone.

Seven days after the above-mentioned ceremony; a sort of four-corned tent called *aramanai* was erected with the above-mentioned branch of the pipal tree at the centre. At the foot of the pipal tree, an altar facing the East was set up. There was no crucifix or cross on the altar. The direction facing the East was chosen in consonance with the Hindu tradition. Branches of mango tree were placed at the four corners of the tent. Leaves of mango tree were hung all round.

The Christian ceremony of the marriage was performed very quietly in the church in the morning. A second and solemn ceremony took place in the evening in the Hindu fashion. The bridegroom left his house in a palanquin surrounded by dancing girls at the sound of musical instruments before the gate of the church. He went in to the church for a short prayer and entered into the palanquin kept outside. He made a tour in the palanquin and went around the town. When he returned to his house, three female relatives carrying a bowl each in their hands received him. Two of the bowls were filled with saffron water and a small herb resembling couch-grass which they considered representation of Lord *Ganesh.* The third bowl was full of rice of different colours with a ball of cooked rice mixed with butter from cow's milk. A wick burning with cow's ghee was inserted in the rice ball. The dancing girls received the three bowls from the women relatives and waved them three times round the head of the bridegroom. This was to protect him from the evil. At the end of the ceremony, the dancing girls emptied bowls at his feet. Afterwards he entered the tent and circumambulated the altar. Then he took his seat facing the altar. The catechist who acted as the ceremony master or *Brahman* took his position by the side of the altar towards the South, with his face to the North as laid down in the Hindu rituals. A large fig leaf on which uncooked rice was spread and it was brought to him along with two yellow copper pots *(kalasas)* filled with pure water, five leaves of mango tree and a coconut. Each of them was encircled several times with a thread.

Two small stools were placed in front of the catechist acting as *Brahman*, one with a bowl filled with uncooked rice of different colours and the other with necklace *(thali)* on it. The stone placed at the foot of the branch of the pipal tree seven days before the wedding was taken out. The catechist put some incense in the container of incense and sung the litany of the Blessed Virgin Mary. Then he took the copper pot *(kalasa)* with his right hand and washed the coconut with the water. He broke the coconut half on the stone and permitted its juice to flow on it. Then he separated the coconut into two pieces. Later the officiating catechist took the bowl containing the *thali* and placed it on the altar. He recited a few prayers in the local language and covered it with the bowl. He incensed the *thali* as well as the statue of Blessed Virgin Mary. The celebrant extended the thali to the parents of the bridegroom and the principal guest for touching it with their right hand for paying their respect. At last the catechist. handed over the *thali* to the bridegroom, who to the accompaniment of music tied it around the neck of the bride.

Afterwards, the catechist took from his waist-belt ashes made out of cow-dung and blessed by the Jesuit missionaries, called *thiruniru.* He scattered it three times on the heads of the newly-married couple sitting down with their half open fists resting on their knees. Then he took a fresh bowl of peas and showered them three times over the two fists and feet and heads of the couple. The relatives followed him. The couple exchanged garlands of flowers three times. The parents and the principal guests too did the same with the couple. Again the catechist took another coconut and a bowl of peas. He took a small quantity of peas by both the hands and placed them in the hands of the bridegroom who returned them to catechist. This was performed three times. At the end the catechist poured some water into the hands of the bridegroom, over the rice and the coconut. Afterwards both the bride and bridegroom rose up from their seats and made a sort of procession round the altar. One of the women relatives took the lead in the procession with a lantern in her hand while another woman followed sprinkling water from the bowl around the altar. A barber came forward to show the couple the way. The bridegroom holding the bride's little finger in his closed hands followed the barber. They passed three times in this way around the altar. Then the couple made a profound obeisance to the altar with joined hands. Subsequently they turned to the door. The catechist took the water vessel and poured the rest of its contents on couple. They ran to the house. The eyewitness blames the Jesuits for permitting these customs, which were usually followed by the members of the higher stratum of Hindu society in Pondicherry, and wonders what harm had been done to the Christian faith by the Jesuits.[36]

Manucci describes still another practice of the higher stratum of the society of Hindus followed by the Christians of Pondicherry. This was the ceremony performed for the funeral. As soon as a Christian passed away, some betel was put into the mouth of the deceased and the teeth were smeared with the juice of that leaf. The dead body was washed from head to foot with a solution of cow-dung. Some marks associated with the *Saivites* were made on the dead body. A throne was prepared for seating the dead body in a bier made of sugarcane. The body was wrapped in the best cotton or silk cloth. The throne was decorated with mirrors, cut cucumbers, piece of betel leaves and some stalks of rice. Some banana plants were kept at the four corners of the bier. The deceased is seated in the throne and carried on the shoulders to the sound of trumpets to the burial place. The Jesuits insisted on following the Hindu traditions while the Capuchins permitted the ordinary Christian burial followed in Europe. The insistence of the Jesuits in this matter was seen from the details of the burial of Andre Muthappa Mudaliar, a broker of the French East India Company during the governance of François Martin. The ceremonies performed on the thirtieth day after the burial by the Christians under the instructions given by the Jesuits again followed the burial by the upper stratum of the society of Hindus. Manucci gives a picturesque description.[37]

With a view to claiming upward social mobility, the Christians converted from any stratum of the society tried to avoid the use of beef in their menu. As discussed above, even the Vedic Brahmins used to eat beef. But in due course of time this was considered abominable to Hindus of higher stratum. The Jesuit missionaries in tune with the missionary methods followed by Roberto Nobili avoided beef and good number of them turned to be vegetarians. The Missionaries who were in the habit of eating beef in India were looked down upon and were considered equal to scavengers or night-soil workers in Europe as explained by Manucci.[38] Hence the Europeans were considered to be equal to *pariahs* by the Hindus. Realising the attitude of the Hindus, the Jesuit missionaries tried to project themselves as people not belonging to the group of *Frangis*, the detested Europeans who used to eat beef and asserted that they were Roman Brahmins, or noble men from Romapuri. They dressed like Brahmins and were therefore respected by the people.[39] This was indicative of the process of sanskritization or upward social mobility.

Principle of Equality and the Prejudices against Lower Castes

The French Jesuits often tried to avoid any distinction between the several strata of Indian society in the places of worship. A Jesuit priest working in Karaikal visited the church in Pondicherry on 16 October 1745 and was shocked to see a wall in the church separating the *pariah* Christians from the local Christians of higher stratum of society, Eurasians and the Europeans during the time of divine worship. This was on the northern side of the interior part of the church. Separation of this sort was in existence for quite some time with the approval of the concerned authorities. The

Jesuit father took immediate steps to remove this barrier. So, he instigated the *pariah* Christians living at the *Paracheri*, the Big *Paracheri*, the Burning ground *Paracheri*, and the Ozhandai *Paracheri* and the village menials like the *thoetis* converted to Christianity to remonstrate. They all went to the senior priest in Pondicherry and complained about the injustice meted out to them in the past and asked for the redressing their grievances. He ordered immediate demolition of the wall and asked them to mix freely with the others in the church. The *Pariahs*, Eurasians, Europeans and Tamilians mixed together for the evening service. The women folk of the native Christians too came forward. The wife of Asarappa Mudali, the sister's son of Kanakaraya Mudali came to the church beautifully clad and bedecked with ornaments to the extent of inviting the wrath of the senior priest presiding over the service. Later Jaganivasa Mudali with the support of several others objected to the change brought about in the church. Kanakaraya Mudali went to the priest and explained the difficulties involved in the innovations. The aggrieved missionary managed to get the governor to issue an order to arrest those Christians who rebelled against him. Rebellious crowds ceased to come to the streets. But on 17 October 1745 a barrier of chairs was put up in the church to separate the *pariah* Christians from the others.[40] This clearly demonstrates how difficult it was for the missionaries to inculcate ideals of equality into the minds of the local Christians.

The missionaries keeping in mind the principle of equality of human beings before God, wanted to keep the place of worship open to all. So, the missionaries interested in building the St. Paul's church in Pondicherry contacted the Christians for contribution. An amount of one thousand *pagodas* was offered. At the time of laying the foundation stone for the Church in 1766 the priests realizing that there would not be enough room for the *pariah* converts suggested to enlarge the structure. The Christians quarreled with the priests for keeping the proposed church open for *pariahas* and declared that they would build a church exclusively for themselves. They came forward with the suggestion of paying for the priest to serve in that church meant for the Christian converts of higher stratum of the society. The priests did not permit them to attend the religious services since they did not listen to the suggestions of the priests. So they stood outside the church showing their protest. The priests applied pressure from the French government to get them round. So, M. Boyelleau summoned eleven of them to his office. They were of *Mudaliar* group. The names of

Mariadass Mudali, Surappa Mudali, Barlam Mudali, Royyappa Mudali the short, Muthaiya Pillai and Thiyagappan figured among the eleven. They complained to M. Boyelleau and his councillors that the priests insisted on their mixing freely with the *Pariahs*, something that was not done earlier. Boyelleau insisted that they should listen to the priests. But, they refused and so the governor got wild with them and asked them to go to thc temple of *Bhugavathi* if they did not like to obey him and the priests.[41] It was reported that all the eleven were summoned to the Council on 8 April 1766 and were severely censured and punished with a fine of one hundred *pagodas* each for disobeying the Council. They were placed in custody till they paid the fine. But they did not do it and were therefore put in prison in the *chavadi*.[42] Kandappa Mudali with the *nayinar* went to the *chavadi* on 25 April 1766 under the orders of M. Boyelleau to meet the imprisoned Christians who refused to obey the orders of the governor as well as those of the priests with a warning that they would be banished from the town if they did not send their family members to church. Pragasa Mudaiar met the womenfolk of the imprisoned and asked them to go to the church as suggested by the priests and the governor. They expressed their reluctance to go to the church and mix with the *pariahs*. They added that they did not feel sorry for their husbands being imprisoned since they were not guilty of any crime. The report given by the Christians imprisoned in the *chavadi* was conveyed to the Governor by Kandappa Mudali. At last they paid the fine on 27 April 1766. But the governor told them that they would be released only if they and their women attended the church. Threatened as they were, they agreed to attend the church at the orders of the governor. Finally on 28 April 1766 they gave a declaration as insisted by Kandappa Mudali to the effect that they along with their family members would attend the church. Thereafter they were released.[43] The conflict between the missionaries and the Christians of upper stratum of society in Pondicherry on the matter of mixing with the Christians of lower status persisted. This can be confirmed in the light of the unwillingness of the Christians of upper stratum to share the expenditure of the festivities on 8 September 1766 in which the *pariahs* were chosen for the choir. This was the feast of Blessed Virgin Mary. So, the *pariahs* themselves bore the expenses for the procession and the erection of the tent for the exposition of the Statue of our lady.[44]

The survey made above clearly indicates that the French missionaries tried several methods to win over the people of India for an egalitarian behaviour. The consideration of *varnas* and *jatis* which had deeper roots in India did not permit the missionaries to bring about a situation in which people belonging to various *varnas* and *jatis* could be considered equal even after conversion to Christianity which in principle does not permit any discrimination based on birth or affiliation to a particular stratum of society. Therefore the missionaries had to accept the existing conditions of society as they were and some tried to experiment a few steps indicative of upward social mobility which could be considered a case of sanskritization. Even the synod of Pondicherry held in 1844 could not do away with the distinction based on birth and so some candidates were denied entry into priesthood. Even the decrees issued by the Second and the Third Republics could not be effective in Pondicherry under the French. On the other hand some of those people from lower *varnas* and *jatis* adopted some customs and manners observed by those of upper strata of the society. Since the customs and manners were inextricably connected with affiliation to a particular stratum of society, one may say that these are indicative of upward social mobility involving social changes.

Though the Indians did not wear any turban while entering the places of worship, the Christians in Pondicherry in the second half of the Eighteenth Century followed the European custom of wearing turbans in the Church.[45] Some of the converted Christians went to the extent of renouncing their citizenship in India and adopted customs and manners of the Europeans. They broke with the traditions of Indian society and argued for equality in all walks of life as one could see in the case of Ponnuthamby who gave up his own name and adopted La Porte to show his disaffiliation to Indian society.[46] Here one could see the influence of westernization along with sanskritization effecting equality.

Hence, the missionaries from France played some role in the social changes in Pondicherry and its environs. But the conflicts based on different *varnas* and *jatis* have not disappeared totally. On the other hand radical tendencies disturbing the social fabric take virulent proportions even in the Twentieth century in Pondicherry and its surroundings in the ecclesiastical circles despite the concerted efforts of the missionaries for centuries together to bring about equality of status.

Notes and References

1. M.N. Srinivas, *Social Change in Modern India*, Berkeley, 1996, p. 6. For the first time it was propounded by M.N. Srinivas in his studies related to the Society in Goorg. See, *Religion and Society among the Coorgs of Southern India*, Oxford, 1952. Later he reiterated his ideas in another work,

Caste in Modern India, Bombay, 1952 pp. 42-66. In fact in his study on the Coorgs of the erstwhile Mysore State, he employed the term "Brahmanization" to denote the adoption of some customs of the Brahmins by the lower castes and giving up of some of their own which were considered impure by the higher castes.

2. M.N. Srinivas, "A *Note* on Sanskritization and Westernization" *Caste in Modern India and other Essays*, London, 1962, p. 42.
3. A.M Shah, and Schroff, R.G., "The Vaishnava Barots of Gujarat : A Caste of Geneologists and Mythographers" in Milton Signer, (ed.,) Traditional India: Structure and Change, Philadelphia, 1959, pp. 40-68; Bernard S, Cohn. "The Changing Status of a Depressed Caste" in Mckim Marriot, Village India, University of Chicago Press, 1955, pp. 53-77, Pocock, D., "Inclusion and Exclusion: A Process in the Caste System of Gujarat" *South Western Journal of Anthropology*. Vol. 13, 1957, L.Rowe William, "Changing Rural Class Structure and the *Jajmani* System" *Human Organization*, Vol. 22, No.1, 1963, pp. 41-44.
4. M.N. Srinivas, "A Note on Sanskritization and Westernization", p. 44.
5. S.L. Kalia, "Sanskritization and Tribalization" *Bulletin of Tribal Research Institute*, *Chinchwara*, April 1999.
6. M.N. Srinivas, "As I have already stated, sanskritization is not confined to Hindu castes but also occurs among tribal and semi-tribal groups such as the Bhils of Western India, the Gonds and Omans of Central India and the Pahadis of the Himalayas" *Social Change in Modern India*, Berkeley, 1966, p. 7.
7. M.N. Srinivas, "Now I realise that in both my book on Coorg religion and my" Note on Sanskritization and Westernisation "I emphasized unduly the Brahmanical model of Sanskritization and ignored the other models-Kshatriya, Vaishya and Shudra", Social Change in Modern India, p. 7.
8. M.N. Srinivas, *Social Change in Modern India*, Berkeley, 1966, p. 47.
9. M.N. Srinivas, *Social Change in Modern India*, Berkeley, 1966, p. 48. He gives the details of the traditional pattern of eating "Traditionally Indians ate their meals sitting on the floor.

The food was served either on leaves or on metal (brass, bronze, or silver) plates. Among the upper castes, and especially among Brahmins, eating was a religious act. The food had to be cooked while the women were in ritually pure state, since it was offered to the domestic deities before being served to the members of the family. The men and the children ate first, adult men being in ritually pure state while eating. This meant removing their shirts and changing into a silk *dhoti (Silk* is ritually superior to cotton) and upper cloth, or a freshly washed cotton *dorthi*, and upper cloth. At the end of the meal the dining leaves became impure and were thrown out. The places where the leaves had rested were purified with a solution of cow-dung". M.N. Srinivas, *Social Change in Modern India*, p. 53.

10. M.N. Srinivas, *Social Change in Modern India*, p. 7.
11. Social structure of "Little Tradition" consists of its own role-incumbents such as the folk artists, medicine-men, tellers of riddles, proverbs and stories, poets and dancers while that of "Great Tradition" is formed by "those persisting and important arrangements of roles and statuses appearing in such corporate groups as castes, sects, or in teachers, reciters, ritual leaders of one kind or another, which are concerned with the cultivation and inculcation of this tradition". Ref. Milton Singer, (*ed.,*) *Traditional India: Structure and Change*, Philadelphia, 1959, p. 12.
12. This consists of a) the classical tradition b) the emergent national tradition c) the regional tradition d) the local tradition e) the western tradition f) the local sub-cultural tradition. Ref. S.C.Dube, "The Study of Complex Cultures" in Unnithan, Indra Devi, T.K.N. and Yogendra Singh, (eds.,) *Towards a Sociology of Culture in India*, Delhi, 1965, pp. 421-23.
13. Yogendra Singh, *Modernization of Indian Tradition*, New Delhi, 1988, p. 19.
14. Louis Dumont, *Contributions to Indian Sociology*, No. I, p. 12.
15. Yogendra Singh, *Modernization of Indian Tradition*, New Delhi, 1988, pp. 23-27.
16. Father Ephraim was sent by his superiors to Pegu for missionary activities. On his way to Pegu he went to Bhagnagar, the

headquarters of the Qutbshahis of Golconda. The Mirza Muhammad, alias Sharifu-I-Mulk, the Sheik of Mecca who married the eldest daughter of Abdulla Qutbshah (1611-1672) interested in keeping the learned persons in Bhagnagar, promised to build church and a house for Father Ephraim. Sheik"s plan was to put some missionary in the service of the Portuguese and the Armenians who used to come to trade with the kingdom of Golconda. Since Father Ephraim was adamant in following the orders of his superiors, he excused himself and decided to proceed from there to Masulipatnam. The Sheik offered him an ox to ride on and two attendants. Ref. Jean Baptiste Tavernier, *Travels in India*, Vol. 1, New Delhi, 1977, (translated from the original of 1676) pp. 132-133. Since he could not get any vessel from Masulipatnam to Pegu, he was attracted by the English who invited him to Madras where the English had a factory since 1639.The site was given to Mr. Francis Day by Sri Ranga Raya, the Raja of Chandragiri. The general office of the dependencies of the kingdom of Golconda was also situated in Madras. The English built a church for Father Ephraim and kept him there to look after the spiritual needs of the Christian merchants coming there for trade in textiles. The authorities of the English East India Company issued an order on 8 June 1642 asking him to look after the spiritual needs of the people. He died in Madras in 1694. His companion Father Zenon died in 1684. Father Ephraim working under the English flag in Madras had to face severe problems with the Portuguese in Santhome and was imprisoned. On account of this there were severe differences of opinion between the Portuguese authorities at Santhome and the English authorities in Fort St. George. Later he had to appear before the Inquisition in Goa. He reached Goa on 15 January 1650 and was kept in the Jesuit house in a cell after an insulting stripping. He was left free in 1651. He was not allowed to celebrate Holy Mass from 28 December 1649 to 5 December 1651 Then he was allowed to go to the Convent St. Francis in Goa to celebrate Holy Mass. The details are furnished in the work of Nicolao Manucci who was in India from 1656 and died in 1717 in Madras in the household granted to him by the

English in perpetuity. Ref. *Storia do Mogur*, or *Mogul India*. Vol. III, New Delhi, 1981, pp. 408-440. The details of his difficulties and his liberation from the prison in Goa on account of the interference of the Sultan of Golconda are narrated in detail by Tavernier. Ref. Travels in India, New Delhi, Vol. I, pp. 176-186. He mentions that the Inquisitors in Goa did not pay any attention to the instructions nor of the French rulers. Only the political pressure on the part of the Sultan of Golconda and his son-in-law played an important role and so on his way back to Madras, Father Ephraim went to Bhagnagar to thank them.

17. *Memoirs of François Martin* (1670-1694) Translated by Lotika Varadarajan, as India in the Seventeenth Century, (Social, Economic and Political) Vol. I, part I, (Hereafter Memoirs of François Martin) New Delhi, 1981, pp. 392-93.
18. S. Jeyaseela Stephen, *Portuguese* in *the Tamil Coast: Historical Explorations* in Commerce and *Culture, 1507-1749*, Pondicherry, 1998, p. 405.
19. D. Ferroli, *The Jesuits in Malabar*, Vol. II, Bangalore, 1951, p. 426; For further details on the subject, Ref. G. Tachard, S.J, *Voyage de Siam des Peres Jesuites Envoyes Parle Roi aux Indes*, , Amsterdam, 1689.
20. The Armenian Archbishop died in his residence near the Church of Our Lady of Angels. The present rue de L'Eveche is named after the Armenian Archbishop.
21. S. Jeyaseela Stephen, *The Diary of Rangappa Thiruvengadam Pillai*, 1761-1768, Pondicherry, 2001, p. 267.
22. Kenneth Ballhatchet, "French Missionaries and Indian Society: The Jesuit Mission to Madure 1837-1902" in *Les Relations Historiques et Culturelles entre la France et l'Inde XVI/"-XX Siecles*, Le Chaudron-Sainte Clotilde, 1987, pp. 227-248.
23. Please see the highlights of the decree in D. Ferroli, *The Jesuits* in *Malabar*, pp. 430-431.
24. D. Ferroli, *Ibid.*, Vol. II, p. 437.
25. Father Maria Lucino presented a tract *Regioni proposte ed examinate in favore del decreto,* a bulky volume running into 493 pages in defense of the decree of de Tournon while the Justification and Answer by Brandolini had three parts with 528, 742 and 168 pages respectively.

26. The present clock tower in the Big Bazaar situated between Jawaharlal Nehru Street and Ranga Pillai street was the place of the residence of the M.E.P Fathers. Ref. Jean Lafrenez, *Precis d'histoire de la mission de Pondichery*, Translated and edited by P.A. Sampath Kumar, and Andre Carof, *History of Poudicherry Mission: An Outline*, Pondicherry, 1999, p. 27.
27. Adrien Lauany, *Histoire des Missions de de L'Inde : Pondichery, Maissour, Coimbatour*, Paris, 1898, pp. 7-8.
28. Rangappa Thiruvengadam Pillai was the nephew of Ananda Ranga Pillai (1737-1761) was the son of Thiruvengadam the younger brother of Ananda Ranga Pillai, known also as Appavu. He wrote a diary related to the period from 1760 to 1781. He was in Tharangambadi (Tranquebar) from 1761.The part of the diary from 1761 to 1766 has been transcribed and published in Tamil by S. Jeyaseela Stephen in two volumes in Pondicherry in 2000 and an English translation was published by the same author under the title *The Diary of Rangappa Thiruvengadam Pillai*, 1761-1768, (Hereafter *The Diary of Rangappa Thiruvengadam Pillai)* Pondicherry, 2001, p. 267.
29. Jean Lafrenez, pp. 48-49.
30. For details of Ponnuthamby an ardent protagonist of cultural assimilation and his opponent Chanemougam, See, Jacques Weber, "Chanemougam: King of French India, Social and Political Foundation of an Absolute Power under the Third Republic", *Economic and Political Weekly*, 9 February 1991, pp. 291-302.
31. Though 1701 is found in the work of Niccolao Manucci, Norbert wrote his Memoirs Historiques dates it to 1700. Ref. Vol. I, p. 62.
32. The procession of this nature is conducted now in the Cathedral of Pondicherry named as Immaculate Conception on 8 December every year with the cart *(Ther)* as in the Hindu temple.
33. Niccolao Manucci, *Storia do Mogor* or *Mogul India, 1653-1708*, Delhi, 1981, Vol. III. pp. 326-28.
34. Niccolao Manucci, *Storia do Mogor*, pp. 328-333. Here he gives the different marks made of ashes by different sects of the Hindus like the Vaishnavites, Saivites and so on.

35. The witness was Niccolao Manucci, a Venetian, who visited India in 1656 and was associated with the Mughal court for over half a century. He was bitter about the way in which non-Christian ceremonies were permitted to be performed by the Catholic missionaries in Pondicherry under the French. He gives the detailed narration from his personal observation. For further details, Ref. Niccolao Manucci, *Storia do Mogor or Mogul India, 1653-1708*, Delhi, 1981, Vol. III, pp. 321-25.
36. Niccolao Manucci, *Storia do Mogor*, Vol. III, p. 326.
37. Niccolao Manucci, *Storia do Mogor* Vol. III, pp. 335-336.
38. Niccolao Manucci, *Storia do Mogor*, Vol. III, p. 304.
39. Niccolao Manucci, *Storia do Mogor*, Vol. III, p. 305.
40. Frederick Price, and K. Rangachari, (eds.,) *The Private Diary of Ananda Ranga Pillai*, Vol. 1, Delhi, Asian Educational Services, reprint, 1985, pp. 284-287.
41. *The Diary of Rangappa Thiruvengadam Pillai*, pp. 219-220.
42. *The Diary of Rangappa Thiruvengadam Pillai*, p. 224.
43. *The Diary of Rangappa Thiruvengadam Pillai*, pp. 230-31.
44. *The Diary of Rangappa Thiruvengadam Pillai*, p. 250.
45. *The Diary of Rangappa Thiruvengadam Pillai*, p. 107
46. Jacques Weber, Chanemougam, op. cit, pp. 291-302.

15

Religious Conversions in Pondicherry and the French (1703-1878)

J.B.P. More

This paper examines the expansion of Christianity in Pondicherry and the problems met by the Catholic Christian missionaries in converting the Hindus. It aims to identify the principal factors that impeded or retarded the progress of Christianity and to pinpoint certain methods employed by some French missionaries and colonisers to attract Hindus to Christianity. The paper is not intended as a study of the caste system, nor is it a chronological account of conversions or an assessment of the number of conversions. Instead, an attempt is made to understand why some Hindus converted at certain times, and why some others resisted conversion.

There are authentic proofs for the existence of Pondicherry as a small or a big village even before the French actually arrived there in 1672-73.[1] The Danes already had a settlement in Pondicherry before 1672 and were trading there.[2] The population appears to have been mostly Hindus, with a small Muslim community. The Hindus of Pondicherry as in the rest of India, were divided on the basis of caste, with every caste having its own locality.[3] There were already four main Hindu temples in Pondicherry when the French arrived; the Perumal temple, the Kalatiswaran temple, the Ellamman temple and the Vedapuriswarar (Shiva) temple.[4]

The Muslim community inhabited the seaside areas even before the French arrived [5] In a map of Pondicherry, drawn by Denyon in 1704, available at the *Bibliothèque Nationale de Paris,* two mosques are seen located behind the Capuchin missionary church on the seaside.[6] There is no trace of these two mosques now, but the Capuchin church still stands almost in the same place on the seaside. The circumstances under which the mosques disappeared are still unclear. These two mosques were located in the White town, where the French established their administrative and residential quarters. The White town included the areas from the seaside to a canal (which exists even now) that cut Pondicherry town virtually into two parts. The area beyond the canal, inhabited by the Indians, came to be known as the Black town. Before the French acquired Pondicherry, it was under the political control of the Muslims. It was initially from an Afghan chieftain, Sher Khan Lodi, subject to the Bijapur Sultan, that the French obtained permission to establish themselves in Pondicherry. Thus the Muslims, though a small minority, were the rulers, while the Hindus, though numerically preponderant were the ruled. That is, even as early as the 17th century, the Muslims had a distinct identity of their own in Pondicherry, with their own mosques, their own locality and their own religion. In the light of the above it is wrong to contend that Pondicherry was founded by François Martin. Instead he can be deemed as the modern promoter of Pondicherry.

One of the conditions under which the local rulers appear to have allowed the French to establish themselves at Pondicherry, was that the French should tolerate the native Hindu religious cults and merchants.[7] The Hindus, living in the world of their own, were probably under the impression that the hereditary caste system, which had religious sanction, would continue indefinitely. But new forces from unknown and distant West European countries were beginning to impinge on their lives and throw up new challenges.

Describing the Hindu society of Pondicherry in the 18th century, Ananda Ranga Pillai distinguishes Tamils (non-*pariah* Hindus) from the *pariahs*.[8] For him Tamils meant non-*pariah* Hindus, or rather the *Shudras*, and not the untouchables. Among the *Shudras*, there were high and low castes. But the untouchable Hindus, long subordinated in the name of custom and the *Shastras*, undoubtedly constituted the weak underbelly of the Hindu society of Pondicherry. It is against this background that we explore the meeting of the two worlds, Hindu and Christian in Pondicherry.

Before the arrival of the French, there were no Christians in Pondicherry.[9] Among the French, there were the colonisers and the missionaries. In 1674, François Martin took charge of Pondicherry and worked to promote French and Christian interests until 1706. He welcomed the French Capuchin missionaries from Madras to serve the religious needs of the Christians in Pondicherry.[10] Later, in the 1680s, the Jesuit missionaries followed them. These missionaries strove hard to convert the local Hindu and Muslim population to Christianity. They seem to have scored some success with the Hindus. In 1709, there were about 1000 to 1100 Indian Christian converts in Pondicherry.[11] By 1725, there were 3000 Indian Christians out of a total population of about 30000 in Pondicherry.[12] These converts consisted of *Shudras* of the low as well as high castes, and the untouchable Hindus.

Policy of Preference and Pressure

The French missionaries had to use all the means at their disposal to convince the Hindus of the values of Christianity. When the state-controlled, French East India Company was founded in 1664, it was thought fit that the Company, apart from its commercial ventures, should strive also to propagate the Christian faith among the Gentiles.[13] As a result, when the Company's political power was being consolidated by François Martin and his successors in Pondicherry, the French missionaries, especially the Jesuits, naturally thought it fit to use French political power and influence to bring about conversions to Christianity.

It appears that from the time of the establishment of French power in Pondicherry, preferences were shown, especially in the employment and economic fields, to those who embraced Christianity. From at least the year 1690, the French East India Company had appointed an Indian Christian as *Diwan* to act as intermediary between the French and the Indians. Lazaro de Mota Mudaliar, a high caste Indian Christian convert, was the *Diwan* in the year 1700. A leading Indian merchant of the French Company, he had not only donated a church known as *Eglise St.Lazare* to the Capuchin missionaries, but had also donated lands and houses to them in the 1680s to assist the conversion of the Hindus.[14] Lazaro de Mota had also donated land to the Jesuits for the construction of a church. About 300 adults were baptised in this church in 1703.[15] Lazaro de Mota's family was in the service of the French Company from the time of François Martin. It is quite certain that Lazaro de Mota, in spite of his incompetence to serve the Company, had been able to elevate himself to the post of *Diwan* and maintain himself in that position until 1708, solely because of his Christian connections.[16]

In 1708, Nainiyappa Pillai, a Hindu of the lower *Idayar* (Yadava) caste, born at Madras, and who was in the service of the French for more than Thirty years, was appointed as the *Diwan* by the French Company. The Jesuit missionaries did not view this appointment favourably. Following the decision of the French king that the post of *Diwan* be reserved for native Christians alone, the Jesuits brought pressure on Nainiyappa and gave him six month's time to convert to Christianity. They wanted the French government to appoint an Indian Christian in his place should he not convert within this period.[17] As he failed to convert, an Indian Christian by the name of Saveri *pillai* was appointed as Assistant *Diwan*.[18] Instigated by the French authorities of Pondicherry and the Jesuit missionaries, Nainiyappa was removed from the post of *Diwan* on trumped up charges. His properties were confiscated and he was thrown into the prison, located within the French fort, known as Fort St.Louis, in Pondicherry, where he died a miserable death in 1717.[19]

Soon after Nainiyappa's death, his son Guruvappa, born in Pondicherry, was appointed as *Diwan*. Unlike his father, he does not seem to have resisted the pressure brought upon him to convert to Christianity. He went to Paris and got himself baptised by Rev. Louis de la Verge de Tressan, Archbishop of Nantes and Chaplain of the Duke of Orleans, at the chapel of *Palais Royal*, according to the parish register maintained at the Saint Eustache of Paris, when he was about 20 years old he seems to have converted not because of any sudden illumination, but probably because it allowed him to recover the confiscated properties of his father. His godfather was the regent, Philippe d'Orléans, of noble blood and his godmother was the duchess, Elisabeth-Charlotte. A few months later, the King of France knighted Guruvappa, who came to be known as Charles-Philippe Guruvappa, as *Chevalier de Saint-Michel*, to honour the services of his father and his conversion to the Christian faith.[20]

The Jesuits also proposed certain other measures, such as open preference to Indian Christians in matters of employment to encourage the expansion of Christianity. The French government generally agreed to implement such propositions during this period.[21] In 1730, another leading high caste Christian, by the name of Pedro Canagaraya Mudaliar, who had donated much to the church, was appointed as the *Diwan*, under the influence of the Jesuits [22] At his own expense, he built a church at Oulgaret near Pondicherry, which was thrown open to the public on 30 November 1745[23] Incidentally, Pedro was conferred by the French government a lifelong commission for the minting of rupees in Pondicherry.[24] On Pedro's death, Ananda Ranga Pillai, a lower caste Vaishnavite Hindu, related to Nainiyappa Pillai, was appointed as *Diwan* by Dupleix, the Governor of Pondicherry, probably because there was no other Indian Christian capable of occupying the post of *Diwan* at that time. [25]

Apart from the Indian Christian *diwans*, many other Indian Christians, who benefited by the favours shown to them by the French, had donated munificently to the cause of Christianity. For example, in the year 1700, land was donated by the family of Colandaiappa, the official high caste Indian Christian interpreter of the French Company, to the missionaries of the Mission Etrangères de Paris, for the construction of a seminary.[26] It appears that Colandiappa was in the servicc of the French, from the time when the French arrived in Pondicherry. It was he who obtained from the King of Tanjore the authentic decree that ceded Caveripatnam, at the mouth of the river Cauvery to the French. Similarly in 1720, land was donated by another Indian Christian, known as Pouchiammal, for the construction of another church.[27] The preceding instances amply demonstrate that pressures, persuasions and preferences were responsible for the conversion of some leading high caste men and families of Pondicherry. In their turn, many of these leading Christians, in order to prove their loyalty to the French and to the missionaries, donated much to the church, probably with a view to obtaining more favours from the French in the economic and employment fields, or simply to retain the favours already shown to them.

The French missionary, Rev. Ducros writes from Ariancoupam village, (not far from Pondicherry) on 17 October 1725: "I have found that from 2 October 1724 to 12 October 1725, 601 baptisms were administered to the *Shudras* (non-Untouchable non-Brahmans) mostly....This is the work of a single missionary, Rev.Turpin".[28]. He further writes: "Some twelve or thirteen years ago, Father Bouchet had only one Christian at Ariancoupam. But today there are nearly 400 and high hopes to convert several families of the high castes".[29]. This evidence suggests that high caste conversions to Christianity during the early decades of the 18th century were quite numerous. This was because the French at that time were mainly concerned with trade, which naturally brought them into contact with high caste (or rather non-pariah) men, who were traditionally dominant in these fields. During this time, the French were among the buyers of cotton and other goods produced in Pondicherry and its neighbourhood for the European market. This provided many non-pariah men the opportunity to involve themselves in trade and in production of goods for the French.

Besides, the French as a colonial power needed Indian subordinates to run the administration. Here too, the non-*pariah* men were better placed to occupy the subordinate jobs provided by the French administration, rather than the pariah untouchables, for obvious historical reasons. Undoubtedly, as already noted, the French preference in the economic and employment fields for those who had converted provided a strong reason for many non-pariah men and families to convert to Christianity, for they alone and not the untouchables, were in a position during those early decades of colonisation to avail of the trade and employment opportunities provided by the French.

Famine and Epidemics

On the basis of French sources, it is clear that famine and epidemics were major causes leading to the conversion of many Hindus, especially pariahs, to Christianity. though we do not always have the exact caste-wise figures of the conversions, the pariahs, who were economically poor and at the most disadvantaged end of the Hindu social hierarchy, seem to have been the most vulnerable during periods of famine and epidemics. During such periods, it was the missionaries who were often zealous in coming to the aid of those afflicted. The French Jesuit priest, Barbier, wrote in 1723: "More than 200 adults were baptised...; such an enduring famine had provided the Fathers a new occasion to exercise their zeal.... Several Gentiles (Hindus) have found along with the preservation of their physical life, an assurance of the eternal life of the soul, through the baptisms that they received.[30] When there was again famine during the 1730s and 1740s, there were a good number of converts to Christianity.[31]

Reverend Poissevin writes in 1747: 'In May 1747, famine stalked Pondicherry.... This created the occasion for the conversion of several pagans'.[32] The conversions during the 1740s were made possible to some extent by the liberal donations of Dupleix, the French governor of Pondicherry, and his wife, which were no doubt utilised to relieve the famine-stricken people.[33] Thus the missionaries were undoubtedly a strong source of physical and psychological comfort to the needy Hindus, who as a result converted to Christianity in sizeable numbers.

Such conversions during the 18th century seem to have taken place not only in Pondicherry, but in many other places of South India, for instance, Karikal, where many people converted during the outbreak of a cholera epidemic in 1755. The French Jesuit missionary, Father de Saint Estevan wrote from Karikal: "During this year an epidemic struck our Christians.... More than 4000 pagans had died around Karikal, of whom some converted at the time of death; we have lost 300 Christians and a number of children whom we have fortunately saved from paganism; we have baptised this year more than 150 adults at Karikal, without counting the several children."[34]

According to Jacques Weber, conversions to Christianity during the 19th century were fewer. His study proves conclusively that the quantitative increase in the Catholic minority in the 19th century was due more to the excess of births over deaths rather than to the conversion of pagans.[35] However it seems that even in the 19th century, famine and epidemics had contributed to many conversions. In 1829, a cholera epidemic devastated Karikal. This led to the conversion of many Hindus to Christianity[36]. During the terrible famine of 1831-32 and that of 1876-78, the missionaries obtained many conversions in exchange for some rice, pieces of meat and other material help. [37] Before the famine of 1876-78, there were 14200 Catholics in Pondicherry. But by 1886, there were 20300. According to the missionary M.J.Baulez, the sudden increase in numbers was due to the great number of baptisms administered during the famine crisis.[38] He maintains that the charity of the missionaries had contributed to the multiplication of conversions between 1876 and 1878.[39]

Additionally, aware that new Christians had to be encouraged through charitable actions Rev. Arul baptised about 1500 famine-stricken Hindus between 1866 and 1870 by distributing some rice and money.[40] Actually the French missionary, Monseigneur Laouenan writes about these conversions as follows: "We gave to every adult (baptised) 18 centimes per day for their food and only during the period of instruction. Some neophytes cost less, others more. In short, including the food... (and) the salary of the catechists in charge of teaching the prayers, the baptism of each neophyte costed about 10 francs on an average".[41] In 1898 alone, famine facilitated the conversion to Catholicism of 2225 pariahs in the villages situated to the north of Pondicherry town.[42] In their turn, the missionaries also seem to have been encouraged in their conversion missions through financial inducements. Towards the last decades of the 19th century, every missionary was given Rs.3 for every adult baptised and Rs.2 for every child baptised.[43]

Besides, the missionaries received liberal donations from Europe, notably from France, to carry on with their proselytising activities, especially during periods of famine and epidemic. Indeed sometimes such activities were held up due to the shortage of money flowing from Europe.[44] The French priest; Fourcade remarked that: "Famine was the most terrible and most heeded of the predications. God knows well the Indians. He knows hunger is the best way to bring them into his beautiful heaven.... There were no high castes who converted, but only low castes".[45] Generally it seems that conversions diminished considerably after the famine and epidemics were over.

The preceding details illustrate the role of the missionaries during period of famine and epidemics, in bringing about conversions in a peaceful and persuasive manner by offering voluntary material and psychological assistance to the needy and helpless Hindus, especially the untouchables, who in all probability would not have converted otherwise. Though one can appreciate the help so rendered by the missionaries, one should not fail to note that the missionaries in their zeal to obtain converts to

Christianity, in the process deprived the people whom they sought to convert of their ancestral religious, cultural, moral and social beliefs and traditions, and even their usual Hindu names. In this one can undoubtedly discern a certain intolerance on the part of the missionaries vis-à-vis non-Christian people and their beliefs and traditions, notwithstanding their peaceful and persuasive means and their pious intentions.

Religious Intolerance

Let us now examine the factors that actually prevented conversions in Pondicherry or slowed down its pace. In contrast to Hinduism, Christianity was a proselytising religion from the very beginning, but western missionaries had to carry on with their proselytising activities in Asia mostly under adverse conditions. Contrary to the persecution of missionaries in parts of the Buddhist world like Japan and China, the missionaries who came into contact with the Hindu world do not seem to have faced any real opposition from the local population.[46] In spite of this, there were a number of factors that impeded the growth of Christianity in the Hindu world.

The foremost of these factors, as far as Pondicherry was concerned, seems to have been the policies adopted by the French colonisers and some missionaries especially in their dealings with the Hindus. Generally it seems that the west European Christian missionaries who came to India, were conditioned by the twin Christian concepts of God and the Devil. Naturally, when they came into contact with the Hindu Gods and goddesses, they dismissed them as simply demons or devils and thought that the Hindus were only fit to be converted.[47] The French missionaries of Pondicherry were no exceptions in this regard, as we shall see. In March 1701, under the influence of Jesuits, François Martin prohibited all Hindu and Muslim religious ceremonies during Easter and on Sundays.[48] The zeal of the missionaries was such that they wanted to eradicate all temples and mosques from Pondicherry, following the example of the great French king, Louis XIV, who destroyed all heresy in France.[49]

It also appears that the Jesuit missionaries, who had established themselves in a place adjacent to the big Shiva temple, just outside the White town, unable to tolerate the existence of a temple, requested François Martin, to take steps to demolish the temple.[50] Thus, on 15 August 1702, François Martin prohibited the Hindus from taking out processions and celebrating their festivals and asked for the temple keys. Contrary to all expectations, Hindus of all castes, numbering about 12000 to 15000, including masons and coolies, who were constructing the French fort and

5000 or 6000 weavers, prepared to quit Pondicherry altogether, leaving behind their shops and houses, rather than accept silently the dictates of the French.[51]

In spite of his religious inclination, François Martin could not afford to lose the population of Pondicherry simply in order to please the Jesuits given that most of the local merchants were Hindus.[52] The population was absolutely necessary for the commercial welfare of the French East India company. As a result, François Martin was obliged to revoke the prohibitions and orders and allow the Hindus to carry on with their usual religious pursuits. Similarly in 1705, when the Jesuits tried to prevent the Hindus from gathering in their temples, all castes including the coolies, shopkeepers and weavers prepared to leave Pondicherry. Once again the French were obliged to concede the demands of the Hindus for fear of endangering their commerce through the depopulation of the town.[53]

But the Jesuits continued with their attempts to restrict Hindu festivities and worship at the temples. They proposed to the government to leave only two temples in Pondicherry for the Hindus to carry on with their worship, just two or three times a week, and to wall and close the doors of the other temples so that they would decay in the course of time.[54] They also wanted to prohibit the building of any new temples and disallow the Hindus from worshipping at their temples during Easter and Sundays and other Christian festivities like Ascension, All Saints Day and Christmas.[55]

Following such proposals, the French government issued orders prohibiting the Hindus from celebrating their festivals on Sundays and Christian feast days.[56] Once again the Hindus of all castes chose to quit Pondicherry. Even the *dhobis* (washermen), *coolies* and *Mukkuwas* (fishermen), prepared to leave Pondicherry, along with the shopkeepers, weavers, etc. [57]. The Capuchins, who were less strident in their missionary zeal, wanted to allow the Hindu ceremonies in Pondicherry to continue without restrictions. But the Jesuits were severely opposed to this. On 4 February 1715, Rev-Bouchet, a French Jesuit, wrote to Dulivier, the governor of Pondicherry: "....It is necessary to destroy the (Shiva) temple now and that is the best means to make the Malabars (Hindus) come back to Pondicherry.... The root cause of all these disorders was Nainiyappa.... As long as Nainiyappa is maintained in the position (of *Diwan*), we will face similar troubles and we could do nothing in favour of the (Christian) religion."[58] But the government seems to have been more favourably disposed towards the proposals of the Capuchins and dissuaded the Hindus from migrating by allowing them to celebrate their festivals.[59]

The inclination of the Hindus to undergo the hardships of migration rather than stay back and defend their interests through other means including violence, is a perfect demonstration of the historical principle of non-co-operation in action against the intolerant intentions and attitudes of the principal political and religious authorities of French Pondicherry. The non-violent exodus of the Hindus from Pondicherry was also an effective method to socially boycott the colonisers and the missionaries. Thus the migration brought to the fore in a striking manner the three principles of non-violence, non-co-operation and social boycott in a way that obliged the French to review the situation. The exodus also shows a certain unity prevailing among the Hindus during this time, despite the caste divisions, for it was not only the high castes who decided to leave Pondicherry for neighbouring territories under the native control, but also the low caste and Untouchable Hindus like the masons and coolies.

It appears that during this period, every caste had its headman, known as the *mahanattar*. These headmen, eighteen in number, were in charge of the affairs of the Hindus of Pondicherry. Available indications show that it was they who were behind the exodus of the Hindus.[60] The French had actually arrested some caste headmen like Chagapamudali, Kalavé Tandaven and Vellaiambalam, who were considered to be the instigators of the troubles in Pondicherry and banished them.[61] This also shows that *Diwan* Nainiyappa Pillai was instrumental in protecting Hindu interests and preventing the accomplishment of the Jesuits' plans. He paid the price for it with his life.

Finally on 11 February 1733, the French East India company promulgated certain rules allowing the presence of Hindus in Pondicherry and the celebration of Hindu festivals and requiring the missionaries to be cautious in their dealings with the Hindus.[62] The Company seems to have come to this decision for the welfare of their commercial interests, which were dependent on the Hindu merchants, artisans and workers. The missionaries could do nothing more than complain about this state of affairs, where commerce prevailed over religion.[63]

However such a policy seems to have been set aside during the period 1742-54, when Dupleix was the Governor of Pondicherry. Dupleix adopted a number of measures favourable to Christianity. for example through the order of 14 November 1746, he prohibited people from working on Sundays; and by the order of 12 January 1747, he permitted the teaching of Christianity to the slaves in French custody. Besides, Madame Jeanne Dupleix, the wife of Dupleix, was specially interested in missionary work. She gave liberal donations to both the Jesuits and the Capuchins. In 1751, she gave two villages, Markanam and Cheyur, that she had received earlier from the Nawab of Carnatic, to the Jesuits so that they might use the revenues from them to propagate Christianity among the Hindus and baptise the pagan children. During the same time, she donated the village of Kadapakkam to the Capuchin missionaries and helped them to construct a church.[64] Thus the missionaries seem to have found in Dupleix and his wife firm allies in advancing the cause of Christianity.

The Jesuits, as we know, had been trying to dislodge the Shiva temple for about fifty years, from the time François Martin was in charge of Pondicherry.[65] This temple was finally destroyed on 8 September 1748. It was situated not on the site of the massive church, which stands almost at the same place even today, but at a place adjacent to the church (as could be seen clearly in the map of Pondicherry town, published by the French in 1741.[66] Presently the temple site is part of the church property.[67] It appears that though the French never allowed the temple to be rebuilt at the same site, permission was given a couple of years later to build a new temple in place of the destroyed one, not far from the old temple site.[68]

The following letters written by Dupleix prove beyond doubt the decisive role of Dupleix in the destruction of the Shiva temple, though many writers, starting from Ananda Ranga Pillai to the 20th century French historians, attribute the actions of Dupleix during this period mostly to the influence of his wife and the Jesuit missionaries.[69] In a letter dated 21 October 1748, written by Dupleix to the Directors of the French company, we read: 'One of the happiest events of the siege is the destruction of the temple which since several long years was a perpetual scandal. It is finally demolished...' In another letter of the same date, Dupleix wrote to Barthelemy, a member of the French council at Pondicherry: 'The Jesuits sang the Te Deum yesterday... The demolition of the temple flatters them immensely and I am in fact very satisfied for having ended a scandal so close and so continuous. God be praised'. These two hand-written letters of Dupleix, which were in the private archives of Marquis de Nazelle, a descendant of the former's brother, were published in 1908.[70] In a third letter, written by Dupleix to his brother on 26 January 1749, available at the *Bibliothèque Nationale* de Paris, we read: 'I am on the best of terms with the Jesuits since I got destroyed a certain temple, which was veritably a perpetual scandal. this action is worth a passport for me to the other world.[71]

About a thousand people appear to have been involved in the destruction of the Shiva temple. Among them were French Jesuit priests and soldiers, and Indian coolies and workers and sepoys.[72] It also appears that Dupleix gave permission to the Brahmins of the temple and other high caste headmen like Arumuga Mudali, Nella Chetty, Andana Nayaken, Kuttiya Pillai and Chinna Mudali, to remove the idols, chariots and other cult objects from the temple.[73] But when they went to take away these things, they had to face the wrath and violence of the priests like Fr. Coeurdoux.[74]

It should be noted that coolies and workers employed by the Jesuit priests to demolish the temple, as well as the Sepoys, were in the pay-roll of the French. It is also held that Madame Dupleix made use of certain low castes and Untouchables Hindus under her control, like the *Pallis*, to threaten and loot the high caste, rich Hindus, and even instigated them to install themselves in the houses of high castes and use their utensils, an abomination to any high caste Hindu in those days.[75]

It should be noted that at the time of the demolition of the Shiva temple, the French also wanted to destroy the mosque, situated just behind the Capuchin church in the plan of Pondicherry drawn by Denyon in 1704, they desisted when the Muslims rose in opposition under Jamedar Abdur Rahman, who had played a crucial role along with other sepoys, against the English invasion of Pondicherry in 1748.[76] It appears that it was Dupleix who created the Sepoy regiment, by appointing two Muslims, probably from Malabar, at their head. Thus Abdur Rahman had been appointed as chief of the infantry wing of the Sepoys, while Sheik Hassan (Hassem) was appointed as the head of the cavalry.[77]

As the French were dependent on Muslim sepoys for political and military purposes, it appears that they could not execute their plans to destroy the mosque. Instead they seem to have gone out of their way to please the Muslim sepoys. In his letter dated 21 August 1748, Dupleix himself declared that Abdul Rahman and his brother, Sheik Hassem were worthy of the gratitude of the French nation for their role in the war against the English, and spoke of the necessity for the French to keep Abdur Rahman and his men closely attached to the French by conferring honours and presents upon them. As a result it appears that Madame Dupleix rewarded Abdur Rahman and other Muslims with rich presents.[78] Thus the French strove to remain in the good books of the Muslims.

However this mosque vanished without trace from the White town some years afterwards. Its disappearance seems to be connected with the transfer of the Muslim population to the other side of the canal, where muslims like even today. It appears that the road in which the mosque was situated was known as '*rue de la Mosquée*'(Mosque street). But along with the mosque and the Muslims, even the name '*rue de la Mosquée*' ceased to exist in the area during the French regime. The Mosque street was re-named as *rue* (street) Baslieu by the French.[79]

Contrary to what happened during the first decades of the 18th century, when Hindus of all castes were united in their opposition to repeated French religious intolerance, this was no longer possible. Within the space of three or four decades the French had been successful in creating a rift between the Hindus; especially some low castes and untouchables like the *pallis* and the coolies in the service of the French, not to speak of the non-pariah and pariah converts, were acting against caste Hindu interests.[80] Even Ananda Ranga Pillai, Dupleix's low caste Hindu *diwan*, seems to have been rendered ineffective and was never, unlike his relative Nainiyappa Pillai, able to use his influence to stop the destruction of the temple. Besides, the Hindus were not able to repeat the social boycott of the French by migrating or staying out of Pondicherry in Indian or British-controlled territories, as they had done before, because the temple was destroyed at a time when English troops were besieging Pondicherry and much of the population including many of the caste headmen had actually left Pondicherry. The remaining caste headmen could do nothing to prevent the destruction of the temple. Actually the destruction seem to have taken place in the midst of their silent and feeble murmurs of protest.[81] Three years later in 1751, Dupleix seems to have been involved in the destruction of the famous temple at Gingy, not very far from Pondicherry.[82] Actually the twelve single-piece granite columns with their classic Hindu sculptural reliefs were dragged to Pondicherry in a hundred ox-carts by Dupleix. These columns were part of the great Senji temple.[83]

From the time of their establishment in Pondicherry until the destruction of the temple and even later, the aggressive stance of the French towards the Hindus and especially towards the non-pariahs would have certainly deterred many of them from converting. It is quite possible that under normal circumstances many of these Hindus would have converted, at least to take advantage of the favours shown to the converts by the French colonisers in the economic and employment fields. In fact, as noted, such favours had fetched more converts to Christianity, especially from the high castes, than had the aggressiveness of some of the missionaries.

Missionaries versus Colonisers

While excessive missionary zeal had slackened the growth of Christianity in Pondicherry, as we have shown, the missionaries themselves held the French colonisers responsible, albeit for different reasons. India in the Eighteenth century was an extremely conservative society and Pondicherry was no exception, as Ananda Ranga Pillai's diary amply proves. Not only the frontiers between the castes and the religions were strictly maintained, but the conventions governing sexual relationships were particularly severe and lapses hardly tolerated. The Portuguese were the first Europeans to come to South India. A French Jesuit missionary of the Madura kingdom, in a letter dated 1 June 1700, attributed the difficulty in converting the Hindus to the conduct of the Portuguese: "The Portuguese never understood in the beginning the differences between the castes....;They never troubled themselves to differentiate between the high and low castes; they employed freely the pariahs and fishermen and made use of them to satisfy their various needs. This conduct of the early Portuguese shocked the Indians and became very prejudicial to our religion; for they (Hindus) considered there afterwards the people of Europe as a despicable and miserable lot with whom one cannot deal without dishonouring oneself. If we had taken wise precautions from those very days, as in the Madura for more than a century, it would have been easy to win all these people... for Jesus Christ".[84] In another letter, dated 30 January 1699, Rev. Martin writes: "...They (Hindus) have no relationship with the Europeans, of whom some by their debauchery and bad examples have spoilt and corrupted the entire Christianity of India.

The horror of the Indians for the Europeans has more than one cause. We have often indulged in great violence in their country. They have seen terrible examples of all kinds of debauchery and vice; but what shakes them particularly is that the Firangis... drink (alcohol) and eat flesh, regarded by them as horrible and they treat those who eat (flesh) and drink as vile".[85] Even Rev. Bouchet, based at Pondicherry, cautioned the missionaries not to identify themselves with the European colonisers, in the following terms: "....All our attention should tend to hide from these people (Indians) that we are what they call 'Firangis'; the smallest doubt that they have in this regard, will be an insurmountable obstacle for the propagation of the (Christian) faith".[86] He further held: "The idolators reasonably perceive the missionaries as persons who want to destroy the religion of the country.... Generally speaking, the Indians, except the Untouchables, hate drunkenness. They never drink liquor that will render them drunken. They actually express against this vice more strongly than our zealous missionaries and this inspires in them partly a great disdain for Europeans".[87]

Many other missionaries had held that the Hindus of South India were very slow in taking to Christianity because of the extreme aversion and contempt that they had for all foreigners in general, due to the scandals and bad conduct of the Europeans which affected even the small number of conversions obtained during this period.[88] It appears that the early missionaries like Francis Xavier and Roberto Nobili obtained more success in converting some of the local populations, than the missionaries of the 18th and 19th centuries, when the Europeans had conquered South India.[89]. As the French missionary, Dubois, wrote in the beginning of the Nineteenth century: "They (colonisers) are spread out at present and they reign in the whole of the peninsula. There is no way to hide (the fact) that the missionaries also are Europeans like them. The people of this country, who always judge things by their appearances, seeing in these foreigners habits and customs and ways opposed to theirs, seeing them behave in a manner contrary to the principles of their religion, seeing them violate without modesty the rules of probity and decency by publicly having concubines, seeing the soldiers abuse openly their women.... seeing them lead shamelessly a life that even the most vile caste among them will not lead without shame, they can only (hold) the Europeans in the most extreme contempt. On account of (the colonisers') manner of living, they hold against their habits, religion and customs, I will not say a prejudice, but an invincible horror; so that after having convinced them of the (Christian) truth and the excellence of the (Catholic) religion, they do not embrace it, because they say it is the 'religion of vile (people), of the horrible Firangis".[90]

Thus the missionaries held the colonisers themselves responsible for the paucity of conversions in South India and established themselves firmly at the political level. Anyhow, there is certainly a large element of truth in the missionaries' contention that the conduct of the European colonisers made conversions extremely difficult, given the conservative nature of Indian society, though the effect cannot be exactly quantified. So it can be said that though there were pressures, persuasions and preferences operating on one side to induce conversions, there were on the other side certain cultural and moral aspects like vegetarianism, which made conversions difficult.

The Caste Obstacle

The European missionaries, especially the French, appear to have realised very soon that caste was a big obstacle for the conversion of Hindus to Christianity. Anybody who desired to become a Christian was ostracised and boycotted by the parents, the family the entire caste and the priests, such that it became very difficult for a potential convert to find a bride within his caste and establish a family, all marriages being caste endogamous.[91] Thus converting to Christianity for those belonging to a caste where there were no Christians implied excommunication and renunciation of the desire to establish a family.[92] This naturally blocked the growth of Christianity. This explains also to some extent why in earlier periods Hindus resorted to mass conversions in the coastal areas of Tamilnadu and Travancore. The egalitarian message of Christianity was the logical anti-thesis of the inequality prevailing in the Hindu world, and it was but natural for the French missionaries who had established themselves in Pondicherry to seek converts from both the high and low castes or Untouchables on an equal footing.

In some areas of Tamilnadu, the *pariahs* were more numerous in converting to Christianity, while the high castes seem to have considered that converting to Christianity would mean converting to *parianism*. Besides, it seems that to some extent the missionaries also were identified with the *pariahs* by the high castes.[93] Such identification of Christianity with *parianism* was a serious obstacle to winning high caste converts. Moreover, conversions did not mean that the converts were ready to abandon the caste altogether, just to be in conformity to Christian values, [94] as the missionaries desired. The high caste converts wanted to maintain in some form the frontier between them and the Untouchables, and the missionaries were obliged to give in. In 1745, a line was drawn separating the high caste Christians from the pariah Christians in the Jesuit church known as '*Notre Dame de la Conception*' of Pondicherry, according to the decision of the Pope.[95] This church was razed to the ground by the English in 1761, when they captured Pondicherry. When the Jesuits thought to rebuild this church without providing for the separation between *pariah* Christians and high caste Christians, it was vehemently opposed by the latter, who even went to the extent of boycotting the church. The opposition was such that the Jesuits had to modify their plans to satisfy the desire of the high caste Christians.[96]

Though the *pariah* Christians and high caste Christians were separated by pillars and stone benches and separate doors in the church, they were nonetheless united within the same church. Moreover the communion table and the altar were common to everyone. that is, the missionaries had made some concessions to the high caste Christians, without totally compromising the egalitarian principle of Christianity. On the other hand, it was a considerable concession on the part of the high caste Christians to have accepted the entry of the *pariah* Christians into the same church as themselves, since in Hindu temples *pariah* Hindus were invariably kept away. Though the high caste Christians had been won over to the egalitarian principle to a certain extent, they did not totally want to renounce their high caste characteristics, hence the separate doors and distinct areas within the church and also the separate cemeteries for the *pariahs*. A similar situation prevailed in other places like the churche of Ariancoupam, Pinneipundi and Kerveypundi.[97]

The missionaries took the problem of segregation in churches before the Sacred Congregation for the propagation of faith in Rome. The Sacred Congregation decided in 1778 to tolerate the separation of *pariahs* from high caste Christians in the churches.[98] In fact, the Papal Bull, *Omnium Sollicitudinum* made no mention of this separation, and above all did not condemn it.[99] In March 1780, the Cardinal in charge of the *Propaganda Fide* in Rome wrote that the separation could be tolerated for the moment, though it was condemned earlier by Pope Gregory XV 'as contrary to Christian humility and charity'[100] Again on 9 April 1783, Cardinal Antonelli of Rome gave the missionaries the right to tolerate segregation in the churches.[101]

Actually the intervention of Rome relieved the missionaries in India of their responsibility in tolerating segregation on the basis of caste was 'a major obstacle for the establishment of Christianity in the country.[102] The high caste Christians, to the contrary, thought that Rome had definitely conceded segregation in the churches, and some even went to the extent of asking for separate churches for high caste Christians.[103] Now, why did the missionaries tolerate this segregation? The answer is not far to find. As the Bishop of Tabraca wrote: "We would like to have a common gathering to avoid scandal.... but after going into the pros and cons, we are very embarrassed. the missionaries all say that a common gathering of the *pariahs* with the *shudras* would bring about the apostasy of almost all high caste Christians and would raise an invincible obstacle to the conversion of high caste Hindus in Pondicherry; even at the slightest change the high caste Christians revolt! On this we have had a number of unhappy experiences; a common gathering without separation.... will essentially end in the loss of a great majority of the Christians".[104] Even the Cardinal in Rome preferred to tolerate segregation in the churches and in the cemeteries, rather than face the consequences for Christendom of not tolerating it.[105]

Thus on the one hand, the missionaries had the task of convincing high caste Christians and even potential converts (high caste Hindus) that separation between them and the pariahs would be maintained in the churches, and on the other hand they had to convince the *pariah* Christians that discrimination would not be allowed in the churches, and if at all allowed to some extent, it was only temporarily. In fact, the fear that segregation might be abandoned some day would have been there in the minds of many high caste Hindus and would have deterred at least some of them from converting to Christianity. On the contrary many low caste and Untouchable Hindus may have naturally felt that discrimination was not going to end even if they converted to Christianity. Here is a case, where identification with certain aspects of Hinduism probably prevented Christianity from spreading further. This contradicts the claims of Susan Bayly who asserts that Christianity spread because of its identification with Hinduism, especially low Hinduism. [106]

The essential features in the interaction between the Hindus and Christians of Pondicherry between 1700 and 1900 had been discussed above shows how Christianity gained a foothold among the Hindus. On the one hand pressures, preferences and persuasion were used by the French to induce conversions, while on the other certain cultural, social and moral aspects of Hinduism made conversions difficult. From the records it is quite obvious that the phenomenon of conversions due to sudden illumination or change of conviction seems not to be very frequent. Even when there seemed to be such type of conversions sometimes, as claimed by the missionaries, it is enough to scratch a little below the surface to find that the real reason for such conversions too will be of purely material nature.

Although the Hindu hereditary caste system was supposed to be legitimised by *karma* and rebirth theories, there is *nothing* in the missionary or other records that we have consulted to indicate that Christian converts of those days made use of the *karma* and rebirth theories to legitimise the caste distinctions among them. In any case, the missionaries never believed in the *karma* and Rebirth theories and there was no place in their churches for such Hindu religious ideas. The converts who frequented these churches were instructed in the fundamentals of the Christian world. Last Judgement and Resurrection replaced the notions of *karma* and rebirth as, similarly, Jesus Christ replaced Shiva, Vishnu, etc.

The principle of human hierarchy and inequality and the notions of purity and impurity among the Hindus were always known. It was not a Dumontian invention, though they were central to Dumontian thought. They do not however have an independent existence, disconnected totally from the core Hindu theory of *karma* and rebirth. Actually they find their legitimacy in the latter, both theoretically and practically. The simple fact that the converted Christians and their descendants hardly resorted to the *karma* and rebirth theories to justify the divisions and differences among them proves that they were fundamentally different from the Hindus as far as the Hindu core is concerned. As a result whatever Hindu might still remain in them, in a modified form could only be survivals of ancestral traditions, which might or might not cease to exist. This is also the case with the Muslims. This can in no way mean that Christians and Muslims do not have an independent existence. In general, the missionaries rarely succumbed to the charms of the local culture. They always maintained their contact with Rome, from where they expected guidance in their dealings with the converts and the local people. Similarly the Indian Christian converts accepted the authority of the church over them. They might have possessed certain Hindu traits, survivals of their ancestral traditions, but this does not imply that the frontiers between themselves and the Hindus were blurred. The missionary and colonial records prove that the converts were classified as 'Malabar Christians' from the time of their conversion, confirming that, religiously speaking, they belonged to the Christian world.

It is also not possible to conclude that there is a religious symbiosis at work between the Christians and Hindus of Pondicherry simply because of some similarities in their customs and habits. After all, Jews, Christians and Muslims of the Middle-East and Europe or rather the Judeo-Christian-Islamic world, have many common beliefs like the belief in an extra-cosmic personal god, in the theories of creation, resurrection and last Judgement and in the idea of the equality and brotherhood of man. But it is noteworthy that in spite of these and many other common features, the Jews, Christians and Muslims have neither lost their specific religious identities, nor have they mixed and mingled to form a complete, indivisible, religious symbiosis. This being the case, why should one expect that in India alone, which historically belongs to a totally different world (ie., the Hindu-Buddhist world, centred around the laws of *Karma* and Rebirth), there should be a religious symbiosis in operation? If at all we can speak of symbiosis, it can be nothing but the one swallowing or trying to swallow the other.

Actually symbiosis may or may not take place if two groups of people, strange to one another, happen to meet and live together or co-exist. Thus the English who were total strangers to Indians before the Sixteenth century, happened to co-exist with Indians for more than two centuries, yet they maintained their separate identity all throughout. We cannot really talk of a symbiosis of Indian and English races and cultures. But the great majority of the Christians and Muslims in India are not strangers to India, like the English. They are as much sons of the soil as the Hindus. But by virtue of their conversions they have drifted away from their Hindu moorings. They are actually breakaway groups. How can we talk of symbiosis in this situation where many Hindus for various reasons have been continuously breaking away from Hinduism and creating for themselves separate identities, whose fundamental notions and principal personalities are alien to Hinduism. In my opinion, all these groups can co-exist, but they are incapable of symbiosis as long as they retain their special characteristics, conditionings and identities and their competitive nature.

Besides, why should one expect, as Louis Dumont does, that Hindu world-view permeates and encompasses everyone who participates in Hindu civilisation?[107] As far as the Indian Christians of Pondicherry are concerned, we could say from the above, that they had actually cut themselves off from their original Hindu moorings by virtue of their conversion and whatever Hindu remains in them are just survivals of ancestral traditions, which may or may not cease to exist gradually or all of a sudden in the future. Egalitarian Christianity was and always has been a competitive ideology, seeking to establish its dominance and supremacy at the expense of all other ideologies, beliefs and traditions, whether egalitarian or non-egalitarian. It believes that it alone possesses the entire truth, as revealed in the Bible, and that it has a civilising mission to convert the whole world. On the contrary, traditional Hinduism, whatever its virtues or vices, was indirectly tolerant and even respectful of the rights of the non-Hindus to freely pursue their customs and traditions without the necessity of conversion.

The Hindus of Pondicherry never sought to convert the French Christians to Hinduism or their way of life. But as we have seen, their tolerance was put to a severe test during the 18th century by the competitive nature of Christianity and the extreme zeal of some French colonisers and missionaries. Even under extreme provocation, the Hindus of Pondicherry preferred to offer passive resistance to protect their interests rather than indulge in violence. This was no doubt one of the earliest instances in colonial India where the age-old principles of non-violence and non-co-operation were put into actual practice. Contrary to the Hindus, the Muslim reaction to Dupleix's intention of destroying their mosque at the same time when he destroyed the Hindu temple, was strikingly different from that of the Hindus. Actually they threatened the French Christians with violence and death if they dared to destroy the mosque in the original Muslim quarters, near the Capuchin church. This shows, without an iota of doubt that the psychological dispositions of the Muslims was not at all the same as the Hindus. This demonstrates once again that Louis Dumont's views that Muslims and other non-Hindus who function within the Hindu system have the same basic psychological dispositions, are totally wrong.[108] It would appear then that Dumont's views and those of many other scholars both Indian and western who more or less toe his line, like Imtiaz Ahmad of Delhi and Susan Bayly of Cambridge, have been prejudiced by the predominance of the Hindu factor or by their intellectual penchants or their ideological commitments. Political considerations, social and academic upbringing might have also impinged on their views, as pointed out by the Islamicist, Francis Robinson, in the case of Imtiaz Ahmad.[109] Besides, it is also absurd and irrational to assume like Louis Dumont that the psychological dispositions of Hindus all over the Indian sub-continent were and are homogeneous. As we know from the preceding, the Hindus reacted to European intrusion on the eastern coastal regions like Pondicherry with the utmost restraint, without resorting to violence. But various other studies have proved conclusively that the Hindus in various other parts of India did not react in a similar fashion to European penetration as the Hindus of Pondicherry.[110]

Egalitarian ideologies like Christianity and Islam have a tendency to gravitate towards cultural or religious homogeneity or uniformity. This had happened in Europe and in the Islamised world and it is happening in many other parts of the world. It would not be an exaggeration to conclude that egalitarian ideologies, in spite of all the virtues attributed to them, have an in-built tendency to be competitive and to eliminate peacefully or persuasively or violently, in the name of some universal ideal or belief, the rich cultural diversity and heritage of mankind. On the contrary, traditional Hinduism, in spite of all the imperfections inherent in its non-egalitarian approach to human existence, had preserved more or less the rich cultural and religious diversity of the Indian people, without attempting to homogenise them, as Christianity had done in Europe and elsewhere, on the basis of a set of beliefs or traditions or dogmas. In short, in the non-egalitarian Hindu world, there was always a great scope for cultural and religious diversity and liberty, while in the egalitarian Judeo-Christian-Islamic world the absence of this diversity and liberty, and conformity to a certain set of beliefs, customs and laws, was the order of the day. Strangely, modern non-religious egalitarian ideologies do not seem to be very different from ancient egalitarian ideologies like Christianity and Islam. This may be because of the fact that they have their roots still in the latter though they may claim to have broken away from it.

Notes and References

1. Alfred Martineau, *Mémoires de François Martin*, II Vols, Paris, Société d'éditions, géographiques, maritimes et coloniales, 1931-32, See Vol. I, pp. 387, 394; Julien Vinson, *Les Français*

dans l'Inde, 1736-1748, Paris, Ernest Leroux, 1894, pp. 111, 115-116. Recensement Général. March 1948–A.P. Carton 448, dossier 22–August 1949, Archives d'Outre-mer, Aix en Provence,

2. Castonnet des Fosses. *L'Inde Française avant Dupleix*, Paris, Challamel, 1887, p. 122; M.V. Labernadie, *Le vieux Pondichéry, 1674-1815*, Pondichéry, Imprimerie Moderne, 1936, pp. 10-12; J. Macau, *L'Inde Danoise-la première compagnie, 1616-1670*, Aix en Provence, Université de Provence, n.d. p. 101. Mss.Fr.6231. Mémoires sur la Compagnie des Indes Orientales, 1642-1720, fl.8, Bibliothèque Nationale de Paris(henceforth BNP).
3. A perusal of Ananda Ranga Pillai's diary confirms this state of affairs. Ranga Pillai who belonged to the relatively low-status *Idayar* caste, was the *Diwan* of Dupleix, the French governor of Pondicherry.
4. Julien Vinson, *op. cit.*, pp. xxxix.
5. Mss.Fr.6231. Mémoires.fl.12, BNP ; See also, Labernadie, *op. cit.*, p. :79.
6. See also Vinson, *op. cit.*, pp. xxviii. Plan général des dépendances de Pondichéry par Denyon, 1704, BNP.
7. *Catalogue des manuscrits des Archives de l'Inde Française*, I, 1690-1789, Paris, Leroux, 1922, p. 1 ; See also, Castonnet des Fosses, *op. cit.*, p. 214.
8. H. Dodwell, (ed.,) *The Private Diary of Ananda Ranga Pillai* (trans. from Tamil), New Delhi, Asian Educational Services, (reprint) 1985, p. 306.
9. Lettre du Père Ducros à l'Abbé Ragnet, directeur de la Compagnie des Indes, 17 October 1725, Ariancoupam. In *Lettres Edifiantes et Curieuses* (henceforth *LEC)* tome 13, Paris, Merigot, 1781, p. 335 See also, Adrien Launay, *Histoire des Missions de l'Inde-Pondichéry, Maissour, Coimbatour*, Paris, Ancienne Maison, 1898, p. I, xxx.
10. Paul Kaeppelin, *La Compagnie des Indes Orientales et François Martin, 1664-1789*, Paris, Challamel, 1908, p. 554; Launay, *op. cit.*, Vol. 1 p. xxx; Martineau, *op. cit.*, 1931: I, pp. 630-31, 634.
11. Lettre de M.Hebert, gouverneur de Pondichéry, 12 February 1709. In Mss.Fr. NAF 9364, BNP ; Mss.Fr.6231, Mémoires, fl.42, BNP.

12. Lettre du Père Ducros à l'Abbé Ragnet, Directeur de la Compagnie des Indes, Ariancoupam, 17 Ocotober 1725. In *LEC*, tome 13, Paris, Merigot, 1781, pp. 335-36.see also, Launay, *op. cit*, Vol. I, xxxii.
13. Mss.Fr. 8972. Déclaration du Roy, 1664, article XXX; *LEC*, tome 10, Paris, Merigot, 1781, p. ix.
14. Mss.Fr.25286. copie de l'acte de donation faite d'une Eglise aux Capucins, 28 May 1676, signé par Lazaro de Mota, BNP ; *Catalogue des manuscrits des Anciennes Archives de l'Inde Française, 1690-1789*, tome I, Paris, Leroux, 1922, p. 6. See also, Kaeppelin, *op. cit.*, p. 554; Launay, *op. cit.*, Vol. I, p. xxx; Vinson, *op. cit.*, 1894: xv.
15. *LEC*, tome VII, M DCCC.XIX, Vernarel et Cabin, p. 470. See also, Launay, op. cit., Vol. I, p. xxxii; Vinson, *op. cit.*, xvii.
16. Mss.Fr. 8971, Affaire des Indes. Lettre de Chevalier Hebert, Gouverneur de Pondichéry au R.P.Tachard, Jésuite, fl.17, BNP. See also, Paul Olagnier, *Les Jésuites à Pondichéry et l'affaire Naniapa (1705-1720)*, Paris, Leroux, 1932, p. 15.
17. Mss.Fr. 6231, fl.46v, BNP.see also, Olangier, *Ibid*: 19-20; Launay, *op. cit.*, Vol. I, p. xxxiii, xxxv.
18. Lettre du gouverneur Dulivier de Pondichéry à Pontchatrain, 18 July 1714. In Olagnier *op. cit.*, pp. 23-24 ; Délibération du conseil souverain de Pondichéry, tome I, Société de l'Histoire de l'Inde Française, Pondichéry, n.d., pp. 140, 143-44.
19. Mss.NAF 9357, fl.14, BNP ; Mss.Fr.6231, fl.56, BNP ; Mss.NAF, 9225, fl.293 ; Lettre de la veuve du chevalier Guruvappa au Supérieur et directeur du Séminaire, 17 January 1726, Pondichéry, Vol. 992 (Inde), Archives des Missions Etrangères de Paris (henceforth AMEP) ; Lettre de M.de Querelay aux Monsieurs du Séminaire des Missions Etrangères, 1 February 1719, Pondichéry, Vol. 960, AMEP.
20. Mss.NAF 9354, Compagnie des Indes, 1714-42, BNP; Lettre de M.de Querelay, 8 September 1709, Vol. 995 (Inde), AMEP.see also, Launay, op. cit., Vol. I, pp. xxxii-, xxxiii. Olangier, op. cit., p. 106.
21. Mss.Fr. 6231, Mémoire des Jésuites, fl.46-47, BNP
22. Launay, op. cit., Vol. I, p. xlvii; Olagnier, op. cit., p. 33.
23. C. Dairianadin, (ed.,) *Mémoire de M.Pedro Canagaraya Mudaliar*. Pondicherry, Santhanam Press, 1984, p. 64; Labernadie, *op. cit.*, p. 204.

24. *Catalogue des manusrits des Anciennes Archives de l'Inde Française*, tome I, Pondichéry, 1690-1789, Paris, Leroux, 1922, p. 6.
25. Mss NAF, Compagnie des Indes, 1742-54, lettre de la Compagnie à M.Dupleix, gouverneur de Pondichéry, 30 September 1746, BNP.
26. Lettre datée du 8 February 1700, Vol. 990 (Inde), AMEP ; Lettre datée du 3 March 1700, Vol. 963 (Inde), AMEP ; Mss.Fr.6231, fl.25, BNP.
27. Martineau, *op. cit.*, p. 7; Labernadie, *op. cit.*, p. 131; Vinson, *op. cit.*, p. xviii; Martineau, *op. cit.*, pp. 547, 549.
28. Lettre du Père Ducros à M.l'Abbé Ragnet, 17 October 1725, Ariancoupam, *LEC*, tome 13, Paris, Merigot, 1781, p. 336.
29. *Ibid.*
30. Lettre du Père Barbier, Jésuite au Père de la même Compagnie, Pinneipundi, Mission de Carnate, 15 January, *LEC*, tome 13, Paris, Merigot, 1781, pp. 296-297.
31. Lettre de Mathon, prêtre, 21 December 1744, Vol. 993 (Inde), AMEP ; Extrait d'une lettre de Père Calmette au Père de Tournemine, Vencataguiry, 16 september 1737, *LEC*, tome 14, Paris, Merigot, 1781, p. 10 ; Lettre du Père Poissevin de 4 et 16 December 1743 à Madame Hyacinthe, Crichnapouram, *LEC*, *Ibid.*, p. 173 ; Extrait d'une lettre du Père Poissevin au Père d'Irlande, Chandernagore, 11 January 1749, *LEC*, tome 14, Paris, Merigot, 1781, pp. 249-51 ; Castonnet des Fosses, *op. cit.*, p. 155.
32. Lettre du Père Poissevin au Père d'Irlande, Chandernagore, 11 January 1749, *LEC*, tome VIII, Lyon, Vernarel et Cabin, MDCCCXIX.
33. *Ibid.* Lettre du Père X de Saint-Estevan à M.Le Comte de-, Pondichéry, 7 December 1754, *LEC*, tome VIII, Lyon, Vernarel et Cabin, MDCCCXIX ; See also, Launay, op. cit., Vol. I, pp. xxxviii-xxxix.
34. Seconde lettre du Père X de Saint-Estevan, Jésuite à M.Le Comte, 15 November 1755, Karikal, *LEC*, tome 15, Paris, Merigot, 1781
35. Jacques Weber, *Les Etablissements français en Inde au XIXe siècle (1816-1914)*, Paris, Librairie de l'Inde, 1988.Vol. I, p. 575.
36. Rapport de M.Cordier, gouverneur intérimaire des Etablissements Français, non classées, 1829, Archives d'Outre-

mer, Aix en Provence ; See also, J.B.P. More, 'Muslim Evolution and Conversions in Karikal, south India', *Islam and Christian-Muslim relations*, 4, 1, 1993, pp. 65-82, see p. 71.

37. Lettre à M.Tesson, Karikal, 10 July 1833, Vol. 998, p. 776, AMEP ; Lettre de M.Bigot à M.Tesson, 10 July 1833, Vol. 998, p. 776, AMEP ; Les Religieuses du Monastère du Bon pasteur, Bangalore, 20 December 1878, Vol. 1006, Série D, AMEP; Launay, *op. cit.*, Vol. I, pp. 293-94; Weber, *op. cit.*, Vol. :I, p. 576.
38. Weber, *op. cit.*, Vol. I, p. 576.
39. Launay, *op. cit.*, Vol. IV, p. 25.
40. Lettre de M.Fourcade à M.Ligeon, Nangatur, 10 October 1874, Vol. 1004, AMEP; Mgr.Laouenan à MM. Les membres du Conseil de la Propagation de la Foi, 4 November 1870-1 November 1871, Vol. 1004, AMEP; Launay, *op. cit.*, Vol. III, pp. 463-64; Vol. IV, p 25.
41. Lettre de Mgr.Laoueana à MM. Les membres du Conseil de la Propagation de la Foi, Pondichéry, 18 December 1869, Vol. 1004, AMEP.
42. Weber, *op. cit.*, Vol I, p. 576.
43. Launay, *op. cit.*, Vol. IV, p. 71.
44. Lettre de Mgr.chevalier aux Missionnaires, Bangalore, 6 February 1878, Vol. 1006, AMEP ; Lettre de Mgr.Laouenan à Mgr. Hugarin, Evêque de Bayeux, Pondichéry, 28 June 1878, Vol. 1004, AMEP ; Lettre circulaire de Mgr.Laouenan aux Missionnaires de son Vicariat, Pondichéry, April 1877, Vol. 1004, AMEP ; Lettre de Mgr.Laouenan aux Missionnaires de son Vicariat, Pondichéry, 31 December 1877, Vol. 1004, AMEP ; Lettre de M.Fourcade à Mgr. Laouenan du 17 April 1877 et 9 June 1877, Alladhy, Vol. 1004, AMEP; Lettre circulaire de Mgr.Laouenan aux Missionnaires, Pondichéry, 8 July 1878, Vol. 1004, AMEP.
45. Launay, *op. cit.*, Vol. III, p. 31.
46. Origine et état actuel de la Mission Française du Carnate dans les Indes Orientales, Vol. 996, AMEP.
47. Lettre de Mathon, prêtre, 19 October 1744, Vol. 993, AMEP ; See also Robert Caldwell, *The Tinnevely Shanars*, Madras, Christian Knowledge society's Press, 1849; J.Macau, *op. cit.*, pp. 28, 66.
48. Mss.Fr.6231, fl.25, 27, BNP ; Série C2 66, fl.16, Archives Nationales, Paris.

49. Extrait de la lettre du Conseil de la Compagnie, 15 February 1702. Mss.Fr.6231, fl.29, BNP ; Lettre de Mathon, prêtre, 19 October 1744, Vol. 993, AMEP ; Olangier, 1932, pp. 22-23.
50. Procès-verbaux des délibérations du Conseil Souverain de la Compagnie des Indes, 9 March 1714, tome I, Société de l'Histoire de l'Inde Française, Pondichéry, n.d., p. 140 ; Launay, op. cit., Vol. I, see foot note p. lxiv.
51. Mss.NAF 9225, Affaire de la Compagnie des Indes, fl.292, BNP ; Mss.Fr. 6231, fl.30, BNP ; Olangier, op. cit., pp. 22-23.
52. Procès-verbaux des délibérations du Conseil Souverain de la Compagnie des Indes. Mss. Fr.6231, fl.29 ; Mss.NAF, fl.293-295.
53. Mss.Fr.6231, fl.37, BNP ; Mss.NAF 9225, fl.295, BNP.
54. Mss.Fr. 6231, fl.46, BNP ; Mss.NAF, 9225, fl.292-93, BNP.
55. Procès-verbaux des délibérations du Conseil Souverain, 9 March 1714 et 16 November 1714, tome I, société de l'Histoire de l'Inde Française, Pondichéry, n.d., pp. 140-41, 150-51 ; Mss.Fr. 6231, fl.46, BNP.
56. Mss.Fr.6231, fl.54-55, BNP; Olanagier, *op. cit.*, p. 25.
57. Procès-verbaux des délibérations du conseil souverain, 4 February 1715, tome I, Société de l'Histoire de l'Inde Française, Pondichéry, n.d., p. 154 ; Mss.fr.6231, fl.55 ; Mss. NAF 9225, fl.293, BNP ; Olangier, *op. cit.*, p. 26, Weber, *op. cit.*, Vol. I. p. 2.
58. Mss. Fr.6231, fl.55 ; Procès-verbaux des délibérations du Conseil souverain, 4 February 1715, p. 15 ; Mss.Fr. 6231, fl.55, BNP; Olangier, *op. cit.*, p. 28, Launay, *op. cit.*, Vol. I.p. liii.
59. Procès-verbaux des délibérations du Conseil Souverain, 4 et 6 February 1715, pp. 155-56, 162 ; Olangier, *op. cit.*, p. 28.
60. Procès-verbaux des délibérations du Conseil Souverain de la Compagnie des Indes, 1724-35, tome II, Pondichéry, Société de l'Histoire de l'Inde Française, 1913-14, pp. 29-30 ; Olangier, *op. cit.*, pp. 23-26, Vinson, *op. cit.*, pp. 205-08.
61. Olagnier, *op. cit.*, p. 25.
62. Launay, *op. cit.*, Vol. I, p. xxxiv.
63. *Ibid.*, p. 69; Weber, *op. cit.*, Vol. I, 2, 481; Vol. II, p. 718.
64. *Catalogue des Manuscrits des Anciennes Archives de l'Inde Française*, tome I, Pondichéry, 1690-1789, Paris, Leroux, 1922, pp. 9, 14 ; The two orders were republished in Launay, op. cit., Vol. I, Appendix III and IV, pp. 459-60 ; Extrait d'une

lettre du Père Poissevin au Père d'Irlande, Chandernagore, 11 January 1749, *LEC*, tome 14, Paris, Merigot, p. 251 ; Lettre de Mgr.Bonnand, Pondichéry, 13 April 1842, Vol. 1000, p. 86, AMEP ; *LEC*, tome VIII, Pondichéry, 7 December 1759, p. 324.

65. Mss.Fr. 6231, fl.27, 29, 46, 54-55, BNP; Martineau, *op. cit.*, p. 490; Olagnier, *op. cit.*, pp. : 22, 23, 25.
66. Abbe Guyon, *Histoire des Indes Orientales, Anciennes et Modernes*, II Vols, Paris, Pierres, 1744.
67. Labernadie, op. cit., p. 81.
68. Délibération du Conseil Supérieur de Pondichéry, 31 January 1750, republished in Vinson 1894, pp. xxix, lxv-lxvi ; Lettre des Pères Capucins à M.Dupleix et à MM. Du Conseil Supérieur au sujet de la reconstruction d'une pagode, 1750, Vol. 993 (Inde), p. 657, AMEP
69. Vinson, *op. cit.*, p. 198, 207; Martineau, *op. cit.*, p. 490.
70. Marquis de Nazelle. *Dupleix et la défense de Pondichéry*, Paris, Honoré Champion, 1908, pp. 41, 357.
71. Mss. NAF 9357, Collection of the papers of Dupleix, Lettre de Dupleix à son frère, 26 January 1749, BNP.
72. Vinson, *op. cit.*, pp. 196, 207.
73. Lettre de Dupleix à Barthelemy, membre du Conseil de Pondichéry, 26 October 1748, in Marquis de Nazelle, *op. cit.*, p. 363 ; Vinson, *op. cit.*, pp. 205-6; Dodwell, *op. cit*, p. 306.
74. Vinson, *op. cit.*, pp. 207-08.
75. Martineau, *op. cit.*, pp. 492, 503; Vinson, *op. cit.*, pp. 196-97, 202, 204, 228-30.
76. Mss. NAF 9357, Papiers de Dupleix, 232, BNP ; Lettre de Dupleix aux Syndic et Directeurs Généraux, 21 October 1748, in Marquis de Nazelle, *op. cit.*, pp. 338-40.
77. Alfred Martineau, *Dupleix et l'Inde Française, 1742-1744*, Paris, Société de l'histoire des colonies françaises, 1923., pp. 83-84; Castonnet des Fosses, *Dupleix, ses expéditions et ses projets.* Paris, Challamel, 1888, pp. 23-24; Labernadie, *op. cit.*, p. 180; Marquis de Nazelle, *op. cit.*, pp. 129, 218, 224, 417).
78. Lettre de Dupleix, 21 October 1748, in Marquis de Nazelle, *op. cit.*, pp. 338-40 ; Martineau, *op. cit.*, p. 504; Vinson, *op. cit.*, pp. 206, 220.
79. Pierre Bourdat, *Eighteenth Century Pondicherry*, The Historical Society of Pondicherry, 1995, pp. 131-132.

80. Dodwell, *op. cit.*, pp. 306.
81. Martineau, *op. cit.*, pp. 481-490.
82. M.P. Sridharan, *Papers on French colonial Rule in India*, Calicut, Progressive Printers, 1997, p. 35.
83. M.P. Sridharan, *op. cit.*, p. 35. It appears that more than a century afterwards in 1870, a larger-than-life size statue of Dupleix was erected over the granite columns containing Hindu sculptured reliefs. The Hindus seem not to have objected to the installation of the statue over Hindu pillars in those days. But after independence from the French in 1954, the Pondicherry government decided to remove the statue, as it was considered hurting Hindu sentiments, given the fact that it was mounted on Hindu temple pillars. For a few years the statue was relegated to the backyard of the French consulate near the seashore and then it found its place at the southern end of the beach.
84. Lettre du Père Martin, Missionnaire de la Compagnie de Jésus au Père Le Gobien de la même Compagnie, Royaume de Maduré, 1 June 1700, *LEC*, tome 10, Paris, Merigot, 1781, pp. 66-71.
85. Lettre de Père Martin, Missionnaire de la Compagnie de Jésus au Père de Vilette de la même Compagnie, Balasore, 30 January 1699, *LEC*, tome 10, Paris, Merigot, 1781, pp. 44-46.
86. Lettre du Père de Bourges, Jésuite à Mme. La Comtesse de Sondé, Mission de Maduré, 21 September 1713, *LEC*, tome 12, Paris, Merigot, 1781, p. 77. See also *LEC*, tome 10, Paris, Merigot, 1781, see Préface.
87. Lettre du Père Bouchet au Père de la même Compagnie Jésuite, *LEC*, tome 13, MDLCLXXXI, pp. 45, 50.
88. Origine, Progrès et état actuel de la Mission Française du Carnate dans les Indes Orientales, 26 May 1802, Vol. 996, AMEP ; Lettre de l'Evêque de Tabraca du 14 October 1777, Pondichéry à M.Alari, prêtre et directeur du Séminaire des Missions Etrangères à Paris, Vol. 995, AMEP ; Lettre de M.Dubois, Missionnaire à M.Boiret, 26 May 1802, Pondichéry, Vol. 996, AMEP ; Lettre du Père Saignes à Sainte Hyacinthe, 3 July 1736, Attipakam, *LEC*, tome 14, Paris, Merigot, 1781, p. 41.
89. Lettre de M.Dubois, missionnaire à M.Boiret, 26 May 1802, Pondichéry, Vol. 996, AMEP ; S. Delacroix, (ed.,) *Histoire Universelle des Missions Catholiques–Les Missions Modernes*,

Vol. II, Paris, Librairie Grund, 1957, pp. 43-48 ; P.Thomas, *Christians and Christianity in India and Pakistan*, London, George Allen, Unwin Ltd, 1954. pp. 44-75.

90. *Ibid.*
91. Mss. NAF, Extrait de la lettre de M.Hebert, Gouverneur de Pondichéry, 15 February 1710, BNP ; Lettre du Père Le Caron, Jésuite à Mesdames les Sœurs Religieuses Ursulines de la Mission du Carnate, 20 November 1720, *LEC*, tome 13, Paris, Merigot, 1781, pp. 201, 210-211 ; Lettre du Père Etienne Le Gac, 10 January 1709, *LEC*, tome 11, Paris, Merigot, 1781, pp. 208, 217-18.
92. Lettre du Père Bouchet, Jésuite au Père Baltus, Jésuite, *LEC*, tome 11, Paris, Merigot, 1781, p. 44 ; Lettre du Père de la Carre au Père Mourgues, Jésuites, Pondichéry, 30 January 1709, *LEC*, tome 11, Paris, Merigot, 1781, p. 216.
93. Lettre du M.Mollet, du 17 February 1788, Vol. 995, AMEP; Seconde lettre du Père Martin, Jésuite à Père de Vilette, Jésuite, *LEC*, tome 11, Paris, Merigot, 1781, pp. 164-65 ; Lettre d'un missionnaire des Indes, *LEC*, tome 15, Paris, Merigot, 1781, p. 127 ; Lettre du Père de la Carre, Pondichéry, 30 January 1709, *LEC*, tome 11, Paris, Merigot, 1781, p. 216.
94. Lettre de l'Evêque de Tabraca à M.Alari, 14 October 1777, Vol. 995(Inde), AMEP ; Mss.Fr. 8971, lettre de M.Hebert, gouverneur de Pondichéry aux plaintes du R.P.Tachard, supérieur des Jésuites de Pondichéry, 20 August 1708, fl.19.
95. Copie d'une lettre à Mgr.l'Evêque de Ceram du 6 January 1781, Vol. 995 (Inde), AMEP ; Launay, *op. cit.*, Vol. I, p. xviii.
96. S. Jeyaseela Stephen, The Diary of Rangappa Thiruvengadam Pillai; 1761-1768, translated from original Tamil, Pondicherry, 2001, pp. 219-220, 224, 230, 231. Lettre du Mgr. Brigot aux Directeurs du Séminaire, 22 October 1777, Pondichéry, Vol. 995 (Inde), AMEP ; See also *Le Progrès*, 25 July 1886.
97. Lettre de M.Perrin, Pondichéry, 14 November 1778, Vol. 995 (Inde), AMEP.
98. Lettre de l'Evêque de Tabraca du 5 March 1780 et la lettre de l'Evêque de Ceram du 23 March 1780, Pondichéry, Vol. 995(Inde), AMEP; see also *Journal de Brigot*, No.31, 12 January 1779, reproduced in Launay, op. cit., Vol. I, p. 102.
99. Copie d'une lettre à Mgr. L'Evêque de Ceram, 6 January 1781, Vol. 995, AMEP.

100. *Ibid.* Lettre de M.Boiret ? du 2 March 1778, Pondichéry, Vol. 995 (Inde), AMEP ; Lettre du 5 March 1780 de l'Evêque de Tabraca, Pondichéry, Vol. 995(Inde), AMEP ; Lettre du 23 March 1780 de l'Evêque de Ceram, Pondichéry, Vol. 995, AMEP.
101. Launay, *op. cit.*, Vol. I, pp. 103-04.
102. Lettre de M.Mollot, 17 February 1788, Vol. 995 (Inde), AMEP.
103. Copie d'une lettre à Mgr. L'Eveque de Ceram, 6 January 1781, Vol. 995 (Inde), AMEP.
104. Lettre de l'Evêque de Tabraca à M. Alari, 14 October 1777, Vol. 995 (Inde), AMEP; see also the letter of Mgr. Brigot addressed to Rome in 1777, reproduced in Launay, *op. cit.*, Vol. I, pp. 98-100.
105. Mss.Fr.8971, Lettre de M.Hebert à R.P.Tachard, supérieur des Jésuites de Pondichéry, 20 August 1708, fl.19; Copie d'une lettre à Mgr. L'Evêque de Ceram, 6 January 1781, Vol. 995 (Inde), AMEP; Lettre de la Propagande à Rome à Mgr. Brigot, 26 September 1778, reproduced in Launay, *op. cit.*, Vol. I, pp101-02.
106. Susan Bayly, *Saints, Goddesses and Kings: Muslims and Christians in South Indian Society, 1700-1900*, Cambridge, Cambridge University Press, 1989, pp. 13, 458.
107. Louis Dumont, *Homo Hierarchicus*, Chicago, University of Chicago, 1970, p. 211.
108. Louis Dumont, *op. cit.*, p. 211.
109. Francis Robinson, 'Islam and Muslim Society in South Asia', *Contributions to Indian Sociology*, Vol. 17, (2), 1983, p. 187.
110. Leena More, *English East India Company and the Local Rulers in Kerala: A Case Study of Attigal and Travancore*, Tellicherry, IRISH, 2003.

16

Social Stratification and Change in Orissa Under the English East India Company and the Crown

Pratyusa Kumar Mandal

Social stratification has generally been understood as the horizontal division of society into groups or categories that are governed by structurally determined relationships in many ways[1]. In India these social categories are mostly found to be consisted of an ethnic or caste group or a number of caste groups levelled off as a social class. From purely conceptual perspectives the caste and class configurations posit some problem about their points of convergence. But substantive super-imposition of colonial influence on Indian society during the 19th century made these points of convergence more frequent. Consequently studies on social stratification in India, especially pertaining to the colonial period, inclined in favour of laying greater stress not only on endogamy which as a traditional mechanism helped in maintaining status and life-style related boundaries among caste groups but also on the economic aspect of stratification which along with its attendant clout acted as a source of maintenance and reproduction of social stratification[2]. Thus social stratification as a conceptual whole emerged as a lucrative domain of research, though the obsessive phenomenon of caste permeating all social processes in India could not be wished away.

In the context of Orissa, the flurry of changes that affected the social fabric in many ways in over fifty years before the famine of 1866 could not particularly prevent caste from determining the system of ranking in the society. Throughout the entire post-famine period also, caste remained the essential bulwark round which every issue of modernisation inescapably gravitated. In some respects there did take place a blurring of caste distinctions due to fundamental economic changes introduced by the British during this period. But in others, there were indications of the caste consciousness becoming more acute than ever before. Caste continued to exert considerable influence on the prospect of upward social mobility of any group in its place of origin. Simultaneously, increasing caste consciousness also impressed upon the existing dominant groups in the local society to make every effort to maintain hierarchical status quo. In view of this reality, without of course denying the flux that the caste structure experienced during this period, it would be quite legitimate to study social stratification in Orissa giving caste its due prominence.

As regards the linkage between social stratification and change, there is no gain saying the naturalness with which the two processes converge both theoretically as well as substantively. Thus any objective analysis of the system of social stratification would not be complete without a reference to its corresponding processes of social change. But in keeping with the theme of the present study the focus here would be more on the issue of social stratification in Orissa from the point of view of its distinctive historical experience.

A Reappraisal of the Sources

However, before entering into the subject of social stratification in Orissa it is pertinent to point out the pitfalls involved in such an attempt. Superficially a vast range of literature pertaining to the period under review is available regarding the social structure of Orissa. But on closer scrutiny a greater part of this literature ensconced in the contemporary gazetteers, accounts of the British scholar-administrators, periodical reports of revenue settlement and the decennial census reports is found fruitlessly overlapping and exceedingly concerned with the weird dynamics of the local society than with the real issues of social stratification. Quite typical of the colonial mind-set, whenever the characteristically conservative society of Orissa required any mentioning, a note was added here and there to place on record only those social changes which were believed to be the blissful outcomes of the so-called beneficial measures of the colonial administration. Even the reconstruction of the local history by the official compilers of the contemporary gazetteers was an amplified version of this biased view of the local society. Attempts were made at every stage to fit in the processes of the local society with the master imperial scheme. The reports of the revenue settlements in this regard, conforming to the demands of the discipline, confined their inquiry into the existing relationships between different social groups and the types and sizes of land-holdings which each such group had in its possession. Thus, the decennial census reports are only of some help as they supply the much needed information on the pattern of population distribution and the associated social structure. But here too the local society did receive a cavalier treatment. Much of the crucial local information necessary to put in place the picture of social stratification was in most cases brazenly merged with the general imperial or provincial statistics. Under such circumstances, a systematic effort to remedy the situation was made only after the country's independence from 1951 onwards by compiling district-wise census data. But it was also the year since when the collection of information on castes and communities was discontinued to the detriment of prospective socio-historical studies. In all fairness, however, it can be said that in spite of these obvious handicaps the census reports are still a dependable body of documents which possess useful material on the situational and structural responses of the different sections of local society to the processes that were set into motion by the colonial and post-colonial governments. Unfortunately in Orissa social historians have made very little use of these reports, despite the fact that a combination of these reports with the rest of the historical sources could go a long way in presenting a discernible picture of the state's social structure as it evolved during the 19th and early 20th centuries.

Pre-Nineteenth Century Social Evolution in Orissa

In ancient times, parts of the present-day Orissa formed the "extensive, populous and fairly civilised kingdom" of Kalinga, which emerged to the full light of history with its invasion by Ashoka Maurya in about BC 261. Prior to it the epic Mahabharata only mentioned about the sacred river Baitarani, associated with Styx of the Hindu mythology. In its early verses the epic enjoined upon the pilgrims from the *Aryavarta* not to visit Kalinga as the *Kshatriyas* there "had become out-castes"[3]. The injunction against pilgrims' visiting Kalinga was perhaps warranted as Orissa by the time of the Mahabharata had not yet come within the full ambit of *Aryavarta* (land of the Aryas). Apparently, other than the predominant *Odras*, from whose name the nomenclature of the place was derived in the Sanskrit works prior to the Fifth Century AD[4], Orissa was peopled mostly by such primitive tribes as the *Savaras*, *Juangs*, *Panas*, and *Kewats*. References in the Mahabharata and subsequently in the *Baudhayana Dharmasutra*, which required persons visiting Kalinga to "offer a sacrifice in penance", possibly pointed to the sporadic early Aryan immigrants, who came amidst the numerous non-Aryan people of Kalinga and lost their castes. The self-proclaimed *Mastan* and the *Sarua Brahmins* of north Balasore, who wore sacred thread though, did not care about observing the usual rites associated with the *Brahmins* during the early Nineteenth Century, were perhaps the descendants of these early Aryan immigrants. However, brisk maritime activities in the succeeding centuries on the Kalinga coast linked Orissa scrupulously with the country's northern plains. Thus one could find the later verses in the Mahabharata proclaim the existence of noble men (allusion to an Aryan) in Kalinga besides *tirthas* (centres of religious merit), which were worth visiting[5].

In between the Sixth and Fourth Century BC, when the whole of the Indo-Gangetic plain was in ferment, heterodox sects like Buddhism and Jainism also found fertile grounds in Kalinga. Buddhism specially received ample royal patronage after Ashoka's conquest of Kalinga and its subsequent annexation with the Mauryan Empire. However, after the Mauryan yoke was overthrown by the Chedis, Jainism gained upper hand in winning royal favour from the dynasty's ablest king, Kharavela. Henceforth the two sects competed with each other and alternately found royal patronage from succeeding ruling dynasties until AD 846, when the first reigning queen of the Bhaumakara dynasty, Tribhuvana Mahadevi, effected a turning point in not only the history of the Bhaumas but also in the socio-religious history of Orissa. "During her rule the country advanced in three branches (of administration), the foes were extirpated, the glory spread abroad and there was (religious) harmony among the people. With her head sanctified with the lotus-like feet of Hari, she enjoyed an unparalleled fortune and thought that there was no other work for her to do."[6] The Neulpur charter of Subhakaradeva I (790) and the Terundia charter of Subhakaradeva II (809) speak about their accepting the Brahminical socio-religious order with the *varnas* put into their respective places despite the fact that personally these rulers were Buddhists in their religious persuasion. Naturally, to give effect to the new policies, there was a need for them to encourage the immigration of Brahmins from *Madhyadesa* into Orissa by offering the latter extensive land grants. Besides, these Bhauma kings also became instrumental in facilitating the use of Sanskrit in royal inscriptions and in the writing of Buddhist texts.

Brahminical Hinduism received a further impetus in Orissa under the rule of the Somavamsi kings (922-1119). Being protagonists of the Brahminical culture, the Somavamsi kings engaged themselves in massive construction activities of temples. Mahashivagupta Yayati I (922-955), who is credited with the extension of the Somavamsi power to the coastal strip of Orissa in 931, particularly established the tradition of seeking Brahminical sanction to his regal authority by inviting ten thousand Brahmins from Kanauj to perform the *Ashwamedha* sacrifice on the bank of the river Baitatani at Jajpur. However, in a land where Brahmanism had just begun coalescing with the long favoured heterodox sects, Yayati I, could not escape the politico-religious compulsion to ascribe to a more syncretic cult. And this compulsion persisted despite his achieving impressive military victories to back his claim to the throne. Thus in 949 he built the Temple of Purushottama at Puri. This marked a turning point not only in the life of Yayati I, but also of Orissa. His successor, Mahashivagupta Yayati II (1025-1040) extended the highly permeable syncretic influence of the Jagannath cult by constructing the monumental Lingaraj temple in honour of Lord Shiva at Bhubaneswar. Like the *daitapatis* (saura servants of the deity) of the Jagannath temple, whose legitimate share in the worship of the Lord had been recognised since the day of the establishment of the temple of Puroshottama, Yayati II appointed *vadus* (*sudra* priests) as the custodians of the Lingaraj Temple. These *sudra* priests have been described in the sixty second chapter of the *Ekamara Purana* as the offspring of a Savara mother and Siddhabhuti, a *Saiva* saint. The Brahmins took a share in the worship of the Lord only much later[7]. Similarly, the custom of offering cooked rice to the deity in the Lingaraj Temple and then partaking of it without observing caste distinctions copiously followed the system that was prevalent in the Purushottama temple.

These initial efforts of the Somavamsi kings to build up a pan-Orissa empire by harnessing the syncretic force of the Jagannath cult was epitomised in the Twelfth Century, after the Eastern Gangas acquired sovereign power over Orissa and its most illustrious king Chodagangadeva built the famous Sri Jagannatha Temple on the shore of Puri between 1134 and 1147 on the site of the pre-existing Puroshottama Narasimha Temple. Of course like Yayati I, for a conqueror in search of legitimacy, there might have been political compulsion behind Chodaganga's construction of the shrine of Jagannath, yet founded upon a syncretic platform it was possible for the Jagannath cult to permeate the whole of the regional life in Orissa. Other than in the religio-cultural domain, the cult's integrative force was cemented across the kingdom by providing for special *debottar* lands called *amrita monohi.* These land grants, meant for the upkeep of the worship of Jaganath at Puri, could still be found in all *parganas* when the British came to occupy Orissa in 1803. Trustee-holders of such grants were usually the Brahmin residents of Puri or its neighbourhood, who collected rents at certain intervals through agents. Not surprisingly, therefore, in early 20th century nationalist Oriya leaders struggling for a separate provincial status for Orissa were repeatedly harking back to this only unquestioned symbol of Oriya national life.

The upswing in the overarching influence of the Jagannath cult continued throughout the period of the Suryavamsi rule (1435 and 1538). The tense political situation arising out of incessant military pressure from both the northern and southern fronts did not allow these rulers any respite from either wars or worries about their personal sovereignty. The theocratic notion of kingship which had been popularised by the Ganga kings Anangabhima III (1211-1238) and Bhanudeva II (1306-1328) was, therefore, more copiously followed by them. Kapilendradeva (1435-1468) particularly cautioned his recalcitrant feudatories of offending Lord Jagannath if ever they defied his authority (the defiance of the Gajapati supposed to be the living icon of the Lord amounted to sacrilegious disrespect for Lord Jagannath). Ironically it was partly due to such internal dissension that Orissa ultimately lost its political independence to the Afghan chief of Bengal, Luleiman Karrani in 1568.

Once politically subservient, Orissa became a theatre of struggle among alien powers for mastery. Not only that the conquerors bequeathed some legacies but they also added components of population which became permanent part and parcel of social structure in Orissa. The Afghans particularly contributed to agricultural expansion by granting *jagirs* to the old soldiers. The Mughals, who conquered Orissa in 1592, effected more changes in Orissa's revenue administration. Theoretically though land belonged to the State, yet the Mughals gave the *raiyats* both *patta* and *kabuliyat* to know the amount of rent they were to pay for their land. Whereas the Hindu Kings formerly depended upon the village headmen called *muqaddams* for collection of land revenue, the Mughal system of *tankha raqmi* (revenue settlement) depended upon intermediary officials like *chaudhuries* and *vilayati kanungoes*, also known as *taluqdars*, for the same purpose. Besides, the Mughals also granted *jagirs* both to Muslim and non-Muslim Bengalis, who along with other revenue officials and chieftains, created various types of sub-tenancies in land. To some extent this had led to hierarchical fragmentation of land rights in Orissa before the Marathas came swooping down to rule upon it. Besides, the Mughal administration also injured Orissa's interests in other significant ways. Politically, instead of upholding the provincial character of Orissa, they reduced it to the status of a mere appendage to the Bengal *suba*. Further, to shatter Lord Jagannath's centrality to Orissa's national life, the Mughals beginning with the reign of Aurangzeb imposed *jijiya* on the pilgrims coming to Puri. Aurangzeb's policy of religious persecution coerced a number of premier families of Orissa to get converted into Islam. The notable Bhatta Brahmin family, who had received land grants from Prushottamadeva Gajpati in 1483, in a village near Rupsa in the district of Balasore had thus to embrace Islam. Till date his descendants are living in the Garhpada village of the said district as Muslims.[8]

However, in the realm of culture the Mughal period bequeathed two important traditions. The tolerant strands among the Hindus and the Muslims were harnessed by the current *bhakti* and *sufi* movements to make *Satyapir* an acceptable common deity for both communities. The *sufi* saints, locally called *fakirs*, could in particular win the indulgence of faith among the common folks in Orissa. Fakir Mohan Senapati recalls in his autobiography how his grand mother prefixed *Fakir* to his name to keep her promise made to two Muslim saints in Balasore after he recovered from illness.[9]

Under the Marathas, who occupied Orissa in 1755 (after the rule of Nawab Alivardi Khan of Bengal), Orissa's maritime fortune was further enhanced. The port of Balasore in northern Orissa particularly bustled with trading activities. This returned the Marathas considerable amount of revenue especially from the export of large quantity of salt to Berar and Bengal. Hostilities between the English East-India Company and the Marathas over this lucrative trade in the end led to the British conquest of Orissa in 1803.

Having such a long survey of Orissa's pre-British history here might look gratuitous. But to comprehend properly the modern Orissan society and the various changes which came upon it, this survey provides an essential background. It is also important to note that during all the tumultuous centuries of her early history Orissan society was steadily crystallized into a cognizable entity with a specific from and inherent functioning rationale. Particularly, under the Somavamsi and the Suryavamsi rules, Orissa acquired a definitive national character woven around the hallowed symbol of Lord Jagannath.

Pre-19th Century Social Organisation in Orissa

The economy of pre-19th century Orissa, at least in the few centuries preceding its annexation by the British, was vibrant despite occasional horrors of famine. Despite the fact that the currency of coins in Orissa predated the Gupta Age as has been attested by the Bhadrak inscription of king Gana, "provisions were exceedingly cheap, *cowries* were the only medium of exchange among the people generally, and there was no demand for a gold or silver currency"[10]. But politically, the kings, in pursuance of their efforts to popularise the theocratic basis of their kingship, had taken enough care to keep Lord Jagannath safely ensconced in the religious and political heart centres of the State. Despite their indulgence in enormous building activities, the Suryavamsi and the Gajapati kings, no Jagannath temples were built outside the precincts of Puri and Cuttack till the late-15th century.[11] For the Brahmins this policy secured the position of primacy in Orissan society, who in turn bestowed legitimacy alike upon both the lawful as well as the usurping successors to the throne. Throughout the medieval period this tacit nexus, between the State's ruling elite and the premier priestly caste, manifested itself in the political sovereigns and their feudatories, in the names of the sovereigns, granting tax-free *brahmottar* lands to the Brahmins for the latter's settlement and upkeep. Among the *lakhiraj* (rent-free) lands of all kinds the *brahmottar* land were the ones which "granted either to individual Brahmins or to a body of Brahmins forming a Shasan or Brahmana village for their maintenance" were distributed very evenly over each *pargana* of the districts.[12] The donees in all these cases were enjoined upon the obligation to invoke divine blessings on the donor's name three times a day. This provision was absent from other *sanads*, as the invocations of Brahmins and Vaishnavas alone were considered of any avail.

Apart from this pre-eminent position enjoyed by the Brahmins, the social structure below remained fluid because of historical exigencies. Firstly, due to virtual militarisation of the State by the Somavamsi and the Suryavamsi kings all castes and communities, not excepting Brahmins at times, were obliged to render military service in times of emergency. But it were the men in arms employed as regular soldiers in the service of the kings, drawn mainly from the numerous tribal communities and cultivating castes, who formed a new sub-caste called *Khandayats*. With land grants and new respectable titles like *Senapati*, *Nayaka*, *Gadanayaka*, *Patra*, *Mahapatra*, *Behera*, *Dalabehera*, *Jena*, *Badajena*, *Pradhana*, *Samala*, *Rauta*, *Khuntia*, *Parichha*, *Parija*, *Padhihari*, *Dandapani*, *Dandapata* etc., these neo-*kshatriyas* claimed intermediary social status and became willing clients of the Brahmins for ritual prestige. In the areas of their relatively new settlement the Brahmins out of self interest and in view of the royalty's dependence on this predominantly *sudra*-turned-*Khandayat* populace validated this vertical social mobility by becoming the latter's obliging priests.[13]

Secondly, because of the kings' necessity to rule with the help of a regular hierarchy of civilian officers and scribes in an overtly centralised political system, large-scale recruitment of civilian officers and scribes took place offering scope for men of lower *varnas* to move up the social scale by holding such offices at the village and local levels, which gradually became hereditary and crystallized into many sub-castes like *Srikarana*, *Pattanayaka*, *Mohanty*, *Kanungo* etc. following their functional responsibility. During the later Ganga period these sub-castes were ascribed the omnibus local caste-name of *Karana*.

However, the ascendance of Jagannath cult and the spread of its syncretic ethos did not allow the stratification on caste lines to assume rigidity in the local society. Traditions were consciously built up around Lord Jagannath hailing him as *Purushottama* (best among men) and *Patitapavana* (liberator of the down-trodden). These two exemplary qualities vested in a single deity led a pan-Orissan nationalistic credo to gain currency. The Suryavamsi kings coming from humble origin consciously cultivated it from the top while from below Sarala Dasa became its great representative personality, who composed the *Mahabharata*, *Chandi Purana* and *Vilanka Ramayana* in Oriya during the 15th century. At a time when Sanskrit literature had kept the social elite captivated, Sarala Dasa, himself a *sudra* cultivator and a man of little social consequence, responded to the call of the time and brought about a revolutionary change in the destiny of the folk language of Orissa by making it an effective vehicle of high literature. This historic achievement had a levelling off effect. Sarala Dasa not only became the maker and originator of a new literary movement in Orissa but also led men of all castes to shake off their prejudice against Oriya language and to conjointly contribute to it.[14] Sarala Dasa particularly lent moral and cultural currency to myriad folk beliefs and social practices in his voluminous works, which are still approved by men of all castes and *varnas* in Orissa.

Fourthly, the propagation and spread of reformist socio-religious movements also contributed to the upward mobility of the lower *varnas* even touching off the lowliest to bring about the new order of social stratification in medieval Orissa. The reformist attitude, which Sarala Dasa had set into motion into the Brahminical perception of a ritually stratified society, was carried forward by other equally respected Vaishnavite saints like Achyutananda Khuntia, Balaram Mohapatra, Yoshovanta Mallick and Ananta Mohanty all of whom belonged to non-Brahmin castes. These saints received royal patronage from Prataprudradeva Gajapati and their works in folk language reinterpreting the Sanskrit scriptures gained wide currency. The story of Sriya *Chandaluni*, depicted in the *Lakshmi Purana* of Balarama Dasa *alias* Mahapatra, which portrayed the legend of goddess Lakshmi going outside the limits of the temple city breaking the norms of social hierarchy to accept the worship of Sriya, a *chandala* (untouchable) woman, being moved by the latter's pious life-style and devotion despite an injunction to the contrary by her husband Lord Jagannath and his elder brother Lord Balabhadra, touched the social conscience of every Oriya. The Purana narrates how the Goddess did not find any women belonging to the so-called upper *varnas* leading as much a pious life as Sriya within the confines of the temple city. No doubt, the Goddess was banished from the temple for her deviant behaviour. But following untold misery suffered by Lord Jagannath and Lord Balabhadra, when she was sought to be brought back by the duo, in this case the perpetrators of *varna* discrimination, she agreed to oblige only on the condition that thereafter no discrimination would be observed within the *Sri Mandira* (Jagannath Temple) in partaking of the *mahaprasada* (cooked offerings to the Lord) that she cooks for the Lords. Not only that the legend became a norm in the Jagannath temple but people throughout Orissa started observing the event religiously on every Thursday of the Oriya month of *Margasira* (November) every year.[15]

The reformist sentiment of the Orissa society became much stronger when Sri Chaitanya came to Puri in 1510. Sri Chaitanya's influence is held by Prof. R. D. Banerjee as responsible for the weakening of the military spirit in Orissa. But other than Vaishnavism, the Sakta-Tantrik and Nath cults also contributed historically to the process of lower caste movements, which not only invested respectability to such castes down the social hierarchy but also brought about some caste assimilation at the lower levels in Orissa. Khageswasr Mahapatra finds many of these *tantrik* teachers (*Siddhacharyas*) to be of untouchable castes like *Kewat*, *Mochi* and *Dom*.[16] However, the contention that the upward mobility of lower *varnas* and the emergence of economically as well as socio-politically dominant intermediary castes resulted in a marked decline in the status of Brahmins in local society[17] does not hold good on several counts.

The Gajapatis revered the Brahmins in a manner which they never did to any other caste group. The induction of non-Brahmins as priests in the Jagannath Temple was a conscious attempt at building up the cult as universalistic. But the internal functioning of the temple and its methods of worship remained for ever Brahminical. The Brahmins at times took to other professions because of political and economic exigencies but that did not interfere in their caste ranking or ritual status. Sarala Dasa himself tells *ad nauseum* that different rites associated with the social life of caste Hindus were conducted thoroughly in accordance with the Vedic rules. The contention that Brahmins ought only to engage themselves in worship and the study of religious scriptures is more of a theoretical postulation having less relevance in temporal life.

In sum, the social order that evolved in pre-British Orissa was, therefore, one in which the Brahmins occupied the top stratum. In the intermediate level, the Khandayats and the Karanas, both castes being drawn from the variegated castes and *varnas*, contended with each other to occupy the rank next to the Brahmins. As a result of increasing sanskritisation and due to the softening of the social posture by the Brahmins from the top and various reformist movements exerting pressure constantly from below, *Sudras* acquired typical social respectability, though there occured a general fall in the social outlook. Under the over-lordship of the Bhaumas the women in Orissa enjoyed a distinctly higher status. But their status received a considerable setback in the succeeding centuries. Pre-puberty marriages became a social practice and sought to be legitimised on the grounds of folk belief that "if a daughter attains puberty in her father's house the manes shall sink to hell". *Purdah* system also gained acceptability among the people. Women covering their head became a standard practice in consequence. Upholding political independence at all costs and martial machismo could have been a possible reason which took its toll on social life in this regard.

The Colonial Period, 1803-1865

Orissa came under colonial rule in 1803. Long before it, since June 1633, the colonialists as traders had associated with Balasore to use it as a spring-board in quest of their commercial and subsequently political interests in Bengal. All these years they had carried saltpetre, taffetas, raw silk, sannas, cotton yarn, turmeric, tincall, dussettes or coarse sail cloth from Orissa and in return brought back broad cloth and lead from Europe. Among the merchandise taken towards the end of the 18th century, it was salt manufactured in Balasore that had been found commercially more lucrative. The English East-India Company used to import salt from Orissa at the average rate of 68, 269 *maunds* per annum into Bengal where it had established a monopoly over both manufacture and sale of salt. Consequent upon the adverse effect which the smuggled and cheaper Orissa salt was giving to the company's trade in Bengal, it had urged the Marathas to grant the Company the exclusive right to buy Orissa salt. But given that the Marathas were earning as much as rupees two lakhs per annum from the salt sold in Bengal they had shunned the proposal off-hand. Thus finding the right opportunity during the second Anglo-Maratha war, the East India Company seized Balasore, Cuttack and Puri through the force of arm and by the Treaty of Deogaon, signed on 17th December 1803, got from the Bhonsla Raja of Nagpur, Raguhji, in perpetual sovereignty "the province of Cuttack including the port and the district of Balasore".

The Marathas despite frequent charges of rapacity had found for themselves some socio-political context in Orissa. They had restored to a great extent the pre-Mughal system of revenue administration by minimising the role of intermediaries in revenue collection. In total only 32 *amils* or revenue commissioners had been kept for collection of revenue from all the 150 *parganas* into which the entire *Mughalbandi* area had been divided. The *amils* managed their job only through two sets of officials namely, the *taluqdars* and the *mukaddams*. The *taluqdars* collected the revenue from the *raiyats* of *pahikasth* villages and the *mukkadams* from the *mukaddami* ones. Further the Marathas respected neither *zamindari* nor *mukkaddami* tenures when it was considered suitable for them to collect direct from the cultivators of the soil[18]. Among other measures, the Marathas even after taking over the administration of the Jagannath Temple in Puri, did not interfere with the ritual status of the Gajapati, who still continued to exercise the regal privilege of conferring titles on the inhabitants of Mughalbandi and the Garhjat countries[19]. It is clear from the records that no title granted by the Maratha Government was considered to confer any distinction in Orissa until confirmed by the Raja of Khurda. Being Hindus, the Marathas also lavishly donated to the Jagannath temple as well as to Brahmins. In times of distress, resulting out of floods or droughts, tax remissions as well as *taccavi* advances to the cultivators were given. The Marathas also expended money in settling agriculture and in building embankments to prevent flooding. One such embankment constructed at the mouth of river Subarnarekha did immense good to the people of Balasore[20]. In short, the Marathas unwittingly arrested the process of further fragmentation of the medieval Orissan society on caste and class lines.

Unlike the Marathas, however, the colonial power had no raison d'etre in seeking socio-political legitimacy, its colonial agenda being long drawn up to be effected in any newly acquired territory. Their supreme motive was to further colonial economic interests using the pretext of ending lawlessness and relieving the country form the misrule of native tyrants to establish a just administration. But, no sooner did the Company Government post itself to regular administration of the country its inner motives started ruefully tumbling out.

Its economic policies brought ruination to native industries and affected a shift from a situation of local economic self-sufficiency to helpless dependence on metropolitan economy. While the colonial rulers remained a class apart its revenue administration created an intermediate class of landed aristocracy, which perpetuated itself by exploiting the cultivating under-class with no constructive obligation in return. Under the garb of organising the administrative system outsiders, mainly from Bengal, were brought in great numbers. This created a pernicious cycle of sub-colonialism and demoralised the erstwhile forward sections of Orissan society who could have worked as a moderating lever between the emergent colonial power and long-term native interests. Monetisation of economy and drain of wealth from the land of its production too ensured: (i) economic deprivation leading to large scale migration of lower-class people to different *Garhjats* (Princely States) and to Calcutta as menial workers and servants; (ii) rise of a class of money-lenders and usurers and, above all, (iii) distressing poverty. The policy of non-intervention in people's affairs did not allow the society to prepare itself to readjust to an entirely new emergent system. The natural advantage was, therefore, hijacked by rank outsiders, who had no social commitment whatsoever.

Consequent upon these developments by the middle of the 19th century, a new social structure evolved in place of the one that existed in medieval Orissa. This social structure with an inclination to be more stratified on economic lines ensured weakening of social empathy between the upper and the lower strata in society. In other words, in the emergent society the earlier system of ritual-ranking steadily gave way to a new system where variegated number of caste-groups began getting clustered into either higher or lower strata commensurate with their economic status. Social mobility hence depended more upon who benefited most out of the government policies.

Caste System

The basic component which permeated and to a great extent defined the Hindu Society was caste. Conceptually a caste was based on the principles of (a) endogamy, (b) hereditary occupation that went with it, (c) the number of taboos it practiced, (d) the amount of authority it exercised on its fellow members and, above all, (e) the position it held in the ritual hierarchy of the society. The first census taken in 1872 in the district of Balasore in Orissa returned as many as 99 castes. These castes were graded into fourteen categories such as, (1) Hindu superior castes, (2) intermediate castes, (3) trading castes, (4) pastoral castes, (5) castes engaged in preparing food, (6) agricultural castes, (7) castes engaged in personal service, (8) artisan castes (9) weaver castes, (10) labouring castes, (11) castes occupied in selling fish and vegetables, (12) boating and fishing castes (13) dancer, musician, beggar and vagabond castes, and (14) persons of unknown or unspecified castes. W. W. Hunter, who reproduced Mr. C. F. Magrath's separate *District Census Compilation for Balasore*[21] rearranged these castes into four broad categories, viz. (1) High castes, (2) Respectable *Sudra* Castes, (3) Intermediate *Sudra* Castes and (4) Low castes. This reclassified order in the view of Hunter stood "as far as possible according to the rank which they hold in local public esteem". Broadly it was a hint at the change which had come about in the local society under the impact of the colonial governance. The fact that Mr. Hunter felt inclined to include *Brahmins, Rajputs, Karanas, Khandayats, Baidyas, Ganakas, Bhatas, Shagird Peshas* and *Baisya-Banias* in the same strata, who traditionally would have belonged to *Brahmana, Vaishya* and *Sudra* categories in a descending order, smacked of new social dynamics that had come to assume a quiet significance in colonial Orissa.

The *Karanas*, whose response to the demands of the colonial state was unequivocal, accounted for the maximum number of educated men in Orissa by the turn of the 19th century. Commenting on their rapid rise in the echelons of colonial administration Mr. O'Malley wrote in 1907:

"Among the more educated classes the Brahmans are obstinate and bigoted, but they are of a refined and educated type; and the writer caste of *Karanas*, or as they are called locally *Mahantis*, have as high a reputation for acuteness as the *Kayasthas* of Bihar. The old reproach of unfitness for government employment can no longer be levelled against them. The purely foreign element has almost disappeared from among the ministerial establishment, and even the domiciled Bengali who has adopted the country as his own is losing ground before the advancing native of Orissa. Young Oriya graduates passing out of the Ravenshaw College at Cuttack are entering the sub-ordinate executive service and at the present rate of recruitment, there will in a short time be a staff of Oriya officers sufficient for the recruitment of the whole Division"[22].

The achievement undoubtedly brought a swift turn around in the social position of the *Karanas* who not before long worked as *daftaris* (head clerks) in the offices of the zam*i*ndars or as *gomastas* (accountants) in the houses of the Teli businessmen. Through matrimonial relations they generally drew social sustenance from both the *Khandayat* and the *Chasa* castes. But with their status substantially enhanced in the 20th century, they began practicing strict endogamy[23]. By 1931, there were as many as 372 literate *Karanas* in every 1000 with one literate female to about 6 literate males. [24]

In comparison, the number of literates among Brahmins by the same time was 136 per male and the disparity was twice as great in the female sex as it was in the male sex. For fourteen literate Brahmin males, there was only one literate Brahmin female. Thus the obvious advantage in the realm of education and government service which the *Karanas* could acquire enabled them to rise vertically up in the changed social set up even at times disputing the position held by the Brahmins in it.

What the *Karanas* achieved in great measure, the *Khandayats* gained in bits and pieces. Once a claimant to the status of *Kshatriyas* in Orissa, the *Khandayat* caste was first woefully out-stripped by the immigrant Bengalis and then by the *Karanas* under the colonial dispensation. The "Sunset laws" wrought havoc with many landlords belonging to this caste in the first flush of the colonial rule on Orissa. Even their services as soldiers were not required by the colonial state. Commenting on this aspect Mr. O' Malley wrote:

"…. The decline in the military spirit among this people is an extra-ordinary point in the development of their character. Though a few years ago orders were passed for the enlisting of Oriyas in the wing of Madras regiment quartered at Cuttack none were found suitable or willing for the employment"[25].

However the tenacity of the *Khandayats* to hold on to land as occupancy *raiyats* and to the "Brahminical culture" preserved their position among the higher castes in Orissa. Slowly they exhibited signs of mobility by taking to English education and government services. Eminent personalities like Fakirmohan Senapati and Madhusudan Das rose from among their ranks. But the *Khandayats* had already conceded a much superior status to the *Karanas*. By 1931, they could claim only ninety seven literates per every 1000 of them.

The downgrading of the *Chasa* caste to share equal rank with the hitherto service castes like the *Bhandari*, *Kamara*, *Kumbhara*, etc., in the same way, happened quiet incoherently with their pre-colonial social status. The fact was poignant and indirectly pointed to their economic marginalisation in colonial Orissa. The *Chasa* as a matter of fact, in not so distant a past, formed the very base of the agrarian social structure in Orissa. Both the *Karanas* and the *Khandayats*, who by virtue of their educational and economic attainments effected an upward social mobility, were actually the offshoots of this once great cultivating caste of Orissa. The widely applied caste proverb, *"Khandayat Badhile Karana, Chhindile Chasa*" meaning when a *Khandayat* moves up the social ladder, becomes a *Karana* but becomes an ordinary cultivator when he goes down still stands as a testimony to this inference.

Traditionally, the Chasas accounted for the upkeep of the institution of *jajmana* and the core of the Oriya folk culture. But when the laws of land-ownership changed all of a sudden and chores of life-style began transformed with the well-to-do putting a premium on the English education and government service, the centrality of the Chasas to the social-economic life of Orissa was lost. In their new status, they increasingly became an inconsequential class of tenants-at-will and, hence, no better than the service castes. By 1931, the caste had only forty to fifty literates per 1000 men.

Another contemporary social anachronism, which Mr. Hunter's reclassification of castes in Orissa pointed out, was the placement of Shagird Peshas and Rajus in two different categories. The Shagird Peshas, who were said to be the off-springs of low caste women by Karana, Bhata and sometimes, though rarely, Brahmin fathers, were put in the list of "higher castes" while the Rajus, supposed to be of mixed parentage of a similar kind were put below the rank of other menial castes like the Chasas, Tambulis, Kultas and Gauras. The categorisation was perhaps not done inadvertently. Social portraits drawn in contemporary literature as also in scores of administrative reports assigns its responsibility to the practice of extra-marital relationships that were prevalent among the men of the upper social strata. It might not have been wholly improbable, therefore, for the *zamindars* and the *noveau riche* bidders of an up-market fortune, with all the power and pelf which the colonial agrarian system had bestowed upon them, to have fostered the social origin of the Shagird Peshas. As a caste, they do not find mention in the annals of the pre-colonial social history of Orissa. Thus, being a possible off-shoot of the neo-elite in the Orissan society, their claim to a higher social rank was not unnatural. In the census of 1872 their number was returned as 3, 373. But gradual omission of this caste in the subsequent census points to its ultimate merger with the classes of its origin.[26]

The Rajus, on the other hand, were a product of the pre-colonial times. A numerous caste in the northern part of the Balasore district, their marginalisation was, however, temporary. While reviewing the social bases of land administration in the district, periodical settlement reports emphasised on their gradual progress in the field of education, government services, trade and businesses. Not surprisingly, their claim to the *Kshatriya* status was projected vigorously sooner than later.[27] Formerly a numerous cultivating caste with the common surname "Raju" they adopted a disparate range of surnames from 'Mohapatra' to 'Das' and established extensive marital relationships with the Khandayats of Orissa.

The rise of the *Telis*, who originally were returned in the 1872 census as belonging to an artisan caste along with the *Darzis* (tailors) and *Sunris* (distillers) to the position of a respectable *sudra* caste is also in keeping with their adoptability to the changed socio-economic atmosphere. At a time, when the cultivating castes suffered on account of repressive revenue administration, the *Telis* from the positions of small time pressers and sellers of oil rose to the status of money-lenders, traders and ultimately as proprietary tenure holders. On their educational attainments the census of 1931 stated:

"Their dealings in trade have led a fair number of their men folk about one in ten to acquire some familiarity with the three 'R's but their females are still very backward".

However, the rise of the *Telis* was adversely affected when *Marwaris* and Gujaratis took control of the market in Orissa. The *Telis* co-existed with them but conceded to the *Marwaris* leading position in the sphere of their hereditary occupation. The *Tantis*, who accounted for the earlier economic prosperity of the district, had to likewise join the ever-swelling rank of land-less labourers. This was notwithstanding the emergence of a class of *Matibansi Ojhas* (non-Brahmin tutors) from amongst them, who were eagerly sought after for teaching arithmetic to village pupils in the period presaging the introduction of English education in Orissa. Their irrelevance pushed them below the pollution level. As the census of 1931 on occupational structure in Orissa shows, these three castes were the most immune to change in their hereditary occupations.

Again commenting on the extent to which castes in Orissa had changed their hereditary occupations, the same census quoted a correspondent from Orissa as saying:

"With the advancement in education and the growth of cosmopolitan views the tendency to stick to the traditional occupation has totally disappeared in towns, where at present, the profession of a man is purely one of his choice or of his guardians. But in distant *muffosils* adherence to such traditional occupations has been determined more by the economic necessity of the villages and their inhabitants than by any sanctity of custom or restriction of caste government or opposition from other castes or communities".

As a direct consequence of this new phenomenon a general desire was observed among many upwardly mobile lower Hindu castes to be recognised as higher castes. For the purpose they attached various mythological and far-fetched appellations to their pre-existing caste names. The following table below presents a list of new names for the upwardly mobile old Oriya castes.

Table I
New names for old castes in Orissa

Bhat	Brahmana Bhat
Karana	Sri karana
Khandayat	Mahanayak, Srhestha,
Teli	Kubera
Raju	Chandavat, Shuktavat Kshatriya
Gaura	Jaduvamsi Kshatriya, Yadava
Barhai	Viswakarma Brahmana
Kamara	Viswakarma Brahmana
Pathuria	Viswakarma Brahmana
Sunri	Saundika Kshatriya
Napita/Bhandari	Nai Brahmana

The instrument to which these castes resorted for legitimising their fresh claims was the caste *sabhas*. These associations proliferated particularly during the 1920s. In most cases the procedure was to select for the caste a new name and pass resolution in regard to issues dealing with food and drink, abandonment of occupations unbecoming of the new claim, postponement of the age of marriage etc. The attitude of the ritually superior castes towards these movements was initially hostile. The abandonment of *begari* (menial work) on the part of certain castes particularly caused great inconvenience to them. When the *Gauras*, for instance, refused to carry palanquins in Balasore as part of their campaign to get recognised as *Jaduvamsi Kshatriyas*, the *Khandayats* and *Karanas*, "whose idea of false prestige combined with an exaggerated notion of *purdah* system" received a rude jolt, picked up rivalry against them. But gradually an attitude of indifference gave way to the feeling of hostility. The Brahmins, who received gracious fees for according these caste names, did so without inhibition knowing fully well that such sanctions would not bring real change in the ritual status of the concerned castes.

In yet another aspect, the changing caste equations even made occasional forays into the endogamy practices of several castes. Progress in public life had already made a dent on the observations of commensal rules. The purification rituals associated with personal contacts after availing motor lorry passenger services between Balasore and Bhadrakh, which were introduced in the 1920s[28], for example, became almost a formality. The 1921 census reported about clear signs of laxity in matters of matrimonial relations between various sub-castes belonging to the same castes. The 1931 census quoting a correspondent from Orissa on this score stated:

"Money works in these cases as a mighty leveller of sub-castes. If a member of a lower sub-caste acquires money, power or authority, he marries into the immediately higher sub-caste and gradually becomes amalgamated into it. Thus most of the sub-castes of the Brahmin castes are gradually being amalgamated into the common genus. The *Chasas* of the Puri district are thus trying to inter-marry into and pass themselves off as members of the *Khandayat* caste while the *Khandayats* in their turn trying to inter-marry into and pass themselves off as the members of the *Karana* caste. This is not due to any relaxing of the rules of inter-marriage or commensality. These rules are as hard and inexorable as ever; but, as social rules have lost their sanction and their binding force, people never fear or scruple to violate them whenever it suits them to do so. The man of power and pelf can shut the mouth of the caste people with gold and break the social rule with impunity".

Mutatis mutandis the same observation was equally applicable to the rest of Orissa including Balasore, which always stood on the precipice of the pan-Orissan social complex. Finally, the caste which survived and expanded through combinations and re-combinations by 1931 were few in comparison to their return as referred to in the 1872 census. The table[29] below gives an indication of the trends in the quantitative expansion of certain selected castes in the Balasore district.

Table-II

Trends in the population of selected castes in the Balasore district

Castes	1872	1931
Brahmana	85, 432	110, 658
Karana	21, 352	22, 354
Khandayat	135, 671	199, 750
Chasa	24, 278	11, 541
Gaura	56, 548	69, 157
Teli	37, 749	43783
Bania	5, 628	9, 200
Guria	11, 009	21, 341
Bhandari	13, 733	15, 500
Kumbhara	10, 589	13, 177

(Table II Contd.)

Castes	1872	1931
Kamara	9, 704	10, 840
Tanti	38, 460	47, 570
Dhoba	16, 675	24, 066
Keuta	34, 442	14, 204
Gokha	17, 212	33, 912
Pana	36, 546	59, 545
Kandara	18, 485	30, 791
Doma	1, 397	1, 959
Chamara	4, 383	7, 792
Mihitar/Hari	3, 320	5, 515

Ritual Bases of Stratification

Doubts began to be raised by 1921 about the efficacy of caste as an institution on account of its dwindling hold on the Hindu society. As discussed above, at least in one abiding aspect, i.e., occupation, caste had been losing its former control. But in relation to practices of endogamy and various taboos caste still held its sway. The relaxation experienced in the society due to various exogenous influences had not yet broken the core of its self-perpetuating vitality. Not only that the castes continued to be ritually differentiated on the basis of the traditional *varna* order but every caste also got internally stratified into an agglomeration of sub-castes, which were linked to each other through mutually perceptible high-low relationships.

Agrarian Bases of Stratification

The agrarian social structure, which evolved under the colonial dispensation to a great extent, conformed to the order of ritual stratification in Orissa. The *zamindars*, placed at the top of the structure, virtually presided over all aspects of social and economic life of the people. In their hands was vested the proprietary rights over the land, portions of which they lent out to individual *raiyats* for cultivation. The *raiyats* in turn paid revenue for their possession to the government through the *zamindars*. This centrality of their role in the system of revenue administration made them pivots in the entire agrarian life cycle. In the best tradition of the English landed aristocracy, the *zamindars* position had been created to make them the agents of expeditious rural development. But the exploitative attitude inherent in the colonial mindset made a farcical outturn of the original conception.

The *zamindars* on their part established *cutcherries* (offices) and appointed managers, *gomastas* and peons for regular maintenance of land records and periodical collection of land revenue. In them was vested an array of power regarding mutations transfer, purchase and sale of land and bestowal of *chakran* lands on village *sevayats* (servants). When the acts regarding agricultural loans and land improvement loans were passed in 1884, they were made the recommending authority for any cultivator to be legally entitled to such a loan. They exercised jurisdiction over forest land, waste lands and even trees standing on cultivators' land. In times of flood or droughts, when agriculture suffered, remissions of revenue and *taccavi* (advance loans) were invariably routed through them. All these enabled the *zamindars* to exercise enormous authority on the inhabitants residing in their estates. The usual methods involved could be either by extending patronage to the favourites or by coercing the disobedient.

The government also allowed a handsome percentage on the revenue to the *zamindars*, which they collected rather religiously to keep the authorities as much in good humour as to line their own coffers. Consequently they lived a life of casual effluence often creating a ring of medieval flourish around their persona. A non-resident among them lived in towns like Cuttack, Midnapore or Calcutta and visited the estates only occasionally. The resident *zamindars* instead stayed in the estates and kept direct contacts with the peasants. As for their obligation towards the lot of the peasantry some of them did take care to run village *chatshalas* (schools), put up post offices, laid roads, maintained irrigation works and organised community festivals. But nothing was ever done as a matter of duty. For availing or not availing any such facility an ordinary cultivator had to shell out either a tax or a *bheti* (ceremonial present). In fact, some British officers lamented an absolute lack of public spirit or a sense of commitment towards the improvement of the estates among the *zamindars*.[30]

The *zamindars*' conduct was, of course, conditioned by the general lack of security to their proprietary rights. Even after the Thirty Years' Settlement became a routine, the sense of insecurity prevailed. The pace at which the estates were multiplied due to partition was alarming. Whereas there were only 803 temporarily settled estates in the district of Balasore in 1837, their number rose to 1417 in the settlement of 1897, and to 2394 in the settlement of 1932. The progressive steps of bestowing rights of occupancy on the cultivators were another source of worry. These often soured the existent relationships between the *zamindars* and their tenants.

But, on the whole, in a sustenance economy where every constituent strata viz., the landlords, tenants and the agricultural labourers had equal stake, the *zamindars* thrived at the cost of the rest.

In terms of social representation the following extract from Mr. D. H. Kingsford's statement[31] would show how the ritually top social strata also dominated the agrarian class structure as *zamindars* in Orissa.

Table-III

Recorded shares of the proprietors in the temporarily settled zamindari estates in the district of Balasore according to selected castes

Castes	*Share recorded in 1837 settle-ment report*	*Percentage of total number of 1504 shares*	*Shares in 1897 settle-ment report*	*Percentage of the total number of 7481 shares*	*Percentage of the total population according to 1891 census*
Brahmins	368	24	1991	27	12
Karana	363	24	1333	18	2.7
Khandait	304	20	2095	28	18.7
Bengali Kayastha	84	6	269	4	0.2
Teli	14	1	417	6	4.7
Tambuli	52	3	370	5	0.8
Bania	16	1	52	1	0.7
Gaura	18	1	95	1	7.4

The Brahmins and *Karanas* along with the Bengali *Kayasthas* held *zamindaries* far in excess of their proportion to the total population of the district. The sub-proprietary tenure-holders also largely hailed from among them. The only qualitative difference to this pattern was made by the *Tambulis, Telis, Banias* and, to some extent, the *Gauras*. These castes acquired *zamindaries* with the surplus income which they earned from their respective businesses. But their presence was not large enough to de-link the agrarian class structure from its corresponding ritual base. The small urban elite, which filled the ranks of the emerging professional class as advocates, pleaders, deputy collectors, clerks, *munsifs*, teachers, professors, inspector and sub-inspectors of schools etc., was also a derivative of this social segment.

For the ordinary cultivators to send their wards for expensive English education in the towns was not an easy option. Pandit Godavarish Mishra, an eminent litterateur and politician from Orissa, while rummaging through the difficult phase of his early life has given a graphic description of this reality.[32] Rack-rented to the verge of starvation and over-burdened with all kinds of social and economic obligations, the average cultivator lived a sedentary life. "The only source of his income was his small holding. His habitation was consisted of a cot enclosed by four mud-walls, which were used as the gables of little rooms. Sometimes, but rarely, the cow-shed was built outside the walls. A patch of green aside the house, neatly "shut in with a fence of prickly shrubs", sparingly supplied him with vegetables. His summer dress consisted of a coarse-cotton *dhoti* (waist-cloth) and a *gamucha* (scarf). Household furniture included a few brass pots and plates and cups, one or two bed spreads, a few mats and various agricultural implements. The owners of comparatively larger holdings possessed one or two palm-leaf manuscripts of the Oriya Mahabharata and the Ramayana. Rice, milk and one or two occasional side-items of dried fish, meat or vegetables formed his usual diet."[33] But despite this miserable existence the cultivators as a class sustained the community life by ensuring vertical solidarity among various castes. Belonging to the numerous *Khandayat*, *Chasa*, *Mastan*, *Mali*, *Gaura* and *Tambuli* castes, they formed the core of the *jajmani* system. With an earning of about ten rupees of a month, an average cultivator family spent around rupees seven for itself. Out of the rest, the family priest, barber, blacksmith and the washer man received around eight *annas*. In addition, the cultivator also obliged men of these service providing castes with annual payments in kind at harvest time.[34]

At the bottom of the agrarian order lived the numerous agricultural labourers. Mostly drawn from among the low and the untouchable castes such as *Gaura*, *Rarhi*, *Tanti*, *Pana*, *Kandara* etc., they formed an enormous army of approximately one lakh persons. Many of them were employed by *zamindars*, *lakhirajdars*, and *bajyaptidars* in good circumstances as *baramasiyas*.[35] But many more still worked for the cultivators either as *nag-mulias*, *thika-mulias* or just migrated to Calcutta to work there as *coolies*.

The *bara-masia* stayed with his master round the year availing free lodging and boarding. He also received an annual payment of rupees twelve and four garments i.e., two *kurtas*, one *gamucha* and one *chadar* (shawl). The *nag-mulia* worked on contract basis for a specific period of the year. His payment included half a *gauni* ($5^1/_2$ *seers*) of paddy per day, an annual present of a new *gamucha* and a *puruna sirupa* (cast-off cloth) of his master. A *nag-mulia* was also allowed a *bhita* (plot of land) to cultivate for his own benefit free of rent. The *thika-mulia* was a casual labourer, who worked only for money-wage at the rate of two *annas* per day.

Below the labouring class, there were plain destitute people. The census reports categorised those people into several castes viz., *Kasbi* (prostitutes), *Chukar* (off-springs of prostitutes), *Khelta* (jugglers), *Mangta* (vagabonds) and *Bhikari* (beggars) without any qualification. Nobody knew about their social antecedents. But that extreme economic deprivation had made them un-solicited dependants on the agrarian system is a fact which can not be easily disputed.

Overall Social Condition

Casually, the society presented a picture of depravity and fatalism. In a way, Orissa's frequent subjection to natural calamities was instrumental in sapping its way towards progress. But a further contributing element to this all-glaring predicament was the division of the society into numerous markedly graded caste groups. The atmosphere was so depressing that "no one outside the priestly caste might even plant a coconut tree". However, actually, the Oriyas whenever provided with some opportunities, proved their capacity for hard work and creative imagination to transform their material circumstances. This was not only borne out from the circumstances of the city-ward emigrants, as has been parodied by the contemporary English commentators, but also found eloquent expression in succeeding times within the natural boundaries of Orissa itself. The 'years of transformation' in the aftermath of the famine of 1865-66 bore out this fact.

The Years of Transformation, 1865 to 1947

Politically the transfer of power in 1858 from the hands of the East India Company to the Crown in England brought in the second phase of British colonialism to Orissa as to the rest of the British Empire in India. The 'Queen's Declaration' on the occasion of this transfer of power had assured "in their prosperity will be our strength, in their contentment our security and in their gratitude our best reward". But actually, the espousal of benevolence had been warranted by the insurrectionary turmoil that the Empire had just pulled through. Other than trying to conciliate the rulers of the native states of India and those sections of the people of India, whose interests had been hit a bit too hard in the perception of the British, the mere shifting of the reigns of power from the Company to the Crown brought little change in the basic attitude of colonial governance. In fact, the assumption of power by the Crown left quite a number of incongruities in the colony's social and economic spheres.

In spite of the avowed declaration to stimulate industry and public utility works while reorienting the administration for the benefit of all 'subjects', the transfer of power achieved little for Orissa. The 'policy of non-interference' was strategically taken recourse to by the administration with characteristic imprudence. It was under such circumstances that the famine of 1866 jolted the colonial regime out of its intransigence and helped begin the second phase of the colonial history of Orissa. Echoing this sentiment in the midst of the calamitous famine the editorial in the *Calcutta Review* wrote in October 1866:

"Through the famine, Orissa has attained the turning point and crisis of her destiny. Every calamity has its moral and the moral of the famine is the adoption of the government of a policy of progress, and of moral and material improvement of Orissa"[36].

Social Stratification and Change in the Post-famine Situation

The innovative administrative policies of the British government in the post-famine period in their most decisive aspect created a new social class, which acted as the catalyst of modernisation in Orissa. Though a distinguishably economic criterion did not play a great role in shaping this class, yet fragments of information regarding ancestry, concentration of habitation, caste, educational attainments, professions and ideas of socio-political and economic advancement of the Orissa division as a whole point to its origin from the elite Brahmin, the land-owning *Karana* and *Khandayat* castes. These two groups forming the crucial middle stratum of the colonial society were compelled by the emergent socio-economic changes to aspire and struggle for a resurgent Orissa often with a deep nostalgia for its past. In the process they had to per force embrace the larger identity of the state foregoing their restrictive social identities and privileges.

The post-famine administrative and economic policies, which the government pursued, allowed the convergence of interests of the rising middle class though in their wider effect such policies wiped out potential economic avenues, which would have facilitated a general economic resurgence of the province cutting across the lines of social hierarchy. The salt industry was thoroughly sacrificed in the imperial economic interest depriving thousands of landless labourers of a substantive mean of alternative employment. Other native industries had no scope for rising above the threshold of compulsive local requirements by overcoming the rapidly integrating imperialist market forces. The market in the Orissa itself had become the preserve of manipulative business interests from outside and their middle men.

Within the administrative division of Orissa itself the forces of integration foreclosed district wise developmental concerns as facilities of modernisation became overly centralised. Distributive economic opportunities and consequent social development became perceptively scarce. Cuttack as the divisional head quarters of the administration became the nerve centre of all activities. Flickers of rising socio-political consciousness, undeniably the products of the combination of changing administrative posture of the government and the emerging sub-continental political environment, flowed from peripheral districts to converge in Cuttack. Strands of public activity then spread out from there to other parts of Orissa. This process consolidated the class identity of those people, who came forward to participate in this ever churning process of public activity. But while fostering its sectional interests, the middle class also found itself plagued by inter-caste conflicts. The Brahmin, Karana and *Khandayat* associations were formed to promote the interests of the members of their respective castes. Superficially, however, there was definite reciprocity between the contending upper castes. The English educated lawyers supported the cause of the landed gentry. The landed aristocracy championed the cause of administrative reintegration of the Oriya-speaking areas. And the middle class press held the colonial administration responsible for the sufferings of all social classes. Theoretically, members from non-upper castes could aspire to and indeed found entry into this widening social stratum. The definite course for them was to take to English education and get government service. Nevertheless, distinctive caste consciousness almost always remained palpable within the emergent middle class.

Outside the boundary of this emergent social stratum the socio-economic scenario continued to present a picture of dismal stagnation. The reforms in land revenue administration haltingly moved towards safeguarding the rights of the tenants. But as cultivation had reached the last limit of arable lands in the districts of Orissa land reform measures could contributed only to further fragmentation of land and more litigation. Recognition of the 'rights of tenancy' created graded feudal interests down the line. Lack of alternative sources of employment created the irreversible process of agricultural indebtedness and resulting pauperisation of the peasantry.

However, since investment in land was still a recognised passport to upward social mobility, aspirants for such mobility increasingly took to businesses and other professions for earning enough to acquire landed property. In the intensely differentiated peasant economy only this emergent body of *khusbas rayats* could acquire stability and prosperity by combining cultivation with concomitant trade.[37] But the small and medium farmers, caught in the widespread "debt-trap", slowly lost their holdings and thereby the only means of their earning and social position. The massive labour force, which thus came into existence in the countryside, had to frequently move around in search of work making out-migration among the landless labourers a long term social predicament in Orissa.

Away from this scenario of a small but conspicuous middle class coming into existence with a perpetrated interest in land and government jobs, Orissa also experienced another kind of social transformation in the 20th century the currents of which was sweeping across the Indian sub-continent in the form of nation-wide freedom movement. The Gandhian ideals of social harmony and rural reconstruction influenced a whole generation of men irrespective of their social standing. Orissa was fortunate in having a crop of such individuals, who harnessed the Gandhian values to bring about social transformation. The attempt did not succeed in the structural plain though it made a considerable impact in the realm of caste and class attitudes of the people.

The saga of social transformation between 1866 and 1947 demonstrates this historical course. Till the 1920s there were efforts by the emergent middle class to garner available opportunities offered by the colonial government. It manifested in the movement that was vigorously launched for the administrative reintegration of the scattered Oriya-speaking tracts and in the concerns that were expressed for the all-round development of the province. Since the 1920s an abiding faith and a sense of participation were expressed in the national movement for *swaraj*. In both these movements, the incipient 'common process' of social transformation could be discerned clearly. The goals of political integration of the province, its economic regeneration and *swaraj* became equal parts of this 'common process'.

At the end it seems as if the Orissan society stood on the crucible of change at the dawn of the 19th century. The occupation of Orissa by the British in 1803 heralded this process of change. It was perhaps a fait accompli for the state to be so occupied after going through a series of shifting subjugations by the Afghans, the Mughals and the Marathas. But never before the colonial occupation had the native society experienced such substantive and intemperate change as it did under the British.

The Afghans, Mughals and the Marathas had ruled largely within the framework set earlier by their Suryavamshi predecessors between the 10th and 16th centuries. They always governed under a felt necessity of maintaining a direct link with the ruled. At times such links were culturally packaged to enjoy unflinching loyalty of all castes and communities. Under the Gangas and then the Suryavamshis such an attempt had made Lord Jagannath the abiding symbol of the politico-cultural integrity of Orissa. The syncretic ethos of the Jagannath cult not only permeated the entire society but also enabled these kings to manage the affairs of the State without entreating a hegemonic intermediate social class. The officers dealt with the subjects only with as much authority as were vested in them by the king. The kings directly patronised all arts and crafts keeping the populace creatively engaged. For all purposes, land, the primary source of economy, belonged to the State. For the protection and further acquisition of this resource, the kings needed support and, what is more, the sustenance of their armies from all sections of the society. Thus the triune necessities, i.e. political, cultural and economic, formed the basis of the pre-colonial social structure in Orissa.

It was also these necessities, which produced the huge social class of peasant-militia called the *Khandayats* in the state. The intra-class differentiation among the *Khandayats* was more in terms of rank rather than on the basis of birth. The Suryavamshi kings themselves rose from the ranks of this proliferating social class. The people, who on the other hand, entered into the jobs of keeping administrative and land records, took the necessary professional name of *Karana*. There was nothing save their profession at this stage to socially differentiate them from the numerous *Khandayats*. Like the *Karanas*, the other professional groups like the painters, sculptors, architects and smiths were all held in high social esteem for the invaluable contribution they made to the prestige and prosperity of the State. As the sole exception to this social milieu, the Brahmans were brought from Kanauj by the kings and were settled in *shashans* in and around the temple-city of Puri from where they proliferated to other smaller principalities but always assimilating measures of local traits and culture. However, the importation of the Brahmins into Orissa, at first to conduct the temple rituals and then to provide sacerdotal sanction to the regal authority of the kings, introduced an element of the Brahminical concept of pollution and purity into the Orissan social structure. Brahmins as the legitimising authority of social action ascribed differing status to different social groups apparently on the basis of their vocations from a preconceived scriptural point of view. The kings also gradually began taking pride in reorganising the society in accordance with the *varna dharma*. But as long as the political economy of the State remained in place, the infusion of the Brahminical nuances did not disturb the pre-colonial social structure much.

Under the Mughals the methods of feudalising the agrarian base of the social economy was adopted for some time. The geographical distance that came into being between the imperial seat of power located in far of Delhi and the subjugated province was partly responsible for this break with its immediate past. But the Marathas soon undid the aberration by re-establishing that direct link between the ruler and the ruled, which existed during the pre-Mughal period. The Marathas also restored the primacy of Lord Jagannath in the religio-cultural domain of the State's life. The social structure, which came to be shaped on the basis of these twin aspects, thus survived without much upheaval although the State suffered economically due to the depredatory nature of the Maratha rule.

The English East India Company had already fine-tuned its colonial policy by the time it occupied Orissa. In the agrarian field, to begin with, the Company created a vested-interest intermediary class by largely vesting the proprietary rights on land in the ex-revenue officials of the Mughals and the Marathas. The feeling of being alien in the place of governance, which cherished autonomy, also made the Company to introduce a series of short-term revenue settlements and thereby to create space for the replacement of a large number of indigenous Oriya proprietors by outside speculators. These absentee landlords along with the immigrant clerks, who were brought into Orissa by the Company officials, acted in unison to give effect to the Company's policy of recasting the agrarian structure of Orissa. The twin principle, which worked at the core of such a policy, was maximum aggrandisement of revenue and increasing consolidation of the colonial hold on the occupied territory. Rules regarding the payment of revenue only through the Calcutta *sicca* rupee, instead of the locally circulating *cowries*, and sale of local estates at Fort Williams in Calcutta to the highest bidders were promulgated especially for these obvious purposes. The persistence of the Company with the system of effecting short-term settlements furthered the cause of these rules as the local *zamindars* failing to pay up the ever-escalating demand of revenue through the Company-introduced *sicca* rupee became increasingly dispossessed of their holdings. At first, the local disquiet to such grievous policies was manifested in the Paik rebellion of 1817. But subsequently the native society acquiesced in a bid to readjust itself according to the colonial priorities.

The establishment of monopoly over manufacturing and sale of salt immediately following the occupation of Orissa to make maximum profit out of this trade and abandon it to make way for large-scale importation of the cheaper and finer Liverpool salt shattered the local economy of Orissa. Shipbuilding, weaving and many other indigenous industries similarly declined because of greater importation of foreign products. The mass of the working classes previously depending on these industries therefore had to shift on to agriculture as landless labourers.

With agriculture emerging as the sole means of livelihood and the string of control over this system lying in the firm grip of the colonial government, a new social structure was formed in the State. At the top of this structure presided the single most important prop of the colonial state, i.e. the *zamindars*. The enormous power, which the Company government vested in them, made the *zamindars* the arbiters of the peasants' destiny. While this class along with the various sub-proprietary tenure holders regaled in the life of pomp and opportunities, the peasant cultivators below them bore the weight of the entire agrarian structure. In terms of the durability of their holding these peasants were divided into two classes, i.e. *thani* and *pahi*. The *chandanadars*, who held small plots of land as homestead, occupied themselves primarily with the trade of grains and other articles of daily consumption. At the lowest level came the sprawling mass of landless agricultural labourers differentiated according to the terms of their employment.

Curiously, the reordering of the social structure under the colonial rule also brought in a new mechanism of social mobility. Since the state disengaged itself from the cultural moorings of the society the determinants of an individual or a group's upward mobility became overtly economic. Everything, from *zamindari* to a business permit was available on sale. But the average Oriya at this point of time was too impoverished to buy social mobility. The catastrophic famine of 1865-66 only demonstrated the extent of their impoverishment.

The famine was also an eye-opener to the colonial regime. Partly guilt-ridden and partly because of a new scheme of governance following the transfer of power from the Company to the Crown, the British-India government introduced a number of administrative measures in Orissa after the famine. The government's realisation that marginalisation of the native Oriyas almost in every area of governance was primarily responsible for the catastrophe, led it to reorient its policies to cater to the Oriya interests. Consequently the government initiated constructive measures in the field of education, communication, irrigation, and public health. A series of measures were also introduced to create definitive rights of tenants on land. These measures taken together opened up the dormant aspirations of the Oriyas. In the immediate context, the policies helped in giving rise to a small group of educated middle class, who became the forbearers of a post-dated resurgent movement.

Initially the forces of social change found expression in vastly isolated instances of socio-cultural reformation movements. At the base of these movements lay the aspirations of creating a homogenous society. Also was aspired by these movements an attempt to turn away the society from the cynical attitude, which it had come to imbibe under the new circumstances. But these movements failed to motivate the people on a large scale. The source of social prevarication apparently was not in the society's hand. Therefore, only an issue that could touch the common chord had to be taken up.

The Oriya language controversy was the first such issue, which infused a sense of commonality among the Oriyas in the last quarter of the 19th century. The success of the movement prepared the stage for a further concerted movement to bring about the unification of all the scattered Oriya-speaking areas. Associations were formed, literatures produced, and a whole host of programmes for the participation of people in the movement were launched. Ultimately, the objective was attained in the year 1936.

But despite going through this tumultuous process, the colonial social structure did not show signs of withering. The beneficiaries of the constructive programmes of the government, who incidentally belonged to ritually higher castes almost, gained the upper hand on other social classes in their newfound roles of leadership. Members from these castes also filled the services under the government. The other castes, which could gather enough resources bought for themselves *zamindaries* and took to some education. The *khusbas raiyats* belonging to the higher and intermediate castes mainly gained from the land reforms policies of the government. They could withstand the fluctuations of the grain market with increasing resources at their command. But other social groups, who largely depended on wage labour continued to languish in abject poverty. The swelling ranks of migrant labourers, who went out of the State regularly to Calcutta and to Assam and even to Burma in extreme cases, came from these social groups. Thus, while at the top a fresh agglomeration of the caste groups took place, at the bottom the low and the depressed castes continued to remain unaffected by the process of change to the better.

The emergent middle class by virtue of its being composite was not free from internal schisms. These schisms surfaced more openly after Orissa was formed into a separate linguistic province and the responsibility of administration fell largely on this class. The virus of factionalism within the Congress, which continued well after the country won independence, was a pernicious effect of this pre-independence caste rivalry.

Notes and References

1. P. Gisbert, *Fundamentals of Sociology*, Bombay: Orient Longman, 1987; p. 366.
2. *Gazetteer of the Balasore District*, Calcutta: (Bengal District Gazetteer Series) 1907, p. 19.
3. *Ibid.*, p. 10.
4. *Ibid.*
5. *Ibid.*
6. K.C. Panigrahi, *History of Orissa: Hindu Period*, Cuttack: Kitab Mahal, 1981, p. 81.
7. *Ibid.*, p. 344.
8. S. C. Dey, "Political History of Balasore through Ages (ancient Period)" in Seminar on *Cultural Heritage and History of Balasore*, District Office, Balasore; 25 and 26th January, 1981; p. 9.
9. Fakirmohan Senapati, *Atmajivana Charita* (translated from Oriya by John Boulton), Cuttack: 1985, p. 5.
10. *Balasore District Gazetteer*, *op. cit.*, p. 26.
11. Herman Kulke, "Kshatriyaisation and social change: a study in Orissa setting", S.D.Pillai (ed.), *Aspects of Changing India*, Bombay: Popular Prakashan, 1976, p. 102.
12. W.W.Hunter, *A Statistical Account of Bengal: The Districts of Puri, Cuttack and Balasore*, Vol. 18, Calcutta: 1877, p. 312.
13. Herman Kulke, *op. cit.*, p. 405.
14. K.C. Panigrahi, *op. cit.*, 209.
15. Surendra Maharana, *Oriya Sahityara Itihasa*, Cuttack: Banirupa, 1988, p. 280.
16. Khageswar Mahapatra, *Charya Gitika*, Cuttack: 1976, p. 8.
17. S.K.Panda, "Social Mobility in Medieval Orissa" in *Indica*, Vol. 21 (2); Sept.1984, pp. 81-85.
18. *Board of Revenue Collections*, Cuttack: Vol. 586, p. 300.

19. B.C.Ray, *Orissa Under the Marathas*, Allahabad: Kitab Mahal, 1960, p. 127.
20. *Balasore District Gazetteer*, Op. cit. p. 111.
21. W. W. Hunter, Op. cit. pp. 268-270.
22. Balasore District Gazetteer, 1907, op. cit.
23. Radhakanta Barik, "Caste System and Economic Backwardness in Orissa", *Social Science Probings*, Vol. 2 (2); June 1985, p. 257.
24. *Census of India, 1931*, Vol. VII, chapter I, Sec. VI, p. 217.
25. *Balasore District Gazetteer*, 1907, op. cit., p. 51.
26. *Census of 1931*, Op. cit. p. 267.
27. *Baleshwar District Gazetteer, 1994*, pp. 138-39.
28. W.W. Dalziel, *Final Report on the Revision Settlement of Orissa, 1922-1932A.D.*, Patna: 1934, Chapter X, p. 92.
29. W.W. Hunter, Op. cit., pp. 268-270.
30. S. L. Maddox, *Final Report on the Survey and Settlement of the Province of Orissa, 1890-1900*, Vol. II, Calcutta: 1900, p. 492.
31. *Ibid.*, Appendix-N (b), p. 520; Census of 1891, Population Tables.
32. Godavarish Mishra, *Ardhashatabdhira Odisa O Tanhire Mo Sthana* (in Oriya), Cuttack: 1973, pp. 26-35.
33. W.W. Hunter, op. cit., p. 289.
34. *Ibid.*, p. 294.
35. S.L. Maddox, op. cit., Vol. II, p. 493.
36. Prabhat Mukherji, "The Orissa Famine of 1866" in *Orissa Historical Research Journal*, Vol. IV. Part-I, 1955, p. 95.
37. *Annual General Administration Reports of the Orissa Division*, 1871-72, p. 7.

PART-V

TOWARD SOCIETY AND NATION–STATE : IMAGE AND PERCEPTION

17

The Inner Dynamism of a Nation State: An Indian Paradigm

G. Subbiah

India, or Bharat, has completed the 55th year of its Independence as a 'nation-state'. What is its single-most important achievement in this long period? If asked, some might, with tongue in cheek, be tempted to reply that the paramount achievement of independent India is: "it is still there". In fact when India, with its bewildering heterogeneity, emerged in 1947 as a nation-state, many did not—some even now do not—believe that it would survive either as a nation or as a state for long. Writing in 1967, A.L.Basham, a celebrated Indologist and a great admirer of Indian culture, remarked: "Politically and economically India faces many problems of great difficulty, and no one can forecast her future with any certainty".[1]

That this apprehension was not totally unfounded is amply attested by the fact that there has been incessant attacks from within and without on the body-politic of India by various secessionist forces and terrorist outfits since its independence. The skepticism on the future of India as nation-state also rests on the perception that India is "neither a state nor a nation-state according to the western meanings of the terms".[2] Yet, India has belied the prediction of the prophets of doom by surviving so far as a nation as well as a state.

India as a nation-state was no doubt born in 1947. But, was not India a nation before 1947? Or, are the idea of a nation and the emergence of a nation-state coeval? On this crucial question, there is no consensus of opinion even among the leading political parties and thinkers of our country, and each holds a divergent view from the other. India, according to one view, was neither a nation nor a state before 1947; according to another view India is a state consisting of many nationalities; according to yet another view, India should better be seen as a federation of states; and, finally there are those who love to perceive India, with all its diversity, as one nation and one state. This bewildering array of opinions stems partly from the definitional problems of the terms involved namely nation, state, etc, but more importantly it is the reflection of the unique position that India occupies as nation-state in the contemporary world. After the disintegration of the Soviet Union, India remains the only largest multi-ethnic, multi-lingual, multi-cultural, and multi-religious nation-state in the world. The destiny of India as a nation-state is therefore "not only important in itself" but also "the crucial test case for whether relatively new nation-states can preserve diversity in religious, ethnic, and cultural terms."[3]

I

Perceiving the Indian Nation

With regard to the question whether the idea of Indian nation is tenable before India emerged as a "nation-state' in 1947, we begin with the following quote from Amartya Sen:

It is for example not a category mistake to think of the Indian nation prior to 1947 as encompassing the residents of the so called 'native states' (such as Travancore) and of the non-British colonial territories (such as Goa) even though they did not 'belong to' the same *state* at all. It is a mistake to think that the idea of nation requires the prior presence of national state.[4]

Leaving aside for a while the issue of definition of terms such as 'nation', 'state', etc, it may be worthwhile to trace the evolution of the terms such as 'India', 'Bharat', and 'Hindu(stan)' which have been the common nomenclatures by which the subcontinent was referred to for several centuries now. Although geographically the sub-continent is well demarcated by natural boundaries, yet, it did not seem to have had a single term or name to denote it until after the mid part of the first millennium B.C. It is around that time the Greeks coined the term 'Indoi', deriving it from the river Indus or Sindhu to denote the region in and around the river Indus. The same region was referred to as 'Hi(n)du(sh)' in the inscription of Darius I (522-486 B.C.) and the region, according to Herodotus, constituted the twentieth and the most populous satrapy of the Persian empire.[5] Initially therefore both the terms 'Indoi' and 'Hi(n)du(sh)' signified the Indus river and the lower Indus region. The foreigners who subsequently entered into the sub-continent through the Indus region then extended the name of the border region to denote the inner regions a well. Megasthenese (late 4th or early 3rd, century B.C.), for instance, located not only Pataliputra in eastern India but also the Pantiya country in the far south in 'Indoi'.[6] The term was thus employed by him to denote the entire sub-continent.

Interestingly when visitors and settlers from outside in the closing centuries of the first millennium B.C., were attempting to give an identity to the subcontinent by coining a single name, the earliest evidences indicating the efforts by the indigenous people to coin a single term to refer to the subcontinent also come during the same span of time. For instance the term 'Jambudvipa' is employed in the first Minor Rock Edict of the Mauryan emperor Asoka to refer to his vast empire, which encompassed practically the entire subcontinent.[7] The use of the term Jambudvipa, however, became sporadic in the early centuries of the first millennium A.D. It is during this period another term Bharatavarsha, which originally denoted a part of north India as indicated in the Hathigumpha inscription of the King Kharavela (Ist century B.C.), came into vogue to denote the whole of the subcontinent.[8] The *locus classicus* of the geographical definition of the term is found in the Vishnu Purana II, 3.1.

Uttaram yat samudrasya
Himadres'chaiva dakshinam
Varsham tad bharatam nama
Bharati yatra santatih

"The country that lies north of the ocean and south of the snowy mountains is called Bharata; there dwell the descendents of Bharata."

In some of the Puranas the subcontinent is also denoted by the term Kumarika or Kumaridvipa.[9] But the term Bharatavarsha retained its appeal and in course of time became the most popular nomenclature to denote the subcontinent eclipsing the other terms.

The perception that all land that lies south of the Himalayas down to Kanyakumari represented a single geographical unit was not confined only to the early Brahmanical or Buddhist sources. The earliest extant literary texts in Tamil language-known commonly as *cankam* literature—which are generally dated to the immediately preceding and succeeding centuries of the Christian era contain interesting data in this regard. It is clearly stated in early Tamil texts that the Venkatam (Tiruppati) hills in the north, Kumari in the south constituted the boundaries of the Tamil speaking region.[10] Yet, the early Tamil poets while showering encomiums on their patron kings of the Tamil region often set the Himalayas as the northern limit of their political realm. The poets praised their patrons as the lord of the land "that is bounded by the Kumari in the south and the great mountain in the north and by the sea in the east and the west".[11] The *cankam* literature informs us that two kings of the Pantiyan family, Mutukutumi Peruvaluti and Netunceliyan held their sway over this vast land.[12] Two other kings of the Chera family, Netunceralataṇ and Cenkuttuvan, are said to have conquered all kings from the Himalaya (Imayam) region to Kumari.[13] Admittedly the expression is both hyperbolic and formulaic as it occurs frequently in the texts. Therefore the question whether these tall claims have any historical basis or not is not the issue here. And, as noted by Kailasapathy, "the heart of the matter is that this was a theme and a formula and as such was used more for purposes of ornamentation than consideration of historical probability or veracity."[14] As part of the ornamentation, certain kings are even said to have imprinted their royal emblem on the Himalayan Mountain apparently after forcing the northern kings into submission.[15] What is noteworthy from the point of view our discussion is that although the early Tamil poets did not assign any name for it, the subcontinent in their perception was a single geographical unit that stretched from the Himalayas to Kanyakumari. In this respect, the perception of the early Tamil poets tallies well with that of the other indigenous authors cited above.

In the light of these references, it may well be contended that the idea of perceiving the subcontinent as a single geographical entity has a long history of at least two millennia and, therefore, to think of the existence of the Indian 'nation' in the pre-modern period is not an anachronism.

II

Three Major Social Processes

It was already mentioned that India is rather unique as a nation because while nations are generally known to be homogeneous, cultural entities, India is a heterogeneous, pluralistic entity consisting of a number of sub-nationalities. How does then one define the character of the 'nation-state' that is called India or Bharat? Is there anything specifically 'Indian' about it? These questions are no doubt easier to pose than to answer. One may even go a step further and argue that any attempt towards a simple, precise definition of Indianness is neither feasible nor even desirable for two reasons: i) any such definition would be so exclusive that the so-called Indians who fulfill the criterion would truly be a minority in the country, and ii) the diversity of the country is such that in whichever way one defines Indianness, the opposite of it will also be equally true and valid and thus rendering the definition meaningless. This, however, does not mean that Indian society is totally devoid of an identity or character of its own. On the contrary, the long history of India provides ample testimony to the fact that Indian society has, drawing from its own rich and colourful past, worked out a mechanism of its own to meet the challenges and demands in every phase of its history down to the modern times. The basic constituents of this mechanism and the general pattern of its operation have been well summed up in the following quote:

> ... it should be possible to identify at least three major processes which were operative through all the phases of Indian history and through early Indian history in particular. These processes were: i) the expansion of state society through the process of local state formation; ii) peasantisation of tribes and caste formation; and iii) cult appropriation and integration ....
>
> Identifying these societal processes and underlining them as the mechanism of integration do not mean taking an epicentric position. On the contrary, they point to the need to understand how historical regions emerge with distinct personalities—not by being submerged by a predetermined pattern but by responding to, and in turn reshaping with a broad range of variations, an ever dynamic pattern whose dominant political, social, economic and cultural dimensions could be recognised at a pan-Indian level.[16]

The above mechanism of integration, which was in operation in early India's history, may be seen *mutatis mutandis* in operation in contemporary India as well. To illustrate this, we shall focus upon the political arena and our choice of the political arena is dictated by the fact that the most important achievement of the 'Indian State' is located in that arena and it includes first of all, "conducting of general elections in the largest democracy on earth and peaceful transfer of power more than once from one party to another (and) surviving many pressures, stresses and strains inflicted on our body politic by malevolent forces both internal and external."[17]

Now, turning to the mechanism of integration, the process of expansion of state and society in early Indian history involved the horizontal spread of monarchical polity, and in contemporary period this has been replaced by the horizontal spread of participatory or democratic polity. Similarly the process of peasantisation of tribes into castes of the earlier phase has been substituted by the process of politicization of particular caste or caste groups by which these groups themselves turn into powerful political groups or parties. To demonstrate how this process is seen operating in contemporary India, we would like to draw attention to the history of the Dravidian movement an important social-cum-political movement in South India.

III

The Dravidian Movement

The history of the movement is both interesting as well as instructive because it had emerged even before India's independence as a major and significant force demanding secession from the Union of India for a separate state of *Dravidanadu*, comprising of the modern states of Andhra Pradesh, Karnataka, Tamil Nadu, Kerala, and Pondicherry in South India. The movement was spearheaded by E.V. Ramasami Naicker, (1879-1973) or Periyar (the great one') as he was popularly known, who founded his party, the *Dravidar Kazhagam* (DK), in 1944. The party, apart from seeking to establish a separate homeland for Dravidians, perceived the Brahmins of South India as champions of Sanskritic culture and equated them with the Aryans who had migrated from North India. The party was therefore bitterly opposed to Brahmanism and the domination of Brahmins in the political and social sphere in South India and waged a relentless battle for the social and political rights of non-brahmin communities in general and of the backward and scheduled castes in particular.

Attracted by its ideology, many talented young men joined the party, notable among them being C.N. Annadurai, popularly known as 'Anna' ('elder brother'), who became its General Secretary. In the year 1949, there occurred a split in the party because Annadurai and some of his trusted followers became disillusioned when their septuagenarian leader married a party worker who was in her mid-twenties, left the party and founded a new party called *Dravida Munnetra Kazhagam* (D.M.K). Growing steadily in popularity, the D.M.K. continued the demand for separate *Dravidanadu* and contested for the first time in the General elections in 1957 incorporating in its election manifesto its demand for secession. Its moderate success in the election did not ring any alarm bells initially in the political circles. Shortly before the General elections of 1962, some senior leaders left the party and formed a new political outfit that however did not survive for long. But the D.M.K. itself was gaining in strength, and in the 1962 elections, it not only secured fifty seats but also emerged as the principal opposition party in the Tamilnadu assembly. It then dawned on the political *pundits* of the country that there was a serious lacuna in the constitution and an amendment was made in 1963 by the Parliament banning political parties that demanded secession from the Indian union from contesting in the elections. In response to the amendment the D.M.K. chose to abandon formally and publicly its demand separate state of *Dravidanadu*. It was not only a defining moment for the DMK party but also for politics in the Tamilnadu state. Even after giving up its demand for secession, the popularity of the DMK remained intact and the party then resolved to fight for autonomy for the state and federal rule at the centre.

The unprecedented agitation spearheaded by the students of Tamilnadu state against the declaration of Hindi as the national language in January 1965 provided an opportunity for the D.M.K. to launch an agitation and expand its support base particularly among the younger generation. The result was that in the General elections of 1967, the party won an absolute majority in the Tamilnadu assembly and formed the government. In 1969, the founder and the first Chief Minister of the party, C.N. Annadurai died after a prolonged illness and he was succeeded by M. Karunanidhi, who also took mantle of leadership of the party. In the General elections of 1971, the party secured an unprecedented victory winning more than three fourths of total seats in the assembly. On 10 October 1972, there was again a split in the party when the then treasurer of the party and a popular film actor M.G.Ramachandran was expelled from the party. Soon after he formed a new party, initially named *Anna Dravida Munnetra Kazhagam* (ADMK) on 17 October 1972 and then in 1975 renamed All India *Anna Dravida Munnetra Kazhagam* (AIADMK). In the General elections of 1977, the AIADMK won an absolute majority in the state assembly and formed the government under the Chief Ministership of M.G. Ramachandran.

Since then the Tamilnadu state has been ruled by either the DMK or the AIADMK and their hold over the political arena of the state has so far remained unchallenged. During this long period there have been so many splits and ruptures, some minor and some major, in both the parties that it is rather difficult to keep a count on them. Currently there are three major parties which can be regarded as legitimate successors of the Dravidian legacy in the political realm of Tamilnadu: the DMK, the AIADMK, and the *Marumalarcci Dravida Munnetra Kazhagam* (MDMK). The MDMK is a splinter group of the DMK, founded by Vai. Gopala Samy (Vaiko).

The parent party, the DK, never contests in any elections on principle although it actively campaigns for one or the other party at the time of local or general elections. The MGR-ADMK, a splinter group of the AIADMK and a member of the National Democratic Alliance (NDA) coalition government at the Centre merged with the Bharatiya Janata Party (BJP) in the month of February 2002.

These splits and mergers, new permutations and combinations, separations and unions which happen with sickening regularity are not, however, peculiar to the Dravidian parties. The record of almost all political parties in India is no different. Is it then possible to discern a method or a pattern behind these splits and mergers? We shall seek to address this question confining our focus on the history of the Dravidian parties. If we take the case of the three major parties mentioned above, the first and foremost point about them is that they all stick to the position that their original demand for secession from the Indian union is forsaken once and for all. Secondly, each one of these parties is found enjoying the unflinching support of specific communities in specific regions of the state and this backing constitutes the core of their political strength. Their support base no doubt enables them to continue as a significant force in the political arena, but that support alone is, however, inadequate to propel any of these parties independently to the portals of power in a general election. A close look at the electoral fortunes of these parties in the past would amply reveal that the electoral success or failure of a given party is directly linked to the constellation of other dominant caste groups or communities that it is able to muster in its support on the eve of the elections. To achieve this, these political parties attempt to do what the regional parties usually do in Indian context. They seek to enforce a commonality of interest upon as large a section of the population as possible by using one or more of the following markers of larger identity: creed, occupation, economic deprivation, or ethnic-cum-linguistic affinity or regional sub-nationalism. Given the fact that all modern nation states derive their inner strength and sustenance from an overarching identity, it is only logical that the regional political parties in India are also always on the look out for locating one or more of such identity markers to build on and sustain their support base.

But their attempts invariably fail to reach a stage of permanent consolidation in social terms because in Indian society, identities were-and still are-basically highly segmented and contextual.[18] The segmented identities are deep rooted and vibrant that concerted attempts to impose a single and uniform identity upon a larger community have not so far been successful in erasing out or even diluting the former. Every individual in Indian society lives with his/her multiple group identity and any one of those identities is invoked and accorded primacy temporarily transcending or eclipsing other identities depending upon the contextual need. In other words there is hardly a single, macro identity in which smaller, micro identities stand fully dissolved.

Each group identity in the Indian context draws its strength from its own cumulative tradition and each group interacts with other groups as and when required as associates. And each group in Indian society consists of innumerable communities, which are divided and sub-divided internally but affiliate with one another depending upon the situational requirements. This applies not only to the groups which are region specific but also to larger ones whose group identity is based on religion or language.[19] The composition of regional political parties in India is but a reflection of this general pattern obtained in Indian society and each one of these regional parties may therefore be described as a conglomeration of specific communities. Consequently the political fortunes of the parties depend not so much on the individual supporters who are committed to the ideology and programmes of the party, but on the diverse groups or communities who are prepared to affiliate themselves at a given point of time to a given political party that promises them an assured or a better share in the political power.

The demographic distribution in every major region of contemporary India is such that each community, whatever may be the basis of its self-identity, is deeply dependent on various other communities for its survival and sustenance. As long as the internal divisions as well as the interdependence between the communities continue to remain at the level as they are at present and at the same time the inter rivalry between these communities is kept at manageable level, the Indian 'nation-state' would certainly have no threat from within.

References

1. A.L. Basham, *The Wonder That was India*, Delhi, 1967, p. 486.
2. A.K Samanta, 'Separatist Movement and the Indian Nation-State', in *Alumni Annual*, Volume XXVII, 1998-99 and Volume XXVIII, 1999-2000, Presidency College Alumni Association, Calcutta, p. 65.
3. Kaushik Basu and Sanjay Subramanyam (eds), *Untravelling the Nation*, Penguin, 1996, p. 3.

4. *Ibid.*, p. 23.
5. Hemachandra Raychaudhuri, *Political History of Ancient India*, OUP, Delhi, 1996, p. 213.
6. B.N. Mukherjee, *Concept of India*, Calcutta, 1998, p. 15.
7. D.C.Sircar, *Select Inscriptions*, Vol. I, Calcutta, 1965, pp. 48-49. The term occurs often in early Buddhist texts denoting a large geographical area in cosmological terms.
8. *Ibid.*, p. 220.
9. *Markandeya Purana LVII, 6-7; LXVII, 8-9; Vayu Purana XLV, 81; Matsya Purana, XIV, 10.*
10. *Tolkappiyam*, Prologue.
11. *Tenkumari varaperunkal kuna kutakata lavellai, Purananuru, 17:1-2; Maturaikkanchi, 70-71.*
12. *Purananuru, 6:1-4; Maturaikkanci, 70-71.*
13. *Patirruppattu*, 11:23-24; 43:6-8.
14. K. Kailasapathy, *Tamil Heroic Poetry*, Oxford, 1968, p. 209.
15. *Ibid.*, p. 210.
16. B.D.Chattopadhyaya, *The Making of Early Medieval India*, OUP, 1997, pp. 16-17.
17. Subash C. Kashyap, *Our Constitution*, New Delhi, 1994, pp. 264-65.
18. Romila Thapar, *Interpreting Early India*, OUP, Delhi, p. 77.
19. Louis Dumont, *Homo Hierarchicus*, Chicago, 1970, Chapter X.

18

Social and National Consciousness of Rabindranath Tagore and the Indian National Movement (1905-1930)

Bipasha Raha

Rabindranath Tagore was deeply concerned and interested in political, social and economic life of the people. Contrary to popular image of a romantic poet he was thoroughly involved with practical problems such as education and rural reconstruction in Bengal. He had contact with the Indian national movement till 1930. Rabindranath's attitude and reaction at every critical stage of the national struggle during this period is very important. The poet's outlook had undergone a continuous process of evolution with passage of time.

At an early age, Rabindranath's father Maharshi Debendranath Tagore entrusted him with responsibility of looking after their zamindari estates. Work on the estates made him realise that Indians should be taught the virtues of self-reliance. This led him to support various small businesses in the 1890s. Though most of them failed they became the precursors of *Swadeshi* enterprises.[1] Tagore was also convinced that India could not regenerate itself without rural rejuvenation. This belief prompted his multifarious experiments in rural development conducted in his estates.

Rabindranath Tagore's involvement with the national movement was too deep for nationalist leaders to ignore him. Though he was never a member of any political party, he spontaneously responded to all issues at critical junctures of Indian politics. He addressed all demands of political, social, religious and economic life of the country. However, his political thinking was not confined to India. Gradually, he came to acquire a world outlook and began to look beyond the narrow political boundaries of his native land. He was essentially an universal man.[2] His faith in an international order was very strong.

The Beginnings of Social and National Consciousness

Tagore first expressed his patriotism in 1877 when he read a poem at Hindu Mela[3] criticising the lavish splendour of Lord Lytton's Delhi Durbar to celebrate Queen Victoria's accession as empress at a time when, the people suffered from famine and the living conditions were deplorable.[4] In letters written from London between 1878-80, he expressed similar sentiments.[5] During the 1880s and especially in the 1890s he gave vent to sharp criticisms of the British viz. on questions of opium traffic with China and the Sedition Act. He was equally critical of what he considered as national degeneration. In 1895, on the occasion of a memorial meeting for Vidyasagar who died in 1891, he bemoaned the loss of manliness among his people.[6] Vidyasagar, he said, was a lonely man entrusted with the task of rearing his people to manhood, for there was none to share his work and ideals.[7]

Tagore was pained to see how the weakness of Indians encouraged an overweening attitude in the colonial rulers against their best traditions in Britain. When in mid-1898, the government tried to introduce an Act to suppress 'seditious' speeches and writings in the newspapers,[8] Rabindranath Tagore expressed his dis-illusionment in a lecture at the Calcutta Town Hall, *Kantharodh* (the throttled).[9] He criticised the pretensions of almost every Bengali politician to represent the interest of the country[10]. The poet also showed increasing antipathy towards dependence of people on the government. This prompted him to initiate indigenous enterprises in the 1890s.

Rabindranath first came into contact with political activities in 1897 when, he helped some of the politicians of Bengal to collect money for the defense of Bal Gangadhar Tilak who was then charged with sedition. Not only financial but also legal help was sent from Bengal as the barristers of Bombay refused to take Tilak's case. In the same year, Rabindranath Tagore also read his address in the Bengal Provincial Congress. At the turn of the Twentieth Century, dissatisfied with life as zamindar, Rabindranath endeavoured to start 'national institutions' in parallel with the government. Determined to disprove the prevalent belief in Indian inferiority he thought of a different paradigm of development. He introduced the concept of *atma shakti* or 'empowerment'. It literally meant one's own strength.[11] This involved preparing the individual to participate in the larger process of development instead of creating institutions without a meaningful relationship between individuals and process of development. He appealed to the people to invest a 'strong personality' with leadership and consider him as their representative. By 'strong' he meant moral. He insisted that Indians must participate themselves in their nation-building process instead of always depending on the state for support. He derived this philosophy from the ancient Indian tradition of social responsibility. He accepted the western idea of democracy while emphasising on the Indian conception of social initiative and social responsibility. He distinguished between state and community. He was a strong supporter of local self-government in every sphere of life. The major services of the community should be performed by individuals and groups working on their own rather than at the direction of the state. Only then there could be real progress. The community could flourish only when it could look after its own welfare.[12] The state should look after only those aspects of social life which could not be dealt with by the individual or the group.

Ideas of Tagore

The poet outlined his political ideas in '*Swadeshi Samaj*'. He urged the people to consolidate on to their constructive work, remove their wants by themselves without depending on external help. Without appealing to British government he advised the people to set up a parallel government on their own. He preached to his countrymen the idea of undertaking independent of government help and control, constructive work for the regeneration of social, economic and educational life by themselves. He advocated a programme for the rejuvenation of Indian villages. He felt that without rural reconstruction there could be no real independence for the country.[13]

It was during the Swadeshi Movement, Tagore launched a protest against the proposal of Lord Curzon to partition Bengal. He was thus drawn into active politics for the first time. On 19th July 1905, Curzon's proclamation of partition was gazetted.[14] Rabindranath protested vehemently, though he did not speak publicly in Calcutta until 25 August, 1905, preferring to stay in Santiniketan. Upto 16 October 1905-the Partition Day, Tagore attended only five meetings.[15] Twenty-three songs which he composed during this period to arouse patriotic sentiments were written while staying away from Calcutta.[16] These songs touched the sentiments of his countrymen.[17] In his writings he emphasised the beauties of Bengal, the revival of her greatness and the need for rousing her inner strength instead of preaching hatred of the British.[18] On the day of Partition, the poet adopted an ancient Hindu festival *Rakshabandhan*-the symbol of brotherhood as a gesture of protest. He joined crowds walking on the streets, singing his songs. This was followed by a mass movement in north

Calcutta. Rabindranath Tagore appealed for money to be donated to a National Fund. A considerable amount around Rs 50, 000, was collected.

One aspect of the anti-partition programme that appealed very much to Rabindranath which he whole-heartedly supported was that of national education. He wanted to help set up indigenous educational institutions which would not be dependent on government support. This aspect of the *Swadeshi* Movement found favour with a section of Bengali politicians, intelligentsia and student community who immediately wanted to boycott government schools and colleges. But Tagore drew back, when number of students visited him at his house in Jorasanko and eagerly informed him that they awaited his approval to their plan of leaving their schools and colleges, he refused to be a party to such decisions as this principle of boycott never thus appealed to him. Referring to this incident years later Rabindranath explained: "The anarchy of emptiness never tempts me, ever when it is resorted to as a temporary measure. I am frightened at an abstraction, which is ready to ignore living reality. Those students were no mere phantoms to me."[19] He however devoted himself to the cause of National Council of Education. He helped it to raise money, wrote a syllabus of studies, gave a systematic course of lectures on literature and in this way he and others began what later became Jadavpur University. But he soon became dis-illusioned and left the Council when he found himself disagreeing with its method of functioning.[20]

From this time onwards, he began to emphasize on the need for rural reconstruction. He had himself initiated work of rural upliftment on his estates much earlier. In the 1890s, he set up arbitration courts, parallel systems to that of government courts. Cases were taken to them by the villagers. Tagore himself was the final court of appeal. Its success was manifested by the fact that for many years, no tenant filed a suit in the magisterial or *munsiff* courts. During the Swadeshi Movement, he appealed to political leaders to channelise public enthusiasm fanned by the announcement of Partition proposal, to constructive work. He suggested that a band of workers be organized to give a new direction to such work. They should undertake work in the spheres of rural health, sanitation, agriculture, cottage industries, water supply, education, communication, credit facilities etc. But such proposals did not catch the imagination of either the leaders or the public. He failed to convince them that for real political progress it was necessary to inculcate among the people the urge to remove their own wants through self-reliance. He identified patriotism with constructive work. It was not till the arrival of Mahatma Gandhi in the political arena and his insistence (in the 1920s) on such work that its importance was realised.

During this time Tagore started a welfare society, *Hitoishi Sabha* on his estate at Patisar covering about 125 villages with more than 60, 000 people. Both the estate and the villagers contributed financially to build up a common fund. Schools, hospitals, tanks, roads and various other welfare schemes were initiated and maintained by the *Sabha.*[21] To meet the credit needs of the people an agricultural bank was opened which advanced loans at low rates of interest to peasants. Arrangements were thus made to motivate villagers to undertake welfare measures by themselves.

Disillusioned with the methods of political agitation adopted by the leaders, Rabindranath Tagore withdrew completely from politics by 1907. That same year he outlined in great detail a programme for constructive work for rural rejuvenation in his address to the Bengal Provincial Conference at Pabna. There he emphasised the need for adoption of the co-operative principle in all types of activities and the involvement of the educated youth in rural work. He emphasised on development of both agriculture and handicrafts industries to help economic regeneration. In all these he insisted on self-reliance.[22]

The poet's withdrawal from active politics was probably prompted by the outburst of violence and terrorist activities that started in Bengal in 1907-08. He was shocked by the growing Hindu-Muslim animosity in Bengal and by killing of British civilians by terrorist. Rabindranath could not support violence of any kind though he greatly admired the tremendous courage and self-sacrifice of young terrorists.[23] He never again wanted to participate in active politics. In fact, he wrote to his son that he had serious misgivings about his participation in the *Swadeshi* Movement.[24] According to one recent view, he was by this time utterly convinced that the only way for Bengalis to succeed in national enterprises was to start on a small scale out of the public gaze and gradually develop them.[25] Rabindranath was particularly in favour of such enterprises that were based on the principle of co-operation viz. the Hindustan Co-operative Insurance Company, whose secretary was his nephew Surendranath Tagore.[26]

By this time, Tagore's vision had widened far beyond the limits of narrow nationalism. The concept of east-west synthesis began to dominate his thought process from now on. He gave a new dimension to India's quest for freedom. He explained that the root of India's malaise was to be located not in her subjection to colonial rule but in her social degeneration.[27] The former was an outcome of the latter. He was rather skeptical about using antipathy towards British rule to forge a bond of unity among Indians. Once the British left India this bond would snap and there would be internal feuds as the people would search for targets of animosity among themselves.[28] To the poet the best solution lay in the fusion of diverse people in India and harmonious synthesis of the East and the West.[29] In 1915, Rabindranath published *Ghare Baire (The Home and the World)*, one of his most widely read novels.[30] It was based on terrorist violence that shook Bengal in 1907 and after. There was serious soul-searching about the *Swadeshi* Movement. Rabindranath gradually found it difficult to reconcile his own growing faith in East-West synthesis with the anti-imperial struggle. He discovered the eternal India transcending narrow nationalism. He wrote his famous poem *Bharattirtha*: "O heart of mine, awake in this holy place of pilgrimage; In this land of India, on the shore of vast humanity".[31] There was thus a shift in his stand towards the national movement.

The Noble Prize

In the meanwhile, Rabindranath Tagore's own relationship with the British government improved for a few years. The Nobel Prize (1913) accorded him an elevated status in the western world and enabled him to exert some influence. The British government conferred the knighthood on him in 1915.[32] The poet exerted his influence privately to persuade the government to enquire into the cases of young men in Bengal against whom there were charges of sedition. Relations however, became embittered concerning Tagore's visit to Japan in 1916, as it was undertaken in the midst of the First World War, and his denouncement of the cult of aggressive nationalism which he described as a concept borrowed from the west.[33] Such views did not appeal to the people of Japan who were fighting the War.[34] Nor did it appeal to the Indian revolutionaries living in the United States of America whom Tagore met in the course of his travel to the country that followed.

However, by 1917 Rabindranath knew that he could not find it in himself to support petty aggressive nationalism [35] which he said was an 'instrument of political hegemony' and an 'ideology to legitimize' the oppression of one nation over the other. His belief in the unity of man and in a moral universe was too strong to make him support aggressive nationalism.[36] Rabindranath's highly controversial book *Nationalism* was published in 1917.[37] In this he once again attacked the western idea of nationalism directly. He also condemned nationalism in Japan, which was contrary to her ancient tradition. In Japan he learnt about nationalism, which emerged fanatic. About a decade and a half ago, through Okakura in Calcutta, Rabindranath was first introduced to Japan's cultural life and he was impressed by the noble aspects of it. But once on the soil of Japan, he was made acutely aware of a 'jingoism' which prompted him from that time to write the essays on nationalism one after another and these he read in America. He also gave his own interpretation of Indian nationalism with its emphasis on humanism and synthesis between East and West. Tagore's love for humanity contradicted with the nationalist movement in India. These views did not appeal to his countrymen as nationalism had entered a new phase of growth in India. His lectures on nationalism were thus 'ill timed'.[38] According to one recent research, it was 'ill timed' because India then badly needed to establish her own identity. Tagore was asserting his faith and conviction in a moral universe, in the ultimate triumph of the innate goodness of man. This conviction was the basis of his internationalism.[39] He was a poet and a humanist, rather than a politician. Writing about India's glorious past he observed: "Her mission has been that of a hostess who has to provide proper accommodation for numerous guests; whose habits and requirements are different from one another. This gives rise to infinite complexities whose solution depends not merely upon tactfulness but upon sympathy and true realisation of the unity of man. In fact, our history has not been of the rise and fall of kingdoms, of fights for political supremacy. In our country records of these days have been despised and forgotten, for they in no way represent the true history of our people. Our history is that of our social life and attainment of spiritual ideals."[40] These beliefs were however, not acceptable then to the Indian youth and politicians at a time when the country was groaning under the ill-effects of the War with which they had nothing to do but the brunt of which they had to bear, a price they had to pay as a result of colonial domination. Tagore's acquaintance with the American way of life and the intensity with which Europe was fighting the War gave birth to a new idea in his mind. The poet was now convinced of the need to align his own country with the larger world. This task of unification could be performed only at Santiniketan. He wanted to make Santiniketan the 'connecting thread' between India and the world. The blindness of nationalism, he felt, led man astray from the path of the good, which could be recovered only through unity. He observed: "I have it in mind to make Santiniketan the connecting thread between India and the world. I have to found a world centre for the study of humanity there. The days of petty nationalism are numbered-let the first step towards universal union occur in the fields of Bolpur. I want to make that place somewhere between the limits of nation and geography."[41] According to one recent research, this was the earliest 'recorded glimmering' in his mind of Visva-Bharati, his university-to-be.[42]

When Rabindranath Tagore returned to Bengal in March 1917, from his trip abroad he felt himself drawn into the political arena as the country was in turmoil. In June 1917, the Home Rule leader Annie Beasant was interned following a government order. Internment of many young men in Bengal without trial followed. While politicians in Bengal refrained from active protest, Rabindranath expressed his unequivocal support for her in a moving statement issued in July 1917. In this way he was influenced by the political situation though he would never get involved in the way that he did in 1905.

The Jallianwala Bagh Massacre

The significant event in the political life of the country that evoked sharp reaction from him was the Jallianwala Bagh tragedy of 13 April, 1919. The police opened fire on a peaceful mob assembled at Jallianwala Bagh killing a large number of persons.[43] The poet waited for a couple of days for Indian leaders to make a fitting protest against this barbaric act. Disappointed with the attitude of contemporary leaders, he took it upon himself to address this crisis in the political life of his country. He wrote: "A great crime has been done in the name of law in the Punjab. Such terrible eruptions of evil leave their legacy of the wreckage of ideals behind them. What happened in Jallianwala Bagh was itself a monstrous progeny of a monstrous war, which for years had been defiling God's world with fire and poison, physical and moral. The immenseness of the sin through which humanity had waded across the blood red length of agony has bred callousness in the minds of those who have power in their hands with no check of sympathy within, or fear of resistance without. The cowardliness of the powerful who owned no shame in using their machines of frightfulness upon the unarmed and unwarned villagers, and inflicting unspeakable humiliations upon their fellow beings behind the screen of an indecent mockery of justice, and yet not feeling for a moment that it was the meanest form of insult to their own manhood, has become only possible through the opportunity which the late war has given to man for constantly outraging his own higher nature, trampling truth and honour under foot."[44]

When he failed to convince the British government and the British public about the heinous crime committed against humanity he wrote a moving letter to Viceroy Lord Chelmsford asking to be relieved of his knighthood.[45] He wrote to him: "The enormity of the measures taken by the government in the Punjab for quelling some local disturbances has, with a rude shock, revealed to our minds the helplessness of our position as British subjects in India. knowing that our appeals have been in vain and that the passion of vengeance is blinding the noble vision of statesmanship in our Government which could so easily afford to be magnanimous, as befitting its physical strength and normal tradition, the very least that I can do for my country is to take all consequences upon myself in giving voice to the protest of the millions of my countrymen, surprised into a dumb anguish of terror."[46] He therefore wished to stand, shorn of all special distinctions, by the side of those of his countrymen who, for their so-called insignificance were liable to suffer a degradation not fit for human beings. So he observed: "All these are the reasons which have compelled me to ask your Excellency, with due deference and regret, to relieve me of my title of knighthood which I had the honour to accept from His Majesty the King at the hands of your predecessor, for whose nobleness of heart I still entertain great admiration."[47]

Rabindranath Tagore's letter printed in the press on 2 June 1919, was widely read in India. But, according to a recent research, this gesture of the poet in spite of its courage and nobility, did not appeal to public imagination as Gandhi's Salt *Satyagraha* at Dandi in 1930 would do.[48] Yet, that its impact was more subtle and appealed to the intellect is undeniable even though the British government did not officially relieve him of the title.

Tagore's rising status as poet and innate humanism made it difficult for him to remain indifferent to the political situation in the country. In a letter to William Rothenstein, the artist, he explained: "I have nothing to do directly with politics. I am not a nationalist, moderate or immoderate in my political aspiration. But politics is not a mere abstraction. It has its personality and it does intrude into my life when I am human. It kills and maims individuals, it tells lies, it uses its sacred sword of justice for the purpose of massacre, it spreads misery broadcast over centuries of exploitation and I cannot say to myself, 'Poet, you have nothing to do with these facts for they belong to politics.' This politics assumes its fullest diabolical aspect when I find all its hideous acts of injustice find moral support from a whole nation only because it wants to enjoy in comfort and safety the golden fruits reaped from object degradation of human races.[49]

Rabindranath Tagore and Mahatma Gandhi

Indian politics brought the poet into contact with Gandhi. Soon the differences in attitudes of these two great contemporaries towards political issues and the nationalist movement became apparent in spite of their mutual admiration. The two met for the first time in 1915 at Santiniketan though, they were familiar with each other's activities before. Thus was laid the foundation of a life-long friendship between them. It also brought into relief the contrast between their personalities and the dynamics of their idealism.[50] Time and again Gandhi sought Tagore's support to his political programmes. By 1919 when Gandhi launched Rowlatt Satyagraha, Tagore's reputation was far too formidable for political leaders to overlook his political views. Rabindranath welcomed Gandhi's ideals of non-violence on 12 April, on the eve of Jallianwala Bagh massacre.

However, conflict between the two was inevitable. Tagore went to Europe and America in mid-May 1920 and returned after fourteen months. In the meanwhile, Gandhi started the Non-Cooperation Movement. The poet thoroughly disapproved of those aspects of the national political programme, which were negative rather than constructive. He advocated a positive programme of national regeneration. He could never support a negative reaction even against imperialism. At the height of the Non-Cooperation Movement he was speaking of co-operation and reconciliation between the East and the West. He could not support the linking of Khilafat issue with the Non-Cooperation Movement as, mixing of religious issues with a political movement was anathema to him. Expressing his reservations about the methods of non-cooperation the poet observed: "Non-Cooperation appear [s] to me to be the progeny of the union of rejection from one party and dejection from the other party and therefore though I tried to shed upon it my best smile, I long hesitated to welcome it to my heart."[51] He was totally opposed to destructive activities viz. burning of foreign clothes and boycott of educational institutions by students. In this, he was reiterating the stand he had taken during the *Swadeshi* Movement.

Rabindranath Tagore returned to India in mid-July 1921. Gandhi came to meet him On 6 September 1921 at his ancestral house at Jorasanko to convince him in person about the necessity of the Non-Cooperation Movement. C.F. Andrews was the sole witness to the lengthy discussions they had. Though neither published what was discussed, Rabindranath gave an account of it to Elmhirst who had come to Santiniketan to work in the institute for rural reconstruction. Gandhi tried to convince Rabindranath on the ground that based on non-violence, his movement for *Swaraj* was similar to the *Swadeshi* Movement which the latter had promoted earler.[52] But Rabindranath disagreed saying that the whole world was suffering from a cult of selfish and short-sighted nationalism. India had always offered hospitality to people of all nations and creeds. There was still much that Indians could learn from the West and vice-versa.[53] The poet firmly believed that India's problem was world-wide and no people of the earth could work out its salvation by detaching itself from others.

Though Rabindranath supported the Mahatma's principle of non-violence, he had deep reservations about the Non-Cooperation Movement remaining non-violent. He did not believe that violent emotions could be controlled by non-violent principles. Even while Gandhi and Tagore were discussing this, some non-cooperators[54] were making a bonfire of foreign cloth picketed from shops in the neighbourhood in the latter's courtyard. This was not non-violence to the poet.[55] Nor was he convinced that the Mahatma's political programme could unite Hindus and Muslims. He had earlier expressed his misgivings to leaders about common hatred towards the British being the platform for unity among Indians.[56] Such artificial unity would disappear once the British left the country. But feelings of hatred that was fanned would then be directed within. Hindus and Muslims would not be able to live in peace. Rabindranath reiterated the same views to Gandhi. He said that only when children of different religions, communities and castes were schooled together could violent feelings that existed be overcome.[57]

Rabindranath also differed with Gandhi on the issue of *charkha* and *khadi.* When Gandhi, after failing to convince the poet about the Non-Cooperation Movement, asked him for support on his spinning programme Tagore replied: 'Poems I can spin, Gandhiji, songs and plays I can spin, but of your precious cotton what a mess I would make."[58] While Gandhi insisted on the profound symbolic significance of spinning, Rabindranath Tagore disagreed that all true Indians should spin. He did not subscribe to Gandhi's view that *Charkha* could eradicate poverty and hunger.

Tagore's disagreement with Gandhi was carried beyond the meeting held at Jorasanko. Immediately after this Rabindranath, even while expressing his admiration for Gandhi, was critical of the unquestioning obedience of the people to the leader.[59] Gandhi replied to him stating that his misgivings were unfounded.[60] But Tagore's fears were not unjustified. On 3 February, 1922, Rabindranath issued a statement warning leaders and the people about the possibility of eruption of violence and two days later, an irate mob of non-cooperators burnt to death several policemen at Chauri Chaura. This forced Gandhi to call off the Non-Cooperation Movement. On 10 March, 1922, Gandhi was arrested on charges of sedition, tried and sentenced to six years term.[61] In Calcutta, as a kind of tribute to him and the philosophy of non-violence, Rabindranath Tagore cancelled his plans to stage his latest play.[62]

In the meantime, Rabindranath concentrated on efforts at rural reconstruction of Sriniketan where work had begun in earnest since 1921. He found it increasingly difficult to reconcile his views on internationalism, humanism and East-West synthesis with the hatred and contempt for others bred by aggressive nationalism. Between 1924-25 he went on his travels again to China, Japan and Argentina, preaching co-operation at a time when his countrymen were swayed by the doctrine of non-cooperation in spite of the apparent failure of the movement. [63] His differences with Gandhi and other political leaders became sharper by late 1920s. In November 1924, the Indian National Congress accepted Gandhi's proposal that all its members must wear *khadi* or hand-spun cloth at all official programmes and also fulfil a minimum spinning requirement.[64] This drew a severe criticism from Rabindranath. He did not agree that spinning could bring about an increase in national wealth. Nor could it ensure *Swaraj.* The poet expressed his apprehensions about a blind faith on a very large scale in the *charkha* in a country which was 'so liable to succumb to the lure of short cuts when pointed out by a personality about whose moral earnestness' they had no doubt. The turning of the *charkha* to the exclusion of modern science and machines could no longer ensure economic well-being. The *charkha*, he noted, was doing harm because of 'undue prominence' which it had thus usurped, whereby it only added 'fuel to the smouldering weakness' that was 'eating into our vitals'. So he said: "How often have my personal feelings of regard strongly urged me to accept at Mahatma Gandhi's hands my enlistment as a follower of the *charkha* cult,[65] but as often have my reason and conscience restrained me, lest I should be a party to the raising of the *charkha* to a high place than is its due, thereby distracting attention from other more important factors in our task of all-round reconstruction".[66]

The *charkha* agitation thus failed to move Rabindranath. The Mahatma reacted rather sharply to the poet's criticism.[67] He accused the latter of being unable to appreciate the needs of the common people and for not being in tune with mass feelings. Yet Rabindranath was unconvinced. He wrote later that he believed that the cult of the *charkha* could spread easily in India only because the temptation to extort concessions from England by putting pressure on Lancashire was strong. During the *Swadeshi* Movement boycott had the same external objective. Indian political leaders were constantly thinking of the effect on British administration, of forcing it to come to terms. All this he felt, was entirely superficial. It was, he observed, 'foolish to think that the country can be awakened by the inanity of ignorant minds'.[68]

Between 1926 and 1930 Rabindranath went on his travels abroad again. He visited Italy, America, Germany, England, Bucharest, Canada as well as to places in the East viz., Java Bali, Malaya and Japan. All this while eminent Europeans viz. Italian scholar Tucci, physicist Arnold Sommerfield and Viceroy Lord Irwin visited his institute at Santiniketan. He was all the more conscious about the need for international co-operation.

In the meanwhile, the poet's alienation from the Indian national movement was complete. His grounds for differences with Gandhi, the undisputed leader of the masses, on vital issues of *charkha*, *khadi* and non-cooperation were incomprehensible to the average Indian masses and political leaders alike. According to one recent research Tagore seemed unpatriotic to the average Indian nationalist for not supporting Gandhi.[69] But to Tagore, national claims could never obliterate human obligations. Aggressive nationalism could only lead to the destruction of mankind. There was a time, he said, when the spirit of the people was hospitable. But this spirit had been overcome by the spirit of the 'nation', with its 'intense consciousness of self-interest concentrated in political organization'. Whenever the spirit of the 'nation' had come, he observed, it had destroyed sympathy and beauty, and driven out the 'generous obligations of human relationships from the heart of men'. Though in contemporary politics it dominated the spirit of man everywhere in the world, it would die like the 'worm which lies in the heart of the fruit that it has devoured'. It would die, he said, but unfortunately 'may meanwhile destroy things of unrivalled worth, the products of centuries of self-control and spiritual training.'[70] To Tagore mere political necessity was unimportant. It was for the sake of humanity that one should turn one's mind towards the spiritual unity of man.[71] That was why he could not agree with the methods of anti-imperial struggle adopted by his contemporaries. His appeal for rural reconstruction and development of *atma-shakti* as the only way for attaining *swaraj* was ignored. In 1930, Gandhi launched the Civil Disobedience Movement. Rabindranath went on his travel to the west and the relationship between the poet and the nationalist movement entered yet another new phase. In fine it may be said that Tagore had a high sense of social consciousness and he chalked out his own programmes on education and rural reconstruction and implemented them in his own way which at that time did not capture the attention of people but it is now known well for he had a vision and was a man of action.

References

1. Sachidranath Adhikari, *Shilaidaha O Rabindranath*, Calcutta, 1974, pp. 102-104.
2. Rabindranath Tagore, *The Religion of Man*, London, 1913, p. 48.
3. Krishna Dutta and Andrew Robinson, *Rabindranath Tagore the Myriad-Minded Man*, New Delhi, 2000, p. 62.
4. Prashanta Kumar Paul, *Rabijibani* Calcutta, revised ed. Vol. I, 1993, p. 254.

5. Rabindranath Tagore, *Chithiparta*, Vol. I, Calcutta, 1993, pp. 62-110.
6. Prashanta Kumar Paul, *op. cit.* Vol. II, Calcutta, 1984, pp. 62-64.
7. Krishna Dutta and Andrew Robinson, *op. cit.* p. 65.
8. *Ibid.*, pp. 122-23.
9. Rabindranath Tagore, *Rabindra Rachanabali* (henceforth *RR*), Calcutta, 1916, Vol. X pp. 424-31.
10. Rabindranath Tagore, 'Rajtika' (The Raj Seal, *Ibid*, Vol. XXVII, p. 248. Written in 1897-98, it is the story of a loyal Bengali. He has no talent but is an admirer of the British. He suddenly finds himself transformed into a patriot. Henceforth, he tries to acquire the admiration of his nationalist followers.
11. Rabindranath Tagore, 'Swadeshi Samaj' (Society and State), 'Atmashakti', *Ibid*, Vol. III, pp. 513-635.
12. *Ibid.*
13. *Ibid.*
14. Sumit Sarkar, *Modern India 1885-1947*, Madras, 1992, pp. 106-112.
15. Prashanta Paul, *op. cit.*, Vol. V, p. 270.
16. Krishna Dutta and Andrew Robinson. *op. cit.*, p. 145.
17. Among the most popular ones were *Banglar mati Banglar jal* (The soil and waters of Bengal) and *Jadi Tor dak shune keu na ashe tabe ekla chalo re* (if no one answers to your call, walk alone). Rabindranath Tagore, *Gitabitan*, Vol. I, Calcutta, 1967, pp. 255 and 244. The last song was a personal favourite of Gandhi.
18. Sumit Sarkar, *The Swadeshi Movement in Bengal, 1903-1908*, Calcutta, 1973, p. 292.
19. Rabindranath Tagore to C.F. Andrews, letter dated 5 March, 1921. Refer C.F. Andrews (ed) *Letters to a Friend*, London, 1928, pp. 131-32.
20. Krishna Dutta and Andrew Robinson, *op. cit.*, p. 146.
21. *Ibid.*
22. Rabindranath Tagore, 'Sabhapatir Abhibhashan, Pabna Pradeshik Sammelani', *Palliprakriti*, Calcutta, 1987, p. 2.
23. Rabindranath Tagore, *The Home and the World*, London, 1985.
24. Letter written to Rathindranath, 7 April, 1910. *Chithipatra*, Calcutta, 1942, Vol. 2, p. 14.
25. Krishna Dutta and Andrew Robinson, *op. cit.*, p. 149.

26. Bipasha Raha, Rabindranath Tagore and the Co-operative Idea, *Bengal Past and Present*, Vol. 119, nos. 228-229, Parts I-II, 2000, p. 116.
27. Rabindranath Tagore, 'Path O Patheya' (Ends and Means), delivered on 25 May, 1908, *RR*, Vol. X, p. 447.
28. *Ibid.*
29. Rabindranath Tagore, "Purba O Paschim" (East and West), delivered in July, 1908, *Ibid*, Vol. XII pp. 272-73.
30. Rabindranath Tagore, *The Home and the World*, *op. cit.*
31. Rabindranath Tagore, *Bharattirtha*, 2 July, 1910 translated by Indira Devi Chaudhurani
32. Krishna Dutta and Andrew Robinson, *op. cit.*, p. 185.
33. *Ibid.*, p. 201.
34. Rabindranath Tagore, *Japanyatri*, English translation by Pramatha Chaudhuri and Indira Devi, Calcutta, 1961, pp. 9-16.
35. Letter to Rathindranath dated 11 October, 1916.
36. Sisir Kumar Das (ed) *The English Writings of Rabindranath Tagore*, 'Introduction', Vol. 3, New Delhi, 1996, p. 21.
37. Rabindranath Tagore, *Nationalism* New York, 1917, pp. 15-16.
38. Sisir Kumar Das (ed), *op. cit.*, Vol. 2, New Delhi, 2001, p. 771.
39. Goutam Ghoshal, 'Tagore and Sri Aurobindo', *Mother India*, September, 2002, p. 811.
40. Sisir Das, *op. cit.*, Vol. 2, p. 40.
41. Letter to Rathindranath, dated 11 October. 1916. *Chithipatra*, Vol. 2, pp. 55-56.
42. Krishna Dutta and Andrew Robinson, *op. cit.*, pp. 204-05.
43. Sumit Sarkar, *Modern India, 1885-1947*, p. 172.
44. Sumit Kumar Das (ed), *op. cit.*, Vol. 3, p. 752.
45. Letter dated 30 May, 1919. E. P. Thompson, *Rabindranath Tagore: Poet and Dramatist*, New Delhi, 1991, pp. 259-60.
46. Sisir Kumar Das (ed), *op. cit.*, Vol. 3, p. 751.
47. *Ibid.*, pp. 751-52.
48. Krishna Dutta, Andrew Robinson, *op. cit.*, p. 217.
49. Letter dated 6 October, 1920. Mary M. Lago (ed) *Imperfect Encounters: Letter of William Rothenstein and Rabindranath Tagore, 1911-1941*, Cambridge, 1972, pp. 277-78.
50. Krishna Kripalini, *Rabindranath Tagore: A Biography*, Visva-Bharati, 1980, p. 257.

51. Letter from USA to C.F. Andrews, dated March 1921, published in *Modern Review*, March, 1921.
52. *A Centenary Volume, Rabindranath Tagore, 1861-1961*, Sahitya Academy, Calcutta, 1961, pp. 14-15.
53. *Ibid.*
54. Rabindranath Tagore, *Letters to a friend*, London 13 March, 1921, Letter to C.F. Andrews
55. Leonard K. Elmhirst, *Poet and Ploughman*, Calcutta, 1975, pp. 20-22.
56. Rabindranath Tagore, 'Path O Patheya' *op. cit.*, pp. 446-47.
57. Krishna Dutta and Andrew Robinson, *op. cit.*, pp. 237-40.
58. Elmhirst, *op. cit.*
59. Rabindranath Tagore, 'The Call of Truth', *Modern Review*, October, 1921.
60. Mahatma Gandhi, 'The Great Sentinel', *Young India*, 13 October, 1921
61. Sumit Sarkar, *op. cit.*, p. 232.
62. Krishna Dutta and Andrew Robinson *op. cit.*, p. 241.
63. *Modern Review*, November 1924.
64. Sumit Sarkar, *op. cit.*
65. Rabindranath Tagore, 'The Cult of the Charkha' in Sisir Das (ed.) *op. cit.*, Vol. 3 pp. 538-48. It was first published in *Modern Review*, in September, 1925.
66. *Ibid.*
67. *Young India*, 5 November, 1925.
68. Letter to Rani Mahalanobis, dated, 16 October, 1929. *Visva-Bharati Quarterly*, October, 1929, pp. 310-11.
69. Krishna Dutta and Andrew Robinson, *op. cit.*, p. 285.
70. Rabindranath Tagore, 'International Relations', 1925, in Sisir Kumar Das (ed.) *op. cit.* Vol. 3, pp. 472-76.
71. Rabindranath Tagore, 'The Way to Unity', 1923, published in *Visva-Bharati Quarterly*, Vol. 1, No. 2, July, 1923. Ref. *Ibid.*, p. 405.

19

Socio-Cultural Reforms in Bengal and the Indian National Movement : A Case Study of Prabartak Samgha in Nation Building (1915-1947)

Amiya Ghosh

It is generally accepted that the grass-root level studies are as remunerating and significant as the macro level studies of the Indian National Movement. Simultaneously, the somewhat erroneous idea that political organizations are the primary structural base of the Indian National Movement has been melting away during last two decades. Through the way of social and cultural reforms, 'Nation Making' movement had started which was not apparently political in character as well as approach. But the contribution of such bodies to the growth of the Indian National Movement at the regional level can never be underestimated. In the history of the Freedom Movement in Bengal, the emergence of Prabartak Samgha, was a pointer to this direction. The paper seeks therefore to trace the emergence of a new line of 'Nation Making' through socio-cultural reforms in Bengal during the Indian National Movement.

Early in 1915, when Bengal was at the height of the revolutionary movement, and the nation was passing through the momentous ordeal of fire, that with the blessing of Aurobindo Ghosh and Motilal Roy, (Revolutionary and founder of Prabartak Samgha) 'Prabartak', a Bengali fortnightly[1] was brought out to preach the gospel of 'creative nationalism'. It was a message of new faith and dynamic hope that was immediately hailed by young educated Bengali revolutionaries as the herald of a new path. It was the call of a nation building through socio-cultural and spiritual re-awakening. The 'Prabartak' was the first to demand both from government and the people 'no patch-work remedy but utter transformation of character' and set itself 'to revolutionize the brain of the nation' as the starting point of a thorough and all-round constructive endeavour.

British rule and the impact of the West acting as an irritant stimulus intensified a search for identity in Bengal or India. The conflict and contradictions between the British and nationalist forces since the late nineteenth century sowed the seeds of both militancy and constructive nation building. All these forces were reflected in certain organizations and one such organizations was Prabartak Samgha. This Samgha with its limited capacity and resources was still engaged in the work of man making for socio-cultural and economic reconstruction on a spiritual basis. The Prabartak Samgha presented a philosophy and programme parallel to the main stream of the freedom movement but Samhga was emphasizing on nation making. The Samgha and its significant role has not so far received attention from the historians of the national movement.[2]

The Swadeshi Movement, which began with the partition of Bengal in 1905, was a landmark in our national history. Anti-partition upsurge, was the starting point of a new approach of two-fold critic of the congress movement.[3] The congress itself was attacked for representing merely the English educated elite alienated from the common people. Instead of prayers and petitions, self-reliance and constructive work became the new slogans. Swadeshi enterprises and stores tried to organize education on autonomous basis at the village level.[4] The emphasis on self-reliance identified increasingly with the revivalist approach to the Hindu religious tradition by the moderates and an appeal to religious sentiments came to be regarded as the most effective technique for bridging the gulf between the educated and common man, as well as an extremely useful moral booster for political activities. From July 1905, self help or *"atmasakti"* seemed to have become for a time to creed of the whole of Bengal. The year was full of Swadeshi schemes.[5] It is noted that at the same time, Rabindranath gradually tried to detach himself from the direct politics, devoting himself to village reconstruction efforts in his central Bengal estates (Silaidaha) and educational experiment at Santiniketan. On the other hand, the first step towards the foundation of the Prabartak

Samgha was taken in July 1905. Motilal Roy organized the *"Satpathavalambee Sampradaya"* (the society who have chosen the true path) with a band of self less youths of Chandernagore. [6]

The history of Freedom Movement in India would reveal Chandernagore, the French settlement in Bengal, played a noble part all along. It could not be denied that France had once played a great part in the moral and political upliftment of Europe. Her remarkable slogan "Liberty, Equality and Fraternity" could not be forgotten and she had always offered the necessary heaven to the political sufferers. According to the Tegart's Report (1913)[7] and Sedition Committee's Report (1918)[8], Chandernagore too gradually became the rallying place of the hunted revolutionary of Bengal. Even Aurobindo, the great revolutionary, had anxiously sought safety and had gone to Chandernagore for this purpose in 1910.[9] Motilal Roy received this political revolutionary of India with open arms and gave him necessary support and succour at Chandernagore. The leader received a lot of suggestions and hints for the enrichment of his devotional life from Sri Aurobindo[10] who was well known for his mystic spiritual wealth developed in distant land at Pondicherry, the capital of French India.

Bankim Chandra by his mantra *"Vandemataram"* brought about the initial awakening of India. His *"Anandamath"* gave the dream formula for its overt realization. Swami Vivekananda touched upon the same chord to inspire the nation in the worship of the motherland. Sri Aurobindo, took upon the call of these great personalities of modern India and made it his own life formula. He endeavoured whole-heartedly to materialize through his national and political *sadhana*[11] (activities). Bankim, Vivekanda and Aurobindo–they were the prophets of the nation-belong to a race of our national *Gurus*. Sri Aurobindo was indeed a new and remarkable man in Indian politics. After 1910, Aurobindo gradually shifted himself from *"tantra"* or revolutionary work and his follower Motilal Roy, realized also that those men who dedicated to the service of the motherland must first possess impeccable character. Man making, through a spiritual training for the development of the divinity from within, should be the first towards nation building. The energy generated by the *Swadeshi* era was wasted due to the absence of the national character.[12] Rabindranath also tried to make this point in his famous novel *"Char Adhyay"* and *"Ghare Baire"*.[13] Rabindranath had repeatedly mentioned that the act of violence was an attempt to shortcut and inconsistent with the basic value of Indian culture and civilization.[14] Aurobindo and Motilal felt the same realization but in a different way. By 1918, Motilal definitely opted for the constructive path of man making in accordance with what he considered as the spirit of Indian civilization.[15]

Prabartak Samgha

The movement of the Prabartak Samgha had an interesting history behind it. From the beginning onwards it had to pass through all the different stages of our national fragment. The seed of the *Samgha* was laid by Motilal Roy at Chandernagore.[16] The earliest influence, which worked in the life of the founder, was the inspiration of Ramakrishna and Vivekananda that led to starting of a philanthropic institution-the *"Satpathvalambee Sampradaya"*, at Chandernagore (1905).[17] The *"Satpathvalambee Sampradaya"* was engaged in famine and flood relief, social welfare and philanthropic activities.[18] The Swadeshi Movement gave the political dimension to Motilal's thought and action. The original idea of simple humanitarian work appeared inadequate in the changed situation. Motilal himself wrote in his *"Jeevansangini"* (novel) 'the Mighty tide of the Swadeshi Movement swept away our mission of service'.[19] In the wake of the Swadeshi Movement, followed the revolutionary cult in Bengal, in which also Motilal threw himself and became one of its leading figures.[20]

Motilal increasingly felt that men who were dedicated to the service of the motherland should first possess an impeccable character. The character building on the basis of education of spiritual and sublimation of the animal instincts into consciousness of man's inherent divinity were essential to national progress.[21] He was fully convinced that only a sustained programme on the nation building could ensure a firm foundation for the future independence of India. The first steps used towards nation building were strength of character, personal detachment and selfless work.[22] This work of making the nation realized in its potentiality and also to stand on its own legs was the essence of the creative nationalism or *"nirmana"*, which became the core of the Motilal's teaching. To propagate his ideas Motilal started a Bengali journal '*Prabartak*' with effect from September 1915. In February 1921, *Samgha* was founded a school named *"Vidyapith"*.[23] It was to accommodate students who had left government controlled educational institutions during non-cooperation movement. This *"Vidyapith"* gave the *Prabartak* group its first institutional base.

The Wings of the Mission

The Mainstream of the *Samgha* energy, deeply inspired by an intensive outlook and creative orientation always moved in the direction of practical nation building. The first business of the *Samgha* had been to establish itself on a firm spiritual foundation of a new society and culture; the second, to ensure for itself a proper practical basis of stable economy. In this connection, an English organ of *Samgha* wrote "our ideal is no spirituality, that withdraws from life, but the conquest of life by the power of the spirit".[24] *Prabartak* preached a new view of social life, which was also a mode of self-expression. In the field of religion, *Samgha* has stood for the external and universal religion. They realized, the religion is dynamic–its "*sadhana*" is "*karma*" or work. All work thus became "*Yagya*" or sacrifice.[25]

Spirituality of the *Samgha* not only revealed the inner being but also sustained and developed its outer environment and orientation. No caste or colour was recognized within the *Samgha*, not to the question of untouchability.[26] *Samgha*-culture was one and indivisible. Nobody in the *Samgha* possesses any personal home or property.[27] Every action is in a form of sacrifice. Earning for the God (people) in the field or factory is less a sacred, task than uttering prayer in the temple.

The Bolshevik Revolution of 1917 had held out new hopes for the downtrodden. The Bengal workers and peasants party was founded in Calcutta in 1924-25.[28] At the same time M.N. Roy tried to resume contact with his revolutionary friends.[29] Prabartak Samgha acknowledged that social and political changes of external nature were necessary. A journal of *Samgha* (The *Prabartak*) wrote "the constructive inspiration that burns in the heart of Russia today brings to us a message of hope that a band of fiery workers if rightly determined to work for the country, can recreate the whole nation and make it of a new humanity".[30] *Samgha* criticized the Bolshevism and said that "It seems to have a communal idea but communism with a vengeance behind its dark cover of the fire and steel."[31] Russia had tried materialistic communism. Motilal said, "It is a crash of ego against ego, not synthesis. But a 'spiritual communism' is the intension of nature–the direct will of the spirit of humanity."[32]

Socio-Economic Thought and its Application

It will not be an exaggeration to reiterate here that the *Samgha* was a mission of integral life, where religion and actual realities of life were not separate entities. Life with all its wealth enriches power and joy. But life purified through renunciation of ego and desires become a channel of divine energy and wealth.[33] This truth had been the spiritual foundation of the socio-economic life of *Samgha*. The *Samgha*'s endeavours in the field of economy are all directed towards the aim of nation making. This had taken shape in the growth and development of both cottages and factories catering to the needs of the nation as well as contributed to the economic upliftment of the people.[34] A cordial relationship of brotherhood in place of that mere employer and employee was to exist between the Samgha and its band of workers in all spheres.[35] They all worked together for the common prosperity of the nation. The following were the Educational Institutions run by Prabartak Samgha.

1. Prabartak Vidyarthi Bhawan, Chandernagore
2. Prabartak Nari Mandir, Chandernagore
3. Prabartak Primary School for Boys, Chandernagore
4. Prabartak Primary School for Girls, Chandernagore
5. Prabartak Junior Basic School, Chandernagore
6. Prabartak Chauspathy, Chandernagore
7. Prabartak College of Culture, Chandernagore
8. Prabartak Vidyamandir, Dafarpur, Howrah
9. Prabartak Primary School, Dafarpur, Howrah
10. Prabartak Vidyapith for Boys, Kamarhaty, 24 Parganas
11. Prabartak Vidyapith for Girls, Kamarhaty, 24 Parganas
12. Prabartak Primary School, Kamarhaty, 24 Parganas
13. Prabartak Primary School, Raina, Burdwan
14. Prabartak Primary School, Frazergunj, 24 Parganas
15. Prabartak Primary School, Darjeeling
16. Prabartak Vidyapith, Chittagong
17. Prabartak Nari Mandir, Chittagong
18. Prabartak Primary School, Kutubdia, Chittagong
19. Prabartak Primary School, Sakpura, Chittagong
20. Prabartak High School, Sakpura, Chittagong
21. Prabartak High Primary, School Ganganagar, Faridpur.

The profit accrued from different financial concerns went to the maintenance of these educational institutions, social progress and relief in distress. The *Samgha* built up a sense and consciousness of true national solidarity in concrete national life.[36]

The first economic experiment was that of carpentry, started for humble experiences in the name of 'Rakshit, Dey and Ghosh Co.' a partnership firm. There later grew a larger joint stock company 'Prabartak Furnishers Ltd' a manufacturing firm of furniture, in the metropolitan area (B.B.Ganguly Street, Calcutta), as the collective economic centre of the *Samgha*.[37] The *Samgha*, fired with this national inspiration, set to discover in a spirit of adventure, a fit place for its agricultural experiments in 1920 at Frazergunj (Sunderban, 24-Parganas).[38] In 1920, provisional factory under the name of 'Mrinalini Bastravayana Karyalaya' was set up with eight handlooms which were soon increased to fourteen. It was started with the aid of paid workers and Japanese yarns, which could soon be replaced by Indian mill-yarn only[39] as the boys of the *Samgha* swiftly learnt the art and themselves became weavers.[40] By the year 1925, the Khadi department opened new branches in Chittagong, Mymensingh, Reingun and Burdwan district.[41]

The Prabartak Jute Mills Ltd[42] was also a daring venture of *Samgha* started in 1935. Due to the Second World War, the production of the mill[43] started only in February 1941. Another economic centre, 'The Prabartak Commercial Corporation Ltd' was engaged in direct export and import, dealing with a wide range of commodities.[44] The following Economic Institutions were run by Prabartak Samgha.

1. Prabartak Bank Ltd. Head office, Calcutta
2. Prabartak Jute Mills Ltd. Belgharia, Calcutta
3. Prabartak Furnishers Ltd. B.B. Ganguly St. Calcutta
4. Prabartak Trust, Head office, Calcutta
   (a) Prabartak printing and Halftone Ltd. Calcutta
   (b) Prabartak Publishers, Calcutta
   (c) Prabartak Jute Agency, Mayansingh
   (d) Prabartak Agriculture Dept., Frerganj
   (e) Prabartak Engineering Ltd., Frerganj
   (f) Prabartak Machinery Treading Co., Calcutta
   (g) Prabartak Hosiery Works, Calcutta
   (h) Prabartak Samgha Press, Chandernagore
5. Prabartak Commercial Corporation Ltd., Head office, Calcutta
6. Pabartak Khadi Dept. Head Office, Chittagong
7. Pabartak Industrial Home, Chittagong
8. Prabartak Dyeing and Printing Works, Chittagong

9. Prabartak Ghee and Oil Unit, Chittagong
10. Rakshit Dey and Co, Chandernagore

Further the economic sectors of the Samgha 'Prabartak Bank and Insurance Compnay.' 'Prabartak Printing and Halftone Ltd' had been taken under an umbrella for the better management. Then 'Prabartak Trust' composed of all dedicated members of *Samgha*, had been entrusted to carry on the economic programme of the mission. The income of the trust was spent for the upliftment of the country and the welfare of humanity. The *Samgha* had established several branches in different districts of Bengal such as Chittagong, Mymensingh, Burdwan and also in Gujarat. Their works were conducted on almost identical lines although on a miniature scale in adaptation to the local conditions. Through hard work and perseverance they had built a dreamland of an ashram and their ideal was plain living and divine thinking, based on the immoral principle of spiritual consecration and relationship. Working centres in Gujarat (at Navasari) had its agricultural field, Mymensingh its handloom factory and jute business, Burdwan its several looms and shops.[45]

Socio-Cultural Activities

In undivided Bengal the members of the *Samgha* carried the message of their master all over the country at Frazergunj, just located on the Bay of Bengal. There existed a village centre with one destitute children home, a rural primary school and a village library and they catered to the educational needs of the local children.[46] In Dafarpur (Howrah District), an ashram was founded as a centre of village work and the *Samgha* had established a primary a high school. Other ventures on similar lines were started and developed by *Samgha* in Mymensingh, Chittagong, Dacca and Barisal.[47] The chief lines of propaganda-work has been attempted by the *Samgha* was cultural, reconstructive and nation making. *Samgha* started a vernacular fortnightly as the organ of the new mission. The voice came directly from the depths of Bengal's soul and it created a new era. It had evolved not only its own literature and organs of self-expression but also its own complete machinery for printing and publishing on economic and business like style. Within nine years, the Prabartak grew from a tiny fortnightly into a classical and cultural magazine of first class importance. In January 1925, the French Government by an ordinance suspended the magazine for three months[48] as a measure to stop the voice of nation making activities, but the same spirit of dedication and creative idealism continued and it inspired the literature issued by the *Samgha*. Publications such as '*Atmasamarpana Yoga*' (The Yoga of Consecration), '*Yogacharyya Vivekananda*' (Life and Message of Vivekananda) and the literary works of Aurobindo[49] (upto1921) have rightly led the nationalist minded public to look up the Prabartak Publishing House.

Prabartak realized to re-indianisation of brain cells, for nation making. Samgha adopted a new education system through all its centres. *Samgha* planned to provide for the young generation of our country a basis of discipline which will enable them to preserve the Indian character intact, while enquiring what is best in the science, art and the culture of the West.[50] Under the guidance of competent *Acharyas* of the Samgha's schools, students of both sexes, in their respective spheres were to practise in life the culture and learning of India in addition to the intellectual fitting received in schools and colleges. Along with this, centres for both the technical and vocational education and training were instituted. A glance at the syllabus of the Prabartak College of Culture would throw light on the formation provided to the students. The following subjects were included in the curriculum.

1. Philosophy

(a) Indian Philosophy
(b) Chinese and Iranian Philosophy
(c) Indian philosophy
(d) Western Philosophy

2. Indian Civilization and History

(a) Evolution of Man and World
(b) Political History of India
(c) Indian Saints and Sages and their contribution to nation building

3. Principles of Sadhana

(a) Its aims and objects
(b) Definition
(c) Ideas and practices
(d) Goal of life divine

4. Principles of constructive organizations

(a) Religion of life (karma, seva, energy, money)
(b) Samgha and its philosophy

5. Bengali language and literature

(a) Origin and development of the Bengali language
(b) Growth of modern Bengali literature
(c) Special study of Prabartak literature

6. Extension lectures

(a) Economics and current problems
(b) Special study-Co-operative movements, Provincial budgets, Local self-government, Socialism, Contributions of Japan, USA and USSR
(c) Chemistry (Bio-chemistry, general chemistry)
(d) Geology and Geography

7. Practical

(a) Carpentry
(b) Printing technology
(c) Weaving
(d) Commerce and trade
(e) Agriculture

These students were to learn the arts and crafts from trained technicians, who actually earned their livelihood through such practical means too.[51]

To conclude it may be said that Curzon's most unpopular measure– 'The Partition Of Bengal' gave a new dimension in Indian politics. At the theoretical level, three major trends can be distinguished in the political life of Bengal.[52] Above all, Rabindranath who in his *"Swadeshi Samaj"*[53] address had already sketched out a blue print for constructive work in villages through a revival of the traditional '*Hindu Samaj*' or Community'. Such development for nation making, what Rabindranath called '*Atmasakti*' (self strengthening) was the another meaning of '*Swaraj*'. The founders of the Prabartak Samgha developed this idea of '*Swaraj*'as the main theme of nation making on the basis of spiritualism. This way the interpretation of the term '*Swaraj*' got a new and broad dimension through the activities of the Samgha. The development of the idea of 'Spiritual Nationalism' led to an awakening of national consciousness. It contributed to the national individuality, socio-economic and cultural *swadeshi* as well as soul force. The involvement of the Prabartak Samgha in the national movement directly or indirectly did a lot for the 'nation making'.

References

1. 'Prabartak', the journal of Samgha, first issue was published on 1st September 1915 at Chandernagore. (A fortnightly Bengali Newspaper, 16 pages)
2. Papiya Chakravarty, *Hindu Response to National Ferment*, Calcutta, 1992, pp. 1-12.
3. Sumit Sarkar, *The Swadeshi Movement in Bengal 1903-08*, New Delhi, 1973, p. 47.
4. *Ibid.*, pp. 47-48.
5. *Ibid.*, p. 56.
6. Indu Bhusan Roy, *Samghaguru Sri Motilal* (Jibanipanji), Calcutta, 1968, p. 12.
7. National Archives, (hereafter NAI) New Delhi, Govt. of India, Home (Political Dept), File No. 171/1915 (Sl.no.1-3).
8. NAI, Sedition Committee Report, 1918, pp. 91-95.
9. Sri Motilal, *Jibansangini*, (an autobiography of Motilal) Calcutta, 1968, (3rd Edn.) p. 49.See, Indu Bhusan Roy, *Samghaguru Sri Motilal*, p. 15.
10. Arun Chandra Dutt (ed.), *Light to Super Light*, (unpublished letters of Sri Aurobindo), Calcutta, 1972.
11. Arun Chandra Dutt, *Message and Mission of Prabartak Samgha*, Chandernagore, 1970, p. 31
12. Papiya Chakravarty, *Hindu Response to National Ferment*, p. 79.
13. *Rabindra Rachanabali* (Collected works of Tagore), Vol. 10, Visva-Bharati, 1365 B.S., p. 79
14. Rabindranath Tagore, *Path O Patheyo*, See, *Rabindra Rachanabali*, Vol. 10, pp. 562-568.
15. Amiya Ghosh, *Bangaleer Bastumukhi Atmasadhana O Prabartak Samgha* (in Bengali), Chandannagar, 2000, p. 44-46.
16. See, *The Message and Activities of Prabartak Samgha*, Chandernagore, 1926, p. 12.
17. Sri Motilal Roy, *Jibansangini*, and See also, Indu Bhusan Roy, *Samghaguru Sri Motilal*, pp. 12-13.
18. Sri Motilal Roy, *Amar Dekha Biplab O Biplabi* (in Bengali), Calcutta, 1984, (3rd edn.), p. 30.

19. Samghaguru Sri Motilal, *Biplabi Said Kanailal* (in Bengali), Calcutta, 1973, p. 30.
20. NAI, Govt. of India, Home (Political and. Confidential). File No. 171/1915, pp. 9-15.
21. *The Prabartak* (Monthly Journal in English), July, 1935, pp. 22-23.
22. *The Standard Bearer* (Monthly English Journal), Vol. 1, No.8, December 1927, pp. 476-477.
23. Indu Bhusan Roy, *Samghaguru Sri Motilal*, p. 22.
24. *The Standard Bearer*, Vol.-1, No.-1, August 1920, pp. 1-2.
25. *The Prabartak*, March 1940, p. 156.
26. Memorandum of Association and Rules, Regulations and By-Laws (Constitution): Prabartak Samgha, 1946, pp. 11-13.
27. *Ibid.*, pp. 16-17.
28. Papiya Chakravarty, *Hindu Response to National Ferment*, p. 96.
29. L.A.Gordon, *Bengal : The Nationalist Movement 1896-1940*, New Delhi, 1979, p. 256.
30. *The Prabartak*, Vol. 1, No.19, June 1932, p. 78.
31. *Spiritual Communism*, (Collection of Articles from The Standard Bearer), Chandernagore, 1922, pp. 22-23.
32. *Ibid.*, p. 38
33. Sri Motilal Roy, '*The Constructive path and principle*', in *The Prabartak*, March 1940, pp. 156-157.
34. Annual Reports Placed at the Third All Bengal Prabartak Conference, Chandernagore, 1937, p. 5.
35. Nehru Memorial Museum and Library, New Delhi, *Interview*-Aurn Chandra Dutt, (First Secretary, of Prabartak Samgha), Oral History Section, interview Dated 14.7.1968, taken by Dr. R. Sharma
36. *Ibid.*
37. Official Records (Prabartak Samgha), Chandernagore Central Office, File No. 1/P/A See also, *9th Annual Report on Prabartak Financial Sectors*, Calcutta, 1940, pp. 3-7. See also Annual Reports of Prabartak Samgha, 1943-1983.
38. *The Message and activities of Prabartak Samgha*, Chandernagore, 1935, p. 33.

39. Prabartak Archives, Chandernagore, Letter from M.K. Gandhi to Sri Motilal Roy, dated 9.5.1927 with Postal Mail Received No. 111033.
40. Amiya Ghosh, *Bangaleer Bastumukhi Atmasadhana O Prabartak Samgha*, p. 204.
41. *The Message and activities of Prabartak Samgha*, Chandernagore, 1926, p. 19-20.
42. Directors Report of Prabartak Jute Mills Ltd., Presented at the meeting of the Shareholders on 25.3.1941, Calcutta, p. 3.
43. Prabartak Trust Office, Calcutta, Directors File, No, Con/II/.
44. Prabartak Archives, Chandernagore, *Personal Diary of Sri Motilal Roy*, dated 9.8.1940,
45. *The Message and activities of Prabartak Samgha*, Chandernagore, 1926, pp. 33-34. see also 10th Annual Report, Prabartak Economic Centre, 1941.
46. Prabartak Ashram, Frezerganj, Official Records, file No.42/XXXIII/1987.
47. Annual Reports Of Prabartak Samgha (Bangladesh) 1989, 1990, 1991-94, Chittagong.
48. Govt. of Bengal, Official Records, Home (political), File No.-Con. 37/1925/(sc) pp. 2-3.
49. The following books were written by Sri Aurobindo and published by Prabartak Publishing House in Chandernagore. For details see, *The Message and activities of Prabartak Samgha*, Chandernagore, 1926.

No.	*Name of the Books*	*Price*
1.	Aurobinder Patra (Letters of Aurobindo)	Six Anas
2.	Dharma O Jatiyota (Religion and Nationalism)	One Rupee and Eight Anas
3.	Gitar Bhumica (An introduction of the Gita)	One Rupee and Four Anas
4.	Kara Kahani (Story of Jail)	One Rupee and Four Anas
5.	Lila	Eight Anas
6.	Sadahana	Ten Anas
7.	The Renaissance in India	One Rupee and Twelve Anas
8.	The Ideal of Karmayogin	One Rupee and Twelve Anas
9.	The Yoga and its objects	Eight Anas
10.	Uttarpara Speech	Four Anas
11.	Yogik Sadhana	Twelve Anas
12.	Purna Yoga	Eight Anas

50. Nehru Memorial Museum and Library, New Delhi Source: *Interview*-Arun Chandra Dutt, dated 14.7.1968
51. Amiya Majumdar, *Samghaguru Motilal O Prabartak Samgha* (in Bengali), Calcutta, 1989, pp. 80-88.
52. Sumit Sarkar, *Modern India, 1885-1947*, Madras, 1983, p. 112. See also, Prospectus of the Prabartak College of Culture, 1942.
53. See, Rabindranath Tagore, *Swadeshi Samaj* (in Bengali), Calcutta, reprint, 1962.

Index

C

D

E

H

I

J

K

L

M

Q

R

S